W9-BJV-061

From Arrival to Incorporation

DISCARD

NATION OF NEWCOMERS
Immigrant History as American History

General Editors: Matthew Jacobson and Werner Sollors

Beyond the Shadow of Camptown: Korean Military Brides in America
Ji-Yeon Yuh

Feeling Italian: The Art of Ethnicity in America
Thomas J. Ferraro

*Constructing Black Selves: Caribbean American Narratives
and the Second Generation*
Lisa D. McGill

*Transnational Adoption: A Cultural Economy of
Race, Gender, and Kinship*
Sara K. Dorow

Immigration and American Popular Culture: An Introduction
Jeffrey Melnick and Rachel Rubin

From Arrival to Incorporation: Migrants to the U.S. in a Global Era
Edited by Elliott R. Barkan, Hasia Diner, and Alan M. Kraut

From Arrival to Incorporation

Migrants to the U.S. in a Global Era

EDITED BY

*Elliott R. Barkan, Hasia Diner,
and Alan M. Kraut*

New York University Press

NEW YORK AND LONDON

NEW YORK UNIVERSITY PRESS
New York and London
www.nyupress.org

Library of Congress Cataloging-in-Publication Data
From arrival to incorporation : migrants to the U.S. in a global era /
edited by Elliott R. Barkan, Hasia Diner, and Alan M. Kraut.
p.   cm. — (Nation of newcomer series)
Includes index.
ISBN-13: 978-0-8147-9960-4 (cloth : alk. paper)
ISBN-10: 0-8147-9960-4 (cloth : alk. paper)
ISBN-13: 978-0-8147-9961-1 (pbk. : alk. paper)
ISBN-10: 0-8147-9961-2 (pbk. : alk. paper)
1. United States—Emigration and immigration—History.
2. Immigrants—United States—History. 3. United States—Ethnic
relations—History. 4. Americanization—History. 5. Globalization—
Social aspects—United States.   I. Barkan, Elliott Robert.
II. Diner, Hasia R. III. Kraut, Alan M.
JV6450.F76 2007
304.8'73—dc22   2007030065

New York University Press books are printed on acid-free paper,
and their binding materials are chosen for strength and durability.

Manufactured in the United States of America

c 10 9 8 7 6 5 4 3 2 1
p 10 9 8 7 6 5 4 3 2 1

To the memory of the late John Higham (1920–2003), whose scholarship and humanity illuminated the migration experience, especially the obstacles faced by those who were once "strangers in the land," and to the millions of today's newcomers whose presence reminds us that we remain, as in the past, a nation of nations.

Contents

Acknowledgments

We would like to extend special thanks to those organizations whose funding enabled us to complete this project: the Immigration and Ethnic History Society, the College of Arts and Science of American University, California State University San Bernardino, the Migration Policy Institute, the Center for Migration Studies, the New York University Ireland House, Columbia University's Center for the Study of Ethnicity and Race, the American Immigration Law Foundation, the Polish American Historical Association, Casa Italiana Zerilli-Marimo, and Harlan Davidson, Inc. In addition, we certainly wish to express our gratitude to NYU Press's editorial director, Eric C. Zinner, and assistant editor Emily Park for patience and support that proved invaluable.

Introduction

Elliott R. Barkan, Hasia Diner, and Alan M. Kraut

"Si, se puede!" (Yes, we can!), chanted the hundreds of thousands of im-migrants and their native-born supporters who marched through Ameri-can cities and in front of the Capitol in Washington, D.C., in the spring of 2006. Appropriating the chant once popularized by protesting farm-workers, the marchers—many of them Latino but Asians and Europeans as well—campaigned for a reformed immigration policy that would al-low undocumented newcomers to remain in the United States and to one day become citizens. A sea of American flags left the clear impression that those who had come, however they had gotten to the United States, wanted to stay. Despite a deadlocked Congress, including a House of Rep-resentatives demanding legislation that would brand undocumented ali-ens as felons who should be arrested and prosecuted, the protesters still believed that tomorrow in the United States must be better than today in Mexico, the Philippines, El Salvador, Honduras, Vietnam, or Ireland.[1]

Such optimism hardly characterized the attitude of all migrants around the Atlantic community. In France, protests against a law facilitating the firing of laborers by their employers especially drew the ire of the many thousands of young Muslim workers who had migrated for jobs, found few, and now despaired of ever enjoying the security and opportunity that had lured them from their homes in North Africa or the Middle East. Less than a year earlier, in England, despair was translated into self-destruc-tion.[2] On July 5, 2005, four young men from Leeds, England, three of them born to middle-class Pakistan parents in Britain and the fourth of them from Jamaica, went to London and blew themselves up on three trains and a double-decker bus. Asked his reaction, a twenty-two-year-old Muslim in Leeds commented, "I don't approve of what [they] did, but I understand it. You get driven to something like this; it doesn't just happen." A few days later, a *New York Times* reporter compared Muslim experiences in Leeds with those of Muslims in the New York metropolitan area. In the former, extensive unemployment, lack of job skills, and uncompleted education both reflected and compounded the years of mistreatment of South Asians in a formerly largely homogeneous nation. Abuse and discrimination had left many of these newcomers feeling marginalized, frustrated, and alienated to the point of embracing the violence advocated by radical Islamists. Throughout human history violence has been the voice of desperation. No longer did these young men believe what Muslims in New York and immigrant marchers in the streets of America did, that they could experience incorporation into their host society.[3]

While the attention of scholars and policy makers in host nations has been primarily focused on the pushes and pulls of migration, and especially on definitions of borders and boundaries and the legal implications of crossing them, some scholars and policy makers have turned their attention to postmigration phenomena. In the United States those who study migration and those who debate legislation are already attending to the challenges facing newcomers and their hosts as migrants are integrated into American society and culture. As during previous migrations, scholars are already examining how today's new arrivals negotiate their place in American society with native-born Americans.

Because we live in a global age that has been fashioned by new technologies of transportation and communication, the incorporation process is somewhat different than in earlier eras, yet there is also much that remains the same. For example, recent congressional debates over whether English should be made the official language of the United States reflect the anxieties of some Americans that their culture and tradition will be insufficiently durable to withstand the stress of new transportation and communication technologies. Can a nation that has had immigration policies but never an immigrant policy, especially one that speaks to the issue of language, successfully integrate the millions of newcomers currently arriving? How will this process proceed? While the technologies may alter the process, the underlying anxieties experienced by newcomers and natives are hardly new.

Indeed, much of the contemporary debate over the integration or assimilation of newcomers into American society prompts a sense of déjà vu. Mass immigration to the United States began before the Civil War, when 4.5 million newcomers arrived between 1840 and 1860, most of them having originated in the nations of northern and western Europe, especially Ireland, the German states, and Scandinavia, with a smaller number from China. While that pattern persisted after the war as well, still more newcomers began arriving from other donor nations. Between 1880 and the 1920s, over thirty million migrants made their way to America's shores. Now an increasing number of migrants left southern and eastern Europe, Canada, China, Japan, Canada, and Mexico for the United States, Canada, Australia, New Zealand, Argentina, and Brazil. If the migrants were heterogeneous, so were the scholars studying them. Examination of this fresh stream of migrants was interdisciplinary in character.

In an era when historians had just begun to professionalize and break from the notion that the past should be left to talented amateurs such as George Bancroft, the leading students of immigration often came from the ranks of social scientists, such as Robert Park, Louis Wirth, William I. Thomas, and Florian Znaniecki at the University of Chicago. These members of the "Chicago School" brought the insights of sociology, economics, political science, and anthropology to their endeavors. Others, such as Jane Addams, Lillian Wald, and Jacob Riis, were urban reformers of a Progressive bent who saw comprehension of migration and migrants as essential to achieving their broader reform agenda that included urban and industrial change.

Some social scientists at universities and reformers at urban settlement houses were dubious, or guardedly optimistic at best, about the inclusion of immigrants in American society. They dubbed the newcomers of their era the "new immigrants" to distinguish them from those "old immigrants" who had arrived from northern and western Europe in the middle of the nineteenth century and whom the social scientists and reformers looked upon as better prepared for life in the United States than more recent arrivals. Sociologist Peter Roberts, author of the 1912 study *The New Immigration: A Study of the Industrial and Social Life of Southeastern Europeans in America,* advocated the rapid assimilation of newcomers. He told his readers, "I believe in the immigrant. He has in him the making of an American, provided a sympathetic hand guides him and smooths the path which leads to assimilation."[4] Others could not have disagreed more. In 1914, Wisconsin sociologist E. A. Ross published *The Old World in the New.* He concluded that "subcommon" immigrants arriving in the United States might actually cripple the American population if permitted unrestricted entry. He contended that "from ten to twenty percent are hirsute, low-browed, big-faced persons of obviously low mentality. . . . These oxlike men are descendants of those who always stayed behind."[5] Nor did Ross prove to be an exception. Madison Grant's *The Passing of the Great Race* (1916) synthesized many nativist arguments into a masterful and widely read volume on the superiority of hereditary over environmental factors in shaping mankind. Grant filtered his data through his own biases. The incorporation of the foreign born would be risky, he believed, because the resulting race mixing would produce a hybrid race that reverted to a "more ancient, generalized and lower type."[6] The lowest type among the immigrants, East European Jews, seemed to Grant both the antithesis of the tall, fair Nordic type he most admired and a likely drain on the vitality of the superior Anglo-Saxon race, which they were bound to undermine over time if they were allowed entry and intermarriage.

As early as 1911, Columbia University anthropologist Franz Boas, himself a German Jewish immigrant, published *The Mind of Primitive Man,* a refutation of the arguments posed by those who regarded the foreign born as racially inferior and inassimilable.[7] In one series of experiments, Boas demonstrated that the American environment had modified the very "racial characteristics" that nativists found so objectionable in new arrivals. Because the slope of the cranium had often been regarded as a reliable index of race, he measured the skulls of second-generation immigrants and discovered that many no longer physically resembled their parents. Long-headed types grew shorter and round-headed types often developed elongated heads. Boas concluded that nutrition and other aspects of living conditions determined these "racial characteristics" more than heredity.[8] He had little doubt that given the opportunity immigrants could be integrated into American society. Though Boas was acclaimed in the scientific community, he was unsuccessful in changing most other anthropologists' views regarding the usefulness of race as an analytic category. Not until 1938 was he able to persuade the American Anthropological Society to pass a resolution defining terms such as *Aryan* and *Semite* as having "no racial significance whatsoever."[9] As historian Eric Goldstein observes, later anthropologists such as Ruth Benedict and Ashley Montagu continued Boas's work and questioned whether the term *race* was applicable to European groups, while terms such as *ethnicity,* "pioneered by Jewish scholars in the 1920s," were increasingly applied to "European descent groups."[10] Neither Boas nor his acolytes ever convinced all lay readers that race was not a useful category to apply to the newcomers of the early twentieth century or that most immigrants could ever be successfully integrated into American society. Not until 1998, ninety-six years after its founding, did the American Anthropological Association find race a useless analytic category, stating that "'race' . . . evolved as a worldview, a body of prejudgments that distorts our ideas about human differences and group behavior. Racial beliefs constitute myths about the diversity in the human species and about the abilities and behavior of people homogenized into 'racial' categories."[11]

Like most anthropologists at the turn of the century, such American historians as Herbert Baxter Adams attributed the greatness of the United States to racial superiority, especially the superiority of the Teutonic race, tracing American democracy to the tribes of the great German rain forests. Adams feared that the newcomers of his era were incapable of preserving the gift of America's Teutonic heritage.[12] Other historians such as Frederick Jackson Turner observed the newcomers firsthand. In 1901, he wrote a series of newspaper articles filled with the stereotypes and clichés of the era. He found Italians "quick-witted and supple in morals." Jews he knew to be "thrifty to disgracefulness, while their ability to drive a bargain amounts to genius."[13] Still, Turner had faith in the American environment to transform new arrivals. He hailed the western frontier as a beneficent force for homogenization, believing that the diversity of stocks "with their different habits, morals and religious doctrines and ideals . . . led to cross-fertilization and the evolution of a profoundly modified society."[14] He also realized the need for more scholarly treatment of immigration.

Of Turner's students, only Marcus Lee Hansen recognized that the peopling of America began in Europe and that historians should understand why some left and others stayed as well as why America seemed so attractive to immigrants. Hansen had little doubt of the ability of newcomers to be incorporated into American society, to the benefit of both the newcomers and their hosts.[15] A quarter of a century later, Oscar Handlin's *The Uprooted* would begin the modern study of the newcomers who had arrived at the turn of the century. Although later scholars criticized the volume for its exaggerations and imprecision, Handlin's almost poetic description of European peasants seeking better lives in the New World made clear his belief that immigrants could and would be incorporated into American life.[16]

Today, the subject of incorporation continues to provide grist for the scholarly mills of both social scientists and historians as they address the experiences of more recent migrants.[17] Social scientists looking at the contemporary immigrations are tackling a dazzling array of topics, issues, and groups. They have a particularly complicated chore given the sheer diversity of immigrants coming to the United States since the 1970s. Historians looking back to the earlier part of the twentieth century and to centuries past basically had a smaller range to consider. Their subjects primarily came from Europe, with those from different European regions coming during fairly specific decades. They also had to be cognizant of the very small migrations of the Chinese, Japanese, and Indians, as well as the trickle from the West Indies and Mexico. Additionally, we know after decades of scholarship by historians that most immigrant groups in the past tended to come from a particular class, those who had little economic stake in the places they left but who were not so poor as to be unable to finance an oceanic immigration and ply their skills in a new economy.

Since the 1970s, however, peoples from the entire world have begun to migrate to the United States, and sociologists, anthropologists, economists, demographers, and political scientists confront an America that draws in immigrants from every continent and every country within those continents, and, to a great extent, at the same point in time (or in overlapping periods). Since the passage of the Hart-Cellar Act in 1965, women and men from all over the world have sought to enter the United States. Millions have done so legally and millions have done so outside legal channels. Millions more aspire to do so. This new migration has drawn to the United States people from Central America, South America, Africa, Asia, and the Middle East. Mexico in particular has sent millions to the United States, and it has become a major staging ground for potential immigrants from other parts of Central America. In addition the last three decades of the twentieth century and the first of the twenty-first found Europeans on the move again. Immigrants from some countries with long histories of American-bound migration, Ireland and Italy in particular, also took advantage of the new policies. Immigrants from the former Soviet Union and Poland found their way to the United States too, while various regions of the Balkans that experienced major ethnic upheavals in the wake of the fall of communism likewise sent their daughters and sons to America during these recent decades.

In addition, social scientists have shown us that the newest immigrants to America are much more economically diverse than previous waves. They include within their ranks the most educated and the least, some of the best off in their homelands and some of the worst off. Immigrants from the Indian subcontinent, the Philippines, and various nations of the Caribbean have included nurses and doctors, scientists, and high-level employees of global corporations. They also have included poorer women and men who have taken some of the lowest-paying jobs in the service economy. This disjunction has left its mark, anthropologists and sociologists have shown, on the kinds of community practices developing in the newest ethnic enclaves.

Furthermore, contemporary immigrants have fanned out to more regions and states than previous immigrants have. Mexican immigrants can be found, and studied, not just in California and the Southwest but also in North Carolina and New York. They have in addition planted their communities in suburbs more frequently than in the old urban neighborhoods, although they have shown up there as well. That too has made for a greater complexity among today's immigrants than among those in the past and has complicated the project of social scientists seeking to study immigration as an on-the-ground phenomenon.

In some cases these groups found small ethnic communities already in existence that they could relate to and depend upon. In other cases, the post–Hart-Cellar immigrants functioned as the pioneers, building their ethnic enclaves from scratch. Some of the contemporary immigrants came to America and found their friends and relatives, their "co-nationals" who had already learned how to negotiate American realities, political, cultural, and economic, and who shared this knowledge with the newcomers. Others, the newest of the new immigrants, had to go through the learning process on their own. All in all, the vast heterogeneity of places from which contemporary immigrants have been drawn, the tremendous differences between them and among them, place the project of contemporary social science analysts in a category far different from what historians of the "old" immigration have confronted.

In addition, most past researchers treated an era in which American law played a minor part in shaping immigrant life and ethnic incorporation. Not so contemporary analysts. They are examining an era in which they cannot disassociate migration and ethnic community formation from the complex legal and administrative system that leaves its mark on family and community life. In essence, to do contemporary analysis requires deep knowledge of the workings of the American legal system, given its profound impact upon the immigrants and their American negotiations.

Historians tend to not see the particular challenges facing their colleagues in the social sciences. They mostly believe that contemporary social scientists, when studying migration and incorporation, neglect the historical dimension. They would prefer that social scientists acknowledge that the phenomena they identify in the present have often appeared before. Historians, too, use the term *incorporation* as they look back upon earlier eras of migration. Consumed with studying phenomena over broad stretches of time in specific geographic locations, hesitating to overgeneralize or engage in model building, historians prefer instead to attend to the specificities of the cases they study.

Yet, when not engaged in methodological wars, social scientists and historians can offer complementary perspectives on migration, ethnicity, and incorporation in a global age. Sociologists and cultural anthropologists describe familiar patterns of chain migration, in which new arrivals follow their friends and relatives to areas of settlement in the host country. Historians test the model by observing how new arrivals from China or India gravitate to preexisting communities of settlement and rely upon family and friends for jobs and assistance during postmigration periods of adjustment, just as East European Jews did in 1910. Social scientists accept ethnicity as a construct that blurs unique national identities, while historians explain how Mexicans, Cubans, and Nicaraguans submerge differences and embrace a common Latino identity after migration to the United States, even as workers from the different regions of southern Italy accepted a common Italian identity in an earlier migration era. And social scientists describe contemporary patterns of Asian and Latino incorporation by tracing occupational patterns, voting patterns, and marital patterns in the global world, even as historians offer examples of these patterns among the Poles, Greeks, or Japanese who arrived at the turn of the last century.

What portrait do these scholarly perspectives offer of today's migrants? In what ways does contemporary immigration differ from the migrations of the past? To what degree do the immigrants who began to arrive in the last decades of the twentieth century represent a more profound crisis for American society than those who left their homes in previous centuries? On the most profound level, the weight of evidence that can be gleaned from the corpus of work created by immigration scholars points to similarities outweighing differences and highlighting the extent to which differences function as matters of degree rather than kind.

Just as scholars of an earlier era conceptualized immigrants as either "old" or "new," depending upon when they arrived and from where they originated, there is a temptation to consider the experience of today's migrants in a binary framework: individuals migrate or remain in place; their hosts welcome them or reject them; newcomers are completely integrated into the host society or are transnational in perspective; migrants cling to home-country traditions and customs or embrace acculturation;

today's migrants experience migration differently from or similarly to those who arrived earlier.

The social scientists and historians who have contributed to this volume offer a far more complicated, nuanced perspective on migration and integration experiences. The migration experiences and the negotiations in which migrants engage as they find their place in American society today are neither completely different nor completely the same as those of individuals and groups who arrived at the turn of the last century. And just as scholars at the turn of the last century perceived profound differences between newcomers arriving in their era and the Irish, Germans, and Scandinavians who came midcentury, so many of today's scholars perceive a gulf between the Europeans—Italians, Russians, Jews, Greeks— of the early twentieth century and those migrants who came at the century's end, who often were not Christian or European, did not speak European languages, and seemed to share few social and cultural characteristics with Americans.

As for the whiteness or nonwhiteness of newcomers, such scholars as Alexander Saxton and David Roediger have redefined the concept of whiteness in relation to the power relationships that exist in American society at a given time. Historian Noel Ignatiev has observed that Irish immigrants who arrived in the middle of the nineteenth century were initially defined as nonwhite, while other scholars, such as Thomas Guglielmo and Karen Bodkin, have explained that later arrivals, as well, were initially defined as non-Caucasian.[18] Perhaps no scholar has done more to explore the complexities of ethnic and racial labels with respect to migrants than Matthew Frye Jacobson in his 1998 volume, *Whiteness of a Different Color: European Immigrants and the Alchemy of Race.*[19] More recently, David Roediger has described the 1920s and 1930s, just when restrictive immigration laws and procedures were being put in place, as the moment when migrant groups who had arrived in previous decades were being fully redefined and incorporated as part of white America.[20]

What similarities and differences can we see between earlier migrations and the current migration, and their implications for American society? As for the act of migration itself, few contemporary scholars imagine a simplistic model of migration in which some individuals move elsewhere permanently and others remain. Migration, especially movement over long distances, oceans, and continents, remains one of several possible decisions made in response to economic and social pressures.[21] Individuals and families calculated strategies to improve their lots in light of these pressures. As John Bodnar and other scholars have observed, in an earlier era the pressures often resulted from larger changes taking place in the development of capitalist labor markets.[22] Moreover, migrants thought in temporary, not permanent terms, with populations moving back and forth across boundaries for jobs and higher wages. In the early twentieth century, Italian laborers from the southern provinces were often characterized by American immigration officials as "birds of passage" because they sailed back and forth to countries in North and South America so often in response to seasonal labor needs.[23] Today, as well, migration patterns are fashioned from labor shortages and abundance. Mexican migrant laborers make semiannual appearances on the stage of American agriculture coinciding with planting and harvesting seasons. And just as newcomers of an earlier era followed family, friends, and compatriots in chain migration patterns, taking advantage of the economic and communal structures that others had fashioned, so, too, do today's Latino and Asian newcomers. A century ago even migrants who intended to remain in their host countries returned to visit family back home, as did the Russian Jews fleeing poverty and Russian pogroms. So, too, contemporary immigrants make visits home, bringing consumer goods and remittances to poorer relatives in addition to the ones they send via mail. Arrivals, whether from Ireland in the 1850s or Guatemala in the 1990s, transformed "back home" even as they sought to draw away brothers, sisters, wives, and children by paying their passage to the United States.

Migration meant redefining identities from the moment of arrival, if not before.[24] Whether we focus our attention on women and men who came to the United States in 1900 from Calabria or in 2000 from the Yucatan, newcomers continued to maintain relationships with friends and family from home villages. Moreover, in their new home the Calabrians came to recast themselves as "Italians" and those from Yucatan as "Mexicans," respectively, finding that they had much more in common with arrivals from Apulia or Sonora than they did with arrivals from Poland or India.

Migrants at the turn of the last century and now neither exclusively cling to the traditions of their homeland nor rush to embrace acculturation. They do both. At one and the same time they seek to preserve traditions, which anchor them in the world, and embrace what they see as cultural innovation, although they may do so cautiously. To succeed in their new home they embrace new cuisines and new styles of dress, language, worship, courtship, marriage, child rearing, and recreation, cobbling all of these together into a collage of practices that inform their everyday lives. In the early twentieth century, groups arriving from southern and eastern Europe often arranged marriages for their children. However, in the factories, in the schools, and on the streets of the United States the youth of different groups met and mingled. Parents often faced the challenge of notions of romantic love that defied their authority and resulted in marriages that crossed religious, ethnic, and racial barriers. Cultural mediators, such as Abraham Cahan, editor of the Yiddish-language daily *Forward,* suggested that in America the matchmaker (*shadkan*) might be replaced by parks and beaches where "boy meets girl." Increasingly generational conflict resulted in compromise and modification of marriage traditions, especially in the second generation.[25] Today as well, the negotiation over whom to marry and the customs of marriage take place as part of a broader negotiation. The *New York Times* marriage notices in August 2002 included the announcement of the wedding of Rakhi Dhanoa and Ranjeet Purewal, two Sikhs. Ms. Dhanoa, a twenty-seven-year-old immigration attorney employed by a New York law firm, is a first-generation American who, unbeknownst to her, became the focus of a Sikh matchmaker at the behest of the young lawyer's mother. The matchmaker invited Ms. Dhanoa to her daughter's graduation party, where she was introduced to Mr. Purewal, the eldest son of Punjabi immigrants, a handsome graduate of Rutgers University who worked as a recruiter for a New York head-hunting firm. The couple dated secretly to avoid parental meddling. Though well educated and modern in every way, the couple insisted upon a traditional Sikh wedding. Why? The bride observed that her family's stability came largely from "religion and family," adding, "When you are growing up as the first generation in America, it's important to have that [traditional] identity." A friend of the bride observed, "You can't escape your ethnicity, so you just have to deal."[26]

Migration has always required the newcomers and the native born to negotiate their relationship. Would newcomers be welcomed or held at arm's length? An immigrant aphorism translated into many languages was "America beckons but Americans repel." Even as opportunity has drawn newcomers to the United States, Americans have often expressed reservations and erected barriers to incorporation. At the turn of the last century some opponents of immigration plumped for restrictions, believing that legislation would be the best way to exclude undesirable newcomers. Others sought to admit newcomers and then to transform them, to Americanize them. The latter included reformers such as Jane Addams, who founded Hull House in Chicago, and Lillian Wald, the founder of New York's Henry Street Settlement. Through classes and by example, Addams, Wald, and others sought to transform migrants into middle-class Americans. They and others provided a comprehensive array of services including counseling, employment bureaus, and emergency relief to those in need of food, clothing, or shelter. Day care centers aided working mothers. Lillian Wald's Visiting Nurse Service brought medical care into the tenement apartments. Another source of assistance and philanthropy was derived from members of an ethnic group who had arrived in an earlier era. Organizations such as the Educational Alliance on New York's Lower East Side were supported by contributions from German Jewish philanthropists who sought to hasten the incorporation of newly arrived East European Jews at the turn of the last century. Similarly, the Italian Welfare League brought assistance to recent arrivals from those who had come years before. Assistance to Catholic newcomers in that era, including southern Italians or Poles, often came from Catholic charities or church coffers that had been nourished by the contributions of Irish Catholic philanthropists who had arrived years before.

At times settlement house workers practiced marked cultural sensitivity. While classes in cooking acquainted newcomers with American foods and patterns of eating, they fostered a culinary exchange. Settlement house workers encouraged immigrants to share their recipes. In Milwaukee, settlement workers helped their pupils compile family recipes from German, Russia, Poland, and elsewhere into the *Settlement Cook Book,* an exercise in cultural sharing. However, cultural faux pas sometimes happened too. Jane Addams recounted an episode that lost Hull House workers credibility in their community. A sick infant was abandoned on the front step of Hull House. In spite of the ministrations of a physician, the child died. When the Hull House workers prepared to have the child buried by the county, an angry crowd gathered in the largely Italian Catholic neighborhood, infuriated by the absence of a priest, and made arrangements to bury the child with religious rites. An embarrassed Addams later wrote, "It is doubtful whether Hull House has ever done anything which injured it so deeply in the minds of some of its neighbors. No one born and reared in the community could possibly have made a mistake like that. No one who has studied the ethical standards with any care could have bungled so completely."[27]

Similarly, today there are those who would repel newcomers by passing restrictive legislation. Modern-day nativists such as Peter Brimelow advocate reduction in the admission of legal immigrants as well as undocumented immigrants, arguing that immigrants have not been as beneficial to the economy as some have claimed but have proven to be considerably more problematic for the future of American culture than immigration advocates have allowed.[28] Others, such as Samuel Huntington, have suggested that particular groups, such as Latinos, are less assimilable than earlier groups.[29] At the same time, others see the newcomers as needing only culturally sensitive treatment to encourage and support their incorporation into American society on terms satisfactory to natives and newcomers alike. Often, the same sensitivity once extended to newcomers in settlement houses has been put into practice in contemporary institutions where newcomers seek culturally sensitive aid. One such place is the hospital or medical clinic. In an earlier era, physicians often attempted to force their definitions of health and therapy upon immigrants. However, more recently physicians, nurses, and hospital staff have come to realize that the most successful therapy often depends upon comprehending the role that culture plays in both disease and therapy, especially with respect to mental illness. At times, newly arrived Asian patients suffer from depression, anxiety, or schizophrenia, but some ailments are culture bound. *Pa-feng* is a phobic fear of wind and cold that occurs in Chinese patients. *Hwa-byung* is a suppressed anger syndrome found among Koreans. An increasing number of institutions employ physicians with the required cultural sensitivities to treat patients and train colleagues. In the Asian-American Family Clinic at Zucker Hillside Hospital in Queens, New York, an immigrant physician and former chaplain in the South Korean Army blends Zen Buddhism, Confucianism, and psychotherapy in treating patients, tailoring each therapy to the patients' culture.[30]

These examples suggest that the immigration experiences of the past and present are not all that different. However, avoiding oversimplification requires acknowledging significant changes that have transformed migration and recast the experience of migrants. The most obvious differences concern communication and transportation between donor and host nations. Letters that traversed oceans in ships that took many days to make the journey have been replaced by speedy electronic communications, including telephone and more recently electronic mail linking migrants with those who remain at home.[31] Parents and their children, neighbors, and friends need not wait to share thoughts, feelings, and experiences. The implications of such speed in maintaining or recasting human relationships are still being explored by scholars. So, too, are changes in transportation.

In an era of inexpensive air travel, the ease of round-trip journeys may well nurture a more extensive web of transnational relationships than the seasonal or long-term migrations possible in the early twentieth century. Newspapers report that international businessmen can begin the day in New York City, tend to their affairs over lunch in a Caribbean nation, and be home in time for a late supper.[32] Dual residences and dual citizenship are becoming increasingly common aspects of such transnational patterns, challenging the very definition of international migration and its implications for "becoming American."[33] Ever since the 1967 Supreme Court decision *Afroyim v. Rusk,* the United States has had to recognize dual citizenship.[34] We cannot know if the children or grandchildren of contemporary immigrants will enter American life more slowly than the children or grandchildren of earlier immigrants because they have grown up in an environment frequently suffused with the words and tastes of their ancestral homelands, but it is likely that the ability to maintain closer connections between places of residence and places of origin will have an impact.

Contemporary migrants face a web of regulatory policies and laws far more extensive than those that engaged migrants of an earlier era. Immigrants arriving in the United States during the nineteenth and early twentieth centuries, with the exception of the Chinese, who were the first targets of restrictive legislation designed to exclude a particular ethnic or national group, faced few legal tests prior to arrival. Many achieved naturalization unencumbered by insurmountable legal obstacles. However, since the 1920s, government has been increasingly obstructionist. No longer is the obstacle an Ellis Island physician or Immigration Bureau interrogator. Today's legal migrant faces a perplexing maze of preference categories, lotteries, and extensive forms. The erection of these legal hurdles has raised high the walls that divide "legal" from "illegal or undocumented" aliens. The ethnic enclaves where undocumented migrants live and work have been shaped by their presence, and the perspective of even legal migrants has been recast accordingly. Increasingly, legal immigrants equate the plight of the undocumented with their own anxieties about incorporation. Those who have nothing to fear become the advocates of those who live in daily fear of being discovered and deported. Families with children born on American soil to undocumented parents face daily risks of disruption.

On the other hand, today's immigrants arrive in an American society that at least rhetorically celebrates "diversity" and "multiculturalism" far more than did American society at the turn of the last century. Current law allows those who reside in the United States to be citizens of another country at the same time that they are American citizens and vote in both places. No longer does taking on American citizenship and participating in the American political process require a divorce from one's country of origin and the renunciation of older political ties and even property rights.

How, then, should social scientists and historians conceptualize what happens after migrants arrive in the United States? Such terms as *incorporation* and *assimilation* have been used to describe the postmigration process. Are they synonyms or do they describe quite different processes? Scholars tend to use the term *incorporation* to describe those actions taken by individual migrants and their families to bring them closer to the host society.[35] Groups do not incorporate, people do. Incorporation involves individuals engaging in ever-widening circles of contact and interaction with the host society, beginning with the workplace and emanating outward into a broad range of informal and less structured encounters in venues such as neighborhoods, schools, sport and recreation facilities, and religious institutions. If this process of incorporation proceeds without substantial resistance, it will eventually include membership in nonethnic organizations, citizenship and suffrage, and possibly social interactions that transcend group boundaries, such as dating and out-marriage.[36]

Assimilation is a more thoroughgoing, two-way social process that requires not only the desire of a newly arrived group to incorporate into society but the consent and cooperation of host society members to accept the newcomers. Assimilation demands that newcomers increasingly abandon ethnic traditions and ethnic exclusivity. It also requires that members of other groups and especially those native to a society accept newcomers as equals in a broad range of encounters, including access to avenues of mobility, influence, and even political power. Segmented assimilation involves access and acceptance into a particular stratum of society often defined by race or religion. Thus West Indian migrants of dark complexion often find that they may achieve assimilation only in the African American community and not in the broader society, where racism remains an obstacle. Some scholars, such as historian Elliott Barkan, contend that incorporation embraces such other social processes as acculturation, adaptation, and integration and is an element of the larger, more comprehensive assimilation process.[37]

As contemporary scholars investigate how incorporation is actually operating in the twenty-first century, they have become increasingly aware that social boundaries once seemingly insurmountable are increasingly permeable, or at least negotiable. A number of factors are responsible for the changing face of incorporation. First, incorporation is far more gendered than it was in earlier eras. As an increasing number of women, whether single or married, have acquired education and entered the workforce, more of them engage in activities that promote incorporation in the public sphere. Second, incorporation and assimilation may take longer than scholars and policy makers anticipate. Evidence suggests that second- and third-generation migrants continue to display behavior promoting incorporation. Although patterns differ from group to group, transnational lives may inhibit rather than promote rapid incorporation and assimilation. Third, incorporation patterns tend to be uneven among groups and within a given group. Recency of arrival, age, gender, education, linguistic aptitude, occupation, religion, place of settlement, and preexisting biases of the host society are just some of the variables that may influence the pace of incorporation and its progress toward assimilation. Fourth, incorporation has been redefined to eliminate the notion that it requires the complete shedding of earlier identities as well as all customs and cultural patterns defining a migrant group as different from the host society.[38] This modification of an older notion requiring complete abandonment of the past has been encouraged by a fifth factor, an enhanced toleration of diversity and pluralism in the United States. Increasing acceptance of diversity encourages integration of minorities into American society without requiring that a group's customs, identities, and even prior national allegiances be immediately and thoroughly abandoned, as was often the case in the nineteenth and early twentieth centuries. Finally, incorporation has been dramatically transformed by the realities of globalization. High-speed communications, travel, and trade have combined to shrink the globe. No longer does confining citizenship to a single nation-state or restricting economic transfers among individuals residing in different sectors of the globe seem prudent or even possible. As historian Peter Kivisto observes, "No adequate theory of assimilation can be developed that does not account for globalization."[39] The same appears to hold for incorporation. Transnational travel, the transfer of remittances across border and boundaries, and many other interactions routine in a global environment redefine but never exclude the possibility of a group's incorporation into a host society or even its eventual assimilation, processes that continue beyond the generation that made the initial move from one location to another.

The process of integration is worth close scholarly examination, although it is hardly unprecedented. Earlier migrants, too, sought to maintain homeland ties and retain cultural, religious, political, and historical affiliations with those who stayed behind, at least until their homelands achieved independence and were transformed or until the pressures of U.S. immigration laws prevailed in cutting individuals off from faraway friends and relatives.[40] As historian Reed Ueda suggests, in the 1920s immigration policy in the United States became a "device for social engineering." A "racially restrictive naturalization policy" by which "the state [could constrict] the boundary of American nationality" resulted in a sharp constriction of opportunities for incorporation and assimilation. Americans temporarily seemed to lose their faith in the power of their economy, culture, and political institutions to make aliens Americans. The cost of incorporation seemed too high and the risks appeared daunting.[41] The expansiveness of an earlier era was canceled by restrictive legislation and later in the 1930s by administrative procedures that accomplished the same ends.[42]

Following World War II, Americans reassessed their reservations about ethnic pluralism. Beginning in 1965, reform in American immigration law reflected the attitudinal shift. In subsequent decades the result echoed new demographic realities as admissions soared from Asia (Southeast, South, and West Asia), Latin America and the Caribbean, and Africa. The end of the Cold War opened the spigot so that East Europeans could join the flow. Some scholars contend that the civil rights movement and feminist movement promoted an expansiveness and revision of social values and attitudes and legitimized and institutionalized the multicultural ethos that encouraged the incorporation of the foreign born. The historian Reed Ueda observes that the federal government, having deployed immigration laws to discourage immigrants' incorporation, now adopted liberal policies and offered an invitation to enter and join the American enterprise. Ueda contends that the 1965 legislation restored "the central role of immigration" and "the cosmopolitan belief in the capacity of all individuals for membership in the American nation," thereby enabling their incorporation into every aspect of American society.[43] The change prompted various groups and communities in the United States to reassess their own boundaries, offering greater opportunity for the social and cultural incorporation of newcomers than ever before. If the 1965 legislation in part shaped a civic culture that was more open to newcomers than the civic culture of earlier eras, this reevaluation of the border and boundaries separating natives and newcomers was echoed in the nation's economic, religious, educational, and political institutions, according to Ueda.

Historian Mae M. Ngai agrees that the quota system of the 1920s created a pernicious division among newcomers. Legal and illegal categories often corresponded to racial differences. While migrants of color were included in the labor force that the United States continued to import, they were often excluded legally in a manner that deprived them of rights and citizenship. However, unlike Ueda, Ngai does not find that the Immigration Act of 1965, the Hart-Cellar Act, was a catalyst for immediate improvement in the status of all migrants. While those who had been the main target of the 1924 legislation, southern and eastern Europeans, now benefited, as did migrants from Africa and Asia, those migrating from Mexico, the Caribbean, and Latin America were severely affected by the law's initial hemispheric ceiling and increased attention to border control. Ngai concludes that, increasingly, illegal immigration was blamed on Mexicans, a problem that could be solved only by rigorous law enforcement.[44]

Ngai and others observe that not until the late 1960s and 1970s did assertions of Black Power, Brown Power, Asian-American Power, and a host of smaller ethnic heritage movements begin to meet with some success.[45] Efforts in the Latino and Asian communities to assert greater political power on behalf of their groups were fueled by the increasing number of new arrivals. From the mid-1960s to early 2005, more than twenty-six million newcomers arrived legally and an estimated additional eleven million arrivals came undocumented.[46] Because of these increasing numbers, newcomers who naturalized could assert power at the ballot box, while all could assert power in the American marketplace as workers and consumers. This power was enhanced by the maintenance of homeland connections permitted by rapid communications and low-cost, speedy transportation. Transnational relationships enhanced the power of migrants, especially because of the way remittances forged financial connections with families and communities remaining in the donor countries. By 2004 remittances from the United States alone had reached $32 billion and were significant sources of national revenue for such countries as the Philippines, El Salvador, and Mexico. So many countries have recognized the importance of these transnational relationships to their welfare that approximately one hundred have granted their nationals the right of dual citizenship—urging them to become American citizens while retaining their original nationality.[47] Although the United States does not formally recognize dual citizenship, ever since *Afroyim v. Rusk* the federal government has accepted limitations of the grounds upon which citizens could be denaturalized. For the most part, citizens must explicitly renounce their United States citizenship in order to be legally divested of it. Thus migrants can potentially exert political as well as economic power in donor and host nations.

While the potential power seemingly accessible to international migrants at the dawn of the twenty-first century appears formidable, the reality may be less so. Some scholars argue that most migrants maintain only limited, intermittent, or episodic ties with their country of origin and former neighbors, a modest relationship that one scholar has labeled "translocalism."[48] Thus, while Colombians and Dominicans often campaign and vote in homeland elections and Mexicans offer financial assistance to improve service and infrastructure to their villages via hometown clubs, others barely keep touch with the relatives and friends who remained behind. Sociologist Alejandro Portes observes that "not all immigrants are transnationals." Indeed, "regular involvement in transnational activities characterizes only a minority of immigrants and . . . even occasional involvement is not a universal practice."[49]

As scholars continue to tangle over the definitions and scope of such terms as *incorporation, assimilation, transnationalism, translocalism,* and *globalism,* there is a growing consensus that these terms do not define mutually exclusive relationships. Within migrant groups from the Hmong to Mexicans these processes often occur simultaneously. Moreover, identity issues, citizenship choices, destinations, gender roles, residential preferences, occupational roles, educational objectives, organizational affiliations, legal status, political participation, and even intermarriage collectively embody an ongoing negotiation between aliens and the United States that has been perennial in American history, long preceding the current wave of migration.

And what of the native born? Public opinion research suggests that Americans do not disapprove of immigration and incorporation patterns nearly as much as Americans did in the nineteenth and early twentieth centuries.[50] At least some of the credit for the diminished opposition to immigration is the direct result of statements by American presidents and other leaders suggesting that newcomers who arrived in the United States legally are not responsible for diminished security or diminished economic opportunity for the native born. In the midst of the turmoil after the attack upon New York City and Washington, D.C., by radical Islamists,

President George W. Bush sought to curb American nativism by urging Americans not to blame all Muslims for what a radical minority had done, a far cry from President Franklin Delano Roosevelt's failure, in the 1940s, to prevent the internment of West Coast Japanese in the face of a national security crisis. While the current debate over immigration policy often waxes passionate, angry critics of current policy most often focus their ire upon America's porous borders and inconsistent policies toward temporary workers and undocumented aliens.

Newspaper reports suggest the almost daily dilemmas and uncertainties confronting those seeking to become part of American society. The *Los Angeles Times* reported the story of four young Mexican Americans who participated in a high school science fair in Arizona and were rewarded for their fine project with a trip to Niagara Falls. Coming back from the Canadian side, they were detained as illegal aliens because as youngsters, ranging in age from two to seven years old, they had been brought into the country by their parents. Their teachers and school principal came to their defense, and in July 2005 the federal government's case against the young men—all four of whom now either were in college or had graduated and were applying for citizenship—was tossed out by a judge. A *Times* editorial applauded the judge's "sensible step blocking their deportation."[51] Why? The extent of incorporation by these four young men proved more compelling to the judge than the government's argument that as illegals they must be deported, whatever their circumstances or accomplishments.

Today as at the turn of the last century, the study of migration is an interdisciplinary endeavor. The objective of this collection of articles by eminent scholars is to offer readers an interdisciplinary perspective on the compelling issues confronting migrants to the United States and their hosts. Five disciplines are represented by those participating in this anthology. Our objective is the incorporation of such scholars from diverse disciplinary backgrounds into the shared territory of migration studies. Included in this collection are the essays of five historians (Gary Gerstle, Paul Spickard, Barbara Posadas, Roland Guyotte, and Timothy Meagher), six sociologists (Roger Waldinger, Karen Woodrow-Lafield, Min Zhou, Xiyuan Li, Mehdi Bozorgmehr, and Anny Bakalian), two anthropologists (Caroline Brettell and David Haines), and two economists (Barry Chiswick and Paul Miller).

By 2005, more than thirty-five million legal and illegal migrants were present in the United States. At different rates and with differing degrees of difficulty most will become incorporated into American society and culture. Some may assimilate, or their children may, as sociologists Richard Alba and Victor Nee predict, although they see racism continuing to set boundaries on the process.[52] Others will resist or fail to negotiate the changes required in going from one society to another. Scholars want to understand the process both from the perspective of the migrant and from the perspectives of the societies they are leaving and joining. How is the United States changing even as it requires change from those who come here? It is probably too early for a conclusive analysis, though scholars and journalists are often split between those who embrace the notion that diversity enriches American society and those who believe for various reasons that diversity degrades American culture and that the current newcomers are simply unassimilable in ways that earlier generations of newcomers were not. Still others echo the perennial fear that immigration is harmful to the American economy, especially to the interest of American workers.[53] As historian Mae Ngai observes, "In the globalized world of the early twenty-first century, when national borders have softened to encourage the movement of capital, information, manufactured goods, and cultural products, the persistence of hardened nationalist immigration policy would seem to demand our attention and critique."[54] Those who joined in the marches of 2006 would agree, and many would remind Americans that in an ever-shrinking "global village" the United States is unlikely to escape continuing to be a nation of nations, numbering among its citizens women and men with contacts, connections, and knowledge of other cultures and other places.

The eleven essays in this collection provide invaluable perspectives on the challenges of incorporation by newcomers into American society in many parts of the nation—and, by inference, patterns of integration in other diverse societies in this age of ever-greater globalization. The themes include policies and formal procedures of legal inclusion; economic entrepreneurialism that becomes a different avenue for learning about America; newcomers measuring their adaptation by negotiating how much of their traditions to hold on to; immigrants discovering both the benefits and drawbacks for their adaptation of relying too heavily on an ethnic enclave; bonding among immigrant spouses (in many cases those in mixed marriages) as a means of coping and also providing networks for adjusting to their new homeland; and language schools and public media with ethnic emphases that both influence perceptions by immigrant/ethnic group members about their own heritage and culture and have a potential impact on responses to, and from, mainstream society.

Two essays provide longer historical perspectives of events during the twentieth century that, we can now see, provided precedents for Americans' periodic fears about foreigners and the perception of threats that they might represent, especially since September 11, 2001. Those perceived threats seem more ominous the more different the newcomers are when compared with American society and culture. Unavoidably, those perceptions have shaped and reshaped the conditions under which such newcomers have been welcomed or shunned by Americans. Finally, to a significant degree, incorporation into American society is profoundly affected by an array of intervening variables that include, on the macro level, government domestic policies, global geopolitical conditions, and U.S. relations with sending countries, and, on the micro level, the degree of attachment immigrants preserve with their home countries, bonds that are often seen by outsiders as far stronger, more persistent, and more prevalent than is often the case. Rather than a widespread transnationalism, we frequently see signs of translocalism—moderate ties that soften as newcomers move out of their communities and into the larger society (or into other groups) and as American-born generations arrive.

David Haines tackles the important feature of nation-state controls over the admission of newcomers, in this case refugee policies. Sovereign nations determine whom they will (legally) admit, under what conditions, and with what limitations and controls. Ultimately, policies focusing on the specific class of special admissions—refugees and asylees—can affect their incorporation into American society and their experience of the boundaries they may or may not encounter, for borders may represent impassable boundaries for some and more passable ones for others. Haines begins with a summary of the tragic events surrounding the German Jewish passengers on the *S.S. St. Louis* in the spring of 1939. They had registered for American visas and now desperately sought to avoid being returned to Germany because their admission numbers had not yet come up. The absence of any real refugee policy, combined with an unsympathetic public and a State Department riven by anti-Semitism, doomed their chances. Historically, Haines observes, "Those refugees with strong constituencies have fared better."

In American refugee policies, the "moral commitments" to respond affirmatively have been based on applicants' class, ethnicity, race, religion, gender, age, and previous ties with the United States and on America's current relations with their homeland governments. Most of the nearly four million refugee admissions since 1945 were linked to anticommunism, and most others to a sense of American personal responsibility due to U.S. involvement in their homelands. A third component, reflecting the new sense of moral commitments, has been the nation's shift to a willingness to take a fair share of refugees as part of broader international efforts. A fourth has been, especially since 1980, a commitment to aid those who have been persecuted or are at risk of persecution. Haines then examines data related to measurement of refugee incorporation, specifically employment and perceptions of self-sufficiency, illustrating not only the complexities of incorporating such newcomers but also the difficulties of measuring how successful that effort has been. Ambivalence about refugee admissions periodically resurfaces, as we see in the last essays of the collection.

Long overlooked by immigration scholars who have focused on the causes of immigration and modes of newcomer adjustment, the propensity to seek U.S. citizenship is actually an important indicator of immigrant incorporation and commitment to the new host society. Karen Woodrow-Lafield is one of a small number of scholars now concentrating on the question of who applies for citizenship, how rapidly, and as a consequence of what variables. National origin is a vitally important factor related to political incorporation, as are gender and the visa category under which one was first admitted, especially the latter. Woodrow-Lafield analyzes provisions for admission to the United States, how the categories of those entering are connected to the likelihood of seeking U.S. citizenship, and how rapidly immigrants apply upon becoming eligible to do so. For example, the motives for citizenship do vary, and the emphasis in immigration law on family reunification certainly has had a bearing for many who do petition for it as a means of hastening the admission of immediate relatives.

The increasing percentage of nonimmigrant persons already residing in the country who adjust their status to permanent resident and then more rapidly petition for citizenship understandably suggests that some elements of incorporation are present earlier for such persons, including language competence, education, occupation, and familiarity with American principles and political institutions. Length of time in the country before applying is similarly often related to the likely degree of incorporation and is significantly linked, for many nationalities, to the percentage who have already been naturalized. Finally, the broader political context in terms of prevailing policies and public sentiments regarding immigrants also influences the decisions immigrants make in this regard.

A critical figure in easing the integration of newcomers into American society is the ethnic entrepreneur, according to anthropologist Caroline Brettell. In an age of globalism, ethnic entrepreneurs do far more than create economic opportunities for others of their ethnic group or offer familiar goods to their customers. Brettell suggests that they transmit the values of American society to newcomers while they encourage migrants' integration into their adopted society and culture. In return for brokering the integration of newcomers, ethnic entrepreneurs who distribute patronage to newer arrivals cultivate new customers and a reservoir of goodwill that translates into popularity and profits. Observing that anthropologists often speak of the economy as "embedded in society" and configured by a particular social system's political and social constraints, Brettell deploys the work of other social scientists to demonstrate how immigrant entrepreneurship is culturally and socially embedded in an ethnic community, with the community more than the entrepreneur being the unit of her analysis.

Although Brettell acknowledges the importance of gateway cities, such as Los Angeles, New York, Miami, and Chicago, for the contemporary immigrant story, she turns to a tier of slightly smaller metropolitan areas that have recently become more ethnically diverse than ever because of migration. In this study her laboratory is the Dallas–Fort Worth area. She focuses upon the Asian Indians in that metropolitan area, a residentially dispersed population including a substantial number of talented, well-educated individuals. With a ready market, an Indian entrepreneur who had been working in a Houston grocery store in Houston moved to Dallas to open his own grocery, the Taj Mahal. His imagination and energy paid off in a successful business catering to Indian tastes, and soon other Asian Indian businesses moved into the same shopping mall where the grocery was located. Once discovered, the mall became a magnet for the Indian community in a five-state area. Many found their way to the Chaat Corner, a fast-food bar at the back of the store. However, for Caroline Brettell the most significant development was that Asian Indians flocked to the Chaat Corner for far more than food. It soon became a locus of migrant activity, where newcomers met old friends; others planned community events and sold tickets; and still others posted fliers about concerts. And for a modest monthly fee other Asian entrepreneurs left stacks of their business cards.

The Taj facilitated not only buying and selling but also the dissemination of information, promotion of interaction, and preservation of cultural practices. Cultural citizenship was nurtured among Asian Indians as they were kept connected to their home culture, their traditions, in the case of Hindus their faith, and such culturally embedded economic practices as bargaining and trust in business dealings. Brettell offers the Taj Mahal in Dallas–Fort Worth as an example of how in a global environment local marketing and consumption in an ethnic population can yield profits for entrepreneurs, while their business establishments and practices assist in maintaining cultural boundaries, practices, and ancient traditions at the same time as these newcomers adapt to the unlikely environment of American suburban communities.

Retaining ethnic identity even as they pursue integration into American society has always been a formidable task for newcomers to the United States. Moreover, the task varies considerably by ethnic group and the size of the community in the United States where the new arrivals take up residence. In their chapter "Filipino Families in the Land of Lincoln," historians Barbara M. Posadas and Roland L. Guyotte analyze this process not as it occurs in a large metropolitan area but as it occurs in a midsized American community in the Midwest, Springfield, Illinois, the sixteenth president's birthplace. Concerned with the role that ethnic organizations play in encouraging ethnic identity retention among midwestern Filipinos, the authors focus especially on the roles played by Springfield's women of Filipino heritage (Filipinas) in determining the content of Filipino ethnic identity and marking the Filipino community's boundaries, which include some and not others.

How did Springfield acquire a Filipino community in the first place? Posadas and Guyotte explain that between 1965 and 1974 approximately nine thousand physicians trained in the Philippines were welcomed into the United States. Some of these physicians and their families, Roman Catholic in religion, established an upper-middle-class enclave in Springfield. There, they educated their children and formed a variety of ethnic organizations to assist families in retaining Filipino identity even as they economically prospered and became respected members of the Springfield community. By the 1990s, a new cohort of Filipinas arrived from the Philippines. These were often the so-called pen pal brides. Some met husbands who worked at U.S. airbases on the islands; others first met their mates through letters or over the Internet. However they met their husbands, these newly arrived Filipinas were frequently quite different from those who had preceded them. They often tended to be younger and less well educated, to have less command of English, and to be of a lower socioeconomic class.

Citing the cases of specific Filipinas, some of whom they themselves interviewed, Posadas and Guyotte observe that the social distance among the Filipinas who arrived in different eras and were from different backgrounds could be bridged if the new arrivals articulated and modeled a gendered devotion to family and religion—usually Catholicism—that echoed the values of the earlier wave of migrants. However, Filipinas were not incorporated but were excluded if they failed to meet social and religious norms. In one case, for example, community members shunned a Filipina, whom they had initially supported when she left the battering American spouse who had brought her to Springfield, after they learned that she had had an affair with her unmarried divorce attorney and when she later became the mistress of a married automobile dealer. Thus the challenges of incorporation can extend beyond the boundaries of mainstream society to include the dynamics of integration and acceptance within the immigrant/ethnic communities themselves.

Barry Chiswick and Paul Miller bring another approach to the question of how newcomers adapt to their new environments and what can facilitate their incorporation. Together, various components of social and human capital—networks of family and friends and personal skills and experiences—and where one enters the country play critical roles in how well the newcomer fits in and the extent to which he or she relies upon the ethnic community in efforts to adapt to a new host society. Chiswick and Miller propose the term *ethnic goods* to encompass the goods and services that are sought by immigrants in their ethnic communities and that are "not shared with the host population or with members of other groups." Such "goods" as the language spoken, clothing, foods, religious services, ethnic schools, and access to potential marriage partners also become more available and, in many instances, less costly the larger the enclave is. That in turn draws more newcomers to the ethnic enclave.

Affected by the presence of such "goods" and social networks is the immigrants' likelihood of accepting lower wages in the enclave, in part because the availability of such "ethnic goods" there is believed to offset the lower income. In other words, not having such goods and services readily available would mean having to pay more to obtain them. Consequently, employment away from such an ethnic enclave would be appealing only if the income were great enough to outweigh being distanced from that community. Consequently, the incorporation of newcomers can be aided by the availability of the networks and the accessibility of such desired goods and services. On the other hand, the more skills, education, lan-

guage competence, and experience one has, the easier it is to be more distant from the immigrant/ethnic enclave and yet begin the processes of incorporation into the mainstream society. Moreover, because the enclaves
are functional in the ways enumerated, they frequently do persist beyond
the immigrant generation.

To test the effects of the enclave, Chiswick and Miller use census data to
analyze English-language proficiency and earnings. Offsetting the benefits
of the ethnic goods somewhat is the finding that those concentrated in
such communities tend to have lower English-language abilities and that
lower earnings are associated with concentration in enclaves and with limited language abilities. In the short run, it would appear that these enclaves
do affect immigrants' incorporation into the mainstream society, at least
until language skills are acquired, and that, usually, once newcomers leave
the enclave their opportunities for more income do improve, in part because of their greater competency in English.

Historian Paul Spickard reminds us that scholars who treat migration
and ethnicity in the United States often neglect the roles that religion and
race, respectively, have played in shaping the experience of immigrants, especially their incorporation into American society. He is troubled that,
with few exceptions, treatments of earlier migrations in scholarly books
and museum exhibits have not adequately analyzed and presented the influence of race and religion in shaping the experience of newcomers as
they have other economic or social variables. He laments that the significance of religion and race amply demonstrated in the "fine historical studies of Asians and Latinos" over the past twenty years have often not been
deployed by scholars who write about Caucasian newcomers.

Certainly earlier scholars interested in the notion of assimilation offered theories about the roles of religion and race. Spickard cites the still
provocative work of Will Herberg in *Protestant, Catholic, Jew* as an example of an assimilation theorist's argument that American religions were
following a path similar to that of many newcomers, discarding dimensions of their institutional identities that smacked of foreignness as they
joined the American cultural mainstream. Herberg did not address race,
but sociologist Milton Gordon did, finding most people of color so "epiphenomenal," in Spickard's words, as to not throw doubt on the for-
mulaic pattern of assimilation that Gordon envisioned. Even the recent
"race-conscious scholarship" by Richard Alba and Victor Nee seems to
Spickard insufficiently sensitive to the racial dynamics that Spickard sees
as distinctive and determinist in eliminating the assimilation into the

American mainstream that was a possibility in the past pattern of Caucasian migrants.

Spickard's contribution to the ongoing dialogue over patterns of incorporation is a discussion of how religious identities have been framed in racial categories and how racial divisions in the American population have affected the identities of religious groups and their relationships in the broader sphere of denominational relations. Relying upon his considerable research and general expertise on Asian groups, Spickard focuses largely, but not exclusively, upon the Japanese American experience, offering several categories of discussion of this intersection of race and religion, including "institutions, leaders, lived religion, and racialization."

Spickard observes that Asian churches and other religious institutions reinforce ethnic identities. In Seattle, the Seattle Buddhist Church, the Japanese Methodist Church, the Japanese Baptist Church, and many others are centers of Japanese community activity as much as they are vehicles for religious worship. Spickard emphasizes the often overlooked but powerful role of religious leaders in preserving ethnic identity and shaping the incorporation process in the United States. In addition to leadership, Spickard notes that Korean American Protestant churches are not just places for worship service but also places where members "speak Korean and eat Korean food together." For a similar effect Spickard notes that Japanese with home altars, *butsudans*, often reported feeling an enhanced sense of their Japanese ethnicity as well as piety as Buddhists.

Finally, Spickard contends that religious identities have often been racialized. He offers as an example the manner in which American religious organizations often reach out to Buddhist churches in a spirit of religious fellowship and diversity because they regard them as by definition "foreign" and therefore in need of special treatment, no matter how many members might be native born or even non-Asian. Concisely, Spickard concludes, with respect to incorporation, "Religion matters. Race matters."

Few issues loom larger in discussions of immigration and ethnicity, past or present, than language. Two key aspects of language have long informed discussions about immigration, ethnicity, relationships within the immigrant community, and importantly the nature of the linkages between the generations. Language has, on the one hand, served as a profound element in the life of the group, both a real and a symbolic example of the differences between being a member of an immigrant community and not. On the other hand, the language of the host society has been one of the most powerful, pervasive aspects of the new land, demanding competence of newcomers so that they might navigate the streets and the various new institutions. In this respect, perhaps no place has been as distinctive as the United States in terms of the expectation that immigrants eventually learn English.

Min Zhou and Xiyuan Li offer here an important window through which to see the various problems and issues raised by the language question. They focus on language maintenance among Chinese immigrants and their progeny in the United States, and they ask how the leaders of the immigrant communities have provided, and still provide, language instruction for youngsters born and raised in America, with its demand for English. Min Zhou and Xiyuan Li, despite not being historians, have shown how important it is to historicize contemporary concerns.

To understand the nature of the Chinese-language schools that predominate in Chinese enclaves at the beginning of the twenty-first century, they tell us convincingly, it is necessary to look back to the Chinese-language schools that emerged at the end of the nineteenth century and the early twentieth. In the past, they show, community leaders created Chinese-language schools to make it possible for the youth to some day return home or be able to function in the ethnic enclave. Present-day Chinese-language schools serve to foster greater economic mobility and to enhance the prospects for Chinese American children to prepare to enter the most prestigious American educational institutions. Min Zhou and Xiyuan Li show that these schools, joint ventures between community leaders, entrepreneurs, parents, and children, have changed with time and have reflected differing historical realities. However, while in both periods they have contributed to the debate over how they might incorporate into American society, in the earlier phase they represented far more the immigrants' desire to resist integration, motivated by a sojourner mentality. In recent years they have stressed cultural preservation but not at the expense of seeking incorporation into American society.

In "The Importance of Being Italian," Timothy Meagher ventures into the area of representation and the ways in which the popular arts, in this case mainstream movies, reflect the ethnic landscape of America. Starting in the 1960s, moviegoers began to see a substantial number of films depicting Italian Americans. Before that time Italians rarely captured the interest of filmmakers, so audiences had few opportunities to "meet" immigrants from Italy and their descendants on the big screen. But from the 1960s to the 1990s, film after film, some of them such blockbusters as the *Godfather* trilogy, explored the details of Italian American ethnicity. In fact, during these decades Americans of Italian descent emerged as the quintessential "ethnics," the stand-in for white Americans who maintained a connection to some place of European origin and who seemed different enough to be interesting, even exotic, yet could be recognizable to all Americans.

Italians came to represent a degree of primitivism without being frightening. They venerated family in these movies and operated according to a code of honor that made them disdainful of bureaucracy and the formal trappings of the state. According to Meagher, the wildly popular movies and widespread diffusion of certain stock images of cinematic Italian Americans fit well into the culture of America during the last decades of the twentieth century, indirectly contributing to Italian Americans' efforts to gain greater acceptance in mainstream American society.

Why, he asks, did this change occur, and how did Italian Americans move from the relative obscurity of the earlier era to the widespread prominence of this later period? What was it about Italian Americans that served the interest of filmmakers, producers, studios, and the American public in the decades after the 1960s as they explored certain aspects of ethnicity?

Meagher indicates that other groups would not as effectively serve what was essentially an exploration of a counter-American image but ultimately a safe one. The Irish had been in America too long to seem different, while Poles and other East Europeans lacked widespread recognition or familiarity to most Americans. Jews lacked the association with the primitive and if anything were portrayed as overly cerebral and overly civilized. Thus the stupendously popular and then constantly repeated image of the Italian American as *the* ethnic had little to do with "real" Italian Americans and much to do with the nature of American culture in these years. Nevertheless, despite the differences between the cinematic and the actual Italian Americans, the overall effect of the former was to add certain favorable attributes to the latter without their initiative (e.g., appreciation of food, family, passion for life), enhancing their efforts to further their integration.

Indeed, the implication here is that as a consequence of the popular media Italian Americans were invited into mainstream America on terms very much linked to their perceived representation of traditional values of family and community as well as to the manner in which their cinematic characters captured America's frustration, despair, and sense of impotence with politicians and officeholders. Thus this mantle of respectability and legitimacy remained a media-generated phenomenon that was actually at variance with the real profile of contemporary Italian Americans. Their incorporation, therefore, was not unqualified but very much an unusual work in progress.

Finally, "The Importance of Being Italian" goes beyond the issue of how American film makers represented "Italianness" and why American audience responded positively to particular themes. Meagher speculates on the ways in which America's most recent immigrants may or may not become incorporated into the nation through popular culture images. New immigrant groups are very likely to become the subjects of films and other works, and those works, to be consumed by large numbers of Americans, could become part of the newcomers' process of incorporation. However, for Italians the projection of the cinematic images took place long after their principal immigration had ended and Italians had ceased to be defined as a problem. For the newest immigrants, on the other hand, this media-related process has begun while their immigration continues unabated, constituting for many Americans a serious social concern. In essence, Americans may in part "meet" the newest immigrants on the screen. How this will affect their representation and, consequently, their incorporation remains to be seen.

Given that the incorporation of immigrants is profoundly affected by the context of reception in the receiving society, Gary Gerstle's "The Immigrant as Threat to American Security: A Historical Perspective" offers a valuable, sweeping overview of Americans' fears of immigrants and immigration in both the past and the present. It takes as its time frame nearly all of American history, going back to the early nineteenth century and moving forward to the most recent years, the period defined largely by the attacks at the World Trade Center on September 11, 2001.

Gerstle balances four historically recurrent themes as he seeks to understand how and when Americans worried about immigrants and the threat they posed to American life. He describes four axes of American concern: immigrants' perceived threats to American security in terms of religion, politics, economics, and race. The central issue involves the repeated ways in which Americans have identified immigrants as religiously, politically, economically, and racially subversive. Implicit here in terms of our theme is the way those responses have adversely affected newcomers' efforts to gradually gain access to American society. Depictions of immigrants' subversion, in both rhetoric and policy, reflected an American ideology that held up, differently at different times, a belief that America had to remain a white, Protestant nation, committed to a capitalist economic order, and based on a republican ideal.

Various eras usually produced distinct fears directed at particular groups. Those fears inspired specific policies to address the anticipated immigrant threat and stimulated hostile imagery and violent mob action. American anxieties especially flourished during times of unrest and wars because their aftermaths proved to be particularly fertile ground for making Americans feel insecure. In effect, accusations made against immigrant groups can serve (and have served) to significantly delay their integration into mainstream American society. In addition, because immigrants are seen in some respects as markedly different, they are also perceived as a threat. If not pressured to depart, as an expression of these various motives, the newcomers are certainly kept, in social and political terms, at arm's length, denied the essential opportunities to incorporate into American society.

In other words, confronted with changed circumstances that they were struggling to understand, Americans had at hand a convenient focus: the immigrant threat, whether to America's religious core, its racial purity, its economic livelihood, or to its political order. Immigrants provided handy exemplars of all that had gone wrong, and targeting them seemed a reasonable way to address the new and troubling realities. The recurrence of this pattern makes it clear that the past and present can and ought to be considered in tandem. We can expect that the earlier difficulties experienced by immigrants seeking acceptance in America will be encountered by new groups in the future—if they are not being encountered already.

The essay by sociologists Anny Bakalian and Mehdi Bozorgmehr draws on both history and contemporary affairs as it explores the ways the United States has defined itself as a nation under attack and how that perception has connected to fears of immigrants and other foreigners. Here is an example of how scholars primarily concerned with recent events can use history. The reaction of the U.S. government in the wake of the terrorist attacks on September 11, 2001, had precedents, and Bakalian and Bozorgmehr argue persuasively that to understand how the government, and public opinion more generally, made sense of the recent crisis scholars should look to the past.

Bakalian and Bozorgmehr give to those concentrating on the contemporary scene several historical examples that they assert should be referred to and understood. They illustrate not only how certain groups could be singled out and further marginalized because of tumultuous domestic and foreign events but also how precarious the quest for incorporation could become in the face of such crises as war and domestic unrest. They take as their first past event the massive campaign launched both at the policy level and through popular outrage stirred up against Germans and German Americans during World War I. In that early-twentieth-century example, they show, we can see all the developments that occurred in the wake of September 11 as the state and the populace seethed with anger at Middle Easterners and South Asians who found themselves in the United States. Likewise, these two scholars suggest that scholars and others concerned with contemporary reactions to the sense of threat from the outside that the events of the fall of 2001 inspired should look back to the Palmer Raids, a response to the "Red Scare" that gripped the United States in the wake of the Bolshevik Revolution in Russia and the wave of strikes that swept through the United States in 1919. Finally, the experiences of Japanese Americans (as opposed to the Issei, Japanese aliens), American born and as such American citizens, following the attack on Pearl Harbor and America's entry into World War II, can provide precedents for thinking about the present.

Because Bakalian and Bozorgmehr have provided historical material here, they are asking an essentially comparative question. How did the reactions of the state and the public in 2001 differ from what had been manifested during World War I, the Red Scare, and World War II? What similarities link the past with the present, and how can the similarities and differences be explained? And what do such examples reveal about the dilemmas that minorities (both white European and nonwhite) face in terms of reconciling their desire to preserve traditional cultures, beliefs, and even homeland ties with their desire to be accepted by mainstream society? Those who have marginal political beliefs and/or are associated with a nation in conflict with the United States could find their security and rights seriously jeopardized.

Our collection concludes with Roger Waldinger's critique of uses of the concept of "transnationalism" that imply that ties to homelands are a relatively recent innovation. He contends that the phenomenon "scholars call 'transnationalism' is fundamentally mislabeled and misunderstood." He sees such activities as "long-distance particularism" not unlike what took place among earlier immigrants. Yet although he discusses the historical parallels for what is now identified as transnationalism, he also notes the contrasts. Especially important is the impact of nation-states today in ways that introduce international uncertainties into such "global interconnections." Moreover, loyalties that transcend borders have often been viewed by the public—with some misgivings—as dual attachments. Implicit in his discussion is also the recognition that many immigrants do not preserve the strong ties identified with transnationalism but have moved toward more limited, periodic contacts—what Barkan has labeled "translocalism."

Furthermore, Waldinger's analysis of the immigrants' social networks and "transborder bilocalism," as juxtaposed to "intrastate bilocalism," raises a number of issues related to the intersections of migration, nation-states, and boundary maintenance and control. The incorporation of new-comers is significantly affected not only by the attitudes and needs of the immigrants but also by nation-state mechanisms that control international migration and the admission of new immigrants. Whatever proponents of transnationalism may argue about "deterritorialization" arising from immigrants' dual loyalties ignores the ongoing presence of elaborate sovereign state controls, which have "increased significantly between the last age of mass migration and today's." In the final analysis, because immigrants are perceived as "internal aliens," there is the latent threat of their being viewed as suspect, making their "long-distance nationalism . . . a hazardous game." Immigrants especially eager to integrate into mainstream society frequently recognize the potential drawbacks of remaining too tightly (and too visibly) wedded to their homelands and make adjustments and compromises to facilitate their incorporation into American society. Their children, especially those born in America and less intimately familiar with their parents' homeland, will commonly move ahead more readily with their own integration.

NOTES

1. Rachel L. Swarns, "Immigrant Groups Plan Campaign to Bring Legal Changes," *New York Times,* April 20, 2006; David Montgomery, "A Banner Day on the Mall," *Washington Post,* April 11, 2006.

2. "While Paris Burns," editorial, *New York Times,* November 8, 2005.

3. Hassan M. Fattah, "Anger Burns on the Fringe of Britain's Muslims," *New York Times,* July 16, 2005; Sarah Lyall, "Lost in Bombings, Diverse and Promising Lives," *New York Times,* July 17, 2005; Nina Bernstein, "In American Cities, No Mirror Image of Muslims of Leeds," *New York Times,* July 21, 2005.

4. Peter Roberts, *The New Immigration: A Study of the Industrial and Social Life of Southeastern Europeans in America* (New York: Macmillan, 1912).

5. Edward Alsworth Ross, *The Old World in the New: The Significance of Past and Present Immigration to the American People* (New York: Century, 1914), 285.

6. Madison Grant, *The Passing of the Great Race* (New York: Scribner's, 1916), 18.

7. Franz Boas, *The Mind of Primitive Man* (New York: Macmillan, 1911).

8. Franz Boas, "Changes in Bodily Form of Descendants of Immigrants," in *Reports of the Immigration Commission,* 61st Cong., 2nd sess., Senate Document No. 208 (Washington, DC: Government Printing Office, 1911), vol. 38.

9. Quoted in Ruth Benedict, *Race: Politics and Science* (New York: Viking Press, 1945), 195–96, and in Eric L. Goldstein, *The Price of Whiteness: Jews, Race, and American Identity* (Princeton: Princeton University Press, 2006), 193.

10. Goldstein, *Price of Whiteness,* 193.

11. "American Anthropological Association Statement on 'Race,' " May 17, 1998, www.aaanet.org/stmts/racepp.htm.

12. Herbert Baxter Adams, "The Germanic Origin of New England Towns. With Notes on Cooperation in University Work," *Johns Hopkins University Studies,* 1st ser., 2 (1882): 1. Also discussed by Peter Novick in *That Noble Dream: The "Objectivity Question" and the American Historical Profession* (New York: Cambridge University Press, 1988), 87–88.

13. Frederick Jackson Turner, quoted in Ray Allen Billington, *Frederick Jackson Turner: Historian, Scholar, Teacher* (New York: Oxford University Press, 1973), 171.

14. Frederick J. Turner, *The United States, 1830–1850: The Nation and Its Sections* (New York: P. Smith, 1935), 286.

15. Marcus Lee Hansen, *The Immigrant in American History,* ed. Arthur M. Schlesinger (Cambridge, MA: Harvard University Press, 1940).

16. Oscar Handlin, *The Uprooted: The Epic Story of the Great Migrations That Made the American People* (Boston: Little, Brown, 1951).

17. An excellent anthology on incorporation that includes the work of social scientists and historians is Peter Kivisto, ed., *Incorporating Diversity: Rethinking Assimilation in a Multicultural Age* (Boulder, CO: Paradigm, 2005). See also Werner Sollors, ed., *Theories of Ethnicity: A Classical Reader* (New York: New York University Press, 1996).

18. Noel Ignatiev, *How the Irish Became White* (New York: Routledge, 1995); Alexander Saxton, *The Indispensable Enemy: Labor and the Anti-Chinese Movement in California* (Berkeley: University of California Press, 1971); David Roediger, *The Wages of Whiteness: Race and the Making of the American Working Class* (New York: Verso, 1991) and *Towards the Abolition of Whiteness: Essays on Race, Politics, and Working Class History* (New York: Verso, 1994). Scholars dealing with other immigrant groups and the whiteness issue include historian Thomas A. Guglielmo, *White on Arrival: Italians, Race, Color, and Power in Chicago, 1890–1945* (New York: Oxford University Press, 2003), and anthropologist Karen Brodkin,

How Jews Became White Folks and What That Says about Race in America (New Brunswick: Rutgers University Press, 1994).

19. Matthew Frye Jacobson, *Whiteness of a Different Color: European Immigrants and the Alchemy of Race* (Cambridge, MA: Harvard University Press, 1998).

20. David R. Roediger, *Working toward Whiteness: How America's Immigrants Became White* (New York: Basic Books, 2005).

21. Alan M. Kraut, *The Huddled Masses: The Immigrant in American Society, 1880–1921*, 2nd ed. (Wheeling, IL: Harlan Davidson, 2001), 17.

22. John Bodnar, *The Transplanted: A History of Immigrants in Urban America* (Bloomington: Indiana University Press, 1985), 1–56.

23. On return migration, see Mark Wyman, *Roundtrip to America: The Immigrants Return to Europe, 1880–1930* (Ithaca: Cornell University Press, 1993). Italian return migration is treated in Betty Boyd Caroli, *Italian Repatriation from the United States, 1900–1914* (Staten Island, NY: Center for Migration Studies, 1973), and Dino Cinel, *The National Integration of Italian Return Migration, 1870–1929* (New York: Cambridge University Press, 1991).

24. See Josef J. Barton's description of this predeparture process in *Peasants and Strangers, Italians, Rumanians, and Slovaks in an American City, 1890–1950* (Cambridge, MA: Harvard University Press, 1975), 64–90.

25. Letter to the editor of the *Jewish Daily Forward, 1930*, in *A Bintel Brief: Sixty Years of Letters from the Lower East Side to the Jewish Daily Forward*, ed. Isaac Metzker (New York: Ballantine Books, 1971), 148–50.

26. Stephen Henderson, "Rakhi Dhanoa and Ranjeet Purewal," *New York Times*, August 18, 2002, reprinted in David A. Gerber and Alan M. Kraut, *American Immigration and Ethnicity: A Reader* (New York: Palgrave Macmillan, 2005), 124–25.

27. Jane Addams, *Twenty Years at Hull House* (New York: Macmillan, 1910).

28. Peter Brimelow, "Time to Rethink Immigration?" *National Review*, June 22, 1992, 30–46, and *Alien Nation: Common Sense about America's Immigration Disaster* (New York: Random House, 1995).

29. Samuel P. Huntington, *Who Are We? The Challenge to America's National Identity* (New York: Simon and Schuster, 2004).

30. Sarah Kershaw, "Freud Meets Buddha: Therapy for Immigrants," *New York Times*, January 18, 2003, reprinted in Gerber and Kraut, *American Immigration*, 297–99. For a fuller discussion of health institutions and their response to immigrants, see Alan M. Kraut, *Silent Travelers: Germs, Genes, and the "Immigrant Menace"* (New York: Basic Books, 1994).

31. An excellent discussion of immigrant letters is to be found in David A. Gerber, *Authors of Their Lives: The Personal Correspondence of British Immigrants to North America in the Nineteenth Century* (New York: New York University Press, 2006).

32. Deborah Sontag and Celia W. Dugger, "The New Immigrant Tide: A Shuttle between Worlds," *New York Times*, July 19, 1998.

33. Alejandro Portes describes the conditions that affect the ability of individuals to participate in transnationalism. See Alejandro Portes, "Conclusion: Theoretical Contingencies and Empirical Evidence in the Study of Immigrant Transnationalism," *International Migration Review* 37 (Fall 2003): 879, and Alejandro Portes and Rubén G. Rumbaut, *Legacies: The Story of the Immigrant Second Generation* (Berkeley: University of California Press, 2001), 46–49.

34. *Afroyim vs. Rusk,* 387 US 253 (1967).

35. Philip Kasinitz, John H. Mollenkopf, and Mary C. Waters, "Worlds of the Second Generation," in *Becoming New Yorkers: Ethnographies of the New Second Generation* (New York: Russell Sage Foundation, 2004), 4.

36. Elliott R. Barkan, "Race, Religion and Nationality in American Society: A Model of Ethnicity—From Contact to Assimilation," *Journal of American Ethnic History* 14 (Winter 1995): 49, reprinted in Kivisto, *Incorporating Diversity,* 190–91; Portes, "Conclusion," 877.

37. Barkan, "Race, Religion," 54–58, reprinted in Kivisto, *Incorporating Diversity,* 194–98.

38. Peter Kivisto, "The Revival of Assimilation in Historical Perspective," in Kivisto, *Incorporating Diversity,* 5–14.

39. Ibid., 25.

40. Peggy Levitt, Josh DeWind, and Steven Vertovec, "International Perspectives on Transnational Migration: An Introduction," *International Migration Review* 37 (Fall 2003): 567–71.

41. Reed Ueda, "Historical Patterns of Immigrant Status and Incorporation in the United States," in *E Pluribus Unum? Contemporary and Historical Perspectives on Immigrant Political Incorporation,* ed. Gary Gerstle and John Mollenkopf (New York: Russell Sage Foundation, 2001), 305.

42. Herbert Hoover preferred the use of administrative procedures by consular officials of the State Department to returning to Congress for even more restrictive legislation in the early 1930s. See Richard Breitman and Alan M. Kraut, *American Refugee Policy and European Jewry, 1933–1945* (Bloomington: Indiana University Press, 1987), 11–51.

43. Ueda, "Historical Patterns," 313.

44. Mae M. Ngai, *Impossible Subjects: Illegal Aliens and the Making of Modern America* (Princeton: Princeton University Press, 2004).

45. These movements had to adapt to gain mainstream legitimacy, and this continues to be true for more recent cases. Kivisto, in "Revival of Assimilation," echoes Will Kymlicka's observation in *Politics in the Vernacular: Nationalism, Multiculturalism, and Citizenship* (New York: Oxford University Press, 2001) that there are four prerequisites for the functioning and integration of a multicultural society, the ground rules that specific groups as well as mainstream society must accept. These are "public spiritedness," a "sense of justice," "civility and tolerance," and a "shared sense of solidarity or loyalty." Most recently, American Muslims

have been pressed to demonstrate their commitment to these four principles in the wake of the September 11 attack on New York's World Trade Center and the Pentagon. Specifically, Muslims living in the United States have been expected by their non-Muslim neighbors to explicitly disavow violence toward nonbelievers as a legitimate aspect of Islamic teachings. In July 2005, following the bombings in London, the Muslim community in the United States did issue a *fatwa* condemning extremism and violence against civilians. See Laurie Goodstein, "From Muslims in America, a New Fatwa on Terrorism," *New York Times*, July 28, 2005.

46. U.S. Office of Immigration Statistics, Department of Homeland Security, *2003 Yearbook of Immigration Statistics* (Washington, DC: U.S. Office of Immigration Statistics, Department of Homeland Security, September 2004), table 2, and Jeffrey Passel, "Estimates of the Size and Characteristics of the Undocumented Population," Pew Hispanic Center, March 21, 2005, 1, www.migrationinformation.org (under "New Resources") (accessed April 18, 2005).

47. Betsey Cummings, "Cash Flow across Border Starts to Get More Savvy," *New York Times*, July 28, 2005.

48. This translocalism model is developed by Elliott R. Barkan in "America in the Hand, Homeland in the Heart: Transnational and Translocal Immigrant Experiences in the American West," *Western Historical Quarterly* 35 (Autumn 2004): 335–41.

49. Portes, "Conclusion," 876–77. See also Kivisto, "Revival of Assimilation," 23.

50. On public opinion, see Elliott R. Barkan, "Return of the Nativists? California Public Opinion and Immigration in the 1980s and 1990s," *Social Science History* 27 (Summer 2003): 229–83, and David M. Reimers, *Unwelcome Strangers: American Identity and the Turn against Immigration* (New York: Columbia University Press, 1998).

51. Nicholas Ricardi, "Judge Rules Students Can Stay in U.S.," *Los Angeles Times*, October 22, 2005.

52. Richard Alba and Victor Nee, *Remaking the American Mainstream: Assimilation and Contemporary Immigration* (Cambridge, MA: Harvard University Press, 2003), 271–91.

53. Steven A. Camarota, "Economy Slowed, but Immigrants Didn't: The Foreign-Born Population, 2004," Washington, DC, Center for Migration Studies, November 2004, 1, www.cis.org/articles/2004/back1204.html.

54. Ngai, *Impossible Subjects*, 264.

Part I

Thematic Approaches to Immigration and Incorporation

Chapter 1

America and Refugees
Morality, Rationality, and Expedience, 1939–2005

David W. Haines

The American experience with refugees over the past sixty years has ranged from acceptance to rejection, from well-wrought program efforts to botched policy decisions, from humanitarian concerns to crass politics. The U.S. Department of State has been both the fabricator of paper walls to exclude refugees and the locus of intense efforts to move them quickly into the United States. Religious and secular voluntary agencies have been lauded for their efforts on behalf of refugees and chided for providing inconsistent services. Refugees themselves have been characterized as true American success stories and criticized as overly dependent on public welfare. The American people, in turn, have often been impressively generous in their welcome of refugees but at other times have been neglectful, uninterested, and sometimes hostile.

Refugees and America have thus had a long, complicated, and often vacillating relationship.[1] But, throughout, the relationship has been an important one. America has often been the major country of support for refugees, and refugees have often been for America the most visible, challenging, and morally significant of newcomers. Refugees, for example, often receive disproportionate media attention, both positive and negative. It is often a surprise to Americans that refugees are such a small numeric segment of overall immigration flows to the United States—about a tenth in recent decades, although far lower since September 11, 2001. This importance of refugees to America, despite their relatively small numbers and relatively modest program costs associated with them, has a very strong moral component. On the positive side, refugees represent those whose life experiences most clearly demand humanitarian respect and action. Because of the moral demands of such action, assistance to refugees often requires practical, incisive actions that are outside the bounds of normal bureaucratic structures and processes. On the negative side, refugees who violate the ideal refugee image by engaging in fraud or persecution of other refugees are subject to very sharp moral rejection. The U.S. government itself is subject to censure when it betrays moral standards for political expedience or when it allows bureaucratic ineffectiveness to undermine humanitarian action for refugees.

All this makes the American experience with refugees highly complex but also useful as a window on how morality, rationality, and expedience interpenetrate more broadly in American institutions, attitudes, and social interactions. Further, the situation of refugees presents an important contrast to the situation of other U.S. immigrants both because of the difficult paths by which refugees come to the United States and because of the far greater involvement of the public and private sectors in their postarrival adjustment. This chapter provides a preliminary account of these refugees, focusing on the moral commitments Americans have toward them and the frequent clashes between those moral commitments and more practical and political concerns. The starting point for the discussion will be 1939 and the ending point 2005.

Moral Commitments

Two events occurred in 1939 that serve as a prologue to the American experience with refugees in the second half of the twentieth century.[2] The first was the ill-fated voyage of the *St. Louis.* Its passengers were largely German Jews fleeing the now visible threat to them from the Nazi regime. As they attempted to land in Cuba and then sailed along the East Coast of the United States, they were denied the right to land, even though seven hundred of them had registered for American visas and had received affidavits of support. Despite their pleas and those of many supporters in the United States, they were rebuffed and thus returned to Europe to face their destinies there.[3] The second event—ultimately a nonevent—was the attempt to pass the Wagner-Rogers bill. The bill was a modest effort to permit some twenty thousand German refugee children to enter the United States. It was carefully crafted, nonsectarian in its phrasing (although the majority of those involved would inevitably be Jewish),[4] and very broadly endorsed by organizations and prominent individuals. Yet even this modest effort to address a well-documented humanitarian need failed. These two examples of the rejection of Jewish refugees set the pattern not only for the denial of new immigration slots but also for the construction of additional barriers—"paper walls," in David Wyman's words—to keep Jews out even when slots were available. That combination of the denial of new admissions mechanisms *and* the undercutting of existing admissions mechanisms buttresses Wyman's more general argument about the full abandonment of Jewish refugees to the Holocaust.[5]

This non–refugee program provides some useful lessons. One is that it matters very much who the refugees of the day are. There was blatant anti-Semitism among many of those opposing humanitarian action for European Jews. There were, after all, special programs for British children during the war to keep them in the United States and thus out of harm's way in Great Britain. Even after the war, when the United States acknowledged the need to resettle some of the many displaced persons in Europe, initial versions of the legislation had an anti-Jewish bias—although that was removed in later versions of the legislation.[6]

This particular theme of rejecting or accepting refugees on the basis of their specific identity has been a continuing one in the U.S. refugee program. Those refugees with strong constituencies have fared better. Those who could unite multiple constituencies have fared best of all—for example, by appealing to the humanitarian impulses of the left, the anti-communist impulses of the right, and the communitarian impulses of co-ethnics and co-religionists. Thus the moral commitment to refugees has been neither unitary nor unchanging. Whatever the merits of an internationalist, pan-refugee orientation, the American experience is very much a parochial one of different kinds of commitment toward different refugees based on their circumstances and identity: their class, their ethnicity, their race, their religion, their gender and age (for example, the frequent emphasis on women and children), the existence of a previous connection to the United States, and current U.S. relations with their homeland governments.

From its very nonbeginning in 1939, the U.S. refugee program thus illuminates what kind of people generate moral commitments strong enough to override the usual divisive force of national borders. There has been much discussion in recent years about the reasons why Americans should move beyond their own borders, whether for personal, economic, or military reasons; the years since 1939 provide an analogous inventory of the reasons why Americans believe those from foreign countries should be allowed to cross the borders into the United States. In more general immigration, much of that discussion is quite practical: Are immigrants contributing or not? In the more specific area of refugees, however, the issues are less practical. Instead, the question is whether there is such an overriding commitment to particular people outside U.S. borders that the United States should bring these people within its borders for limited—if any—practical gain.

Moral Commitments and Refugee Admissions

A review of the origins and numbers of refugees admitted to the United States since the Second World War indicates some specifics of this moral commitment. One theme is anticommunism. The United States has been consistently willing to accept as refugees those who flee (or wish to flee) communist regimes.[7] Anticommunism in itself is enough to explain virtually all refugee admissions up until the 1990s: 416,000 displaced persons after World War II who might otherwise have been repatriated to recently communist countries in eastern Europe;[8] 37,000 Hungarians fleeing after the failed uprising there in 1956; a million Cubans who have arrived since Castro's ascension to power in 1959; 1.3 million refugees from Vietnam, Laos, and Cambodia beginning in 1975; and refugees from various other communist countries, particularly the former Soviet Union and eastern Europe. That acceptance of refugees from communist countries has had some very practical political advantages. It has, for example, provided useful press coverage on people voting with their feet for freedom. Yet even such practical, political advantages rest largely on a moral commitment to stand for a particular kind of political and economic system and to recognize in word and deed that people fleeing a competing kind of political and economic system (sometimes even an "evil" system) have every reason to do so and every right to claim refuge in the United States.

However, the Cuban and Southeast Asian examples go well beyond anticommunism as a general stance to reflect very bitter relations with two specific communist regimes. Although the acceptance of early Cuban refugees might be construed as simple anticommunism, the dynamics of the Cuban expatriate community and the extent to which many people moved back and forth between Cuba and the United States before 1959 suggest something far more personal. Likewise, those fleeing from Cambodia, Laos, and Vietnam were not simply fleeing communism but also fleeing situations made worse by American involvement. This is not, then, simply an ideological commitment but also one that invokes a moral commitment to help those placed in harm's way by U.S. action. Refugee admissions are thus a partial restitution either for American inaction (letting Castro achieve power, leaving South Vietnam open to what was ultimately a North Vietnamese invasion) or for actions that made things worse (the Bay of Pigs, collusion in the assassination of Ngo Dinh Diem).

Although these two commitments—one of ideology and one of personal responsibility—help account for much of U.S. refugee admissions policy, they do not fully account for all refugee admissions or for the tenacity with which refugee admissions from some places have continued. Another kind of commitment—and also a moral one at least in part—is for the United States to take a fair share of refugees as part of broader international efforts. That is clear in the U.S. refugee program in the 1990s, especially with the increased numbers of refugees from Africa.[9] It helps explain earlier flows as well. Thus the United States came fairly late to the resettlement of displaced persons after World War II. Other countries had already indicated a willingness to accept displaced persons (although often for reasons more practical than moral).[10] More recently, much Southeast Asian resettlement after 1979 was part of a cooperative international effort to ease pressure on the countries of initial asylum in Southeast Asia. Those countries had begun to forcibly push refugees back to sea or across land borders—often to their deaths. In these cases, the United States was not only meeting its commitments of ideology and responsibility to the refugees but also making a fair-share contribution to resolving an international problem. Indeed, *fair share* is a recurring term in refugee policy deliberations.

There is one more crucial moral commitment: the one reflected in the refugee definition of the United Nations 1951 Convention and 1967 Protocol on Refugees—and of the U.S. refugee program itself since the incorporation of that definition into the Refugee Act of 1980. That is the commitment to aid people who have been subject to such a degree of persecution that they must flee their home and their country. What is perhaps most crucial (and difficult) about this definition is how individualized it is. Although there are roughly thirty million refugees and internally displaced persons in the world today,[11] the identification of refugees is technically subject to an individual determination based on both objective events and personal psychodynamics. Essentially, that legal standard involves a fear of persecution, not persecution per se. In practical terms, this requires a meticulous process for determining status, including the right to derivative refugee status for people who may not themselves meet the standard but who are the spouses, siblings, children, parents, or other relatives of those who do meet that standard. This last moral commitment thus poses particular difficulties for status determination.

To return to the somewhat apocryphal nonbeginning of the U.S. refugee program in 1939, it is clear that there was a disavowal of all these kinds of moral commitment: of any ideological reason to save the Jews, of any sense of responsibility for the position in which the Jews found themselves, of any need for a fair-share contribution to a broader international problem, or of any need to recognize the situation of even a few individual refugees. Yet there is an important addition to be made to that bleak assessment. If we look at the White House, and at a president who was swayed only with great effort to intervene on refugee issues, we also see down the hall another Roosevelt who was assiduously addressing refugee issues and engaged in individual correspondence with refugees.[12] Sometimes Eleanor would send notes down the hall to FDR. "FDR, can't something be done?" she wrote to him on a denied visa for a man in Portugal. "FDR, something does seem wrong," she wrote about a set of visas that had been approved but not issued. As Bethany Burns suggests from her review of archival documents at Hyde Park, there is a thread linking Eleanor Roosevelt's correspondence at that time with the broader role she would take after the war on behalf of displaced persons.[13] In that sense, the formal beginnings of the U.S. refugee program, perhaps most usefully seen as the 1948 Displaced Persons Act, lay in the nonbeginning of that program nearly a decade earlier, in the work of Eleanor Roosevelt and others like her who saw both the general humanitarian demands posed by groups of refugees and the extraordinary personal experiences of individual refugees.

Refugee Admissions and Refugee Resettlement

The United States, through these multiple commitments, has admitted nearly four million refugees for resettlement since the Second World War. Those included in these overall numbers arrived under a variety of specific legal statuses. Many, for example, entered under the provisional parole authority of the U.S. attorney general. Even when their legal status was regularized, *refugee* status was not necessarily invoked. Cubans, in particular, have largely been regularized under 1966 legislation (the Cuban

Adjustment Act) that does not include the word *refugee* at all. On the other hand, in some statistics various kinds of status are counted as "refugee" even though in technical legal terms they are not: for example, Amerasians, Orderly Departure Program (ODP) immigrants, Cuban-Haitian entrants, and asylees. In addition, there are a wide range of other legal and illegal immigrants whom many people would also consider fully admissible as refugees because all the arguments about moral commitments apply to them as well—except perhaps that a broad "flight from totalitarianism" is substituted for a narrower "flight from communism." The largest such group were those from Central America who arrived in the United States in the 1980s.[14]

These definitional issues aside, admitting refugees to the United States has raised several persistent challenges. Those challenges are often very political. Without strong constituencies, the number of refugees admitted is likely to drift downward. Many of the challenges, however, are more practical and operational. Often they are simply logistic. Thus, from the time of the post–World War II displaced persons onward, there has been a concern with the "pipeline" through which refugees can be transported to the United States. (Even today the U.S. Department of State has a budget category for "pipeline development.") Sometimes the pipeline has developed additional twists, turns, and holding tanks because of uncertainties at the ends of the pipeline and more routine administrative concerns to regulate the flow of refugees. Sometimes there has also been a desire to provide health screening, cultural orientation, and language training for refugees before their arrival in local U.S. communities. For example, refugee processing centers (RPCs) were set up for Southeast Asian refugees on U.S. territory in 1975 and then overseas following the massive boat exodus of the late 1970s.[15] Even the logistics after refugees reach the United States are complex. Initial destinations must be chosen and coordinated among resettlement agencies. Those agencies, in turn, must move new arrivals into appropriate housing, through health screening, and toward education and employment.

These practical challenges reflect the sheer scope of what is required in the refugee resettlement process. Refugee resettlement involves a level of social engineering virtually unknown in the United States. After all, the refugee program aims to take people whose lives have been utterly disrupted, whose kin and community networks—those most elemental of "safety nets"—have been attenuated and ruptured, whose expectations may never have been to come to America, who may know no English, and who may have no exposure to an urban, industrial society, and, despite all this, turn them into functioning, successful Americans. It is hardly surprising that refugees sometimes do not make a rapid transition. It is also not surprising that those attempting to assist refugees sometimes drift into quasi-parental views of "their" refugees, for it is perhaps only in parenting that Americans have a model of such broad responsibility for some other person's complete social transformation. In turn, the frustration when adult refugees do not make this transformation quickly helps explain why persons assisting refugees sometimes skip over the difficulties of adult refugees and focus instead on the social transformation of refugee children.

This task of social transformation is especially difficult because of the diversity of refugees coming to the United States. Since there is no uniform set of characteristics shared among those entering as refugees (other than the refugee experience itself), there is also no common starting point for this process of social transformation. In recent years, as the U.S. refugee program has become more representative of global refugee flows, the degree of diversity in national and ethnic origin has become impressive. Refugee groups with more than ten thousand arrivals since 1982 include Afghans, Bosnians, Cambodians, Cubans, Hmong, Iranians, Iraqis, Lao, Liberians, Poles, Romanians, Russians (and those from other parts of the former Soviet Union), Somalis, Sudanese, and Vietnamese. Furthermore, there are many other smaller groups of refugees, and there is often ethnic and religious variation within these national-origin groups. For example, Iranians include Bahais, Christians, Jews, and Muslims; Russians include both Jews and Pentecostal Christians. The latest group of refugees from Somalia is hardly Somali in an ethnic sense: they are Bantu people who were trafficked north into Somalia as labor and often as slaves. This range of cultural diversity is, for many, the glory of the refugee program, despite the many practical difficulties it poses—translation, for example.

There are other kinds of diversity as well. Perhaps most important are age and gender. Gender is unpredictable in its effects, working to favor sometimes women and sometimes men, but populations with gender imbalance (for example, lack of young women or lack of older men) face social and economic challenges. Age, in turn, has enormous effects on how quickly people adapt to the United States—the younger usually the better. Educational background, occupational background, and English-language competence are also usually crucial.[16]

Given great diversity in all these areas, and the lack of any standard starting point for this ambitious social transformation, measuring progress toward resettlement goals has inherent difficulties. To the inevitable and seemingly reasonable program question "How are refugees doing?" there can be only conditional answers because the degree of progress hinges on the starting point. One can argue, for example, that the more the U.S. program is helping refugees most desperately in need, the more difficult the course of their adjustment to the United States will be. Consequently there is a temptation to select from any group of refugees those who will do best after resettlement and therefore make the resettlement program look as if it is working well. There is also a temptation to pass over refugees entirely in favor of other immigrants who—whether legal or illegal—will make fewer program demands and promise a clearer and more immediate economic benefit.

Refugee Resettlement and Employment: Data Considerations

These problems in assessing refugee adjustment to the United States are severe. They can be seen even in what is probably the most common measure of progress in refugee resettlement: employment. There are extensive quantitative data addressing refugee employment. For example, annual surveys of refugees have been conducted in one form or another by the federal government since 1975.[17] Data from the late 1990s suggest impressive improvement in the situation of the refugees. Whereas in 1995 labor force participation was 50 percent for refugees (versus 67 percent for the general U.S. population), the figure had risen to 69 percent by 1999 (versus a U.S. rate of 67 percent).[18] Similarly, refugee unemployment was 15 percent in 1995 (versus a U.S. rate of 5 percent) but had dropped to 3 percent (U.S. rate: 4 percent) by 1999. Yet the portrait in 1999 matches, in many ways, that of 1979, twenty years earlier. At that earlier time, the economic adjustment of Vietnamese refugees appeared to be rather good. They were employed at higher rates than the general U.S. population and also appeared to be working longer hours. Although there was downward occupational mobility, their status report was one of relative success, and likewise relative success for the refugee resettlement program.

Between these two dates of 1979 and 1999, however, the employment status of refugees was far less encouraging. If 1986 and 1993, for example, are compared with 1999, the contrast is pronounced.[19] For first-year arrivals, the overall employment ratio (which combines the effects of labor force participation and unemployment) was 23 percent in 1986 and 25 percent in 1993, compared to the very respectable figure of 51 percent in 1999. That is, in 1986 and again in 1993, the employment ratio for first-year arrivals was less than half of what it was in 1999. For those who had been in the United States for five years, the overall employment ratio was 40 percent in 1986 and 26 percent in 1993,[20] compared to 67 percent in 1999.

These data are striking in their contrast of comparatively poor employment "outcomes" in the late 1980s and early 1990s with comparatively impressive employment outcomes at the end of the 1970s and the end of the 1990s. The data could be taken to represent the decline and resurrection of the refugee resettlement program. Or they could reflect shifting economic conditions, good in 1979 and 1999 versus the relatively difficult times of the early 1980s. Or perhaps the data reflect shifts in the characteristics of arriving refugees. That is certainly the case for the early 1980s, when new arrivals had more limited educational, occupational, and English-language skills. Certainly within different arrival cohorts the effects of background characteristics are crucial. For 1999 survey data, for example, the employment situation varies widely depending on the world region from which the refugees came. Those from Asia, for example, appeared to be doing fairly well in employment terms, those from the former Soviet Union and Africa far less so. These are not simply cultural differences; they are rooted in elemental issues of demography and human capital. Refugees from the Soviet Union, for example, were far older; those from Africa had far less education. Advanced age and low education are severe obstacles in U.S. employment. Indeed, younger refugees from the Soviet Union and better-educated Africans are more often employed than the apparently more successful refugees from other countries.

Refugee Resettlement, Employment, and Self-Sufficiency: Policy Considerations

Refugee resettlement is thus aimed at an enormous social transformation for which even the most rudimentary measure of progress (employment) indicates as much about the starting point of the process, and the conditions under which it occurs, as it does about progress per se. Although there are statistical ways to begin to sort out the respective contributions of human capital, program actions, and resettlement context, they are not easily used even for relatively large populations, such as Cubans and Vietnamese, let alone for the numerous smaller populations and the cultural, ethnic, religious, and linguistic subgroups within the larger populations. There is an even more fundamental problem: the very inadequacy of employment as a program measure. Why is immediate employment so crucial? Why not have people go to school so they can get better jobs later on? Why not have parents stay home with their children, keeping them out of trouble and helping them do their schoolwork so that in the future the children can have better jobs or can themselves do a better job of helping their own children with their schoolwork, and so on?

The 1980 U.S. Refugee Act gives mixed guidance on this issue of employment.[21] The actual wording in the act can be taken to mean either a goal of any work now *or* a goal of the best possible work in the future, specifically "employment commensurate with existing skills and abilities." This ambiguity reflects the failure to resolve the debate that was in process at the time the Refugee Act was passed in 1980. At that time, for example, there were programs for retraining professionals so that they could practice their former profession. "Employment commensurate with existing skills and abilities" did not automatically mean that if a refugee doctor had limited English competence the only employment option was manual labor. It was only in the context of the new Reagan administration in 1981, when notions of "welfare dependency" began to infiltrate the refugee program, that this notion of appropriate employment came to mean what it usually means now: employment of any kind and as soon as possible. A focus on immediate employment, however, avoids the question of occupational futures: What kind of employment, with what future increases in wages and benefits?[22] Only such longer-term data can address a broader notion of employment and how it relates to refugee integration into American society.

At the risk of making this discussion even more convoluted, some brief comment is needed regarding the Refugee Act's other major goal for refugee resettlement: achieving self-sufficiency. Part of the problem with assessing "self-sufficiency" mirrors that for employment. Is the goal marginal self-sufficiency now or a more stable self-sufficiency in the future? There are also questions about the very meaning of self-sufficiency. Self-sufficient in what respect? Living in a decent neighborhood? Having health care? Raising children with some parental involvement? It is in areas like this that policy analysis and cultural studies come together: apparently objective program outcomes turn out to be quite conditional to cultural meanings. Rather than addressing those broader questions, self-sufficiency (like employment) is often treated in U.S. refugee resettlement at the rudimentary "have-it-or-not" level, which is then translated operationally into "receiving public assistance or not."[23]

This inability to establish basic program goals, much less any reasonable progress markers toward meeting those goals, helps explain some of the inconsistency of the U.S. refugee resettlement program over time and of U.S. public opinion about refugees. It is, as noted, fundamentally impossible to give a simple, straight answer to the seemingly reasonable program question "How are refugees doing?" Any answer is highly contingent. It just depends: on which refugees, with what characteristics, having gone through what experiences before arrival, and living in what kind of America, both generally (economic boom? recession?) and in terms of specific locale (good schools? crime on the streets? helpful employers?).[24] This inability to answer a simple program question poses an overarching challenge to the refugee program. It causes enormous frustration to the many people who want to say, "Refugees are doing great," because they know that on some level that is true. It is likewise a frustration to the many people who want to say, "Refugees are having serious problems," because they know that is true on some level as well.

There is a brighter side to this dilemma. Much of the difficulty lies with the diversity of the refugee population and the fact that refugees are *not* selected simply for how well they will do in adapting to the U.S. labor market. This does not mean there are no temptations toward such preselection. Much of the early interest in post–World War II displaced persons, for example, was by countries seeking to fill employment needs: Belgium wanted coal miners, Canada wanted farmworkers and domestics, Britain wanted factory workers and domestics, Iraq wanted doctors. Furthermore, much of the process of selecting displaced persons was geared toward the convenience of a good fit with a resettlement country, whether that involved Australia's interest in those of British stock, a preference by many countries for those from the Baltics, or even a somewhat accidental particular connection like that between Argentina and Slovenians.[25] Despite such temptations—which continue into recent times—the moral commitments to refugees suggest that the fit between refugees and the societies that resettle them need not be a smooth one. Smooth adjustment should simply not be the primary purpose of a refugee program.

Concluding Thoughts: 1939 and 2005

This chapter began by setting a beginning date and an ending date for a review of refugees and America: 1939 and 2005. The selection of those dates suggests an implicit comparison: between now and then, between how events developed then and how they may develop now. In many ways, the comparison yields sharp differences. There is now, unlike then, a functioning refugee program, a commitment to accept refugees from most parts of the world, and a large, relatively open immigration policy of which refugees are but a minor component. The levels of discrimination by race and religion of 1939 stand in sharp contrast to a contemporary refugee program that is manifestly responsive to all religions and has finally demonstrated a relatively proportionate attention to refugees from Africa.

In other ways, however, the comparison between 1939 and 2005 yields similarities. Now, as then, there is a frequent American belief that problems in the world ought to be (and are being) handled "there" rather than "here in the United States." Now, as then, there are concerns about the dangers posed by newcomers to American society—and even to its security. Finally, now, as then, the result has been the failure to admit refugees into the United States even when admission slots for them have been available. Contemporary interdictions at sea and summary deportations at airports would seem quite in place in 1939. Furthermore, the delay in arrivals after September 11, 2001, has not been remedied by a catch-up period and has been followed by what appear to be permanently reduced refugee flows.[26] Even though the refugee program returned to some extent to "normal" flows in fiscal years 2004 and 2005, a conservative calculation is that in fiscal years 2002 and 2003 some fifty to eighty thousand refugees did not arrive who would otherwise now be in the United States. Furthermore, the new "normal" rate of admissions is less than 60 percent of what would be projected from the years from 1975 to 2000 (i.e., fifty-three thousand in fiscal year 2004 versus an average of ninety-two thousand from 1975 to 2000).

Despite these limitations, this small refugee resettlement program continues to shed much light on both the world from which the refugees come and the world in which refugees find themselves in the United States. In the refugee experience lies an invaluable story of the world and its horrors, but also a story of how American moral commitments coalesce into action: how Americans collectively and individually, through private and public sectors, on the basis of secular and religious commitments, set about solving complex social problems. Those American efforts are not always successful. Yet they indicate much of the best that America can be, should be, and even must be in the twenty-first century. As the history of the United States and the history of U.S. immigration once again coalesce, it is the fate of refugees that is likely to hold the key to understanding Americans' moral connection to the rest of the world—rather than more instrumental concerns with the economic benefits of immigrant labor and the ease with which immigrants fit into American society.

NOTES

This is a revised version of a paper originally developed for the 2003 Transcending Borders conference of the Immigration and Ethnic History Society. I am indebted to the other participants there and to the audience at two other occasions during which I further developed this paper: as the keynote speech at the 2004 annual meeting of the American Studies Association of Korea and as a public lecture at Miami University of Ohio in spring 2005 (special thanks to Mary Jane Berman and Oliver Mogga).

1. For general reviews of the refugee program, see Julia Vadala Taft, David S. North, and David A. Ford, *Refugee Resettlement in the U.S.: Time for a New Focus* (Washington, DC: New TransCentury Foundation, 1979); Gil Loescher and John Scanlan, *Calculated Kindness: Refugees and America's Half-Open Door* (New York: Macmillan, 1986); Gil Loescher, *Beyond Charity: International Cooperation and the Global Refugee Crisis* (New York: Oxford University Press, 1993); Norman L. Zucker and Naomi Flink Zucker, *The Guarded Gate: The Reality of American Refugee Policy* (San Diego: Harcourt Brace Jovanovich, 1987) and *Desperate Crossings: Seeking Refuge in America* (Armonk, NY: M. E. Sharpe, 1996); Barry N. Stein and Sylvano M. Tomasi, eds., "Refugees Today," special issue of *International Migration Review* 15, nos. 1–2 (1981); and Dennis Gallagher, ed., "Refugees: Issues and Directions," special issue of *International Migration Review* 20, no. 2 (1986). For a recent reassessment of the U.S. refugee program, see David Martin, *The United States Refugee Admission Program: Reforms for a New Era of Refugee Resettlement* (Washington, DC: Migration Policy Institute, 2005).

2. There would also be good reason to begin this story in 1938 with the Evian Conference. See David S. Wyman, *Paper Walls: America and the Refugee Crisis, 1938–1941,* (1968; reprint, New York: Pantheon Books, 1985), 41–51; and Loescher, *Beyond Charity,* 44–45. I use 1939 here instead because of the way the story of the *St. Louis* has endured as a symbol of the rejection of refugees. That vision of ships pushed back to sea returned in the late 1970s with the Vietnamese boat exodus—though with a loss of life that makes the later 1942 voyage of the *Struma* (which

was pushed back and then sank with only two survivors) more harrowing in its implications than that of the *St. Louis*. Vice-President Walter Mondale, for example, invoked the ill-fated *St. Louis* as a way to increase public support for the Southeast Asian boat people (see Loescher and Scanlan, *Calculated Kindness,* 145). The year 1939 is also useful because of the pairing of the *St. Louis* incident with the failure to pass the Wagner-Rogers legislation. The pairing highlights the two themes of energizing crisis and plodding legislation that have often characterized the American response to refugees.

3. D. Wyman, *Paper Walls,* 38–39.

4. Certainly the majority of those involved would have been Jewish, but there was also some question of what proportion were Jewish by actual religion and what proportion were Jewish simply in the Nazi sense of having Jewish forebears. David Wyman (*Paper Walls,* 86) estimates that some 50 to 60 percent of those who would have benefited from the Wagner-Rogers bill were Jewish by religion.

5. David S. Wyman, *The Abandonment of the Jews: America and the Holocaust, 1941–1945* (1984; reprint, New York: New Press, 1998).

6. Leonard Dinnerstein, *America and the Survivors of the Holocaust* (New York: Columbia University Press, 1982); Mark Wyman, *DPs: Europe's Displaced Persons, 1945–1951* (1989; reprint, Ithaca: Cornell University Press, 1998).

7. Many refugees are, in fact, accepted by the United States before they actually flee. "In-country processing" (i.e., processing of refugees in their countries of origin) became increasingly common in the 1980s not only for Vietnamese through the ODP but also for those from the Soviet Union and its successor states, and, in smaller numbers, for other refugees as well. Bill Frelick provides a usefully scathing critique of in-country processing and how it works to the disadvantage of those in greatest danger. See Bill Frelick, "Hardening the Heart: The Global Refugee Problem in the 1990s," in *Refugees in America in the 1990s,* ed. David W. Haines (Westport, CT: Greenwood Press, 1996), 372–82.

8. The Displaced Persons Act of 1948 provided for 205,000 persons, but this was increased to 415,744 when that act was amended in 1950.

9. The broadening of the geographical origins of refugees to the United States is nowhere clearer than in relation to Africa. Although the Refugee Act of 1980 theoretically opened the way to broader geographical representation among refugees admitted to the United States, the entire Africa contingent numbered less than three thousand in 1981. But by 2001, the African contingent was nearly nineteen thousand, with Somalis and Sudanese accounting respectively for five thousand and six thousand admissions. As a percentage of refugee arrivals, Africans increased during that twenty-year period from less than 2 percent to over 25 percent of refugee arrivals.

10. Various countries, in Europe and including Canada, saw the displaced persons camps as sources of needed labor to compensate for postwar labor shortages. The jobs to be filled, of course, were not always ideal. The Belgians, for example,

were the first to take a sizable number of displaced persons from the camps, but that was for twenty thousand coal miners. Women were often sought as domestic workers, and many had to be advised to avoid mentioning any higher education, since that would make them overqualified for such jobs and thus unacceptable for placement out of the camps. See Robert A. Divine, *American Immigration Policy, 1924–1952* (New Haven: Yale University Press, 1957); M. Wyman, *DPs*; Dinnerstein, *Survivors*.

11. Probably the best source of overall refugee numbers is the annual *World Refugee Survey* conducted by what is now the U.S. Committee for Immigrants and Refugees.

12. These examples come from Bethany Burns's "Eleanor Roosevelt and the American People in the Refugee Crisis of 1938–41" (PhD diss., George Mason University, 2002). The nature of these cases is, as she notes, consistent with the notion of Joseph P. Lash, the Roosevelts' biographer, regarding the different roles and sensibilities of Eleanor and Franklin Roosevelt: that he often brought up "difficulties," while she pointed out the possibilities." See Joseph P. Lash, *Eleanor and Franklin* (New York: W. W. Norton, 1971), 636. But that view is also consistent with a distinction between Eleanor's personal, individualized humanitarianism and Franklin's interest-group-oriented politicism.

13. Burns, "Eleanor Roosevelt."

14. Margarita B. Melville, "Salvadoreans and Guatemalans," in *Refugees in the United States: A Reference Handbook,* ed. David W. Haines (Westport, CT: Greenwood Press, 1985), 167–80; Robin Lorentzen, *Women in the Sanctuary Movement* (Philadelphia: Temple University Press, 1991); Allan F. Burns, *Maya in Exile: Guatemalans in Florida* (Philadelphia: Temple University Press, 1993); Susan Bibler Coutin, *The Culture of Protest: Religious Activism and the U.S. Sanctuary Movement* (Boulder, CO: Westview Press, 1993); Sarah J. Mahler, *American Dreaming: Immigrant Life on the Margins* (Princeton: Princeton University Press, 1995); Terry A. Repak, *Waiting on Washington: Central American Workers in the Nation's Capital* (Philadelphia: Temple University Press, 1995); Victoria Rader, "Refugees at Risk: The Sanctuary Movement and Its Aftermath," in *Illegal Immigration in America,* ed. David W. Haines and Karen E. Rosenblum (Westport, CT: Greenwood Press, 1999), 325–45.

15. Some kind of camp experience is very common for refugees. That experience is highly variable. See Lynellyn D. Long, *Ban Vinai: The Refugee Camp* (New York: Columbia University Press, 1993); W. Courtland Robinson, *Terms of Refuge: The Indochinese Exodus and the International Response* (New York: Zed Books, 1998); Liisa H. Malkki, *Purity and Exile: Violence, Memory, and National Cosmology among Hutu Refugees in Tanzania* (Chicago: University of Chicago Press, 1995); James W. Tollefson, *Alien Winds: The Reeducation of America's Indochinese Refugees* (New York: Praeger, 1989); Adelaida Reyes, *Songs of the Caged, Song of the Free:*

Music and the Vietnamese Refugee Experience (Philadelphia: Temple University Press, 1999). The United States had such camps on U.S. soil in 1975. See Gail Paradise Kelly, *From Vietnam to America: A Chronicle of the Vietnamese Immigration to the United States* (Boulder, CO: Westview Press, 1977); and William T. Liu, Maryanne Lamanna, and Alice Murata, *Transition to Nowhere: Vietnamese Refugees in America* (Nashville, TN: Charter House, 1979).

16. The one clear exception to the importance of English-language competence involves cases in which Spanish functions as a lingua franca in lieu of English. That explains the reason why English-language competence sometimes is not a crucial factor in statistical analyses of Hispanic refugee and immigrant adaptation to the United States. Yet even there, the importance of English in addition to Spanish is usually recognized. See Alejandro Portes and Rubén G. Rumbaut, *Immigrant America,* 2nd ed. (Berkeley: University of California Press, 1996); and Alejandro Portes and Rubén G. Rumbaut, *Legacies: The Story of the Immigrant Second Generation* (Berkeley: University of California Press, 2001).

17. Findings for these surveys are in annual reports to the Congress, the most recent of which are online at www.acf.dhhs.gov/programs/orr/reporting/. Linda Gordon provides a useful overview of the surveys through the mid-1980s; see Linda W. Gordon, "National Surveys of Southeast Asian Refugees: Methods, Findings, Issues," in *Refugees as Immigrants: Cambodians, Laotians, and Vietnamese in America,* ed. David W. Haines (Totowa, NJ: Rowman and Littlefield, 1989), 24–39.

18. These are figures of the total sampled refugee population, which was limited to arrivals over the preceding five years. The numbers thus refer to the five-year population in each of the years noted.

19. Because the data for 1979 differ greatly in how they were calculated, the discussion here is largely limited to years with general consistency in conduct of the surveys and presentation of the findings (i.e., 1986, 1993, and 1999). I have also not included more recent data because the shifts in the program both before and after September 11, 2001, have been very sharp. There is, in fact, some decline in employment indicators seen in the 2002 survey, but it is modest.

20. This figure of 26 percent is probably aberrant. The pattern of data from 1993 is relatively similar to that from 1986 for all other lengths of residence.

21. U.S. Code 1522 (a)(1)(B) is hardly subtle in its directive that "employable refugees should be placed on jobs as soon as possible after their arrival in the United States," reflecting section 412 (a)(1)(B)(i) of the Immigration and Nationality Act. Yet section 413(b)(5) of that same act implies a broader goal in that it requires reporting on "evaluations of the extent to which . . . the services provided under this chapter are assisting refugees in achieving economic self-sufficiency, achieving ability in English, and achieving employment commensurate with their skills and abilities." Furthermore, the original House bill itself had an even broader scope "to assist adult refugees in gaining skills and education necessary to become

employed or otherwise self-sufficient, including facility in English, vocational and technical training, professional refresher training and other certification services, and social and employment services."

22. David W. Haines, "The Pursuit of English and Self-Sufficiency: Dilemmas in Assessing Refugee Program Effects," *Journal of Refugee Studies* 1, no. 3/4 (1988): 195–213; Steven Gold and Nazli Kibria, "Vietnamese Refugees and Blocked Mobility," *Asian and Pacific Migration Journal* 2, no. 1 (1993): 27–56.

23. Self-sufficiency as a program goal also raises formidable methodological problems. What is self-sufficiency as a social science variable? Is it to be construed as an attribute of individuals, of households, of families (which sometimes involve wider nets of people beyond the household), or of some combination of all of these? The simplest answer is to treat self-sufficiency as an attribute of households, but even that requires analysis of the interaction effects of people as individuals, as parts of households, and as conditioned by the totality of the household.

24. For some examples, see David W. Haines and Carol A. Mortland, eds., *Manifest Destinies: Americanizing Immigrants and Internationalizing Americans* (Westport, CT: Praeger, 2001).

25. M. Wyman, *DPs.*

26. As the late Arthur Helton put it, efforts on behalf of refugees "should surely be more than the administration of misery" and driven by something more than the "selective apathy and creeping trepidation" he saw in the aftermath of September 11. See Arthur C. Helton, *The Price of Indifference: Refugees and Humanitarian Action in the New Century* (New York: Oxford University Press, 2002), 290, 29.

BIBLIOGRAPHY

Caplan, Nathan, Marcella H. Choy, and John K. Whitmore. *Children of the Boat People: A Study of Educational Success.* Ann Arbor: University of Michigan Press, 1991.

Coutin, Susan Bibler. *The Culture of Protest: Religious Activism and the U.S. Sanctuary Movement.* Boulder, CO: Westview Press, 1993.

Dinnerstein, Leonard. *America and the Survivors of the Holocaust.* New York: Columbia University Press, 1982.

Haines, David W., ed. *Refugees as Immigrants: Cambodians, Laotians, and Vietnamese in America.* Totowa, NJ: Rowman and Littlefield, 1989.

———, ed. *Refugees in America in the 1990s.* Westport, CT: Greenwood Press, 1996.

Kelly, Gail Paradise. *From Vietnam to America: A Chronicle of the Vietnamese Immigration to the United States.* Boulder, CO: Westview Press, 1977.

Loescher, Gil, and John Scanlan. *Calculated Kindness: Refugees and America's Half-Open Door*. New York: Macmillan, 1986.

Robinson, W. Courtland. *Terms of Refuge: The Indochinese Exodus and the International Response*. New York: Zed Books, 1998.

Wyman, David S. *The Abandonment of the Jews: America and the Holocaust, 1941–1945*. 1984. Reprint, New York: New Press, 1998.

———. *Paper Walls: America and the Refugee Crisis, 1938–1941*. 1968. Reprint, New York: Pantheon Books, 1985.

Wyman, Mark. *DPs: Europe's Displaced Persons, 1945–1951*. 1989. Reprint, Ithaca: Cornell University Press, 1998.

Zucker, Norman L., and Naomi Flink Zucker. *Desperate Crossings: Seeking Refuge in America*. Armonk, NY: M. E. Sharpe, 1996.

Chapter 2

Migration, Immigration, and Naturalization in America

Karen A. Woodrow-Lafield

Early studies on the great European immigration were soon followed by others pointing to differences by country of origin in the percentage of immigrants who made the transition from permanent residency to naturalized citizenship. Reflecting debates about the mixture of immigrants with respect to race and ethnicity, these studies noted that some immigrant groups from countries of southern and eastern Europe were lagging behind others on several measures of socioeconomic success, including naturalization. Many immigrants simply did not stay permanently. Wage convergence between Europe and America led to a lowering of emigration from Europe before World War I, and this may also have accounted for high return migration from the United States between 1910 and 1930, including those who intended only temporary stays. One-third of all immigrants who came to America between 1900 and 1980 subsequently emigrated.

Following the immigration of 19 million persons in the first three decades of the twentieth century, there was a period of lower immigration. The numbers of lawfully admitted immigrants were 0.5 million in the 1930s, 1.0 million in the 1940s, 2.5 million in the 1950s, and 3.3 million in the 1960s. Fewer new immigrants were joining natives and earlier immigrants during this period, whose events included the Depression, the Second World War, the postwar boom, and increasing urbanization. Scientific commitments to the classical assimilation perspective seemed to waver as differences by ethnicity were revealed to be persistent and pervasive. Nevertheless, identificational assimilation as naturalized citizens (blending one's identification with that of the host society) seemed to be happening more readily than other types, such as marital and structural assimilation,[1] for the percentage of naturalized citizens increased.

Ever since the Immigration and Nationality Act of 1965 set forth new immigration laws that dispensed with national origins quotas, most immigrants granted lawful permanent residence have been admitted under family-sponsored preference categories or as immediate relatives of U.S. citizens, while many others have come under employment sponsorship, humanitarian criteria (including asylum and refugee provisions), and other categories. The unmarried and married adult sons and daughters or siblings of citizens, with their spouses and children, may receive visas subject to numerical limitation. Parents, spouses, and minor children who are immediate relatives of citizens may be sponsored without such limitation. Permanent residents may apply for visas for only their spouses and children, subject to numerical limitation. Individuals may be sponsored by employers who need their skills or capabilities if the U.S. government deems their work to be sufficiently important in the labor market, again subject to limitation.

Immigrants under humanitarian criteria include refugees and asylees who have demonstrated, with respect to their origin countries, that they are "unable or unwilling to return to that country because of persecution or a well-founded fear of persecution, based on the alien's race, religion, nationality, membership in a particular social group, or political opinion," according to the 1951 Geneva Convention. The Refugee Act of 1980 established the first permanent and systematic procedure for the admission and resettlement of refugees and provided for adjustment to lawful permanent resident status for refugees who had been physically present for at least one year and for asylees for at least one year after asylum was granted. Some recent immigrants were admitted under diversity-based criteria, as specified in the Immigration Act of 1990 (IMMACT), following an earlier program under the Immigration Reform and Control Act of 1986 (IRCA) that made visas available to individuals from countries that are less represented among immigrants.

At the time of the 1965 act, immigration had been gradually rising, especially among Mexicans after termination of the Mexico-U.S. *bracero* programs (because family members were immigrating) and among Asians. The act replaced the quota system with a preference-based one that set an annual visa limit of 170,000 immigrants for the Eastern Hemisphere, with a maximum of 20,000 from any one country. Under amendments in 1976, the preference system was extended to Western Hemisphere countries with an annual visa limit of 120,000 immigrants for the Western Hemisphere and again with a ceiling of 20,000 per country. In 1978, hemisphere limits were replaced by an overall worldwide limit of 290,000 immigrants under preference categories. Nevertheless, Mexican and other Western Hemisphere immigrants increased, particularly through the sponsorship of immediate relatives as earlier immigrants naturalized and obtained visas for spouses, children, and parents.[2] Then, as now, Mexicans showed lower naturalization levels than most other nationalities, a finding that may have been related to their education, occupational status, and knowledge of English, as well as their geographic proximity, economic reasons for migrating, and reluctance to relinquish Mexican nationality.[3]

Among those immigrants of the twentieth century who settled, many were naturalized after fulfilling the residence requirement, even after lengthy periods of residence. Most individuals must have at least five years as lawfully permanent residents. In fact, the 1930 to 1980 censuses showed that foreign-born persons, including many of European origins, were likely to be long settled and to hold naturalized citizenship, a well-documented correlation. But whereas on average the foreign-born population was aging from 1910 to 1970, it has become younger since 1970, reflecting a dramatic shift in U.S. immigration trends: in both the 1990 and 2000 censuses, noncitizens outnumbered naturalized citizens, and the high percentage of the foreign-born population who reported that they had arrived in this country during the most recent five-year period (1995–2000) meant that many were not yet eligible for naturalization.

The trends of the 1970s, 1980s, and 1990s that have so altered the foreign-born population are significant increases in unauthorized migration for short-term stays as well as the considerable presence of an unauthorized long-term resident population; predominance of family ties as the basis for admissions of lawful permanent residents; and increasing numbers of nonimmigrants who have entered for education, work, and business. A temporary, unauthorized migrant may settle permanently. That is, immigrants who are lawful permanent residents include not only those newly arriving in the United States with permanent resident status but also those who initially entered the country as lawful temporary residents and who later adjusted to permanent resident status. Both groups subsequently become eligible to apply for naturalization. Nearly three million formerly unauthorized persons made this adjustment in 1989–91 after they received temporary resident status under IRCA's amnesty provisions. However, they could not have qualified for citizenship by 1990 even though about two million of them had lived in the United States since 1981. Unauthorized migration increased in the late 1990s, and eight or nine million unauthorized residents in 2000, including four million Mexicans, were obviously ineligible for naturalization. Nonimmigrant arrivals, including temporary travelers for business and pleasure, foreign students, and special workers, rose markedly in the 1980s and 1990s, and many of those eventually adjusted their status to lawful permanent residence. Changes to U.S. immigration have occurred in the context of incorporation of nations into global markets, paralleling the historical period 1865–1915, with international exchanges of people (ranging from professional to unskilled workers) as well as goods.[4] Contemporary immigrants may be strongly committed to living in the United States in that the relative attractiveness of their origin countries is not likely to improve quickly in terms of social and economic measures. Return migration is probably at a lower rate than the historical rate of one emigrant to three immigrants.[5]

Obtaining lawful admission for permanent residence is based on a considerable mix of demographic and socioeconomic characteristics and admission circumstances. An immigrant is an alien receiving lawful permanent residence, and he or she is either newly arriving or adjusting status (i.e., already living) in the United States. Such an individual is qualified to receive an immigrant visa or is a close relative of someone who is the principal immigrant. Generally speaking, an immigrant is admitted as a family-sponsored preference immigrant, an immediate relative of a citizen (not numerically limited), an employment-sponsored preference immigrant, or another type of immigrant, such as an adjusting refugee or asylee. He or she may have no friends or family members living in the United States but the likelihood is greater that the individual has friends or close or extended family members who have already established U.S. residence, since so many are now joining or accompanying family members given migration networks and the family reunification provision. Probably only a small percentage of immigrants could be considered original immigrants without any consanguineal or affineal family members already living in the United States. The immigration event occurs at various points in the life cycle: some immigrants are children who come to the United States with immigrating parents or are joining their parents; some are immigrating adults of working and parenting ages; and others are elderly immigrants joining their adult children.

Several empirical sources report country-of-origin differences in the proportion of immigrants naturalizing in a particular year or from a single cohort (administrative data) and in the proportion of immigrants who have been naturalized over time (earlier censuses and surveys). From official sources based on administrative records, Asians are acquiring citizenship or completing the naturalization process after fewer years of residence than North Americans. Official reports following two immigrant cohorts of 1977 and 1982 show how naturalization levels vary by duration of residence, origin, and immigrant visa class. With regard to visa class, professional or highly skilled immigrants and refugees have shown higher naturalization rates, and parents of citizens have apparently been less likely to naturalize than other categories of relatives. However, Asians who are apparently naturalizing more quickly are also more likely to have characteristics associated with higher naturalization, such as holding managerial and professional occupations or having refugee histories. Because length of residence is so relevant and because immigrants of various origins present different profiles on immigrant visa classes, rigorous research has much to offer on this question.

This essay analyzes these variables and considers the theoretical bases for explaining naturalization patterns and variations, which draw on current theories of immigrant incorporation. The discussion then turns to the dual challenges of empirical resources and modeling strategies for studying the naturalization patterns or trends of contemporary immigrants. Key findings on origin, mode of entry, and admission circumstances are presented in relation to the naturalization of recent immigrants. Finally, questions are posed for future research on studies of migration, immigration, and naturalization. As the U.S. foreign-born population continues to change dramatically in an era of increasing international migration, the study of naturalization as incorporation of immigrants is becoming increasingly important.

Theoretical Background

Acquisition of U.S. citizenship is presumed to signify intentions of long-term settlement, eligibility for political participation, and adaptation in language and knowledge of civics and history as well as socioeconomic adaptation in making one's way in this society. These are generally regarded as positive reasons for naturalizing that reflect the theme of Americanization. There are also less noble, more utilitarian reasons for becoming naturalized, such as gaining access to privileges reserved for U.S. citizens, ranging from labor force opportunities to sponsorship of family members for immigrant visas. Since the 1990s, several other meanings are attaching to possession of U.S. citizenship, whether actual or tangential: it may be seen as providing the ideal safeguard against deportation, the surest protection of access to public benefits, or the single document that most facilitates international travel.

Examining naturalization requires first considering the theoretical explanations of immigration. Neoclassical theory can account for some migration decision making, as there may be poor prospects for economic livelihood in the origin community. Individuals who decide to maximize expected income through migration may relocate the entire household or leave other household members in the origin country.[6] Strong evidence suggests some positive selectivity of immigrants from origin countries on skills, temperament, or vigor, but that association is not fixed and depends on contexts, migration dynamics, and social networks. The forces of social capital theory (such as ties to parents, siblings, and community members with U.S. experience) and the new economics of migration explain Mexican immigration to the United States better than the cost-benefit calculations of the neoclassical model. The migration of wives and children and the birth of children in the United States increase the odds of making more U.S. trips and lower the odds of returning to Mexico. The long-term financial risk of returning to Mexico, given the fluctuation of Mexican interest rates, and the higher valuing of Mexican migrants' education and skills north of the border explain the sustained migration.

Prompted by questions of potential chain migration or immigration multipliers associated with visa categories of admission for 1971 immigrants, Jasso and Rosenzweig empirically examined multilevel explanations for naturalization: on the micro level, labor force attachment and the family reunification incentive; on the macro level, influences of economic development and governmental structure in the country of origin, U.S. relations with the country of origin, and English as the official or dominant language in the country of origin. Whether an immigrant naturalized after a decade was shown to be associated with origin-country contexts, specific visa category, adjustee status, and other characteristics, and there were differences for men and women. For both sexes, naturalization was higher among employment-sponsored immigrants and refugees than among those who had come as family members of aliens or of citizens.[7]

Macro-level factors in immigrating lawfully and becoming naturalized include both the receiving state's and the sending state's stance toward multiple citizenship or nationality, other sending-state policies concerning current and former citizens living abroad, and receiving-state policies in

accepting new residents. The United States has not enforced the requirement of renunciation of original nationality, and several nations (including Colombia, Vietnam, and Jamaica) have long permitted their citizens to
retain their original citizenship. Policies in some other countries (Cuba,
China, Korea) are clearly against duality of citizenship. With substantial
immigrant remittances becoming an economic boon, a number of nations
(Brazil, Ecuador, Mexico, and the Dominican Republic) changed laws in
the 1990s to recognize dual citizenship and retention of nationality rights
for their citizens and to address concerns about losing home ties. After a
decade of debate, Mexico has now passed legislation that permits voter
participation by mail from the United States. An increase in Dominican
naturalizations was apparent even before the policy changes were made,[8]
possibly in consequence of political engagement among Dominican immigrants, so many of whom are concentrated in New York City.

Other country-of-origin factors affecting naturalization may be the
multiple cultural influences related to gender roles, marriage, family, and
work, as well as distance from the receiving country and ease of travel to
origin communities. The ease of contemporary transnational travel, communications, and financial transactions diminishes financial and emotional costs of return migration and dual-residence lifestyles.

Visa class of admission subsumes several measures of both human capital and social capital, but admission categories remain explanatory for
several socioeconomic outcomes.[9] The immigrant visa class of record may
not reflect other aspects of human and social capital if it was simply the
most expedient among several eligibility categories. Many immigrants are
not newly arriving but are adjusting from a nonimmigrant category, and
others are not known to have a previous nonimmigrant stay.[10] Those immigrants who are adjusting their status may have more extensive skills for
living here because they are part of a larger pool of students, temporary
workers, visitors for business or pleasure, exchange visitors, and other
nonimmigrants and have redefined their duration of residence from temporary to permanent.

Factors influencing emigration from the sending country and immigration to the receiving country differentially affect men and women. Although women's representation varies among migration streams, that is,
the female share is lower for developing countries than for developed
ones, more women than men migrate to the United States and other major receiving countries.[11] The temporal contexts of family integration (i.e.,
composition of past migration and degree of maturity of the migration

stream) affect the sex composition of flows of numerically limited immigrants and immediate relative immigrants.[12] The extent of representation of parents and employment-sponsored immigrants in past migration flows may increase immigration of women under provisions allowing the entry of immediate relatives. Involvement of women as spouses, parents, or children of U.S. citizens is higher for origin countries with a U.S. military presence, a strong economy, and greater distance from the United States. Women are more likely to be represented among the numerically limited preference categories when they come from a poor economy with gender equality in education and higher access to information about the United States.

As temporary migratory patterns evolve into settlement patterns, women and children are more likely to be incorporated as migrants. Among Colombians, Dominicans, Hondurans, and Salvadoreans in New York City, women were more likely to focus on voting and obtaining citizenship, whereas Latino men were more focused on retaining an orientation to their origin community and their social relationships within the ethnic group because these sustained a sense of their prior status—something important to them, given their typical U.S. experience of downward mobility.[13] The women, in contrast, expanded their human capital, became more empowered in the household and community, and adopted settlement strategies. Despite female immigrants' initial disadvantages in terms of employment opportunities, their parental responsibilities may lead them to make more social contacts and build more social capital that promotes adaptation and a sense of permanence.

Within gender categories, immigrants of different visa categories were differentially likely to have naturalized.[14] Among men, refugees and spouses of permanent residents were the most likely to have naturalized. Among women, those admitted under categories indicative of having fewer relatives in the United States—for example, those admitted as spouses of siblings, sisters-in-law of citizens, and holders of labor certification—were the most likely to have naturalized, and sisters of citizens were the least. Women from the Western Hemisphere seemed to have less likelihood of naturalizing, perhaps because so many were joining or accompanying husbands, in contrast to those possessing labor skills, who were more assertive in taking steps to naturalize. It seems plausible that women may have a greater need for family reunification, since more members of their family networks live abroad.

Adults who are older when they are admitted as immigrants are less likely to naturalize than are younger immigrants, who are more likely to be working and interested in seeking citizenship in order to obtain advantages in the labor market, such as government jobs. Younger immigrants may also be more likely to have relatives abroad for whom they are seeking immigrant visas. Being married signifies a certain access to social capital for acquiring the skills to pass the naturalization tests as well as for understanding the importance of citizenship. Having a spouse enables or permits a split-portfolio strategy so that one member of the couple holds citizenship in the new country and the other maintains original citizenship and nationality rights.[15] Additionally, younger and married immigrants are more likely than older immigrants to have foreign-born and U.S.-born children and to seek status consistency within the family through naturalization that conveys citizenship to minor children born outside the United States. Those admitted as spouses of U.S. citizens also have a residence requirement of only three years for becoming eligible to apply for naturalization.

Empirical Resources and Methodology

Given a resurgence of immigration and immigrant studies that parallels the demographic changes of the past four decades, explaining naturalization outcomes for contemporary arrivals is a complex task that must span various units of analysis, time periods, reception contexts, and social networks.[16] Empirical possibilities for studying naturalization are limited by imperfections in traditional data sources, as has often been noted.[17] Cross-sectional sources—censuses and national surveys—are limited by survey universe, focus on current rather than initial characteristics, and reporting of current naturalization status without date of naturalization. The longitudinal New Immigrant Survey is advantageous in building socioeconomic histories for exploring more traditional causal relationships of achieved or acquired characteristics with the timing of naturalization.[18]

An alternative approach is to use linked immigration records and naturalization records to explore the ways in which initial characteristics, admission categories, mode of entry, and origin and other demographic characteristics are associated with the timing of naturalization. In progress are a series of studies based on 5.2 million immigrants aged twenty-one years or older at lawful admission between 1978 and 1991, of whom 1.8 million, or 35.6 percent, had naturalized by 1997. These cohorts gained admission under similar laws before the preference system was altered under the IMMACT. The data exclude immigrants legalized under the IRCA of 1986. The major limitations are that emigration is an unknown, competing outcome; children's outcomes are poorly measured; and causality cannot be fully assessed. Individuals may have departed after redefining their stays as temporary rather than permanent, so some covariate effects may be underestimated.

Because the data were collected for administrative purposes, they include a limited set of covariates at admission—country or region of birth, age group, sex, married status, immigrant visa class, whether the individual is making an adjustment from nonimmigrant status, occupational background reported, and fiscal year of admission. Visa class of admission is more useful than occupation reported at admission because employment-sponsored immigrants are likely to give the occupation in which they will work but non-employment-sponsored immigrants may answer on the basis of their prior occupation in their origin country, which may not correspond with the occupation they will obtain in the U.S. labor market.

Visa class of admission includes both numerically limited visa categories (family sponsorship and employment sponsorship) as established prior to the IMMACT according to principal or derivative status (spouse or child of principal) and exempt or numerically unlimited visa categories (such as those for immediate relatives and for those admitted under humanitarian criteria), for a total of fourteen categories. Among family preferences, the first (unmarried son or daughter of citizen), second (spouse or child of alien), fourth (married son or daughter of citizen or spouse of same), and fifth (sibling of citizen or spouse of same) preferences are seven dummy variables. The third (professional worker or spouse of same) and sixth (skilled worker or spouse of same) preferences yield four categories. There are two immediate relative categories—spouses and parents as principals—and the last category includes refugees, asylees, and other admissions. These covariates on visa class indicate potential human capital or labor force attachment for immigrants under employment-sponsored categories. They also indicate potential social capital, ranging from "not known as having any resident family members" to "known as having a U.S. resident spouse or having parents, siblings, or children residing in the United States."

The primary goals in this research project on immigration and naturalization are three. The first is to demonstrate the value of administrative records for social scientific analyses of the immigration-to-naturalization transition for immigrants who entered the United States in different years. The second is to describe the timing and occurrence of naturalization by characteristics at admission, disaggregated for countries of origin. The third is development of statistical models for naturalization as a temporal process, with time as a lawful permanent resident until becoming naturalized as the dependent variable. These models give insights about immigrant characteristics associated with naturalizing more quickly than, and are preferable to, simpler analyses of whether immigrants are naturalized or not naturalized at a specific point in time.

The Timing of Naturalization

Among adult immigrants who entered the United States during 1978–91, the majority came from Asia and Latin America rather than from European countries, and the major admission categories were those for spouses and parents as exempt immediate relatives and those for refugees, asylees, or others. Among numerically limited categories, the second preference, for spouses and children of aliens, showed many immigrants, and the fifth preference, for siblings of citizens, had a substantial number. More females than males were found as spouses of aliens, as spouses of employment-sponsored immigrants, and as parents of citizens. Two-thirds of these immigrants were in their twenties or thirties, nearly three-quarters were married, and more than one-half were women. Not all immigrants were newly arriving because more than one-third were adjusting from a nonimmigrant status.

For an immigrant cohort, the probabilities of naturalizing for years of residence typically followed an "inverted U" shape, rising after the fifth year of residence to a peak in the seventh year and then declining to lower levels. In the early years of residence, the highest probabilities appeared for Southeast Asian and African immigrants and the lowest probabilities for Central and North American immigrants, for whom the probabilities of naturalizing gradually increased over the second decade of residence.

Ten leading sending countries (China, India, Korea, the Philippines, Vietnam, Jamaica, Mexico, Cuba, the Dominican Republic, and Colombia) accounted for about half of immigrants in the post-1977 period. Of nearly two million adult immigrants from these ten countries in 1978–87 (table 2.1), 42 percent were naturalized after living here lawfully from ten to eigh-

TABLE 2.1
Naturalization for Adult Immigrants Admitted in 1978–87

Country of Birth	Immigrants and Naturalization Observed by 1996	
	% Naturalized	Total Immigrants
Ten Countries	41.8	1,938,744
China	51.2	187,377
India	44.1	172,757
Korea	38.1	197,358
Philippines	61.7	306,363
Vietnam	65.4	216,561
Jamaica	37.3	114,180
Mexico	18.2	416,725
Cuba	40.3	131,753
Dominican Republic	23.6	125,096
Colombia	45.5	70,574

SOURCE: Karen A. Woodrow-Lafield et al., "Naturalization for U.S. Immigrants: Highlights from Ten Countries," *Population Research and Policy Review* 23, no. 3 (2004): 187–218.

teen years.[19] More than half of Vietnamese immigrants (65 percent), Filipino immigrants (62 percent), and Chinese immigrants (51 percent) had naturalized, whereas less than half of the others had done so (Colombians, Indians, Cubans, Koreans, Jamaicans, Dominicans, or Mexicans), with the smallest percentage among the Mexicans (18 percent).

In a study that I conducted with my colleagues, immigrant transition to naturalized citizenship was shown to differ by country of origin on the basis of statistical models that accounted for visa class of admission, age, sex, marital status, nonimmigrant background, and year of entry.[20] After at least a decade of residence, immigrants from the Philippines, Vietnam, and China were more likely to have naturalized than immigrants from India, Korea, Cuba, Colombia, Jamaica, the Dominican Republic, and Mexico; they also naturalized more quickly. As of 1996, Filipino, Vietnamese, and Chinese immigrants were six to eight times as likely to naturalize as Mexican immigrants.

Categories for visa class of admission were associated with different propensities to naturalize. Both employment-sponsored immigrants and certain family-sponsored immigrants, who were likely to have fewer rather than more relatives here, were likely to naturalize quickly. In the 1980s and early 1990s, the majority of immigrants receiving their green cards as professionals or skilled workers, and their spouses, naturalized faster than immigrants under family-sponsored categories. They might have been the most advantaged with educational levels that facilitated their gaining approval in the process, or they might have been highly committed to maximizing their employment opportunities as inclusive of positions for which citizenship was required. It is not possible to know whether those immigrants receiving visas as employment sponsored already had family members living in the United States (spouse, parent, sibling, or child), and they might need to sponsor these family members. Certainly, they already had an attachment to the labor force that eased the transition to living in America. Spouses of employment-sponsored immigrants might possess similar levels of education and labor force skills, and they might naturalize to gain rights to sponsor their own parents and siblings. Spouses of citizens and spouses of permanent resident aliens also naturalized quickly. Here it is interesting to note that, among Eastern Hemisphere male immigrants of 1977 who were either adjustee spouses or employment immigrants, those more likely to naturalize were those who advanced occupationally over 1977–1990.[21] The sisters- and brothers-in-law of citizens and the sons- and daughters-in-law of citizens naturalized faster than some other family members. Least likely to naturalize were parents of citizens.

Controlling for visa class of admission and country of birth, my initial study found that male and female immigrants were naturalizing at similar times.[22] The gender effect for the propensity to naturalize is probably obscured in that analysis, and studies are in progress to more fully investigate the differences between men and women in the process of naturalizing given that sex composition of immigrants is highly structured by origin and visa class of admission. Different origin backgrounds have varying gender concepts, cultural contexts, degrees of demographic diversity, and social capital levels. Gendered perspectives are valuable in focusing not only on the determinants of migration but also on the incorporation of men and women immigrants in host societies.[23] From analyses comparing naturalization for men and women, preliminary findings show that, within Asian origins, males may be likely to naturalize more quickly than females. In contrast, among those of Latin American origin, females may be likely to do so more quickly than males, perhaps because they value civic participation and more permanent settlement for their families.[24]

Certain findings from my initial study are consistent with prior research. Those who had some prior nonimmigrant experience (experience of having lived in the United States as a foreign student, temporary worker, visitor, refugee, or asylee) naturalized more quickly than counterparts without such experience (i.e., newly arriving immigrants). The effect of past nonimmigrant experience may be underestimated. This additional time for learning English and finding out about opportunities for residence, employment, and education is valuable for some individuals, first in making the transition to permanent resident status and then in making the transition to naturalized citizenship. Immigrants' degree of prior experience is probably increasing over time, and its effect on naturalizing may be greater. Younger immigrants or married immigrants were more likely to naturalize than older or unmarried individuals. More recent immigrants seemed to be more likely to naturalize after shorter durations of residence than earlier immigrants, and this could reflect changes in receiving contexts, familial sending contexts, and rising economic pressures to leave origin countries and cultural acceptance of likely migration abroad.[25]

Work is in progress that intensively focuses on the distinctive patterns in naturalizing over time by national origins. Statistically speaking, the best models will give better results for understanding the ways in which characteristics of visa class of admission, U.S. residential history, and admission year are associated with naturalizing sooner rather than later and how these associations may differ for men and women. For Latin American immigrants, might the best models be based on a pattern of increasing probability of naturalizing that is at low levels in the first decade of residence and consistently higher year by year throughout the second decade of residence? For Asian immigrants, might the best models be ones that allow for a pattern of the likelihood of naturalizing that at first quickly increases and then shifts to a decline in the second decade of residence? Utilizing the linked administrative records data, are statistical methods that control for unobserved sources of heterogeneity, such as socioeconomic characteristics at admission, changing socioeconomic characteristics over time, family ties in origin communities, and intention to return, appropriate or useful in modeling the timing of naturalization? For countries with complicated economic or political histories, such as Cuba and El Salvador, do the particular challenges pose impossible difficulties for modeling naturalization without more comprehensive data?

Conclusion

Given the volume and heterogeneity of immigration and the frequently unanticipated consequences of changes to immigration laws and policies, naturalization has a new significance in contemporary America. Country of birth, admission criteria, and mode of entry were influences for the timing of naturalization in the 1980s and 1990s. Balancing family-sponsored and employment-sponsored criteria is the crux of contemporary controversies of immigrant integration and immigration policy. The basic structure of immigration admission policies has been unchanged over 1970–2000, but proposals to drastically reduce levels or to greatly restrict family-based categories arise intermittently. In *At Heaven's Door*, George Borjas argued that immigrant admission policies should be altered to emphasize employment qualifications and curtail family unification, on the basis of his finding that immigrant skill levels relative to native skill levels had been declining since the 1980s.[26] An alternative argument demonstrated skill levels of new immigrants as rising relative to those of natives, at least since the mid-1980s.[27] The debate revolves around data sources, methods, and countries of origin, and the question is particularly at issue regarding Mexican immigration, given the intertwined histories of the United States and Mexico.

Differentials in naturalization by origin and admission criteria are not per se arguments for greater selectivity on immigrants because policy making is based on weighing evidence about immigrant contributions and needs of the economy with the importance of preserving the family reunification principle of current immigration law. Looking at how naturalization takes place over two decades highlights the progression of Latin American immigrants to citizenship and illustrates specific subcategories of immigrants that are slower in naturalizing. The transition to naturalization is one aspect in the debate about adaptation, assimilation, and social equality involving immigrant groups, the second generation, and third- and higher-generation natives. Race and ethnicity are being redefined as complex sociopolitical structures as the population is differentiated along lines of origin, citizenship, length of residence, and generation. It seems plausible that Western Hemisphere immigrants became more likely to naturalize after extension of the preference system and limits on how many visas would be issued annually per country. Understanding the consequences of U.S. admission policies and contemporary immigration with its heterogeneity across time and cohorts requires a closer focus on patterns of transitions to citizenship by mode of entry and admission criteria within origin by sex.

Record numbers of immigrants became eligible to naturalize in the mid-1990s, and naturalization numbers have been historically high, peaking at 1,044,689 naturalizations in 1996, including 227,905 IRCA beneficiaries, and averaging 644,700 for 1994–99 and 614,000 for 2000–2004. In 1991–2004, there were 7.8 million naturalization approvals out of nearly 10 million applications. Naturalization increases in 1995–96 may have occurred among both recent and earlier cohorts for several possible reasons. Immigrants of the 1970s who held original residence cards (i.e., who had not yet been naturalized) needed to take some action because the U.S. Immigration and Naturalization Service (INS) had begun issuing cards with a ten-year expiration date in late 1993, and their old cards became invalid on March 20, 1996. Further, a "new politics of nativism" arose with legislation directed at restricting immigrants' use of public assistance benefits.[28] In 1994 California passed Proposition 187, which dealt with unauthorized persons' access to benefits, and in 1996 Congress passed the Personal Responsibility and Work Opportunity Reconciliation Act (PRWORA), which barred lawful permanent residents admitted after August 22, 1996, from receiving most public benefits for five years and made such access for permanent residents already living in the United States on that date a matter of state option. Immigrants may have perceived themselves as needing to hold citizenship following anti-immigrant legislation in California and public concerns about immigrants' utilization of public benefits.

In the mid-1990s, the INS Citizenship USA program may have been very effective in creating citizenship assistance centers and generally orienting many immigrant service providers and county welfare offices toward promoting the benefits of naturalizing.[29] Some immigrant advocacy organizations that developed literature for immigrants applying to naturalize in the 1990s are the Massachusetts Immigrant and Refugee Advocacy Coalition, the New Jersey Immigration Policy Network Catholic Community Services, the Emerald Isle Immigration Center, and Travelers and Immigrants Aid. Due to the sheer volume of applicants, administrative delays in processing applications for naturalization delayed many immigrants' transition to naturalized status between 1995 and 2000. Thus, in analyzing recent naturalizations, one must take into account the self-protective behavior of immigrants fearing loss of rights and possible deportation in the post-welfare-reform period, along with the easing of dual-nationality laws by homeland governments and processing complications at the former INS.

Although this essay points to the lesser likelihood of naturalizing among Mexican immigrants, the influence of origin for naturalizing may become altered over time as either origin contexts or reception contexts change. The Mexican-born population is naturalizing more than ever before.

Asian countries accounted for the greatest number of naturalizations for two decades, but in 1996 North America became the leading region of birth among naturalizing immigrants, with Mexico as most prominent among persons naturalizing throughout 1994–2004. In that period, more than half of Mexicans naturalizing were legalized under IRCA and had been resident for ten to fifteen years or more as unauthorized aliens. The total number of IRCA legalized aliens who have naturalized is nearly one million, of whom about half are from Mexico. Now that the Mexican Nationality Act of 1998 has ensured that Mexicans who opt to obtain U.S. citizenship will not lose Mexican nationality or any of the rights of Mexican citizenship, Mexicans may now be more motivated to become U.S. citizens. Further contributing to the likelihood of naturalization is that, over time, Mexican immigrants also acquire skills and improve their English abilities and become less intimidated by the application process.

From census to census, there is a curious consistency as to immigration and prevalence of citizenship within the United States that stems from the global realities of the international marketplace and broadly unchanged immigration policies over three decades. As of 2000, 42 percent of the foreign-born population of 31.1 million had entered in the 1990s. The percentage of foreign-born persons increased from 4.2 to 6.0 percent between 1970 and 1980, from 6.0 to 7.9 percent between 1980 and 1990, and from 7.9 to 11.1 percent between 1990 and 2000 as a consequence of global demographic and socioeconomic changes and the mechanisms established by the 1965 Immigration and Nationality Act. Yet the percentages of foreign-born persons that entered in the preceding decade were nearly identical in 2000 (42 percent), in 1990 (44 percent), and in 1980 (40 percent). Precisely the same percent was naturalized in 2000 (40 percent) as in 1990, lower than in 1980 (49.5 percent), and lower than in 1970 (64 percent). Apparently, a higher percentage of foreign-born persons were unauthorized in 2000 (about 25 percent) than in 1990 (15–20 percent). The majority of foreign-born persons here for two decades had become naturalized citizens by 2000, with 86 percent of Asian-origin persons naturalized, and similar levels for Europeans (81 percent), Africans (80 percent), Caribbeans (80 percent), South Americans (77 percent), and non-Mexican Latin Americans (77 percent). Among long-resident Mexicans in 2000, 52 percent were naturalized. These are consistently higher levels than in 1990.

Regardless of whether the United States controls various aspects of migration, migration will probably continue and escalate. Those settling now in new lands may not be experiencing the same macro-level disruptions as immigrants of the earlier twentieth century. Many are coming with less human capital, and their pathway to naturalization and socioeconomic success may be more circuitous. As family immigrants advance occupationally, their naturalization may resemble that of employment immigrants, as suggested by Jasso and Rosenzweig.[30] The kind of research described here elaborates our understanding of linkages among migration, immigration, and naturalization and our interpretation of current observed patterns for contemporary immigrants who are highly heterogeneous. Any alarmism about disparities seems unjustified given the short history of recent immigration, and these findings point to a measure of optimism about future levels of naturalization.

NOTES

This research was supported by a grant from the National Institute of Child Health and Human Development (NICHD) (R01 HD37279). The cooperation of the Statistics Office in the former U.S. Immigration and Naturalization Service, now the Office of Immigration Statistics in the Department of Homeland Security, is acknowledged in making this work possible. The contents are solely my responsibility and do not necessarily represent the official views of the NICHD or the National Institutes of Health. Thanks to Adam McKeown and Guillermina Jasso for their comments and discussion.

1. Elliott R. Barkan and Nikolai Khokhlov, "Socioeconomic Data as Indices of Naturalization Patterns in the United States: A Theory Revisited," *Ethnicity* 7, no. 2 (1980): 159–90.

2. Katharine M. Donato, "U.S. Policy and Mexican Migration to the United States: 1942–1992," *Social Science Quarterly* 75, no. 4 (1994): 705–29; Guillermina Jasso and Mark R. Rosenzweig, *The New Chosen People: Immigrants in the United States* (New York: Russell Sage Foundation, 1990).

3. Benigno E. Aguirre and Rogelio Saenz, "Testing the Effects of Collectively Expected Durations of Migration: The Naturalization of Mexicans and Cubans," *International Migration Review* 36, no. 1 (2002): 103–24; Alejandro Portes and John Curtis, "Changing Flags: Naturalization and Its Determinants among Mexican Immigrants," *International Migration Review* 21, no. 2 (1987): 352–71; Alejandro Portes and Rafael Mozo, "The Political Adaptation Process of Cubans and Other Ethnic Minorities in the United States: A Preliminary Analysis," *International Migration Review* 19, no. 1 (1985): 35–63.

4. Douglas S. Massey and J. Edward Taylor, eds., *International Migration: Prospects and Policies in a Global Market* (New York: Oxford University Press, 2004).

5. Karen A. Woodrow-Lafield, "Emigration from the United States: Multiplic-

ity Survey Evidence," *Population Research and Policy Review* 15, no. 2 (1996): 171–99; Karen A. Woodrow-Lafield, "Estimating Authorized Immigration," in *Migration between Mexico and the United States: Binational Study,* vol. 2, *Research Reports and Background Materials,* ed. Mexican Ministry of Foreign Affairs and U.S. Commission on Immigration Reform (Austin: Morgan Printing, 1998), 619. Also available online at www.utexas.edu/lbj/uscir/binpapers/v2a-5woodrow.pdf.

6. Douglas S. Massey et al., *Worlds in Motion: Understanding International Migration at the End of the Millennium* (New York: Oxford University Press, 1998).

7. Jasso and Rosenzweig, *New Chosen People.*

8. Michael Jones-Correa, "Under Two Flags: Dual Nationality in Latin America and Its Consequences for the United States," *International Migration Review* 35, no. 4 (2001): 997–1029.

9. Guillermina Jasso et al., "The New Immigrant Survey Pilot (NIS-P): Overview and New Findings about U.S. Legal Immigrants at Admission," *Demography* 37, no. 1 (2000): 127–38.

10. Woodrow-Lafield, "Estimating Authorized Immigration."

11. Hania Zlotnick, "The South-to-North Migration of Women," *International Migration Review* 24, no. 1 (1995): 229–54.

12. Katharine M. Donato, "Understanding U.S. Immigration: Why Some Countries Send Women and Others Send Men," in *Seeking Common Ground: Multidisciplinary Studies of Immigrant Women in the United States,* ed. Donna Gabaccia (Westport, CT: Greenwood Press, 1992), 159.

13. Michael Jones-Correa, "Different Paths: Gender, Immigration, and Political Participation," *International Migration Review* 32, no. 2 (1998): 326–49.

14. Jasso and Rosenzweig, *Chosen People.*

15. Guillermina Jasso, "Migration and the Dynamics of Family Phenomena," in *Immigration and the Family: Research and Policy on U.S. Immigrants,* ed. Alan Booth, Ann C. Crouter, and Nancy Landale (Mahwah, NJ: Lawrence Erlbaum, 1997), 63.

16. See, for example, Charles Hirschman, Philip Kasinitz, and Josh De Wind, eds., *The Handbook of International Migration: The American Experience* (New York: Russell Sage Foundation, 1999).

17. Jasso and Rosenzweig, *Chosen People.*

18. Jasso et al., "New Immigrant Survey Pilot."

19. Karen A. Woodrow-Lafield et al., "Naturalization for U.S. Immigrants: Highlights from Ten Countries," *Population Research and Policy Review* 23, no. 3 (2004): 187–218.

20. Ibid.

21. Guillermina Jasso and Mark R. Rosenzweig, "Do Immigrants Screened for Skills Do Better Than Family Reunification Immigrants?" *International Migration Review* 29, no. 1 (1995): 85–117.

22. Woodrow-Lafield et al., "Naturalization for U.S. Immigrants."

23. Shawn Malia Kanaiaupuni, "Reframing the Migration Question: An Analysis of Men, Women, and Gender in Mexico," *Social Forces* 78, no. 4 (2000): 1311–48.

24. Jones-Correa, "Different Paths."

25. Woodrow-Lafield et al., "Naturalization for U.S. Immigrants."

26. George Borjas, *Heaven's Door: Immigration Policy and the American Economy* (Princeton: Princeton University Press, 1999).

27. Guillermina Jasso, Mark R. Rosenzweig, and James P. Smith, "The Changing Skill of New Immigrants to the United States: Recent Trends and Their Determinants," in *Issues in the Economics of Immigration,* ed. George J. Borjas (Chicago: University of Chicago Press, 2000), 185.

28. Jorge Durand, Douglas S. Massey, and Emilio A. Parrado, "The New Era of Mexican Migration to the United States," *Journal of American History* 86, no. 2 (1999): 521.

29. Greta Gilbertson and Audrey Singer, in *Immigration Research for a New Century: Interdisciplinary Perspectives,* ed. Nancy Foner, Rubén G. Rumbaut, and Steven J. Gold (New York: Russell Sage Foundation, 2000), 157; Hans P. Johnson et al., *Taking the Oath: An Analysis of Naturalization in California and the United States* (San Francisco: Public Policy Institute of California, 1999).

30. Jason and Rosenzweig, *New Chosen People.*

Chapter 3

Immigrant Enclaves, Ethnic Goods, and the Adjustment Process

Barry R. Chiswick and Paul W. Miller

Why do immigrants tend to live clustered together in immigrant concentrations, to be referred to here as immigrant "enclaves"? Why don't they distribute themselves across a destination country in the same manner as the native-born population? Immigrant enclaves appear to be a characteristic of the foreign born in the United States and other immigrant-receiving countries, not only today but also in earlier time periods.[1]

This essay will focus on the contemporary United States. It will demonstrate the existence of immigrant concentrations or enclaves. It will then introduce the concept of "ethnic goods" as a factor explaining these enclaves and, finally, report the results of statistical analyses on the effect that these enclaves have on two dimensions of immigrant adjustment, their English-language proficiency and their labor market earnings.

Immigrant Enclaves

According to the 2000 Census of Population of the United States, about 11 percent of the population was foreign born. Foreign-born individuals are not distributed across the states in the same manner as the native-born population (table 3.1). The "Big 6" immigrant-receiving states are California, New York, New Jersey, Florida, Texas, and Illinois (table 3.2). Each of these states in 2000 had at least 4 percent of the total foreign-born population, ranging from 30 percent in California to 4 percent in Illinois. Fully two-thirds (68 percent) of the foreign born in the United States lived in these states. While overall 11 percent of the population was foreign born, the foreign-born proportion of the population in these states ranged from

TABLE 3.1
Percentages of Selected Immigrant Groups Residing in Top States of Residence versus Percentages of Native Born, 2000

Other Latin America, and Caribbean		Europe (Excluding Former Soviet Union)		Canada		Native Born (Born in U.S.)	
State	Percent	State	Percent	State	Percent	State	Percent
FL	26	NY	14	CA	17	CA	10
NY	23	CA	14	FL	11	TX	7
CA	16	FL	8	NY	7	NY	6
NJ	8	NJ	7	WA	6	FL	5
All Other[a]	27	All Other	57	All Other	59	All Other	72
Total	100	Total	100	Total	100	Total	100

SOURCE: U.S. Bureau of the Census, *2000 Census of Population,* Public Use Microdata Sample, 5 percent sample.
NOTE: Detail may not add to total due to rounding.
  [a] All other states and Washington, D.C.

TABLE 3.2
Foreign Born in the "Big 6" and in the United States, 2000

State	% of State Population That Is Foreign Born	% of the U.S. Foreign-Born Population in Selected States
California	26.9	29.8
New York	18.2	11.3
New Jersey	17.5	4.8
Florida	16.9	8.7
Texas	13.8	9.0
Illinois	10.7	4.3
All other states[a]	5.8	32.1
Total U.S.	11.0	100.0

SOURCE: U.S. Bureau of the Census, *2000 Census of Population,* Public Use Microdata Sample, 5 percent sample.
  [a] Includes Washington, D.C.

27 percent in California—yes, one in four Californians was foreign born —to 11 percent for Illinois (table 3.2).[2] On closer inspection, however, it is clear that immigrants are not distributed in the same manner as the native-born population even within these states. The immigrant proportion is most intense in Southern California and the San Francisco Bay Area, along the Texas border with Mexico, in southern Florida, in the New York City metropolitan area, and in Illinois in Cook County (Chicago).

Nor do immigrants have the same geographic distribution regardless of country of origin (table 3.3). Immigrants from Mexico are concentrated in the states that border Mexico, that is, in California, Texas, and Arizona. Asian immigrants are disproportionately concentrated in California and

TABLE 3.3
*Percentages of Selected Immigrant Groups Residing in
Top States of Residence, by Place of Birth, 2000*

		Place of Birth			
Mexico		Asia		Former Soviet Union	
State	Percent	State	Percent	State	Percent
CA	45	CA	37	NY	27
TX	20	NY	10	CA	22
IL	6	TX	5	IL	6
AZ	5	IL	4	WA	5
All other[a]	24	All other	44	All other	40
Total	100	Total	100	Total	100

SOURCE: U.S. Bureau of the Census, *2000 Census of Population*, Public Use Microdata Sample, 5 percent sample.
NOTE: Detail may not add to total due to rounding.
[a] All other states and Washington, D.C.

New York. Immigrants from the former Soviet Union are to be found disproportionately in New York and California, especially in the New York City metropolitan area and Los Angeles. Immigrants from other parts of Europe and especially from Canada have a much wider geographic dispersion.

The literature suggests that there are three fundamental determinants of immigrant location in a destination (Bartel 1989). The first is the "ports of entry," seaports in the past and airports in the contemporary world. A second is "family and friends," or the results of chain migration. Immigrants tend to favor locations where others of the same country of origin have settled, especially relatives, friends, and others from their same local area. Finally, an important issue is "where the jobs are," that is, immigrants tend to settle where they have the most attractive employment opportunities for the skills that they bring with them or that they expect to acquire at the destination.

With the passage of time in the destination, immigrants engage in internal mobility. The effects of "ports of entry" diminish rapidly, and even the "family and friends" effects became less important as immigrants learn the destination language and acquire labor market information on their own. As a result, the relative importance of "where the jobs are," that is, the strictly economic incentives, increases over time. This explains, in part, why the European and Canadian immigrants have a greater geographic dispersal than the more recent immigrants from Mexico and Asia. Yet in spite of internal mobility that results in some dispersal of immigrants, immigrant enclaves do persist, often beyond the first generation. They persist because they offer economic advantages.

Communication costs for the immigrants can be reduced by living and/or working in a linguistic concentration area (Bauer, Epstein, and Gang, 2005). Not all members of the group need dominant language proficiency, and the earlier arrivals and those more efficient in language acquisition are more likely to become proficient. They can serve as either direct or indirect translators for communication between the enclave and the host society. The absolute demand for this specialized function increases with the size of the linguistic minority group, but the relative demand, that is, the proportion of the group requiring this skill, decreases with the size of the linguistic minority. The demand for this specialized function decreases as the members of the group learn the dominant language or, as is less likely, some of the native population learns the immigrant language.

Even aside from issues of language skills, immigrant/ethnic concentrations provide information networks that can be very valuable in social interaction, consumption activities, and employment activities. Natives of an area have acquired location-specific human capital, which includes information obtained directly and indirectly through established networks. Not being connected to host-country information networks when they arrive, immigrants have an incentive to create information networks through living in geographic concentrations with other new and longer-term immigrants from the same origin.

Ethnic Goods

Immigrants tend to differ from the native or host population along many dimensions related to ethnicity. They may differ in the foods they eat, the clothing they wear, the holidays they celebrate, the religion they practice, the media they read or hear (e.g., newspapers and radio), their social organizations, and the languages they speak, among other characteristics.[3] There is frequently a tension among immigrants between preserving the culture of the "old country" in the new setting and adopting the culture of the host country.

Let us call "ethnic goods" the consumption characteristics of an immigrant/ethnic/religious minority group that are not shared with the host population or with members of other groups.[4] These consumption characteristics include market goods and services, such as ethnic-based clothing (e.g., saris), foods (e.g., kosher meats), and religious services (e.g., Eastern Orthodox church services). They also include the goods and services consumed that are "home produced," that is, that cannot be directly obtained in the conventional marketplace but are "produced" in the home or community.[5] These include friendship networks, marriage markets, and family and group celebrations of national/ethnic/religious origin festivals and holidays. Market goods and services may be purchased but are combined with one's own time, and perhaps the time of others, to produce these goods and services. Thus celebrating one's national holiday may involve market goods and services (e.g., for food) and one's own time and the time of others, as it is more meaningful to celebrate in a group than alone.

To the extent that "ethnic goods" are distinctive and are important in the market basket, immigrants from a particular origin have a different market basket than the native born and immigrants from other origins. The full cost of consumption of these ethnic goods varies with both the price of purchased market goods and services and the value of the time used in their production. It also varies with the importance and distinctiveness of the ethnic goods and the size of the group.

The assimilation process is a two-way street. Mostly, it is immigrants adjusting to the American scene. But Americans also adopt or absorb aspects of immigrant culture. Chinese food, Italian pizza, celebrations of St. Patrick's Day, and Yiddishisms in the English language are examples. In a TV interview, a Korean immigrant teenager she indicated that she wanted to be just like other American teenagers, she wanted to eat pizza and bagels. When this story was told to a class, the students did not see the humor. They too were unaware of the immigrant origins of pizza and bagels.

To some extent the cost of ethnic goods can be reduced if the host society "adopts" the ethnic good. The "Americanized" version of the ethnic good, however, may well differ from the version consumed in the country of origin or by members of the ethnic group in the destination.

There are certain fixed costs and economies of scale in the production and distribution of ethnic goods. Social interaction with others of the same origin (including finding an appropriate marriage partner) may involve little in the way of conventional market goods and services but importantly involves the number of other individuals. The cost would decline (presumably at a decreasing rate) with increasing group size.[6] For example, up to a point, an ethnic religious institution (e.g., church, mosque, temple, or synagogue) or an ethnic school for the children of immigrants has a lower per capita cost for members for the same type of facility providing the same level of services to the congregants or students if it is in a larger rather than in a smaller ethnic community. There are fixed costs for buildings and hiring religious officials, among other items. The probability that enough individuals will show up on a given occasion for the religious service or celebration will rise with the size of the group.

Or consider a marriage market. The probability of finding a "good match" is greater in a larger group, all other factors being the same. As a result, the cost of search decreases with the size of the group in a given location. The group size can be enlarged by including searches in more distinct communities, but doing so increases the cost of search.[7]

To extend the analogy, consider randomly drawing sets of balls from a bin full of balls that are 95 percent white and 5 percent red. A white ball is a "bad match" and a red ball is a "good match." The probability that there will be at least one red ball in the set (a good marriage match) increases as the number of balls in the set increases, say from five to ten to twenty. While this probability increases, it does so at a decreasing rate as the size of the set increases. The principle applies to marriage markets, friendship networks, good matches, religious institutions, and so on.

The cost of "importing" into the community ethnic-specific goods (e.g., saris, Chinese vegetables, kosher meats) also varies with the size of the market because of economies of scale. Indeed, as the size of the community increases, the manner of "importation" may change from a family making a trip to a larger nearby community to collective/cooperative efforts to place periodic bulk orders, to the establishment of a single (monopoly) outlet, to many competitive outlets selling the product. The larger the community, the lower the "full price," which includes one's own time in the activity and the cost of waiting, as well as conventional market prices.

In summary, the cost of living in an area depends, in part, on the relative cost of ethnic goods, broadly defined, and the importance and distinctiveness of ethnic goods in the person's market basket. The larger the particular ethnic/immigrant/religious community, the lower the cost of ethnic goods. The size of the share of ethnic goods in the individual's market basket and their distinctiveness are both likely to be linked to the similarity of the group's culture of origin to the culture of the host society, the extent of the group's integration into the host society, and the duration of immigrants' residence in the destination and among the native-born descendants of immigrants.

Ethnic goods have implications for individuals' incentives to live in an ethnic concentration area, as well as for geographic differences in earnings. If ethnic goods, defined broadly, are an important part of the market basket, the person faces a higher real cost of living where ethnic goods are more expensive—largely because fewer co-ethnics live there—than where they are less expensive, namely in an area of high ethnic concentration. Thus an ethnic immigrant might be equally receptive to two similar jobs, one in a high concentration area and the other in a low concentration area, only if the latter provided a higher nominal wage that was just sufficient to compensate for the higher cost of living.

For that reason, workers would tend to gravitate to areas where their real wage was higher, that is, their nominal wage was adjusted for their cost of living. For members of an ethnic/immigrant group, there would be an inverse relation between nominal wages received and the size of the person's ethnic group. In other words, this ethnic goods hypothesis says that the negative relation between ethnic group concentration and earnings is compensating for different costs of living. Moreover, ethnic goods can result in different geographic concentrations of various immigrant groups and differences in the pattern of regional wage differentials across immigrant groups and between immigrants and natives.

When a new immigrant group initially arrives in a country, it may be indifferent to alternative locations in the destination that are equally attractive in terms of job opportunities and ports of entry. The initial settlers would tend to be immigrants with a lower demand for ethnic goods, since they were the most willing to leave the lower-cost ethnic goods in their place of origin. Subsequent immigrants from this immigrant group would not be so indifferent to the alternative destinations, for ethnic goods would be cheaper where their co-ethnics had already settled. With the immigrant community established, those with a higher demand for ethnic goods would find immigration that much more attractive. In this manner, "ethnic goods" generate ethnic enclaves.

New ethnic concentrations away from the original center in the destination country can be formed under any of several scenarios. An individual with a very low demand for ethnic goods may settle elsewhere and gradually (and perhaps inadvertently) serve as a nucleus for others to follow. An individual with a high demand for ethnic goods may randomly receive a very high wage offer from the distribution of wage offers and settle in a new area. This person may serve as a nucleus and may even have an economic incentive to subsidize the migration of others to join him in the new location so as to lower his cost of ethnic goods. Moreover, if for exogenous or unrelated reasons wages increase in an area outside the enclave, and if the gap between wages in this area and wages in the enclave becomes sufficiently large, incentives to migrate may arise. If the wage differential compensates for the higher cost of living because of ethnic goods, a second enclave can be established, and the first may even shrink or disappear or be replaced (succeeded) by a newer immigrant population. Thus the number of enclaves or areas of concentration will vary systematically with the size of the immigrant/ethnic group and the distinctiveness and intensity of the demand for ethnic goods. And these enclaves need not be static but may change over time.

This discussion has focused on "ethnic goods" and immigrant/ethnic/religious minorities. The analogy may be extended to any group with consumption patterns that are distinct from the majority population. If their particular market basket includes goods and services that are sufficiently distinct, are a relatively large share of that market basket, and are subject to significant economies of scale (the cost declines with larger group size), these "affinity group goods" will influence location choice and regional differences in earnings among members of the group. For example, the analysis could be applied to the gay community, since the cost of meeting others with a similar sexual orientation declines with a larger size of the group. This would explain concentrations in particular geographic areas.

Consequences of Enclaves for Language Skills

Limited destination-language proficiency is likely to reduce the earning potential of immigrants (Chiswick and Miller 1992, 1995). It raises the cost or lowers the efficiency of job searches and in many jobs may restrict access (e.g., if there is a need to pass a test that requires proficiency) or lower productivity. There may also be discrimination in the labor market by the native population (as employers, co-workers, or consumers) against those who are less proficient in the dominant language or who speak it with an accent. Working within a linguistic enclave is a mechanism for sheltering oneself from, or mitigating the adverse labor market consequences of, limited destination-language proficiency.

Living and working within a linguistic concentration area has feedback effects on destination-language proficiency. The more an individual can avoid communicating in the destination language, the slower his or her likely rate of acquisition of dominant-language skills. Consider two individuals: one lives in a large linguistic concentration area where he or she can work, consume, socialize, and engage in other activities using the origin language, and the other lives in a linguistically isolated area where communication can be done only in the dominant language. The latter may have a more difficult initial adjustment but will have a stronger incentive to acquire destination-language skills and greater exposure that will facilitate learning the destination language.

Testing the Hypotheses

Economic theory can suggest "what may be" but cannot by itself determine "what is." For that one needs to examine data.[8] Earlier in this essay it was demonstrated that the foreign born have a different distribution across the states of the United States than do the native born and that these immigrant enclaves differ by country or region of origin. In this section results are reported for the effect of immigrant enclaves on two key aspects of the immigrant adjustment process, English-language proficiency and labor market earnings. The previous section argued that enclaves are associated with poorer destination-language proficiency. The earnings analysis offers a test of the ethnic goods hypothesis regarding the formation and consequences for earnings of these enclaves. As we have shown, the ethnic goods concept generates the implication that reported earnings will be higher, other things being the same, the smaller the relative size of the enclave in which the immigrant lives.

The data for this analysis are from the 1990 Census of Population, Public Use Microdata Files, using a 5 percent sample of the population. The analysis is limited to adult (age twenty-five to sixty-four years) men who were born in non-English-speaking countries. The census provides data on a wide array of relevant variables that either are of primary concern or are "held constant" statistically in the analysis. These include age, years of schooling, marital status, country of birth, language spoken in the home (specific foreign language if a language in addition to or other than English is spoken), proficiency in English among those who speak another language, and labor market earnings. The statistical analyses were performed for all adult male immigrants (excluding those from developed English-speaking countries) and separately for Mexican and other immigrants.

It is necessary to define the relevant reference group for the enclave. Country of birth might be a candidate. Yet some immigrants from a similar cultural and linguistic background come from several different countries. Spanish, for example, is the primary language of immigrants from Mexico and many of the countries in the Caribbean, Central America, and South America. German is spoken in Germany, Austria and parts of Switzerland. And some countries of origin are bilingual (e.g., Belgium) or multilingual (e.g., India). Language is an important element in group cohesion, and language and culture are closely linked. For this reason, the respondents' linguistic backgrounds are used as the determinants of enclaves.[9] The language the immigrant speaks at home if he is not a monolingual speaker of English is used for this purpose. For immigrants who speak only English at home, perhaps because this is the only language of their spouse and children, the language of their country of origin is used. Thus the enclave measure used for each respondent in this study is the proportion of the population in the state in which he lives who speak his language of origin.[10] This is computed for the twenty-four languages other than English most frequently spoken by immigrants from non-English-speaking countries.

A measure of the respondent's proficiency in English is also developed. Immigrants who report that they speak only English at home, or that they speak another language but that they speak English "very well" or "well," are considered proficient. Those who report that they speak English "not well" or "not at all" are considered not proficient. Under this definition 75 percent of the immigrant males in the sample are proficient: 54 percent of those born in Mexico and 83 percent of those born in other countries.

The analysis for English-language proficiency indicates that the larger the minority-language concentration measure in the state for a respondent, the lower the respondent's English-language proficiency, among immigrants overall and among both Mexican and non-Mexican immigrants. Going from a concentration measure of zero to the mean value of 7.8 percent lowers the probability of being proficient in English by 3.1 percentage points. This is 4.2 percent of the mean proficiency of 0.73, or 73 percent. Among immigrants from countries other than Mexico, going from a zero concentration level to the mean level of 3.9 percent lowers proficiency by 1.2 percentage points. This is 1.4 percent of the mean proficiency in this group of 83 percent. For immigrants from Mexico, however, going from a zero concentration level to the mean level of 18 percent lowers proficiency by 18 percentage points. This is 33 percent of the mean proficiency in this group of 54 percent. Thus the concentration measure is associated with lower proficiency, especially among immigrants from Mexico.

The analysis of annual earnings indicates that, other things being the same, the lower the respondent's own language proficiency and the larger the size of the enclave, as measured by the minority-language concentration index, the lower the earnings (Chiswick and Miller 2005). Going from not being proficient to being proficient raises earnings by about 15 percent for all immigrants, as well as for Mexican immigrants and for other immigrants considered separately. This implies that if the cost of acquiring proficiency is approximately the equivalent of a full year's potential earnings the rate of return on the investment is about 15 percent. If the cost of acquiring proficiency is only a half a year, the rate of return is 30 percent, and if the cost is the equivalent of two full years of potential earnings, the rate of return is 7.5 percent.[11] Given the definition of proficiency used here, it would seem that investment in language proficiency is a highly profitable investment for immigrants, even if the calculation is based solely on labor market earnings and ignores the benefits in consumption and social activities.

Even when the respondent's own language proficiency is held constant statistically, the enclave measure matters. The larger the size of the minority-language concentration measure, the lower the earnings of the immigrants. Among all immigrants studied, going from a zero concentration area to the mean level (7.8 percent) lowers earnings by about 4.4 percent. This is comparable to the effect on earnings of one less year of schooling (4.5 percent). Among non-Mexican immigrants, going from zero concentration to the mean level of concentration (3.9 percent) lowers earnings by about 2.7 percent. This is about half of the effect of one less year of schooling (5.4 percent). Among Mexican immigrants, however, the mean minority-language concentration measure is much higher (18 percent), and going from a zero concentration to the mean concentration lowers earnings by about 6.0 percent. This is the equivalent of about two less years of schooling, since each year of schooling raises their earnings by about 2.7 percent.

Thus living in a linguistic concentration area lowers earnings. The depressing effect on earnings of living in a concentration area near the mean compared to living where few speak one's mother tongue is larger among Mexican immigrants than among other immigrants from non-English-speaking countries.

Conclusion

This essay has been concerned with the reasons for, and some consequences of, immigrants living in geographic concentrations, referred to here as enclaves. Data are reported that show that immigrants in the United States are far more concentrated geographically than the native born and that the nature of this concentration varies across immigrant groups. The geographic concentration is most intense for recent immigrant groups and for those from origins that are less similar to the United States in terms of language and culture.

The concept of "ethnic goods" is introduced to explain these patterns. Ethnic goods and services are consumption characteristics of an immigrant/ethnic/religious minority group that are not shared with the host population or with members of other groups. Ethnic goods and services may be purchased in the conventional marketplace or produced in the home or community.

The full cost of ethnic goods may decline with the growth in the size of the group because of economies of scale. If so, ethnic goods will encourage the formation of enclaves. This has feedback effects on destination-language skills and earnings.

Analyses of U.S. Census data indicate that adult male immigrants are less proficient in English if they live in a larger linguistic enclave, that is, in an area where many others are of the same linguistic background. Analyses of their earnings also indicate that, other variables being the same, the poorer the person's English-language skills and the larger the size of the linguistic enclave, the lower the person's earnings. These findings hold overall, as well as separately for Mexican and other immigrants.

The analyses suggest that the ethnic goods concept is very useful for understanding immigrant's living in enclaves, their English-language proficiency, and their earnings.

NOTES

An earlier version of this article was published as "Do Enclaves Matter in Immigrant Adjustment?" *City and Community* 4, no. 1 (2005): 5–35, in which economic modeling and econometric analyses are the bases for the technical exposition. Some sections of this essay are drawn from that larger study.

1. Other economic analyses of the determinants of immigrant or ethnic concentrations include Bartel (1989), Cutler and Glaeser (1997), Lazear (1999), Bauer,

Epstein, and Gang (2005), and Sierminska (2002). Lazear (1999, S99) describes concentrations as forming "in large part because doing so enhances trade" in market and nonmarket goods and services.

2. Other states with 11 or more percent of the population foreign born tend to have small populations—Arizona (14 percent), Connecticut (11 percent), Delaware (14 percent), District of Columbia (17 percent), Hawaii (19 percent), Massachusetts (12 percent), Nevada (17 percent), Rhode Island (11 percent), and Washington (11 percent). West Virginia had the smallest percent foreign born, 1.4 percent.

3. Ross (2002) develops a model in which preferences for social interaction by the majority or a minority (whether negative as in prejudice or positive as in cultural affinity) result in social segregation of neighborhoods.

4. For research on network externalities, see Economides (1996) and Katz and Shapiro (1985).

5. This is analogous to the raising of children, a home-produced "good" that involves the time of parents as well as market goods and services (e.g., food, clothing, school supplies).

6. For a study of consumer network markets and group size, see Etziony and Weiss (2001).

7. For example, a graduate student of one of the authors explained that she was about to leave Chicago for New York because, for her ethnic group, Chicago was too small a "marriage market" and New York offered a larger pool of eligible spouses. Internet dating is a technological change that lowers the cost of searching over a wider area.

8. The details of the statistical analyses are reported in Chiswick and Miller (2005).

9. Bertrand, Luttmer, and Mullainathan (2000) also use language as the basis for their "networks" (concentrations) in an analysis of welfare participation.

10. The appropriate size of the area is not obvious. In the context of ethnic goods a neighborhood would be too small. Sampling variability also enhances measurement error problems for smaller areas, especially for languages that are not as widely spoken as Spanish. Tests indicate that the general patterns do not vary with whether the state or the metropolitan area serves as the basis for computing concentration measures.

11. By formula, b = rk, where b is the effect of being proficient on annual earnings, k is the cost of the investment measured in the number of full-year equivalent potential earnings, and r is the rate of return on the investment.

REFERENCES

Bartel, Ann. 1989. "Where Do the New Immigrants Live?" *Journal of Labor Economics* 7 (October): 371–91.

Bauer, Thomas, Gil S. Epstein, and Ira N. Gang. 1995. "Enclaves, Language, and the Location Choice of Migrants." *Journal of Population Economics* 18 (November): 649–62.

Bertrand, Marianne, Enzo F. P. Luttmer, and Sendil Mullainathan. 2000. "Network Effects and Welfare Cultures." *Quarterly Journal of Economics* 115 (August): 1019–55.

Chiswick, Barry R., and Paul W. Miller. 1992. "Language in the Immigrant Labor Market." In *Immigration, Language and Ethnicity: Canada and the United States,* ed. Barry R. Chiswick, 229–96. Washington, DC: American Enterprise Institute.

———. 1995. "The Endogeneity between Language and Earnings: International Analyses." *Journal of Labor Economics* 13 (April): 246–88.

———. 2005. "Do Enclaves Matter in Immigrant Adjustment?" *City and Community* 4, no. 1:5–35.

Cutler, David M., and Edward L. Glaeser. 1997. "Are Ghettos Good or Bad?" *Quarterly Journal of Economics* 112 (August): 827–72.

Economides, Nicholas. 1996. "The Economics of Networks." *International Journal of Industrial Organization* 14:673–99.

Etziony, Amir, and Avi Weiss. 2001. "Coordination and Critical Mass in a Network Market: An Experimental Evaluation." Unpublished paper, Department of Economics, Bar Ilan University, October.

Katz, Michael, and Carl Shapiro. 1985. "Network Externalities, Competition and Compatibility." *American Economic Review* 75:424–40.

Lazear, Edward P. 1999. "Culture and Language." *Journal of Political Economy* 107 (December): S95–S126.

Ross, Stephen. 2002. "Segregation and Racial Preferences: An Analysis of Choice Based on Satisfaction and Outcome Measures." Paper presented at the conference on Discrimination and Unequal Outcomes, Le Mans, France, January.

Sierminska, Eva. 2002. "Immigrants and State Clustering: Effect of Welfare Benefits." Unpublished paper, Department of Economics, Johns Hopkins University, October.

Chapter 4

Asian Americans, Religion, and Race

Paul Spickard

Things We Don't Talk About

There are two things we don't talk about much in U.S. immigration history: religion and race. They are crucial to an understanding of how immigrants of color have been incorporated into American society over the last couple of centuries and how they have not. Both religious and racial limits have been placed on the opportunities of non-European immigrants to become full members of U.S. society, limits that have not been placed on immigrants from Europe. For immigrants of color from Asia, racial and religious limits have interacted to reinforce each other, in ways that will be explored in the second part of this chapter.[1] We need to talk about race and religion more than we do.

The first part of this essay will speak in theoretical terms about the perspectives I perceive to be underrepresented in studies of U.S. immigration history. The second part of the chapter explores, through illustration, some ways that consideration of race and religion together can illuminate the experiences of Asian Americans. It points to means, not experienced by White immigrants, by which Asian immigrants and their descendants have been defined by the dominant group in American society as essentially and irredeemably foreign in both racial and religious terms. Together, the two sections suggest both what is missing from most studies of immigration history and what important things can be learned if that missing analysis is supplied.

Race

On a trip to New York a few years ago I visited Ellis Island. The museum there prides itself on telling "the story of America's immigrant heritage."[2] Well, it tells part of that story. It tells the story of White immigrants. Later that day I shared dinner with an old friend from college, a Brooklyn woman of Jewish and Japanese parentage. When I told her where I had spent the day, she responded immediately: "I hate Ellis Island. Not because of what's there—because of what isn't there." The story of my friend's Jewish family who came to New York from central Europe is there. But the story of her Japanese family is missing.

It is not just that the people who came from Japan are absent from almost all the Ellis Island pictures and exhibits; after all, most Japanese immigrants came to West Coast places like Seattle and San Francisco, not through New York. The real problem is that Ellis Island, along with most scholarly and popular writing about immigration, ignores race. And race has made the experiences of migrants from Asia, Latin America, and Africa fundamentally different from those of European migrants. Ellis Island is not a template for the experiences of immigrants of color. They're different, and race makes the difference.

Let me give just one example of the difference race makes. Historians of European immigration and the exhibits at Ellis Island rightly bemoan the fact that entrants waited in line for hours after their ships docked, that they were forced to endure rudeness and callous medical inspections, and that 2 percent experienced the tragedy of being sent back to Europe. But the situation for Asians who entered the United States through Angel Island in San Francisco Bay was much worse. There, would-be immigrants endured detentions lasting anywhere from two weeks to two years of isolation, privation, and repeated interrogation. And the rate of refusal and repatriation was more than ten times higher than it was at Ellis Island. The difference was race: in addition to the medical and other hurdles placed before European immigrants, immigrants from China (and later from Japan and other Asian nations) were barred on a racial basis. To enter, Asians were required affirmatively to prove that they were already U.S. citizens or that they were not laborers. The triumphalist story of immigration and assimilation offered by the Ellis Island model may work for White migrants; it does not work for migrants of color.[3]

Some may argue that the growing number of historical studies of Asian and Latin American immigrants has rectified the problem—that while the Ellis Island exhibits may lack focus on race, the scholarship in the field does not and that surely in time Ellis Island will catch up. It is true that there are many fine historical studies of Asians and Latinos.[4] But the racial analysis of works such as these seems not to have penetrated the work of people who write about White immigrants. For nearly all of the latter, Ellis Island is still the template, and if the experiences of immigrants of color are different, then they are merely exceptions to the rule. Such historians simply ignore the Whiteness of White immigrants and assume that immigrants from Europe sooner or later become unproblematically American. I contend that what they become is *White* Americans—quite a different thing.[5]

Of course, some issues and patterns *are* common to the experiences of many immigrant groups, irrespective of race: the rigors of the journey, the shock of the new, the alienation of the second generation from their parents, and a host of other processes. But I want to be wary of the unspoken assumption that every group in America is going through more or less the same process of assimilation and incorporation into a non-ethnic American mass. The assumption of some immigration scholarship, of most immigration-and-religion scholarship, and of all assimilation scholarship is that all American ethnic and racial groups proceed along the same pathway; perhaps they are at different points on that pathway, but they all march relentlessly "into the twilight of ethnicity," when they will just be undifferentiated Americans. It is true for White immigrants. There is little evidence that it is true for immigrants of color.[6]

I have written at some length about the shortcomings of the assimilation model of migrant experiences, as well as about the relative strengths of two other models: the transnational diasporic model and the racial formation model.[7] I will not rehearse those arguments here in full. Briefly, the strength of the assimilation model, as presented at Ellis Island and elsewhere, is that it shows change over time and generation. It emphasizes the transformations in manners, language, religion, clothing, food, and other cultural attributes that occur within individuals as they migrate to new homes and take on new identities. The weaknesses of the assimilation model mainly surround its inability to address certain very large differences among groups—in short, its failure to understand race. It privileges English immigrants as if they were naturally Americans from the time they stepped off the boat and does not explore the changes through which they went as immigrant processes. It ignores the immigrant qualities of African slaves—radical language and identity change, to name just two. It ignores the impact of immigrants (mostly Europeans) on the people who were here before, Indians and Mexicans. And it has one master narrative through which it homogenizes all immigrant groups, the inevitable and unproblematic transition from foreigner to undifferentiated American.

The assimilation model also fails to take account of the fact that people did not make simple, straight-line migrations from an old country to a new country. The transnational diasporic model helps us here.[8] It focuses on the connections between places of origin and new places; on the going and coming; and on migrations not just from, say, Italy to the United States, but also (and in larger numbers) to other places (in the Italian case, to other parts of Europe and to South America). The transnational diasporic model, however, has this shortcoming: it tends to miss the changes that occur over generations in particular locales, as it focuses mainly on the migrant generation.

The panethnic or racial formation model is the most helpful of these three if one wants to understand the experiences of immigrants of color.[9] It observes that in U.S. history there has not been a single movement from foreign to American; rather, there have been several panethnic formations. Migrants of various African ethnicities like Fon, Fulani, Asante, and Yoruba became Black Americans. Migrants of various European derivations became Whites. Lakota, Chickasaw, Navajo, and others became American Indians, yet tended also to retain a second level of ethnic affiliation as members of tribes. Chinese, Koreans, Vietnamese, and others formed an Asian American panethnicity yet also retained their identities of national origin. It remains to be seen whether and to what extent Cubans, Dominicans, Mexicans, and a host of other peoples may form a meaningful Latino panethnicity, for all that they are viewed as one mass by most Anglos.[10] In similar terms, it is not at all clear yet to what extent various peoples of Middle Eastern and North African origin may become a meaningful panethnic group, despite the current virulence with which they are racialized together by non–Middle Easterners.[11]

Each of these three models—assimilation, transnational, and racial formation—has something to teach us about the experiences of immigrant peoples in the United States. The one that has been most often left out of immigration studies is the most important: race.

Religion

Immigration history has only sporadically and selectively had much to say about religion. Surely, insofar as U.S. immigration historians have dealt with migrant groups whose primary markers of difference from other Americans are religious ones (Jews are the most prominent example), religion—or at least religiously marked institutions and divisions between peoples—has been in play. It is not that religion is left completely out of studies of Judaism, but for the vast majority of historians (as opposed to theologians or religious leaders) religion is only a minor factor. More often than not, historians of American Judaism have attended very little to the content and experience of religion and far more to social organization. From justly revered books like Moses Rischin's *Promised City* and Irving Howe's *World of Our Fathers* to recent classics, we learn a great deal about life in the *shtetl*, the journey to America, slum life, working conditions, social life, the labor movement, socialism, involvement in American politics, Yiddish literature and theater, scholarship, the press, painters and sculptors—but we learn far less about the content of religion directly.[12] It is not that there aren't people writing about the religious aspects of Judaism— surely they are plentiful—but immigration *historians* have been surprisingly reticent even with regard to this religiously defined group.

The same is true for nineteenth-century Irish immigrants, who were much vilified for the Catholic identity that most of them carried. Even in those two cases, far more has been written about other sociologically and politically defined phenomena than about the inner life of the spirit, the corporate experience of communal worship, the life of ceremony, the orientation to the transcendent. And for scholarly books and policy reports on most other U.S. immigrant groups or on immigration generally, religion is treated only as a very minor issue, if at all.[13]

All these shortcomings are even more true for those of us who work in ethnic studies as opposed to immigration studies. In Asian American studies, from our beginnings in 1969–70 down to the very recent past, we have operated almost unanimously on a theoretical base of soft-core Marxist orientation that, worse than treating religion as mere superstructure, ignored it entirely.[14] None of the major texts on Asian American history has more than a few incidental words to say about religion.[15] The shelf of books on Asian American religion is small indeed.[16] Analyses of immigrant peoples and religion often underplay the significance of race by appealing to a sense of naive universalism as a way around racialized politics and policies. This is probably one of the reasons that many social scientists, and particularly people who work in ethnic studies, have been dismissive of religion as an issue in ethnic communities.[17]

Race and Religion Together

The two shortcomings come together. What scholarship there is on the religious lives of immigrant communities in the United States is heavily influenced by the Ellis Island paradigm. So seldom do people write seriously about religion and immigration together that those who do frequently turn for their theoretical starting point to Will Herberg's still much-cited 1955 study, *Protestant, Catholic, Jew.*[18] Herberg built on the work of University of Chicago sociologists, who believed that all immigrants, no matter where they came from or the circumstances surrounding their migration, moved through a predetermined social process in the United States, which the sociologists called the "race relations cycle."[19] Immigrants started out as total foreigners, culturally speaking. They gradually became less and less foreign, dropping the language, culture, and habits that kept them removed from the larger American mainstream, that is, native Whites. The second and subsequent generations gradually consolidated their separate ethnic identity into symbolic forms as they became less and less foreign, more and more "American."[20] Herberg followed the Chicago sociologists' lead with his contention that American religion was moving through a similar social process, contracting around three very general, broadly defined religio-ethnic categories: Protestant, Catholic, and Jew.

Herberg—and other assimilation theorists who followed him, such as Milton Gordon, Richard Alba, and Victor Nee—stumbled over the question of race.[21] The two major exceptions Herberg saw to his typology, Latinos and African Americans, he dealt with in a footnote. He considered them "measurably outside the division of American society. . . . Their primary context of self-identification and social location remains their ethnic or 'racial' group." It was clear to him that Latinos and African Americans had not assimilated and therefore did not fit the pattern, but he was unable to explain why this was so. Although he did see the potential for the absorption of Latinos into the model, he wrote that "the future of the Negroes constitutes a much more difficult problem, about which very little may be said with any assurance."[22]

Gordon at least addressed race. Yet he shunted it aside by contending that Indians were so separated from other Americans (they all, in his view, lived on reservations), Mexicans were so new to the United States (!), and African Americans were so hugely discriminated against that for them assimilation would be much slower than normal. Gordon had nothing to say about Asians at all. For Gordon, then, people of color were epiphenomenal and so did not challenge the pattern of assimilation established by White groups. For Gordon, as for Herberg, people of color could safely be ignored.

Alba and Nee, writing after a generation of race-conscious scholarship made Gordon and Herberg's approach untenable, did address the various communities of color in the United States. But they were so preoccupied with measuring what they regarded as indices of assimilation—housing, jobs, incomes, mother-tongue shift, and intermarriage rates—that they failed to see the racial dynamics at work in the lives of people of color. In fact, they went so far as to stop just short of predicting that Asians and Latinos would be absorbed into the White race and cease to exist as distinct racial groups by sometime around the middle of this century.[23]

The massive understatement of the importance of race in the theoretical work by Herberg, Gordon, and other assimilation theorists elided race by sweeping it under broad ethno-religious categories or retreating into measuring minutiae. But ultimately the problem is just too large to remain hidden. For Latinos and African Americans, as well as Asian Americans and Native Americans (who did not even warrant so much as a footnote in Herberg and barely more than that in Gordon), race, not ethnoreligion, is still operative as the primary source of social and political identification. Herberg suggested that to be American is to be Protestant, Catholic, or Jewish, and he made no allowance for racial groups who do not fit this paradigm. In effect, Herberg and those who followed his model reaffirmed the long-held sentiment that non-Whites are somehow non-Americans. They recapitulated the pernicious and all-too-common conflation of "White" and "American."

Japanese Americans, Asian Americans, Religion, and Race

This chapter is about immigration, religion, and race. In particular, I talk about the ways that religious identities have sometimes been racialized, and also how racial divisions have frequently been inserted into religious relations, as Asian Americans have interacted with the larger society.[24] Both race and religion make Asians foreign in the eyes of majority Americans. In this illustration, I will speak about the roles religion has played among Asian Americans, using mainly Japanese American examples, although I will move outward from time to time toward other groups—Chinese, Koreans, South Asians—and toward the Asian American panethnicity that has been forming over the past forty years. I pay particular attention to four aspects of religion in Asian American communities: institutions, leaders, lived religion, and racialization.

Institutions

Religious institutions have long been the most important institutions, after the family, in every Asian American community. In Seattle's Japanese American community in the decades before World War II, one important institution was the Northwest Japanese Association, whose Issei (first-generation) leaders spoke for the community to government authorities, both Japanese and American. There were newspapers such as the *Japanese American Courier,* the *Great Northern Daily News,* and *Hokubei Jiji*; shops, restaurants, and residential hotels; the Nippon Kan theater; and Seattle Gakuen, where American-born kids learned to read and write Japanese. All these institutions catered solely to the Japanese American community.

But none organized so much of Japanese American community life as the churches: Seattle Buddhist Church; Japanese Methodist Church; St. Peter's Episcopal Church; Nichiren Buddhist Church; Japanese Baptist Church; and the Japanese Holiness Mission. Seattle Buddhist Church, from the 1920s to the present, has been the single most populous and vibrant center of community activity. People have gone there to pray and to meditate, to learn flower arranging, to take English and Japanese language classes, and to meet with friends and gossip. The Buddhist Church sponsored the Imperials, a drum and bugle corps that reached national prominence in the 1960s and brought pride to the community. The church, the park nearby, and the street between have for generations been the site of the Bon Odori festival, the largest community gathering, where each summer many hundreds of people come for food, music, and dancing that last several nights. Most of the churches had gymnasiums; together they sponsored Japanese and then Asian basketball leagues from the 1930s onward. When a movement emerged in the 1970s and 1980s to recall and write the history of the World War II concentration camps, to call the government to account for past wrongs, and to make pilgrimages of ritual remembrance, it was in the churches that the organizing for such things took place.[25]

The same can be said of other Asian American communities. In every town of any size across the United States, there is at least one Chinese evangelical Christian church. It is often the only place where more than a few dozen Chinese Americans regularly come together at one time (though nearly all visit the local Asian food market, too). Even among people who have few or no religious commitments, the Chinese Christian church is a place that everyone knows is a sponsor of Chinese American community activities and an emblem of identity. It is a place where people go to be Chinese, as well as to be people of faith.[26] Hinduism is scarcely an "ism" in India, but in the United States, among a wide swath of South Asians, it has become a vibrant faith community that draws in people who had little connection with religion in their original homeland.[27] The same is true for Korean Protestantism. No Asian community is so thoroughly identified with one faith as are Korean Americans with fairly hard-core evangelical Protestantism.[28] Pastors are the most prominent Korean American leaders, and people come to the churches even if they personally have no particular beliefs, because that is where Koreanness is practiced in the United States.[29]

So religious institutions reinforce each of the various existing Asian American ethnicities. But in the last couple of decades religious institutions have also helped create and reinforce a new Asian American panethnicity. Many readers will know that the idea "Asian American" was born in the 1960s and 1970s as a self-conscious political project, by which Chinese, Japanese, Filipinos, and later others began to band together to defend themselves in a hostile society and to pursue common goals. Activists began to build pan–Asian American institutions—Asian American studies programs, the Asian American Mental Health Training Center, and so on and on. Since the middle 1980s, those pan-Asian institutions have begun to include churches.[30] There has been, not just the Chinese Baptist Church, but also the Asian American Community Church. Many college campuses today have not just the Korean Christian Fellowship but also the Asian American Christian Fellowship. In fact, being a member of the Asian American Christian Fellowship is a badge of belonging that has tremendous emotional saliency for many undergraduates. A theology of pan-Asian Christian church growth has emerged as well.[31]

Leaders

Religious leaders and thinkers have been key individuals in all Asian American communities. This fact has been ignored by the scholars of Asian American studies. No Seattle Japanese leader in the 1930s was more important than Rev. Tatsuya Ichikawa of the Buddhist Church. In Hawai'i, Bishop Yemyo Imamura was a sixteenth-generation Buddhist priest and the father and grandfather of two more generations of Japanese American priests. He presided over the Buddhist mission for the entire island chain from 1901 until his death in 1931. He was among the most prominent leaders, not only of his church, but of the Japanese community at large. He mediated a potentially violent strike by Waipahu sugarcane workers against White plantation owners and overseers, and the Buddhist church under his leadership provided the sites for subsequent labor organizing.[32]

While Japanese American Buddhist leaders were very important before World War II, government policy sent them into eclipse in the concentration camps. Most priests and some lay leaders were taken into custody by the FBI in the first days of the war and imprisoned apart from the rest of the Japanese American population for many months. The authorities doubled the racialization of such people; that is, they added to racial otherness an assertion of organic otherness on account of religion. The general Japanese American population was imprisoned because most non-Japanese Americans regarded them as racially unassimilable and irredeemably foreign and because they suspected Japanese Americans of being in league with America's enemies. But Buddhist leaders were singled out for special suspicion and harassment because other Americans thought their religion was foreign, strange, and subversive. Japanese American Christian leaders did not undergo such special incarceration, and, in fact, some in the camps became prominent community leaders who cooperated with the War Relocation Authority. When Buddhist leaders were reunited with the general Japanese American population behind barbed wire, they did not resume their prewar community leadership roles. The government required that all meetings be held in English, and leadership, even of Buddhist worship, passed from the hands of Issei to the second generation. (The exception was the Tule Lake Segregation Center, where the government housed those Japanese Americans they regarded as disloyal. There, during the latter part of the war, some Buddhist leaders again began to stand out.)[33]

Once the war was over, the Japanese American population was quite demoralized. It took two decades for community institutions to begin to make a comeback. Buddhist churches and leaders took part in the restoration of their community, but in the decades after the war Christian churches and leaders were more prominent.[34]

The role of religious leaders has been ignored by Asian American studies scholars. By the same token, religious studies scholars have failed to acknowledge the immigrant quality of Asian American religious figures. In religious studies literature, D. T. Suzuki is celebrated as the man who brought Zen to the Euro-American intellectual world, but his story as a Japanese immigrant to America just does not appear.[35] Rudy Busto tells us the story of Nyogen Senzaki, a contemporary of Suzuki's, who came to San Francisco in 1905 in the hold of a steamer, worked as a houseboy, taught Japanese language for pennies, and then lost his job and was run out of town in the agitation surrounding the 1908 "Gentlemen's Agreement." In the hinterlands he worked as an agricultural laborer, then went back to the city to work as a porter, cook, and hotel manager. World War II found him in a boardinghouse in Los Angeles, where he was seized and incarcerated. After the war he drifted, penniless, back to L.A. and resumed the project he had been working on all along while wandering from job to job: writing poetry, giving public lectures on Zen, and teaching mainly Japanese American disciples. As Busto remarks, "Curiously, the Zen in America narratives tend to depict him as merely waiting out the war, completely detached from the turmoil and racism of the internment experience and the internal factionalism rife among the Japanese internees."[36] In fact, he was actively teaching Zen Buddhism to Japanese American disciples. With this leader as with others—such as Yoshiaki Fukuda, the founder of Konko-Kyo Shinto in the United States, who stepped up to provide support for Japanese Peruvian inmates who were seized and taken to prison camps in the United States and then not allowed to return home at war's end—there is room in the religious studies literature for their religious contributions, but not for their immigrant and racial situations. And in the ethnic studies literature, there is no room for them at all, for in that literature religious leaders are unimportant.

As Jane Iwamura notes, "Mainstream [religious studies] scholars often ignore, deface, or depersonalize Asian American religious leaders who cater strictly to their ethnic communities, because in their eyes, these leaders lack the universalistic appeal of authentic religious leaders (a la Suzuki and Senzaki). . . . If ethnic religious leaders don't reach out to white folks they are folded into the undifferentiated Asian American religious masses" and ignored. To such people, Suzuki is important, but Imamura is not worth mentioning. Indeed, what is purported to be the definitive history of Buddhism in the United States contains many references to men such as Suzuki and Senzaki, who served White audiences, but makes almost no mention of their connection with Asian American Buddhists and no mention at all of Asian American community Buddhist leaders like Imamura.

Jane Iwamura notes further that "Asian Americans have their own invest-ments in participating in the orientalization of figures like Suzuki—we never question [White] standards of religious authenticity, but rather re-inforce conventional measures. In this schema, the Dalai Lama becomes more authentic than Bishop Imamura—even for local ethnic communi-ties and especially for their progeny."[37]

More recently, some Asian immigrant religious leaders have taken on a much higher profile. For communities such as Sikh Americans, the reli-gious leaders *are* the community leaders, by and large, so the people who speak for the community in seeking permits to build a Gurdwara are lead-ers both religious and secular. Sometimes that profile has been too high: Muslims (including Southeast Asian Muslims) have been singled out for government racial and religious profiling and make up the majority of the people who have disappeared into U.S. government custody as the Bill of Rights has been shredded by John Ashcroft and Alberto Gonzalez's Jus-tice Department. No one knows their number. Two thousand, perhaps? But their disappearance on racial grounds, and on religious grounds that have been racialized to mark Muslims as essentially, organically, irrevoca-bly foreign and hostile to the United States, is a story of immigration, reli-gion, and race.[38]

Lived Religion

Throughout Asian American history, lived religion has been a key cul-tural resource for maintaining—in fact for creating—ethnic solidarity. Yes, Korean American Protestant churches are places where people come together to be social with other Koreans and to work out Korean commu-nity issues. Yes, they are places where they speak Korean and eat Korean food together.[39] But they are also places where many people experience, express, and share a vibrant, living faith in the Jesus Christ they perceive in the Bible. And there is a Korean American community-bonding national-istic feeling that goes with that faith. This is not about social categories. It is not just that so many Korean Americans bear the evangelical label. As Jung Ha Kim says, "There seems to be a peculiar affinity between Korean Americans living in the United States as a people and Christianity as a re-ligion."[40] It is that the faith itself binds Korean Americans together. It is an expression and an emblem, for them, of their very Korean Americanness. A few years ago I was listening to a Los Angeles radio talk show while parked on the 134 Freeway. I don't remember the names of the principals being interviewed, but one was the pastor of a large Korean American Church, the other a White fundamentalist minister. The Korean pastor said to his White counterpart, not in exactly these words but with this meaning: "Yes, we Korean evangelicals believe all the same things you White fundamentalists do. But God gave those truths to us first, and we have pursued them with more purity of purpose." He said these things without a trace of irony or even an acknowledgment of his condescension.[41] A particular brand of Christian connection makes Koreans more Korean.

Individual, private worship also has a galvanizing ethnic effect. Every Japanese American person I know who has a *butsudan* (a home altar) feels not just more Buddhist when he or she is burning incense or arranging flowers and artifacts there, but also more Japanese American. The same is true for Hindu keepers of home shrines and for Chinese and Thai Americans who burn incense in their homes and shops to *baisin* their ancestors.[42]

Sometimes the lived religion that makes ethnicity is not affiliated with a formal church. Joanne Doi writes of the power of pilgrimage to make ethnic connection. For a quarter of a century, Japanese Americans have been making annual pilgrimages to Tule Lake and Manzanar, the places where they or their parents and grandparents were imprisoned. These are enormously emotional journeys, and there is ethnic bonding in the journey. As Doi writes: "The Tule Lake pilgrimage provides the opportunity to embrace our liminal nature by connecting to the lived experience and legacy of the Issei and Nisei generations in both their suffering and [their] spiritual strength. It allows us to enter into this deeper level of existence. It returns us from the pitfall of considering the American heritage as exclusively an extension of European tradition in contradistinction to our Asian cultural traditions, and begins to shed light on our world of meaning as Japanese Americans."[43]

Jane Iwamura regards such pilgrimages as evidence of "the birth of a new civil religion" among Japanese Americans that binds them together and makes their unity more meaningful. It is not insignificant that the profoundly racialized experience of being imprisoned together on account of their race calls forth the memory that glues them together and spurs them to act. Iwamura writes:

> Timothy L. Smith . . . speaks of migration as a "theologizing experience." The uprootedness and displacement that immigrants inevitably experience is written into new forms of religious belief and practice. While the fruits

and unanticipated trials of immigration certainly prompted religious innovation among turn-of-the-century Japanese Americans, it would not serve as the defining moment of Japanese American ethnic identity. Far more inexplicable and traumatic would be the legalized and wholesale discrimination that would ensue. Spiritual crisis would come through internment.

Racial prejudice has had a harrowing effect on Japanese Americans. Indeed, such prejudice renders the experience of migration less significant, as it does for other racialized peoples. The documents, sites, and rituals of Japanese American civil religion . . . the institutionalization of memory becomes the occasion for education, political action, and healing. While one hopes that intolerance and discrimination are a thing of the past, [Japanese Americans] are well aware that there is no guarantee that this is or ever will be the case. This vigilant attitude is indeed at the heart of Japanese Americans' critical faith.[44]

Religion and the Racial Connection

Religion matters profoundly in the immigrant communities of which I have been speaking, as it does, I expect, in nearly every other immigrant community. It matters not just as some mechanical measurement of how much the group has assimilated to "American"—that is, White—norms. It is a hugely significant and complex issue in its own right and an important means of ethnic glue, in fact of ethnic and panethnic formation.

But there is more than that at work with the populations about which I write. Everything about which I have written here has been framed powerfully by race. Religious identities have sometimes been racialized. For example, during World War II, White Americans incarcerated essentially the entire Japanese American population on a racial basis. But the authorities singled out Buddhist leaders as especially foreign and put them in separate prisons along with people who had active connections with the Japanese government. Inside the camps, the War Relocation Authority encouraged Christian activities and discouraged Buddhist expression. Japanese American Buddhists were, in effect, doubly racialized.

On the other hand, racial divisions have frequently been inserted into religious relations as Asian Americans have interacted with the larger society. Partly this may be related to the status of eternal foreigner that plagues Asian Americans. I have never met an Asian American who has not experienced being questioned by some White person (and not just once, but many times in their lives): "Where are you from?" "I'm from Oakland." "No, where are you really from?"[45] It is a truism among students of Asian American religions that 90 percent of the Buddhists in the United States are Asian Americans—Cambodians, Lao, Chinese, Japanese, Koreans, Vietnamese, Thai, and others—but 90 percent of the writing on Buddhism in America is about White Buddhists. I don't know if the numbers are precisely correct (no one has counted formally), but they can't be far wrong.[46]

Such issues come to ironic light in Carolyn Chen's ethnographic work in two large Southern California Taiwanese American churches, one evangelical Protestant, the other Buddhist. Because they were Christians, the Taiwanese evangelical church did not represent a threat to American cultural hegemony, and they did not feel the need to do public relations work in the community. They simply went about their business of being evangelical Christians in a monoethnic setting. By contrast, the Buddhist megachurch was very aware that they were seen as a foreign presence because they represented what many Americans imagined to be a foreign religion. They held World Peace Days, contributed to civic causes, and became involved in sponsoring local political events. So when the metropolitan Council of Churches (up until that time mostly White and entirely Christian and Jewish) came to the conclusion that they ought to diversify their membership, they invited the Taiwanese Buddhist church to join their board. The Taiwanese evangelicals probably wouldn't have joined them anyway, because they saw themselves as true Christians and didn't want to have truck with mainline Protestants, much less Catholics and Jews. But the council wasn't looking for them anyway; when they thought of Asian religious people, they thought of Buddhists, even though there probably are more Chinese Americans affiliated with Christian churches than with Buddhist institutions.[47]

Religion matters. Race matters.

NOTES

Most of what I think I know about these matters I learned from several friends, among them Rudy Busto, Peter Yuichi Clark, Carolyn Chen, Diane Fujino, Sheba George, Yvonne Haddad, Kimberly Hoang, Jane Naomi Iwamura, Russell Jeung, Khyati Joshi, David Kim, Fumitaka Matsuoka, Liza McAlister, Pyong Gap Min, Lori Pierce, the late Steffi San Buenaventura, Daniel Spickard, Naomi Spickard, Sharon Suh, Tim Tseng, Bill Wallace, Pastor Joe Wong, David Yoo, and my colleagues in the Asian and Pacific Islander American Religions Research Initiative. I am reasonably sure that none of them would want to be held responsible for everything I have written here, but their knowledge, generosity, and good company should be acknowledged. I am also grateful to the Oregon State University Center for the Humanities and the University of California, Santa Barbara, for providing excellent places to write. A much earlier version of this chapter was presented at the conference "Transcending Borders: Migration, Ethnicity and Incorporation in an Age of Globalism," held at New York University on November 1, 2003. I am grateful to the leaders of that conference, who are the editors of this book, not only for the opportunity to participate, but also for their patient help in making this essay more precise.

1. The same is true of immigrants from Africa and from Latin America, although those peoples are outside the purview of this essay.

2. Ellis Island Immigration History Museum, *Island of Hope, Island of Tears: The Story of Ellis Island and the American Immigration Experience*, DVD (Washington, DC: Guggenheim Productions, 1969).

3. Of 49,764 Chinese who applied for entrance between 1908 and 1932, 11,697 were sent back, or 23.5 percent. Add to that figure 10,673 more who were deported after arrival between 1898 and 1930. The refusal rates for Europeans who came through Angel Island were similar to those at Ellis Island. Erika Lee, *At America's Gates: Chinese Immigration during the Exclusion Era, 1882–1943* (Chapel Hill: University of North Carolina Press, 2003), 142–44, 227–28; Him Mark Lai, Genny Lim, and Judy Yung, *Island: Poetry and History of Chinese Immigrants on Angel Island, 1910–1940* (San Francisco: Chinese Culture Foundation, 1980).

4. To take just a few examples, on Asian Americans: Eiichiro Azuma, *Between Two Empires: Race, History, and Transnationalism in Japanese America* (New York: Oxford University Press, 2005); Yong Chen, *Chinese San Francisco, 1850–1943* (Stanford: Stanford University Press, 2000); Catherine Ceniza Choy, *Empire of Care: Nursing and Migration in Filipino American History* (Durham: Duke University Press, 2003); Dorothy B. Fujita-Rony, *American Workers, Colonial Power: Philippine Seattle and Transpacific West, 1919–1941* (Berkeley: University of California Press, 2003); Madeline Y. Hsu, *Dreaming of Gold, Dreaming of Home: Transnationalism and Migration between the United States and South China, 1882–1943* (Stanford: Stanford University Press, 2000); Lon Kurashige, *Japanese American Celebration and Conflict: A History of Ethnic Identity and Festival in Los Angeles, 1934–1990* (Berkeley: University of California Press, 2002); Lee, *At America's Gates*; Karen Isaksen Leonard, *Making Ethnic Choices: California's Punjabi Mexican Americans* (Philadelphia: Temple University Press, 1992); Huping Ling, *Chinese St. Louis: From Enclave to Cultural Community* (Philadelphia: Temple University Press, 2004); Charles J. McClain, *In Search of Equality: The Chinese Struggle against Discrimination in Nineteenth-Century America* (Berkeley: University of California Press, 1994); Gary Y. Okihiro, *Cane Fires: The Anti-Japanese Movement in Hawai'i, 1865–1945* (Philadelphia: Temple University Press, 1991); Eileen H. Tamura, *Ameri-*

canization, Acculturation, and Ethnic Identity: The Nisei Generation in Hawai'i (Urbana: University of Illinois Press, 1994); John Kuo Wei Tchen, *New York before Chinatown: Orientalism and the Shaping of American Culture, 1776–1882* (Baltimore: Johns Hopkins University Press, 1999); David K. Yoo, *Growing Up Nisei: Race, Generation, and Culture among Japanese Americans of California, 1924–49* (Urbana: University of Illinois Press, 2000); Judy Yung, *Unbound Feet: A Social History of Chinese Women in San Francisco* (Berkeley: University of California Press, 1995).

On Latinos: Rodolfo Acuña, *Occupied America: A History of Chicanos,* 3rd ed. (New York: Harper and Row, 1988); Edward J. Escobar, *Race, Police, and the Making of a Political Identity: Mexican Americans and the Los Angeles Police Department, 1900–1945* (Berkeley: University of California Press, 1999); Neil Foley, *The White Scourge: Mexicans, Blacks, and Poor Whites in Texas Cotton Culture* (Berkeley: University of California Press, 1997); María Christina García, *Havana USA: Cuban Exiles and Cuban Americans in South Florida, 1959–1994* (Berkeley: University of California Press, 1996); David G. Gutiérrez, *Walls and Mirrors: Mexican Americans, Mexican Immigrants, and the Politics of Ethnicity* (Berkeley: University of California Press, 1995); Martha Menchaxa, *Recovering History, Constructing Race: The Indian, Black, and White Roots of Mexican Americans* (Austin: University of Texas Press, 2001); David Montejano, *Anglos and Mexicans in the Making of Texas, 1836–1986* (Austin: University of Texas Press, 1987); Eduardo Obregón Pagán, *Murder at the Sleepy Lagoon: Zoot Suits, Race, and Riot in Wartime L.A.* (Chapel Hill: University of North Carolina Press, 2003); Clara E. Rodríguez, *Changing Race: Latinos, the Census, and the History of Ethnicity in the United States* (New York: NYU Press, 2000); Vicki Ruiz, *Cannery Women, Cannery Lives: Mexican Women, Unionization, and the California Food Processing Industry, 1930–1950* (Albuquerque: University of New Mexico Press, 1987), and *From Out of the Shadows: Mexican Women in Twentieth Century America* (New York: Oxford University Press, 1998); George J. Sánchez, *Becoming Mexican American: Ethnicity, Culture and Identity in Chicano Los Angeles, 1900–1945* (New York: Oxford University Press, 1993); Zaragosa Vargas, *Labor Rights Are Civil Rights: Mexican American Workers in Twentieth-Century America* (Princeton: Princeton University Press, 2005).

5. Some would argue that the vogue of Whiteness studies that began in the 1990s and occupies an extraordinary number of scholars today constitutes serious attention to race of the sort for which I ask here. I have analyzed that literature at length elsewhere (Paul Spickard, "What's Critical about White Studies," in *Racial Thinking in the United States,* ed. Paul Spickard and G. Reginald Daniel [Notre Dame: University of Notre Dame Press, 2004], 248–74, and "Does Multiraciality Lighten? Me-Too Ethnicity and the Whiteness Trap," in *New Faces in a Changing America: Multiracial Identity in the 21st Century,* ed. Loretta I. Winters and Herman L. DeBose [Thousand Oaks, CA: Sage Publications, 2003], 289–300). Some of that literature, such as George Lipsitz's *The Possessive Investment in Whiteness: How White People Profit from Identity Politics* (Philadelphia: Temple University

Press, 1998), is indeed excellent racial analysis, although Lipsitz does not deal with immigrants. Most of that literature is not useful racial analysis. There are a very few prominent historical studies of immigrants and Whiteness, such as Jennifer Guglielmo and Salvatore Salerno, *Are Italians White? How Race Is Made in America* (New York: Routledge, 2003), and Thomas A. Guglielmo, *White on Arrival: Italians, Race, Color, and Power in Chicago, 1890–1945* (New York: Oxford University Press, 2003). Sadly, their racial perspectives have not yet permeated mainstream studies of European immigrant history.

6. Richard D. Alba, *Italian Americans: Into the Twilight of Ethnicity* (Englewood Cliffs, NJ: Prentice Hall, 1985); David A. Hollinger, *Postethnic America: Beyond Multiculturalism* (New York: HarperCollins, 1995). A couple of new books even predict that by 2050, Latinos and Asians will be White: Richard Alba and Victor Nee, *Remaking the American Mainstream: Assimilation and Contemporary Immigration* (Cambridge, MA: Harvard University Press, 2003); George Yancey, *Who Is White? Latinos, Asians, and the New Black/Nonblack Divide* (Boulder, CO: Lynne Rienner, 2003).

7. See Paul Spickard, *Almost All Aliens: Race, Immigration, and Colonialism in American History and Identity* (New York: Routledge, 2007), ch. 1, and "Pacific Diaspora?" in *Pacific Diaspora: Island Peoples in the United States and Across the Pacific* (Honolulu: University of Hawai'i Press, 2002), 1–21.

8. James Clifford, "Diasporas," *Cultural Anthropology* 9, no. 3 (1994); Roger Rouse, "Mexican Migration and the Social Space of Postmodernism," *Diaspora* 1, no. 1 (1991); Sau-ling C. Wong, "Denationalization Reconsidered: Asian American Cultural Criticism at a Theoretical Crossroads," *Amerasia Journal* 21, no. 1–2 (1995): 1–27; Lisa Lowe, "Heterogeneity, Hybridity, Multiplicity: Marking Asian American Differences," *Diaspora* 1, no. 1 (1991): 24–44; Vijay Mishra, "The Diasporic Imaginary: Theorizing the Indian Diaspora," *Textual Practice* 10, no. 3 (1996): 421–47; Robin Cohen, *Global Diasporas* (Seattle: University of Washington Press, 1997); Darshan Singh Tatla, *The Sikh Diaspora* (Seattle: University of Washington Press, 1999); Lynn Pan, *Sons of the Yellow Emperor: A History of the Chinese Diaspora* (New York: Kodansha, 1994); Jiemin Bao, *Marital Acts: Gender, Sexuality, and Identity among the Chinese Thai Diaspora* (Honolulu: University of Hawai'i Press, 2005); Adam McKeown, *Chinese Migrant Networks and Cultural Change: Peru, Chicago, Hawai'i, 1900–1936* (Chicago: University of Chicago Press, 2001); Donna R. Gabaccia, *Italy's Many Diasporas* (Seattle: University of Washington Press, 2000); Adam McKeown, "Conceptualizing Chinese Diasporas, 1842–1949," *Journal of Asian Studies* 58 (1999): 306–37.

9. Yen Le Espiritu, *Asian American Panethnicity* (Philadelphia: Temple University Press, 1992); Michael A. Gomez, *Exchanging Our Country Marks: The Transformation of African Identities in the Colonial and Antebellum South* (Chapel Hill: University of North Carolina Press, 1998); Stephen Cornell, *The Return of the Native: American Indian Political Resurgence* (New York: Oxford University Press,

1988); Gary B. Nash, *Red, White, and Black in Colonial America* (Englewood Cliffs, NJ: Prentice-Hall, 1968); Matthew Frye Jacobson, *Whiteness of a Different Color: European Immigrants and the Alchemy of Race* (Cambridge, MA: Harvard University Press, 1998); Michael Omi and Howard Winant, *Racial Formation in the United States,* 2nd ed. (New York: Routledge, 1994).

10. See Arlene Dávila, *Latinos, Inc.: The Marketing and Making of a People* (Berkeley: University of California Press, 2001); William V. Flores and Rina Benmayor, eds., *Latino Cultural Citizenship* (Boston: Beacon Press, 1997); David E. Hayes-Bautista, *La Nueva California: Latinos in the Golden State* (Berkeley: University of California Press, 2004); Joan Moore and Harry Pachon, *Hispanics in the United States* (Englewood Cliffs, NJ: Prentice-Hall, 1985); Rodríguez, *Changing Race*; Roberto Suro, *Strangers among Us: Latino Lives in a Changing America* (New York: Knopf, 1998).

11. See, for example, Yvonne Yazbeck Haddad and Jane I. Smith, eds., *Muslim Minorities in the West* (Walnut Creek, CA: AltaMira Press, 2002); Elaine C. Hagopian, *Civil Rights in Peril: The Targeting of Arabs and Muslims* (Chicago: Haymarket, 2004); Michael W. Suleiman, ed., *Arabs in America* (Philadelphia: Temple University Press, 1999).

12. Moses Rischin, *The Promised City: New York's Jews, 1870–1914* (Cambridge, MA: Harvard University Press, 1962); Irving Howe, *World of Our Fathers: The Journey of the East European Jews to America and the Life They Found and Made* (New York: Harcourt Brace Jovanovich, 1976). See also Chaim I. Waxman, *America's Jews in Transition* (Philadelphia: Temple University Press, 1983); Stanley Feldstein, *The Land That I Show You: Three Centuries of Jewish Life in America* (Garden City, NY: Doubleday, 1978).

13. For example, the comprehensive *Handbook of International Migration* does not even address the issue of religion; Charles Hirschman, Philip Kasinitz, and Josh DeWind, eds., *The Handbook of International Migration: The American Experience* (New York: Social Science Research Council and Russell Sage Foundation, 1999). In fairness, there is a newly growing number of books specifically about religion and immigration: e.g., Helen Rose Ebaugh and Janet Saltzman Chafetz, eds., *Religion and the New Immigrants: Continuities and Adaptations in Immigrant Congregations* (Walnut Creek, CA: AltaMira Press, 2000), and *Religion across Borders: Transnational Immigrant Networks* (Walnut Creek, CA: AltaMira Press, 2002); Yvonne Yazbeck Haddad, Jane I. Smith, and John L. Esposito, eds., *Religion and Immigration: Christian, Jewish, and Muslim Experiences in the United States* (Walnut Creek, CA: AltaMira Press, 2003).

14. David K. Yoo, "Introduction: Reframing the U.S. Religious Landscape," in *New Spiritual Homes: Religion and Asian Americans,* ed. David K. Yoo (Honolulu: University of Hawai'i Press, 1999), 1–15.

15. E.g., Ronald Takaki, *Strangers from a Different Shore: A History of Asian Americans* Boston: Little, Brown, 1989); Sucheng Chan, *Asian Americans: An Inter-*

pretive History (Boston: Twayne, 1991); Lon Kurashige and Alice Yang Murray, eds., *Major Problems in Asian American History* (Boston: Houghton Mifflin, 2003); Josephine Lee, Imogene L. Lim, and Yuko Matsukawa, eds., *Re-Collecting Early Asian America: Essays in Cultural History* (Philadelphia: Temple University Press, 2002). An exception is Min Zhou and James V. Gatewood, eds., *Contemporary Asian America* (New York: NYU Press, 2000).

16. Happily, it is beginning to grow: see, e.g., Yoo, *New Spiritual Homes*; Pyong Gap Min and Jung Ha Kim, eds., *Religions in Asian America: Building Faith Communities* (Walnut Creek, CA: AltaMira Press, 2001); Jane Naomi Iwamura and Paul Spickard, eds., *Revealing the Sacred in Asian and Pacific America* (New York: Routledge, 2003); Tony Carnes and Fenggang Yang, eds., *Asian American Religions: The Making and Remaking of Borders and Boundaries* (New York: NYU Press, 2004); Raymond Brady Williams, *Religions of Immigrants from India and Pakistan* (New York: Cambridge University Press, 1989); Fumitaka Matsuoka, *Out of Silence: Emerging Themes in Asian American Churches* (Cleveland: United Church Press, 1995); Brian Masaru Hayashi, *"For the Sake of Our Japanese Brethren": Assimilation, Nationalism, and Protestantism among the Japanese of Los Angeles, 1895–1942* (Stanford: Stanford University Press, 1995); Paul Rutledge, *The Role of Religion in Ethnic Self-Identity: A Vietnamese Community* (Lanham, MD: University Press of America, 1996); Jung Ha Kim, *Bridge-Makers and Cross-Bearers: Korean-American Women and the Church* (Atlanta: Scholars Press, 1997); Anne Fadiman, *The Spirit Catches You and You Fall Down: A Hmong Child, Her American Doctors, and the Collision of Two Cultures* (New York: Farrar, Straus and Giroux, 1998); Fenggang Yang, *Chinese Christians in America* (University Park: Pennsylvania State Press, 1999); Ho-Youn Kwon, Kwang Chung Kim, and R. Stephen Warner, eds., *Korean Americans and Their Religions* (University Park: Pennsylvania State Press, 2001); Russell Jeung, *Faithful Generations: Race and New Asian American Churches* (New Brunswick: Rutgers University Press, 2005); Khyati Joshi, *New Roots in America's Sacred Ground: Race, Religion, and Ethnicity in Indian America* (New Brunswick: Rutgers University Press, 2006).

17. R. Stephen Warner and Judith G. Wittner, eds., *Gatherings in Diaspora: Religious Communities and the New Immigration* (Philadelphia: Temple University Press, 1998); Diana L. Eck, *New Religious America: How a "Christian Country" Has Now Become the World's Most Religiously Diverse Nation* (New York: HarperCollins, 2001). For a comment on the latter, see Lori Pierce, "The Eck Effect: The Racial Conundrum of Religious Diversity," paper presented at the Intercollegiate Parliament of the World's Sacred Traditions, Lake Forest, IL, September 21, 2003.

18. Will Herberg, *Protestant, Catholic, Jew* (Garden City, NY: Doubleday, 1955). See, for example, Richard Alba and Albert J. Raboteau, eds., *Religion, Immigration, and Civic Life in Historical Comparative Perspective* (New York: Social Science Research Council and Russell Sage Foundation, forthcoming); R. Stephen Warner

and Judith G. Wittner, eds., *Gatherings in Diaspora: Religious Communities and the New Immigration.* It is worth noting that almost no one in ethnic studies reads Herberg or thinks he has anything to say about peoples of color.

19. Robert E. Park, *Race and Culture* (Glencoe, IL: Free Press, 1949).

20. Herbert Gans, "Symbolic Ethnicity: The Future of Ethnic Groups and Cultures in America," *Ethnic and Racial Studies* 2, no. 1 (1979): 1–20. Note that here "American" means "Anglo-American" and middle class; cf. Milton Gordon, *Assimilation in American Life* (New York: Oxford University Press, 1964).

21. Gordon, *Assimilation in American Life*; Alba and Nee, *Remaking the American Mainstream.*

22. Herberg, *Protestant, Catholic, Jew,* 55. I am grateful to Lori Pierce for the insights—indeed for much of the language—in these paragraphs.

23. Alba and Nee, *Remaking the American Mainstream,* 288–91.

24. See also Joshi, *New Roots*; and Henry Goldschmidt and Elizabeth McAlister, eds., *Race, Nation, and Religion in the Americas* (New York: Oxford University Press, 2004). One can read analyses of the racialization of religion in South Africa in T. Dunbar Moodie, *The Rise of Afrikanerdom* (Berkeley: University of California Press, 1975), and Marjorie Hope and James Young, *The South African Churches in a Revolutionary Situation* (Maryknoll, NY: Orbis, 1981); in China, in Dru C. Gladney, *Muslim Chinese: Ethnic Nationalism and the People's Republic* (Cambridge, MA: Harvard University Press, 1991), and Jonathan N. Lipman, *Familiar Strangers: A History of Muslims in Northwest China* (Seattle: University of Washington Press, 1997); and in Fiji, in Brij V. Lal and Tomasi Rayalu Vakatora, eds., *Fiji in Transition* (Suva: University of the South Pacific School of Social and Economic Development, 1997), and Ralph R. Premdas, "Religion and Reconciliation in the Multi-Ethnic States of the Third World: Fiji, Trinidad, and Guyana" (PhD diss., McGill University, 1991).

25. Paul Spickard, *Japanese Americans: The Formation and Transformations of an Ethnic Group* (New York: Twayne, 1996): esp. 65–68; Madeline Duntley, "Public Voice, Identity Politics, and Religion: Japanese American Commemorative Spiritual Autobiography of the 1970s," in *Revealing the Sacred in Asian and Pacific America,* eds. Jane Naomi Iwamura and Paul Spickard (New York: Routledge, 2003), 291–307; Joanne Doi, "Tule Lake Pilgrimage: Dissonant Memories, Sacred Journey," in Iwamura and Spickard, *Revealing the Sacred,* 273–89; Jane Naomi Iwamura, "Critical Faith: Japanese Americans and the Birth of a New Civil Religion," in Alba and Raboteau, *Religion, Immigration.*

26. Yang, *Chinese Christians in America,* and "Tenacious Unity in a Contentious Community: Cultural and Religious Dynamics in a Chinese Christian Church," in Warner and Wittner, *Gatherings in Diaspora,* 333–61; Timothy Tseng, "Trans-Pacific Transpositions: Continuities and Discontinuities in Chinese North American Protestantism since 1965," in Iwamura and Spickard, *Revealing the Sacred,* 241–71.

27. Prema Kurien, "'We Are Better Hindus Here': Religion and Ethnicity among Indian Americans," in *Religions in Asian America*, eds. Pyong Gap Min and Jung Ha Kim (Walnut Creek, CA: AltaMira Press, 2001), 99–120, "Becoming American by Becoming Hindu: Indian Americans Take Their Place at the Multicultural Table," in Warner and Wittner, *Gatherings in Diaspora*, 37–70, and *Kaleidoscopic Ethnicity: International Migration and the Reconstruction of Community Identities in India* (New Brunswick: Rutgers University Press, 2002); Joshi, *New Roots*.

28. On June 24, 2000, the 2.5-million-member Presbyterian Church USA elected Syngman Rhee its first Korean American moderator, on the fiftieth anniversary of the start of the Korean War. He was chosen partly because of his theological conservatism. "Rhee Elected Moderator on 50th Anniversary of His Flight from North Korea," *212th General Assembly News* (Long Beach, CA, Presbyterian Church USA), June 24–July 1, 2000, http://horeb.pcusa.org/ga212/News/ga00020 .htm (accessed September 27, 2003).

29. Jung Ha Kim, "Cartography of Korean American Protestant Faith Communities in the United States," in Min and Kim, *Religions in Asian America*, 185–213, and *Bridge-Makers*; Kwan, Kim, and Warner, *Korean Americans*; Karen J. Chai, "Competing for the Second Generation: English-Language Ministry at a Korean Protestant Church," in Warner and Wittner, *Gatherings in Diaspora*, 295–331. I am well aware that there are substantial numbers of Korean American Catholics and Buddhists, but the Protestants dominate Korean American community life. On those other faith communities, see Sharon Suh, "'To Be Buddhist Is to Be Korean': The Rhetorical Use of Authenticity and the Homeland in the Construction of Post-immigration Identities," in Iwamura and Spickard, *Revealing the Sacred*, 177–91; and chs. 12–15 of Kwon, Kim and Warner, *Korean Americans*.

30. Another pan-Asian creation is the growing number of restaurants that serve pan-Asian fusion food, a singular contribution to world culture.

31. Ken Uyeda Fong, *Pursuing the Pearl of Great Price: A Comprehensive Resource for Multi-Asian Ministry* (Valley Forge, PA: Judson Press, 1999); Jeung, *Faithful Generations*; Jeung, "Asian American Pan-Ethnic Formation and Congregational Culture," in Min and Kim, *Religions in Asian America*, 215–43, "New Asian American Churches and Symbolic Racial Identity," in Iwamura and Spickard, *Revealing the Sacred*, 225–40, and "Creating an Asian American Christian Subculture: Grace Community Covenant Church," in *Asian American Religions*, ed. Fenggang Yang and Tony Carnes (New York: NYU Press, 2004), 287–313; Rudiger V. Busto, "The Gospel According to the Model Minority? Hazarding an Interpretation of Asian American Evangelical College Students," in Yoo, *New Spiritual Homes*, 169–87; Jeanette Yep et al., *Following Jesus without Dishonoring Your Parents* (Downers Grove, IL: InterVarsity Press, 1998).

32. Lori Pierce, personal communication, October 2003; Tetsuden Kashima, *Buddhism in America* (Westport, CT: Greenwood Press, 1977); Richard Hughes

Seager, "Jodo Shinshu: America's Old-Line Buddhists," in *Buddhism in America* (New York: Columbia University Press, 1999), 51–69; Louise H. Hunter, *Buddhism in Hawai'i: Its Impact on a Yankee Community* (Honolulu: University of Hawai'i Press, 1971); Ronald Takaki, *Pau Hana: Plantation Life and Labor in Hawai'i* (Honolulu: University of Hawai'i Press, 1983); Edward D. Beechert, *Working in Hawai'i* (Honolulu: University of Hawai'i Press, 1985).

33. Dorothy Swaine Thomas and Richard S. Nishimoto, *The Spoilage* (Berkeley: University of California Press, 1946).

34. Duntley, "Public Voice, Identity Politics"; Hayashi, *"For the Sake of Our Japanese Brethren."* It is worth noting that as late as the 1960s some leaders of Japanese American Christian churches were White, not Japanese Americans. Rev. Emory Andrews was pastor of Seattle's Japanese Baptist Church and as revered a figure in the Japanese community of the 1950s as Rev. Ichikawa was in the 1930s.

35. Seager, *Buddhism in America*; Jan Nattier, "Who Is a Buddhist? Charting the Landscape of Buddhist America," in *The Faces of Buddhism in America,* eds. Charles S. Prebish and Kenneth K. Tanaka (Berkeley: University of California Press, 1998), 183–95; Rick Fields, "Divided Dharma: White, Ethnic Buddhists, and Racism," in Prebish and Tanaka, *Faces of Buddhism,* 196–206.

36. Rudiger V. Busto, "Disorienting Subjects: Reclaiming Pacific Islander/Asian American Religions," in Iwamura and Spickard, *Revealing the Sacred,* 19.

37. Jane Iwamura, personal communication, October 7, 2003; Seager, *Buddhism in America.*

38. Jaideep Singh, "The Racialization of Minoritized Religious Identity: Constructing Sacred Sites at the Intersection of White and Christian Supremacy," in Iwamura and Spickard, *Revealing the Sacred,* 87–106, and "American Apartheid for the New Millennium: Men of Profile," paper presented at the meeting of the Asian and Pacific American Religions Research Initiative, Berkeley, August 8, 2003.

39. Sharon Suh, "Buddhism, Rhetoric, and the Korean American Community: The Adjustment of Korean Buddhist Immigrants to the US," in Alba and Raboteau, *Religion, Immigration.*

40. Kim, "Cartography," 186.

41. See also Pyong Gap Min, "A Comparison of Korean Immigrant Protestant, Catholic, and Buddhist Congregations in New York," in *Religion and the Incorporation of Immigrants,* ed. José Casanova and Aristide Zolberg (New York: NYU Press, forthcoming).

42. Shampa Mazumdar and Sanjoy Mazumdar, "Creating the Sacred: Altars in the Hindu American Home," in Iwamura and Spickard, *Revealing the Sacred,* 143–57.

43. Doi, "Tule Lake Pilgrimage," 282.

44. Iwamura, "Critical Faith."

45. Lisa Lowe, *Immigrant Acts: On Asian American Cultural Politics* (Durham: Duke University Press, 1996); Mia Tuan, *Forever Foreigners or Honorary Whites?*

The Asian Ethnic Experience Today (New Brunswick: Rutgers University Press, 1998).

46. Nattier, "Who Is a Buddhist?"; Fields, "Divided Dharma."

47. Carolyn Chen, "Cultivating Acceptance by Cultivating Merit: The Public Engagement of a Chinese Buddhist Temple in American Society," in Iwamura and Spickard, *Revealing the Sacred,* 67–85, "The Religious Varieties of Ethnic Presence: A Comparison between a Taiwanese Immigrant Buddhist Temple and an Evangelical Christian Church," *Sociology of Religion* 63, no. 2 (2002): 215–38, and *Getting Saved in America* (Princeton: Princeton University Press, forthcoming).

Part II

Case Studies

Chapter 5

"Meet Me at the Chat/Chaat Corner"
The Embeddedness of Immigrant Entrepreneurs

Caroline B. Brettell

In the summer of 1972 I was conducting field research on Portuguese immigrants in the city of Toronto, Canada. At that time, many recently arrived Portuguese were living in the Kensington Market area, an urban neighborhood of modest and low-cost housing in downtown Toronto that had traditionally been a receiving area for immigrants. On Augusta Street, at the heart of this neighborhood, produce stalls, bakeries, fish markets, and restaurants catering to a Portuguese clientele, but also in some cases to a broader "Canadian" clientele, lined the streets. On other streets, one could find a Portuguese-language bookstore, several Portuguese travel agencies, other restaurants, and the Portuguese Social Club. This was an ethnic enclave, although the Portuguese were just the most recent immigrant group to settle in Kensington.

In an article that I wrote about the Portuguese in Toronto I described what I called "ethnic entrepreneurs." These individuals, I suggested, were middlemen, but not in the same way that Edna Bonacich has described immigrant entrepreneur middlemen who are both oppressors and oppressed, exploiting those beneath them (co-ethnics and other minorities) for the sake of those above them (large corporations).[1] Rather, I conceptualized the role of ethnic entrepreneurs as patrons and cultural brokers. At the same time that they were catering to the material needs of the Portuguese immigrant community and building a business around this role, they were also providing services that mediated between newly arrived immigrants and the Canadian host society. For example, not only did the travel agents help Portuguese immigrants with airline tickets to go back to Portugal or to bring family members to Canada, they also helped them to write letters, place phone calls, fill out various forms, or apply for insurance and national health care. Sometimes they even acted as legal advisers at the Immigration Appeal Board or as witnesses at civil marriage ceremonies. These services were offered for free or for a small fee, the broader goal being to build a loyal customer base. Acting as a broker, I argued, the ethnic entrepreneur transmits the values of the larger society to the newcomers and expresses concern for and interest in their integration. Through patronage, on the other hand, he furthers his own goals by his ability to dispense favors to immigrants. Ethnicity, I concluded, is partially sustained in urban areas as a good business venture.

I drew on other examples of "ethnic entrepreneurs" to reinforce the point—the owner of the takeout chicken store who was a freelance impresario bringing Portuguese entertainers to the Toronto community and organizing a "Miss Portugal, Canada" contest; or the bookstore owner who not only made soccer games from Portugal available to patrons via a short-wave radio in his store but also provided books for the Portuguese-language school sponsored by the First Portuguese-Canadian Club, which he co-founded. Even the priest acted as an ethnic broker. He delivered the mass in Portuguese each Sunday at a nearby Catholic church, offered a broad range of social services of which Portuguese newcomers could avail themselves in their own language, and acted as the leader of the community in relationships with the city of Toronto and a host of government officials. In return, he earned the loyalty of his flock.

My approach in this analysis was anthropological. It drew on key anthropological concepts of patrons and cultural brokers, and it attempted to situate these economic actors into a broader framework. Anthropologists for a long time have insisted that economic activities must be studied and explained holistically—that is, as part of a complex system that includes social, cultural, and political activities and relations. Another way of talking about holism is to talk about embeddedness. In his book *Economic Anthropology* Stuart Plattner argues that economic anthropologists interpret the economy as "embedded in society" and explain it relative to the social and political constraints (and one might add opportunities) of the social system. This approach focuses on the link between the local and the global.[2]

Anthropologist Stephen Gudeman goes further, suggesting that the economy consists of two realms that he labels "community" and "market" respectively. By the former, he means "on the ground associations and imagined solidarities that people experience." The market, by contrast, involves more impersonal, anonymous, global, and short-term exchanges. He continues, "We might call these two aspects of economy the Up-close

and the Far-distant. . . . Sometimes the two faces of economy are separated, at other times they are mutually dependent, opposed or interactive.
But always their shifting relations are filled with tension."[3]

The concept of embeddedness has been picked up by sociologist Mark
Granovetter to address the social capital and social networks that immigrant entrepreneurs and other economic actors draw upon to achieve economic success. Indeed, Granovetter has argued that while anthropologists
use an oversocialized conception of human action that manifests itself in
the idea of embedded economies, economists use an undersocialized one
(disembedded markets). He takes both disciplines to task, arguing that in
the nonmarket economies that anthropologists routinely study there is a
good deal of instrumental action that is ignored by them and that in the
market economies that economists study there is more embedded action
than economists recognize.[4]

Although I acknowledge the instrumental aspects of individual entrepreneurship in this essay (after all, these are people trying to make a living), it is the community or "up close" nature of entrepreneurship and the
ways in which it is culturally and socially embedded that I explore here. I
choose not to focus on why individual immigrants move into self-employ-
ment and entrepreneurship, or to address the question of whether entrepreneurship (or the ethnic economy) is an effective avenue for economic
and social mobility. Both topics have already been extremely well covered
in the literature.[5] Rather, I emphasize the "ethnic" part of immigrant entrepreneurship, taking the community rather than the individual as the
unit of analysis.

The data for this essay are drawn from my research on Asian Indian immigrants in the Dallas–Fort Worth metropolitan area (henceforth DFW).
This research is part of a larger study of the incorporation of immigrants
in this Sunbelt city.[6] I have chosen for discussion one segment of entrepreneurship from a broad range of enterprises that involve Asian Indian immigrants—those that focus on the ethnic consumer market—because
they best illustrate the centrality of such businesses to the construction of
community.

Immigration to DFW

The study of immigration in the United States is often associated with
four gateway cities—Los Angeles, New York, Chicago, and Miami—and

indeed these four metropolitan areas still have the largest foreign-born populations according to the 2000 census. In recent years, however, second-tier metropolitan areas in the Midwest and West (Denver, Minneapolis), or in the South and Southwest (Atlanta, Dallas–Ft. Worth, Phoenix) have received large numbers of new immigrants, making them more ethnically diverse than ever. In the Dallas PMSA (the primary metropolitan statistical area composed of six counties including Dallas, Collin, and Denton counties), the foreign-born population increased from 8.8 percent in 1990 to 16.8 percent in 2000; comparable figures for the Fort Worth–Arlington PMSA (including Tarrant County) are 6.2 percent and 11.4 percent, respectively. The DFW area is clearly an emerging gateway region of immigration.[7]

This reputation as a new urban destination for immigrants has been building since the 1970s, although it was accelerated in the 1990s. Between 1970 and 1990, the proportion of foreign born in the two key counties, Dallas and Tarrant, doubled—from 5.1 to 10.6 percent and from 3.5 and 6.8 percent, respectively. Between 1990 and 2000 the foreign born in Dallas County increased from 10.6 percent to 20.1 percent and in Tarrant County from 6.8 percent to 12.7 percent. Demographer William Frey classified Dallas as tenth among the metropolitan areas that received the highest volumes of immigration between 1985–90 and 1990–95.[8] In the 2000 census it remained number 10 in a list of the ten metropolitan areas with the largest foreign-born population. The increases in other nearby counties also reflect the trend. The foreign born in Collin County were 6.0 percent of the total population in 1990 and 13.3 percent in 2000. The comparable figures for Denton County were 5.4 percent and 10.1 percent.

The largest group settling in the area during this recent decade of rapid growth were Mexican nationals. The 2000 census enumerated 433,534 individuals born in Mexico in North Texas—57.6 percent of the total foreign-born population. Of these, 295,678 (or 68.2 percent) resided in Dallas County and 104,438 (or 23.9 percent) in Tarrant County. In Dallas County this represented a 197.4 percent increase from 1990 and in Tarrant County a 194.1 percent increase. Table 5.1 shows the comparable changes for other foreign-born populations between 1990 and 2000.

Of note in particular is the increase in the foreign-born populations in the more suburban counties, best illustrated in table 5.1 by Collin County. Collin County was ranked number 8 of twenty-five counties across the United States that demographers Camarota and Keeley label "New Ellis Islands," counties where the number of new legal immigrants between 1991

TABLE 5.1

Regional Distribution of Foreign-Born Population by Nationality Group, 1990 and 2000

	Total Pop.	Total Foreign Born	Mexico	Vietnam	El Salvador	China	Korea	Pakistan
Collin Cty								
1990	264,036	15,611	3,617	586	250	696	546	230
2000	491,675	65,279	17,479	2,675	841	5,634	2,265	928
% change	86.20	318.20	383.20	356.50	236.40	709.50	314.80	303.50
Dallas Cty								
1990	1,852,810	196,328	99,411	8,084	8,235	2,451	5,347	1,389
2000	2,218,900	463,574	295,678	16,934	22,351	5,223	7,333	4,390
% change	19.80	136.10	197.40	109.50	171.40	113.10	37.10	216.10
Denton Cty								
1990	273,525	14,674	3,541	1,000	423	466	664	146
2000	432,976	40591	15,939	2,038	834	941	1,764	1,450
% change	58.30	176.20	350.10	103.80	97.20	101.90	165.70	893.30
Tarrant Cty								
1990	1,170,103	79,363	35,509	6,076	755	1,253	1,620	796
2000	1,446,219	183,223	104,438	14,875	2245	2,581	2,639	2,196
% change	23.60	130.90	194.10	144.80	197.40	106.00	62.90	175.90
Dallas City								
1990	1,006,831	125,862	75,507	3,772	4,271	1,296	1,803	429
2000	1,188,204	290,436	208,688	6,235	10,443	3,101	2,686	1,331
% change	18.00	130.80	176.40	67.70	144.50	139.30	49.00	210.30
Fort Worth City								
1990	447,619	40,300	26,068	2,129	391	342	390	284
2000	535,420	87,120	64,469	4,195	946	565	897	401
% change	18.00	116.20	147.30	97.00	141.90	65.20	130.00	41.20

SOURCE: U.S. Census, 1990 and 2000, Fact Sheets for communities, www.factfinder.census.gov.

and 1998 was equal in size to at least 50 percent of the existing foreign-born population in 1990.[9] More broadly speaking, the Dallas PMSA saw the proportion of the foreign born increase from 12.2 percent to 24 percent in the central city between 1990 and 2000 and from 5.8 percent to 11.7 percent in the suburbs. In the Fort Worth–Arlington PMSA the proportion of foreign born in the central city increased from 8.5 percent in 1990 to 15.9 percent in 2000, while the increase in the suburban areas was from 3.6 percent in 1990 to 6.6 percent in 2000.

This increasing diversification of suburban areas as a result of immigration has been equally characteristic of other emerging gateway cities. For example, the foreign-born population in suburban Atlanta increased from 4 percent of the total suburban population to 10.7 percent between 1990 and 2000, while comparable figures for the central city were 3.4 percent and 6.6 percent. A trend that anthropologist Sarah Mahler first noted in her study of El Salvadorans on Long Island is borne out by the data from these new cities of immigration in the U.S. South and Southwest. Suburbs are no longer simply bedroom communities but, as Robert Manning has characterized them, "dynamic growth poles of employment, consumption, leisure, culture and public administration."[10] As Joseph Wood has written, "Like other American frontiers in other generations, suburbs are now the geographical spaces in which Americans of all sorts of origins are creating America."[11] One such foreign-born population settling in the suburbs of the DFW metropolitan area is Asian Indians.

Asian Indians in DFW

In 1980, the first year that they were listed as a separate group, the U.S. Census counted 387,223 Asian Indians in the United States. This figure had more than doubled in 1990 to 815,447, and by 2000 the estimated number of Asian Indians in the United States had risen to 1.7 million. The growth of the Asian Indian population in DFW has followed these national trends. A small number arrived in the early 1960s to work at the nuclear plant at Comanche Peak and in other scientific or technical fields at local universities or with local companies such as Texas Instruments and Collins Radio. These were individuals who had spent some time elsewhere in the United States, often as students, before moving to the DFW area. They were the ones who in 1962 founded the India Association of North Texas —an umbrella organization that survives to this day and also plays an instrumental role in fostering a sense of community by bridging the religious and regional diversity among Asian Indians.

The number of Asian Indians in DFW began to expand in the 1970s as high-tech industries developed. In Dallas County, Asian Indians settled in Richardson, a close-in northern suburb of Dallas with, at least at the time, a very strong public school system. But only after 1980, and particularly after 1990, did that the population really expand. Table 5.2 presents the number of Asian Indians in the DFW SMSA/CMSA between 1980 and 2002 and for the four counties of the DFW metropolitan area in 1990 and 2000. The population more than doubled during each decade. Simultaneous with this rapid increase, the population moved north from Richardson to Collin County, particularly toward Plano and west toward Irving (still in Dallas County but close to the border with Tarrant County). Map 5.1 shows the distribution of Asian Indians in the metroplex based in 2000 U.S. Census data, with each dot representing ten households randomly distributed by census tract.

TABLE 5.2
Asian Indian Population by County and Major City,
DFW Metroplex, 1980–2000

County	1980*	% Change 1980–1990	1990	2000	% Change 1990–2000
Collin			703	5,753	718.34
Dallas			6,408	16,030	150.15
Denton			758	2,911	284.00
Tarrant			2,478	5,336	115.33
TOTAL			10,347	30,030	190.22
Dallas City			2,256	5,339	136.65
Fort Worth City			646	1,417	119.34
DFW SMSA/PMSA	5,006	152.89	12,660	42,852	238.48

SOURCE: U.S. Population Census, 1980, 1990, 2000, Fact sheets for communities, www
.factfinder.census.gov.
  * In 1980 the total figure is for the entire SMSA. There are no figures at the county
level for Asian Indians in particular. Rather, Asians and Pacific Islanders are grouped
together.

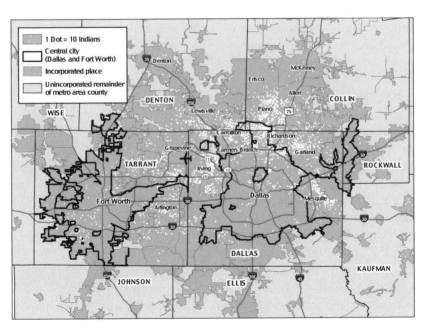

Map 5.1. Residential Distribution of Indians in the DFW Metro Area, 2000

128   CAROLINE B. BRETTELL

The growth and dispersion of this community were simultaneous with the dramatic boom in the telecommunications corridor to the north of the city of Dallas, where the headquarters of companies such as Nortel, Alcatel, SBC, and Erikson are located, and to a lesser extent to the west toward Fort Worth, where companies like Nokia and Verizon built headquarters along Highway 114 in Irving, Texas. In the 1990s many Asian Indians moved to the area on H1B visas or on F1 visas that were then converted to HIB visas. Some of these individuals have since become legal permanent residents. Others, after the economic bust of 2001, have returned to India.

Another group of Asian Indians who have settled in Irving and Arlington, the mid-cities (or close-in suburbs) sandwiched between Dallas and Fort Worth, are referred to by members of the Asian Indian community as the second wave—among them less well-educated family members who were sponsored by earlier immigrants, now naturalized citizens, under various family preference categories. Many of these immigrants became small business owners in convenience stores, dry cleaners, motels, restaurants, small groceries, and other specialty shops serving their own community. In this group are also individuals of Indian ancestry born and raised in Africa—the so-called "twice migrants."

In the mid-1980s the DFW Hindu temple was established in Irving, Texas. Prior to this, local-area Indians met in a rented warehouse in Plano, a suburb north of the city. In 1984 the founders had purchased land in the far suburban north with the idea of building a permanent temple there. Not only were the fund-raising efforts slow, but local Anglo inhabitants protested the presence of a Hindu temple. Under duress, the Indians decided to sell the land and look elsewhere. They found a new site in Irving, Texas, that was convenient to both the Dallas and Fort Worth communities. In 1991 the new temple building, Ekta Mandir, was inaugurated, and since then a cultural center has been added to the compound.

As the DFW Indian community grew, other places of worship were established, some rather informally at first—the Sikh temple, the Swaminarayan temple, the Jain temple, the Marthoma Church for South Indian Christians, additional Hindu temples, and small mosques for those who wanted an alternative to the large mosque in Richardson that gathers together Muslims from a range of national populations. These religious institutions are scattered around the metropolitan area, in north Dallas or in various close-in suburbs.

This is, in short, a residentially dispersed immigrant population, characterized by a large number of high-human-capital professionals who can live anywhere. In the face of such dispersion, it is worth asking how Asian Indians immigrants have built community and whether an ethnic community requires an ethnic neighborhood—something clearly absent in the case of this population in this city. Sociologists John Logan, Richard Alba, and Wenquan Zhang have recently defined the ethnic community as "ethnic neighborhoods that are selected as living environments by those who have wider options based on their market resources."[12] This definition is too narrow and relies too heavily on a co-residential understanding of community. It seems more appropriate to draw on the concept of heterolocalism formulated by geographers Wilbur Zelinsky and Barrett A. Lee. *Heterolocalism* refers to "recent populations of shared ethnic identity which enter an area from distant sources, then quickly adopt a dispersed pattern of residential location, all the while managing to remain cohesive through a variety of means."[13] Zelinsky and Lee suggest that heterolocalism can be observed in both metropolitan and nonmetropolitan settings, and clearly it incorporates some of the ideas embodied in the concepts of transnationalism and deterritorialization. While there are many mechanisms by which cohesion can be maintained among residentially dispersed immigrant populations in large metropolitan areas, here I focus on the role of immigrant entrepreneurs.[14]

A Social and Cultural "Mecca" for Ethnic Community

Between 1632 and 1643 Shah Jahan built the Taj Mahal in the town of Agra in north central India to commemorate his wife Mumtaz, who had died giving birth to their fourteenth child. This magnificent structure, though built by a Mogul emperor, has come to symbolize a predominantly Hindu India around the world. It is a structure that carries the same national iconic value for India that the Statue of Liberty carries for America or New York and that the Eiffel Tower carries for France or Paris. In each case these are destinations, meccas, places sought out by numerous people.

In 1983 an Indian immigrant who had been working at an Indian grocery store in Houston since his arrival in the United States in 1981 moved to Dallas with a plan to open his own grocery business. He had one contact in Dallas—someone who had shopped at the Houston store where he worked who told him that there was no equivalent facility for the growing Asian Indian community in Dallas. "I had been reading books and they all said that Dallas was the town to be in, that it was going to grow, that it was a boom town. That sounded to me like the place to be."

When he and his wife arrived in town he picked up a telephone book and began to look up typical Indian last names to see where people lived. He found out that they were largely in Richardson and North Dallas. His telephone book analysis was confirmed when his contact told him that there were only three places where he should open his store: Beltline and Interstate 75, Spring Valley and 75, or Arapaho and 75. He chose the Beltline area and soon identified a three-thousand-square-foot location in the old Richardson Heights shopping center. Within six weeks he was open for business, drawing on the help of friends in the community to build the shelves and other fittings for the store.

During the first year he lost money, but by June of 1984 he began to make a small profit. At the beginning he and one employee worked in the store, and on weekends his wife, who had a job in a nearby bank, helped out. Slowly he acquired more space, first seven hundred square feet on one side and then seven hundred on the other. He proudly announced, "I rode the wave of growth of the Indian community. I have been lucky." In 1995 he moved his store to its present location, taking over an old office furniture store and six thousand square feet elsewhere in the same shopping center. He has expanded two more times since then, adding two thousand square feet in 1997 and an equivalent amount in 2002. His inventory has grown with his expansion from food and produce to sweets, frozen foods, typical kitchen utensils including *masala* boxes, and most recently herbal and beauty products. He makes at least three trips a year to India to look for new things that he can carry in his store. He brings them to an exporter there, who then arranges for the bulk shipping. Today he employs thirty-five people, thirty-one full time and four part time. The people behind the specialty and checkout counters are Indian—indeed, the owner's brother works full time. But there are several Hispanic employees who stock shelves and work behind the scenes. One of the employees is on the road constantly, picking up shipments from the airport and making deliveries to local restaurants that the store services. Seven people work in the warehouse. Ninety-five percent of the customer base is Indian, about 1 percent is British, and the rest is American. It is worth noting that while this is a decidedly Indian grocery store that attempts to create an Indian atmosphere, as I discuss further below, it has absorbed aspects of American marketing practice—its scale, the diversity of what it sells (which in

India would be provided by several merchants selling particular items), and the attention to American health standard practices.

By the late 1980s several other Asian Indian stores had moved into this shopping center—a travel agency, a video store, a sari store, a jewelry store, and one restaurant. Today there are eight Indian-owned businesses in this center in addition to the Taj Mahal, and across the street there are seven others, including two smaller grocers, a grocery/video store, a sweet shop, a beauty salon, and two sari/appliance stores. These stores find the shared strip mall location mutually beneficial. As one business owner said, "I was in another location but it was demolished, so in 1994 I moved to this location. It is good for business because it is a central place where Indians can come and take care of lots of things. There is a similar atmosphere in all the shops."

In short, this shopping mall has become the physical center for the Indian community in the metroplex if not a broader five-state area. On any weekend the store and the mall are full of Indian families who come to pick up weekly staples. Indeed, more than 50 percent of business for the Taj and the other shops is done on weekends. As the Taj owner observed,

> I have between three thousand and four thousand regular customers. They call me by my first name and say hello. They get upset when I move things around in the store. Some of my customers live in small towns in Oklahoma, Arkansas, Louisiana, and New Mexico. There are no Indian groceries there. Someone from southern Oklahoma might have a family member coming from India. They come to pick him up at DFW and they stop by the store. They are on our mailing list and they get our fliers. Sometimes I send these people in other states UPS packages with the things they need. We offer people good service and they have bonded with us.

This bonding is important, but it is a social relationship that extends well beyond the bond between the owner and his customers because people come to the Taj for more than shopping. They come for the social atmosphere and to find other people in the community. On Saturday mornings young, single HIB visa holders gather at the Chaat Corner (the fast-food bar at the back of the store) for good food and fellowship.[15] Those who are members of charitable organizations like "Art of Living" and "Asha" also use it as a meeting place where they can plan or sell tickets for upcoming events. Sometimes the meeting is serendipitous. He explains, "Someone will come in and run into someone they knew back in India but have not seen for a long time. Other people have been transferred down here, and then they come in to the store to make contacts."

In the Chaat Corner there is a bulletin board where people can post fliers for concerts and recitals. If there is a tragedy in India, like the 2001 earthquake in Gujarat, and local organizations such as the India Association of North Texas want to collect money, they place a donation box in the store. There is also a board adjacent to the Chaat Corner where, for a fee of $5 a month, small business owners can leave multiple copies of their business cards. Some people have been doing this since the beginning, finding it a cheap and fruitful form of advertising. High above and throughout the store are banners advertising other businesses—a physician, a real estate agency. The fee for this form of advertising is $100 a month. The Taj owner explains, "In India if a doctor moves into a neighborhood and wants to drum up business, he will post a banner like this in the local neighborhood grocery. It is very common, and people who come here are used to seeing this kind of advertising."

There are also banners for community events—in August for example, one advertising the annual Anand Bazaar, an outdoor event held each year at Lone Star Park, the local race track, to celebrate Indian Independence Day. For years the Taj Mahal grocery has sponsored the petting zoo at the bazaar. The Taj Mahal, like several other small businesses in DFW, is a place where tickets to community events like the Anand Bazaar, classical dance performances, or a concert featuring the famous Bollywood composer A. R. Rahman, are sold. "Individuals who are sponsoring an event know that if they want to be successful they need to sell their tickets at the Taj because three thousand families a week will pass through." In all these ways the Taj Mahal, like several other businesses in this community and in other immigrant communities, serves as an information broker for the entire community.[16]

But the Taj Mahal does not merely provide a context for social interaction, information sharing, and economic promotion; it also plays an instrumental role in preserving cultural practice and hence in fostering cultural citizenship through its involvement in important annual festivals.[17] One is Diwali, the Hindu festival of lights popular in North India that marks Rama's return to the throne after a long exile. Diwali takes place in October or November. For many years now the store has installed a large *rangoli* painting in a side room. To create a *rangoli*, a form of Hindu folk art, powdered colors (or colored sand) are sprinkled on the floor to form a design. While the designs are often abstract and, in India, are placed at the entrance to people's homes as an expression of hospitality, at the Taj Mahal the paintings are more pictorial and cover a space that is about ten by twenty-two feet. One year, the "wonders" of the world, including an image of the real Taj Mahal, were represented, and in the fall of 2001 there was a patriotic design to commemorate 9/11. The *rangoli* takes four hundred to five hundred hours to make and it is left in place for six weeks. Families bring their children to watch the creation process and to see the finished product.

A second important festival is Holi, observed particularly in Rajasthan and Gujarat to celebrate the end of winter in March. In India, this is a festival of symbolic inversion where the normal rules of behavior are suspended; women pretend to battle with men, hashish is added to milk, and everyone can become a target for the colored powders and water that are thrown. The Taj Mahal owner stocks these colored powders in his store during the spring. A third festival is Raksha Bandhan, celebrated in July and August all over North India. During this festival sisters tie a thread of dyed cotton or silk and glitter, the *rakhi,* on the wrists of their brothers. The thread is a symbol of love and a request for a brother's protection. In India brothers and sisters gather together, sometimes traveling long distances, to go through the ritual of tying the thread.[18] To recognize this festival the Taj Mahal owner stocks the store with the ritual threads, placing them in a display right at the entrance to the store. Women who live in DFW buy them and send them back to India if that is where their brothers are residing. A fourth festival supported by the Taj Mahal is Ganesh Chaturthi, a popular festival that takes place in September. To honor Lord Ganesh, Indians prepare shrines (*mandals*) with the decorated clay image of the elephant god. As part of the ritual these clay gods must be dissolved in water; in Bombay they are destroyed in the Arabian Sea following a procession of sometimes as many as 250 idols. The Taj Mahal owner sells the clay Ganesh idols in the store, again placing them in a prominent place at the entrance at the appropriate time of year. Each year families that observe this festival come to buy a statue. Indeed on a Saturday in late August I noticed several of the gaudy pink-bellied Ganesh idols in many shopping carts, and by the next day the Taj was sold out.

In short, through the merchandise that is sold the Taj Mahal plays a role in keeping Asian Indian immigrants (or at least those of the Hindu faith) in touch with their ritual traditions and hence with their culture. The varied merchandise, ranging from food to ritual objects (which are themselves connected), brings people from the community to the store on a regular basis and is thus good for business. For similar reasons the owner of the Taj Mahal also reaches out to various regional associations; to newcomers to the city, who receive information on the store in their welcome packets; and to the Indian student associations at the major universities in the area. He is particularly supportive of campus events, often providing free food, because in doing so he fosters, among the younger generation, an interest in Indian culture and in the material products that sustain that culture. The result is that they too come to the store.

The Behaviors and Values of Cultural/Economic Embeddedness

From an anthropological perspective it makes perfect sense that a grocery store such as the Taj serves as the mecca for the residentially dispersed Asian Indian immigrant community in DFW and the surrounding states. Food, as a material substance that is culturally embedded and defined, has always been a mechanism by which group membership and identity are reinforced. Indeed, in India food is "closely tied to the moral and social status of individuals and groups . . . [and] is believed to cement the relationship between men and gods, as well as between men and themselves."[19] But other culturally embedded behaviors and values are also essential to the business success of immigrant entrepreneurs. The larger goal is to create a cultural atmosphere, as the Taj Mahal does, that allows people to "feel at home" in their community.

One familiar behavior is haggling or bargaining, rooted in frugality. Bargaining is a game of strategy where seller and buyer both feel that they have been successful. Several entrepreneurs operate their businesses with full cognizance of this culturally embedded economic practice. Take, for example, the owner of the biggest Bollywood video store, who happens to be a Pakistani serving a largely Desi (South Asian) clientele. He described his strategy for economic success as follows:

> I noticed that one place nearby was selling videos for $2.50. Another was renting them for $1. Our quality of inventory was good and the store was nice looking, but I had to do something else to get the volume of sales up. Indian people like bargains; bargaining, that is their habit. They are frugal and they shop around. The Indian community is not ready for Blockbuster, they want things cheaper. So I put up a big sign that said that videos were

available for rent for 49 cents on weekdays and for 99 cents on weekends. I put ads in the newspapers and did whatever else I could to get people in. Within two months the volume of business had increased 700 percent (the previous owner had been losing money badly), and word of mouth helped to spread the news further. People came in, liked the product, the store, and the price.

The next thing I figured out is that a lot of people were coming from great distances like Irving to pick up films, so I offered people a film for a whole week for $2. People would take five and ten films at a time, keep them a week, and return them the following week. This was convenient for them because they would come to the area to shop on Saturdays and then return the following week and not have to make special trips just to return the films.

From there the owner moved to offering an annual plan where people could pay $250 for 100 movies, ten at a time. He mailed them to wherever his customers lived and hence extended his client base to South Asians living in small towns in Oklahoma, Louisiana, and Arkansas, places where Bollywood movies were not easily accessible. He even had one customer in New Hampshire. At one point there were 900 customers on this plan, but by 2002 the number had dwindled to between 100 and 125. He said that the decline was the result of competition from satellite TV—another area of business opportunity. He advertises in local newspapers that cater to the Indian and Pakistani communities but claims that the best strategy is direct mail: "I get telephone directories and I look up common Indian and Pakistani names (Patel, Khan), and I send them a letter about the store and our plans. I even do this for Waco and Austin. I do a bit on radio too, but my best source for drumming up business is the direct mailing." This entrepreneur's business is built on an ethnic clientele and on a well-developed interest in films made in their home country or region. Another market niche where this is equally true is in wedding planning. Many Asian Indians still have arranged marriages, but whether arranged or not, they are celebrated in the traditional Indian way, with the appropriate rituals and room decorations. These weddings have become familiar to non-Indians in the United States through films such as *Monsoon Wedding* and *Bend It Like Beckham*.

There are several wedding planners in the DFW area who are serving a growing wedding economy.[20] One of these is quite prominent and associated with a company that advertises and operates nationally. Another, a younger woman who was just getting started when I interviewed her, commented in particular on the downside of bargaining in relation to her business. "My most difficult problem is dealing with men in the community. They try to haggle with you; they try to get a better deal. . . . I also have trouble getting them to pay up. And sometimes they ask to talk to my father even though it is my business."

She has developed a culturally effective strategy to deal with these problems—she throws something in for free, like a red carpet, and that "usually makes them happy." Although she has been told by her clients that her major competitor will negotiate with people, she prefers to operate with set prices and then "sweeten the package." She also asks for full payment two weeks in advance, and some of her customers protest "because they have not seen the service. But I have bills to pay, so I tell them they will just have to take a chance." She commented that she was in fact surprised at all the haggling because many of the fathers of the bride are well-to-do and can well afford it and want to spend on their daughter's wedding. "It is a cultural thing." As if to confirm this observation, one other businessman, an individual of Indian ancestry born in Zambia who had once been involved in the Indian grocery business, said he had sold that store because he "could not handle it." Indians want everything for cheap, at lower than cost, he said. He did not like it, so he want back to the dry-cleaning business, which has a largely non-Indian clientele, fixed prices, and no haggling.

Another area where bargaining is expected within the Indian community is in the jewelry business. One jeweler in the DFW area brought his business from Africa. He opened his first store in Arlington because it was cheaper to rent mercantile space, but once the business started to grow he realized that most of his customers were in the North Dallas, so he opened another store in Richardson that was more convenient to his primary clientele. Noting that there is a "cultural aspect" to the Indian jewelry business, this entrepreneur went on to say that Indians, even second-generation Indians, think about the purchase of jewelry in a very different way from Americans: "Buying jewelry is an investment, and they put a lot of time, money and effort into selecting the perfect items. Many are buying the jewelry as a form of insurance or savings bank. It is like money to them. They will spend $1,000 to $20,000 on a good set of jewelry, not because it looks good or that they will get a lot of wear out of it, but because in times of need it can be melted down for money in gold and it can be used as a dowry for their daughters."

This jeweler now employs all Indians because "only Indians have the learned knowledge of what Indian customers are seeking when they come jewelry shopping. They know how to sell it better because of their cultural knowledge." He does all the ordering of new jewelry and he is in charge of the expansion projects. He keeps a close tab on his employees to make sure they are giving the customers the highest-quality service because, as he said, "without trust my business would not exist."

Trust is a significant culturally embedded economic value. In Gudeman's view, trust, together with confidence, mutuality, benevolence, goodwill, caring, and respect, underwrites trade.[21] It is inherent in the relationship between the Asian Indian jeweler and his customers, the Taj Mahal owner and his customers, and other ethnic entrepreneurs and their customers within the DFW Asian Indian community. It is perhaps best exemplified by and most vital to those individuals who work in the increasingly competitive travel business, a business that has been hard hit by the Internet, by the events of September 11, 2001, and by a host of new rules set by the airlines.

In the Dallas area there are a half a dozen major travel agencies that serve the Indian community. One of these agents has located his business near the Taj Mahal. Seventy-five percent of his clientele is Indian, and the other 25 percent is largely composed of other South Asians. The customer base, he says, is built on contacts, referrals, trust, stability, and his knowledge and connections that facilitate "return-home" travel. The business relationship is personalized. As this agent explained, "People come back because they have received good service from you, and they know that you know the product. Some of my clients have moved to the West Coast, but they still use me because they know that they can trust me to get them a good deal. . . . My business is very time intensive. People even call me at home. They want an answer right away; they want a ticket at the last minute." That this agent keeps customers who have moved away is evidence of his accumulated social capital.

Yet maintaining the "up-close" dimension at a distance does not always succeed. Three of the four entrepreneurs discussed here have tried to extend their businesses into the U.S. Indian diaspora: the travel agent opened a branch in Houston, the video store owner opened a branch in Chicago on Devon Street at the heart of that city's Asian Indian community, and the Taj Mahal owner opened a second store in Atlanta. Finding the commuting difficult in a business where his presence was important, the video store owner sold his enterprise to a local Chicago Indian after two years. The travel agent's Houston expansion lasted only six months. "I had a special deal with Pan Am, but it went sour, so I closed the agency and returned to Dallas full time. My brother had been helping in the agency in Dallas, but he went out on his own in the diamond trade, so I had work to do when I returned." By contrast, the branch of the Taj Mahal in Atlanta thrives and has become an important outlet for the Taj Mahal brand products that this owner has developed: large sacks of staples like rice, lentils, and flour. The single market offered by the DFW metroplex would not be big enough for the scale of the bulk packaging enterprise, so expansion made good business sense.

Conclusion

This essay explores the cultural dimensions of immigrant entrepreneurship to emphasize the role of small business owners in creating community, fostering a familiar marketplace atmosphere, and promoting cultural citizenship; that is, "the right to be different . . . with respect to the norms of the dominant national community, without compromising one's right to belong."[22] It is worth setting these activities in a broader historical context. Clearly, the immigrant entrepreneur was as characteristic of the third wave of immigration (between 1880 and 1924) as he or she is today. The entrepreneurs of the past may have started small, perhaps as pushcart peddlers, but within residentially concentrated ethnic neighborhoods they found a ready and exploitable market and clientele. As Donna Gabaccia tells us, in 1899 the "Jews of the Lower East Side of New York City boasted 140 groceries, 131 kosher butchers, 36 bakeries, 9 bread stands, 14 butter and egg stores, 24 candy stores, 7 coffee shops, 10 delicatessens, 9 fish stores, 7 fruit stands, 2 meat markets, 10 sausage stores, 20 soda water stands, 5 tea shops, 11 vegetable stores, 13 wine shops, 15 grade wine shops, and 10 confectioners."[23] These were all businesses that catered to Jewish customers.

The need for a ready and exploitable market and clientele is equally essential for immigrant entrepreneurs today, but they must operate, in many instances, in postwar motorcar cities that are laterally spread out such that people do not very often live, work, and shop in the same neighborhood. In these metropolitan areas residentially dispersed immigrant groups have constructed symbolic nodes. In some cases these are commercial centers that become the focus for social relationship and cultural identity. This is as true for the Asian Indians in DFW as it is for Asians in other cities such as the Vietnamese in the Washington, D.C. area. North of the border, in Toronto, the second- and third-generation Portuguese have moved out to the suburbs, but the Kensington Market area still remains as the heart of their community. "The Portuguese return to Kensington to do their weekly shopping, go to church, and participate in cultural events; and some of the first generation still reside there, in a place where they feel comfortable and where they can live in Canada the Portuguese way."[24]

Entrepreneurs, no matter who they are and where they are, are engaged with the processes of both marketing and consumption. From an anthropological perspective, consumption involves a set of social and cultural practices that make and maintain distinctions among social groups and hence establish boundaries. For the first generation of Portuguese who arrived in Toronto in the late 1950s and through into the 1970s, the ethnic entrepreneurs of Kensington served as intermediaries on whom the immigrants could depend to help them negotiate the rules and regulations of Canadian society. They straddled an ethnic boundary for an immigrant population with low human capital and limited English-language skills. The entrepreneurs serving the Asian Indian or broader South Asian population in the DFW metropolitan area do not necessarily straddle a boundary for what is in general a high-human-capital immigrant population. Yet they are equally involved in maintaining distinction through their efforts to create meaningful localized spaces in the face of suburban residential dispersion and to construct ethnic community through the values, practices, and products that they market.

NOTES

1. Caroline B. Brettell, "Ethnicity and Entrepreneurs: Portuguese Immigrants in a Canadian City," reprinted in Caroline B. Brettell, *Anthropology and Migration: Essays on Transnationalism, Ethnicity and Identity* (Walnut Creek, CA: AltaMira Press, 2003), 127–37; Edna Bonacich, "'Making It' in America: A Social Evaluation of the Ethics of Immigrant Entrepreneurship," *Sociological Perspectives* 30 (1987): 446–66.

2. Stuart Plattner, *Economic Anthropology* (Stanford: Stanford University Press, 1989), 3.

3. Stephen Gudeman, *The Anthropology of Economy* (Oxford: Blackwell, 2001), 1.

4. Mark Granovetter, "Economic Action and Social Structure: The Problem of Embeddedness," *American Journal of Sociology* 91 (1985): 481–510, and "The Economic Sociology of Firms and Entrepreneurs," in *The Economic Sociology of*

Immigration: Essays on Networks, Ethnicity and Entrepreneurship, ed. Alejandro Portes (New York: Russell Sage Foundation, 1995), 128–65.

5. James T. Fawcett and Robert W. Gardner, "Asian Immigrant Entrepreneurs and Non-entrepreneurs: A Comparative Study of Recent Korean and Filipino Immigrants," *Population and Environment: A Journal of Interdisciplinary Studies* 15 (1994): 211–38; Ivan Light and Steven Gold, *Ethnic Economies* (New York: Academic Press, 2000); Roger Waldinger, "The Two Sides of Ethnic Entrepreneurship," *International Migration Review* 27 (1993): 692–701, and "The 'Other Side' of Embeddedness: A Case-Study of the Interplay of Economy and Ethnicity," *Ethnic and Racial Studies* 18 (1995): 555–80.

6. That project, "Immigrants, Rights and Incorporation in a Suburban Metropolis," was supported by the National Science Foundation (BCS 003938) through the Cultural Anthropology Program. Other co-principal investigators involved with the project are James F. Hollifield, Dennis Cordell, and Manuel Garcia y Griego. Any opinions, findings, and conclusions or recommendations expressed in this essay are my own and do not necessarily reflect the views of the National Science Foundation. I would like to express sincere appreciation to all the individuals in the DFW Asian Indian community who generously agreed to participate in this research.

7. On "emerging gateways," see Audrey Singer, *The Rise of New Immigrant Gateways* (Washington, DC: Brookings Institution, 2004).

8. William H. Frey, "Immigration, Domestic Migration, and Demographic Balkanization in America: New Evidence for the 1990s," *Population and Development Review* 22 (1996): 741–63.

9. Steven A. Camarota and John Keeley, *The New Ellis Islands: Examining Nontraditional Areas of Immigrant Settlement in the 1990s.* (New York: Center for Immigration Studies, 2001).

10. Sarah J. Mahler, *American Dreaming: Immigrant Life on the Margins* (Princeton: Princeton University Press, 1995) and *Salvadorans in Suburbia: Symbiosis and Conflict* (Boston: Allyn and Bacon, 1995); Robert Manning, "Multicultural Washington D.C.: The Changing Social and Economic Landscape of a Past Industrial Metropolis," *Ethnic and Racial Studies* 21 (1998): 342. See also Richard D. Alba et al., "Immigrant Groups in the Suburbs: A Reexamination of Suburbanization and Spatial Assimilation," *American Sociological Review* 64 (1999): 446–60.

11. Joseph Wood, "Vietnamese American Place Making in Northern Virginia," *Geographical Review* 87 (1997): 70–71.

12. John Logan, Richard Alba, and Wenquan Zhang, "Immigrant Enclaves and Ethnic Communities in New York and Los Angeles," *American Sociological Review* 67 (2002): 300.

13. Wilbur Zelinsky and Barrett A. Lee, "Heterolocalism: An Alternative Model of the Sociospatial Behaviour of Immigrant Ethnic Communities," *International Journal of Population Geography* 4 (1998): 281. Heterolocalism is now also charac-

teristic of some immigrant communities in traditional gateway cities. One might, for example, take note of the significance of the Jackson Heights area for residentially dispersed Asian Indians in the New York area or that of Devon Street for an equally residentially dispersed Indian population in Chicago. Johanna Lessinger labels the Jackson Heights area of Queens a "Little India": "In the absence of clearly defined Indian immigrant residential enclaves, this 'little India' offers a focus and a center to a population geographically dispersed throughout the greater metropolitan area by regularly concentrating large numbers of Indians in one place as shopkeepers, employees and customers." Johanna Lessinger, *From the Ganges to the Hudson: Indian Immigrants in New York City* (Boston: Allyn and Bacon, 1995), 28.

14. A broader analysis would also examine the role of other mechanisms that are mentioned by Zelinsky and Lee. "Much of the glue that holds [the deterritorialized ethnic community] together exists in the shape of ethnic churches, business associations, athletic leagues, social and service clubs, bars, cultural centers, festivals, and other institutions that may or may not be situated in neighbourhoods where some modest degree of clustering can be detected" (Zelinsky and Lee, *Heterolocalism,* 288–89).

15. *Chaat* or *chat* in Hindi means "fast food." There is no pun intended here, but the double meaning in English translation only underscores the point of a space of interaction and communication.

16. For another example, see Arlene Dallalfar, "Iranian Women as Immigrant Entrepreneurs," *Gender and Society* 8 (1994): 541–61.

17. I borrow my use of the term *cultural citizenship* from Rosaldo and Flores, who define it as "the right to be different . . . with respect to the norms of the dominant national community, without compromising one's right to belong, in the sense of participating in the nation-state's democratic processes." Renato Rosaldo and William V. Flores, "Identity, Conflict, and Evolving Latino Communities: Cultural Citizenship in San Jose, California," in *Latino Cultural Citizenship: Claiming Identity, Space, and Rights,* ed. William V. Flores and Rina Benmayor (Boston: Beacon Press, 1997), 57.

18. In India the *rakhi* can also be given to a close male friend. The ritual then places these individuals in a symbolic relationship of "*rakhi* brother" and "*rakhi* sister" and hence of special affection equivalent to that extended to blood relatives.

19. Arjun Appadurai, "How to Make a National Cuisine: Cookbooks in Contemporary India," *Comparative Studies in Society and History* 30 (1988): 10. See also Donna R. Gabaccia, *We Are What We Eat: Ethnic Food and the Making of Americans* (Cambridge, MA: Harvard University Press, 1998); Sidney Mintz and Christine M. Du Bois, "The Anthropology of Food and Eating," *Annual Review of Anthropology* 31 (2002): 99–119.

20. Karen Leonard and Chandra S. Tibrewal, "Asian Indians in Southern Cali-

fornia: Occupations and Ethnicity," in *Immigration and Entrepreneurship: Culture, Capital, and Ethnic Networks,* ed. Ivan Light and Parminder Bhachu (New Brunswick, NJ: Transaction Publishers, 1993), 141–62, have described a similar trend in Southern California.

21. Stephen Gudeman, *Economics as Cultures: Models and Metaphors of Livelihood* (London: Routledge, Kegan Paul, 1986), 18.

22. Rosaldo and Flores, "Identity, Conflict," 57.

23. Gabaccia, *We Are What We Eat,* 64.

24. Carlos Teixeira, "The Portuguese in Toronto: A Community on the Move," *Portuguese Studies Review* 4 (1995): 69.

Chapter 6

Filipino Families in the Land of Lincoln
Immigrant Incorporation in
Springfield, Illinois, since 1965

Barbara M. Posadas and Roland L. Guyotte

The Filipino American community in the Land of Lincoln—Springfield, Illinois, and nearby cities—provides a site for examining the experiences of post-1965 immigrants in a setting in which they are *not* a substantial "minority" population. It underscores the diversity of Filipino immigrants in the United States.[1] It also offers an opportunity to explore the ways in which gender has shaped the lives of female immigrants in their adopted home over the course of a generation. Immigrant family, organizational, and religious ties emerged and developed among a fairly stable population that included professionals, practicing physicians, and salaried employees of the State of Illinois who arrived in the locale from the early 1970s through the 1980s. In the 1990s, as the initial cohort aged, and as some of their adult children remained in the area as part of the Filipino American "community," newer immigrants from the Philippines joined them. Although some have also been professionals, the more recent arrivals have also included Filipinas, women who enjoyed fewer of the advantages possessed by the initial cohort and whose incorporation into the ethnic community has been shaped by the parameters set by women of the earlier group.

Springfield, the capital of Illinois, lies two hundred miles southwest of Chicago and one hundred miles northeast of St. Louis. With a population of approximately 112,000 in 2000, Springfield is predominantly white (81 percent) but also has a substantial African American presence (15.3 percent). Asians constitute only 1.5 percent of the city's residents, while Hispanics are an even smaller 1.2 percent.[2] Because Springfield is the state capital, as well as the county seat of Sangamon County, the business of government provides employment for large numbers of Springfield residents. Higher education is available at three public institutions: the University of Illinois at Springfield, the Southern Illinois University School of Medicine, and Lincoln Land Community College. Those seeking a Catholic institution can attend Springfield College in Illinois or one of the professional schools of St. John's Hospital, which includes the St. John's College Department of Nursing and the School of Dietetics. As the home of Abraham Lincoln, Springfield draws over one million visitors each year to its historic sites: Lincoln's Home and Neighborhood, Lincoln's Tomb, and nearby New Salem. Similarly, the Illinois State Fair draws huge crowds to the State Fairgrounds every August. During sessions of the Illinois General Assembly and Illinois State Senate, state lawmakers are temporarily in residence for long periods of time, typically finding quarters in one of the city's twenty-eight hotels and motels.

Given its population mix and constant flow of temporary residents and visitors, Springfield has not become a city in which Filipino Americans are immediately visible as a presence on its streets. This is especially true because of the small numbers of Philippine- and American-born Filipinos living in Springfield. In 2000, 171 residents claimed Filipino ancestry.[3] But Springfield residents do not comprise the entire Filipino American community. In the nearby towns and small cities of central Illinois, Filipino immigrants have also found places to live, work, and raise their families. Philippine- and American-born Filipinos total 5 in Carlinville, 106 in Decatur, 38 in Jacksonville, 34 in Lincoln, 5 in Litchfield, 3 in Pana, 6 in Shelbyville, and 20 in Taylorville, all within a radius of sixty miles. Thus, in 2000, the Land of Lincoln was home to a Filipino American community of just under four hundred.[4]

Although the central Illinois Filipino American population is tiny by comparison with many enclaves on the East and West Coasts and in Chicago, the story of these immigrants nonetheless offers insight into the means by which ethnic community is forged *despite* the absence of large numbers. To some extent, large numbers can offer a degree of insulation from the broader society, particularly with regard to social interaction. Urban neighborhoods and suburbs with high concentrations of Filipino Americans enable Filipino immigrants and their families to settle nearer to each other than is possible when numbers are small. Larger numbers also facilitate the development of ethnic institutions in fixed sites. In Chicago, for example, Filipino Americans have supported a community center since the 1970s. Still, Filipinos in central Illinois have found the means by which to forge their own ethnic societies and associations through which, over the last thirty years, Filipino American ethnic identity has been fostered. This study now turns to that network of community organizations, and then to the role played by women in creating the content and defining the boundaries of being Filipino American in the Land of Lincoln.

Filipino Americans came to Springfield and other central Illinois communities from the early 1970s through the 1980s because of U.S. government policies that encouraged the immigration of foreign-trained medical personnel. In these years, Filipino physicians and nurses benefited from long-standing ties between the United States and their homeland. Specifically, they were educated in the English language and trained in curricula developed by the American medical profession.[5] Those who came to central Illinois were part of a cohort of more than nine thousand Philippine-trained physicians who entered the United States roughly between 1965 and 1974.[6] Approximately fifty physicians, mostly male, but some "husband and wife" teams, settled with their families in central Illinois during these years. Educated in the Philippines, often already married, and sometimes bringing young children, these immigrants made their way in a strange land with the advantages that their education, profession, and family support system gave them. Subsequent federal legislation in the 1970s, however, reduced the numbers of foreign medical personnel, and the opening of the Southern Illinois University Medical School, which graduated its first class in 1975, began to supply locally trained physicians to the region. Reduced opportunities and demand thus produced in Springfield a discrete population of immigrant men and women born in the late 1930s and the early 1940s who practiced their professions and raised their families in the United States but whose numbers were not continuously replenished by medical newcomers from the Philippines. The vibrant community and organizations that they built are aging with them, leaving ultimate survival to their grown children and to a small number of newer immigrants, many of whom do not come from the professional ranks.

Philippine-born women have always played a large role in the development of this community. Before the arrival of the physicians and their families, the first Filipinas in Springfield were the wives of Americans—post–World War II war brides and military spouses from subsequent years. Corazon Jasmines Clark, for example, married her husband in the Philippines before coming to the United States in 1947. Their American husbands invariably held middle-class occupations, often as engineers employed by the Illinois Departments of Public Health or Transportation. Their large, interracial families (four, six, and nine children respectively among some of the early community leaders) set a tone of inclusiveness for the family-centered organizations that would be built later when more Filipinos arrived. Three of the first six presidents of the Central Illinois Philippine American Society (CIPAS), founded in 1970, were the "Anglo" husbands of Filipinas. After the organization's first decade, four Philippine-born women served as president between 1981 and 1991.

Like other immigrant professionals, Filipino physicians came to central Illinois by a circuitous rather than a direct route.[7] They typically made several prior stops of from one to three years elsewhere in the United States. But once the first to arrive became established in Springfield in the early 1970s, they increased in number there and in the smaller, neighboring towns and cities. Several were Philippine medical school classmates or had interned or taken medical residencies together under the U.S. government's Exchange Visitor Program. Some of these medical workers were single when they arrived from the Philippines but met and married compatriots in the United States, as did Drs. Edwin Siroy and Sally Santelices.

In central Illinois, some found employment at state institutions, while others entered private practice in such specialized fields as anesthesiology, emergency medicine, pediatric cardiology, and psychiatry. Several worked in clinics with countrymen: in Pana, Drs. Gloria and Virgil Dycoco practiced together; in Shelbyville, Drs. Urbano Dauz and Virginia B. Caballero-Dauz practiced alongside Dr. Edwin Siroy; and in Springfield, Drs. Reynaldo and Rachel Gotanco settled, he to practice in a clinic while she raised four children and worked part time. These networks proved professionally and socially supportive for Filipinos and their families, even though life in central Illinois placed them far away from emerging Filipino American communities in major metropolitan areas. The physicians' cohort in central Illinois in the 1970s anticipated Ann Bagchi's contention that in the 1990s career opportunities sometimes overrode the chance to live near countrymen.[8]

Springfield's Filipino immigrants soon created a small, energetic community centered in several organizations—the Central Illinois Philippine American Society (CIPAS), the Association of Filipino Physicians in Southern Illinois (AFPSI), and the Filipino American Historical Society (FAHS). The first of these emerged after Drs. Vicente Perez and Virgilio Pilapil and their wives, Emilia and Elena, met with four other couples in

1970 shortly after their arrival in Springfield and formed the Philippine American Society. In 1973–74, the organization changed its name to the more geographically precise Central Illinois Philippine American Society (CIPAS). The group held their first gathering, a *lechon* (roast pork) picnic on a member's front lawn, attended by nineteen different families and six single individuals, spending $74.00 for the pig and $15.85 for beer. In December, the society held its first Christmas dinner dance at the Springfield Elks Club, where decorations and entertainment mixed two cultures: crossed U.S. and Philippine flags set in floral centerpieces and the ubiquitous "Tinikling," danced by couples as bamboo poles clapped at their feet. The group quickly developed a calendar of social events including the summer picnic, an October general meeting, a Christmas dinner dance drawing as many as three hundred revelers, and such recreational activities as bowling tournaments, golf outings, and a casino night. To these gatherings, otherwise not unlike those of other American social and professional organizations, Springfield's Filipinos have brought an ethnic dimension by usually including Philippine food, traditional attire, and folk dances.

CIPAS has also retained the Philippine custom of including even small children at formal events. Children have been not only present but also prominently involved, often performing for their parents' friends and associates. However, in the United States, as opposed to the Philippines, mothers have not been able to rely on the ubiquitous *ya ya* (nanny) to supervise the youngsters. Instead, Filipina mothers have had to enlist their husbands in the task or, if possible, rely on mothers and mothers-in-law who have come from the Philippines specifically to help with child care. Despite the difficulties in this and other aspects of child rearing in the United States, Filipina women of this generation have always emphasized and taken pride in their role as mothers. Dr. Virginia B. Caballero-Dauz, CIPAS's 1993 president, declared: "The children were made the highlight of my presidency—they took part in the entertainment and it was stressed that they are our best natural resources."[9]

In the early 1980s, controversy arose within CIPAS over whether the organization should remain focused primarily on social activities or devote energies to fund-raising and charitable work in central Illinois and in the Philippines. A new constitution, put forward in 1982 during the presidency of wife, mother, and civic activist Elena Pilapil, the group's first female president, envisioned the latter course. It committed CIPAS "to encourage voluntary participation and involvement . . . in charitable, civic, and cultural activities that enhance the life of the communities," "to function as a not-for-profit organization in charitable, civic and cultural fund-raising events that CIPAS supports," and "to foster friendship and cooperation among Pilipinos [sic] and Americans in Springfield and the surrounding areas of Central Illinois." Opposition to the new constitution resulted in an unplanned mail balloting of the general membership.[10]

Having shifted away from the purely social, CIPAS took on a variety of charitable, often health-related ventures in the Philippines that were sometimes the special projects of individual CIPAS leaders. In addition, as it defined Filipino Americans as an ethnic presence in central Illinois, CIPAS also raised money for non–Filipino American charitable organizations in Springfield and participated in an Asian Night and in the Springfield Ethnic Festival, where members successfully sold Philippine snacks at the large community gathering.[11]

Although CIPAS has tried over the decades to reach out to Filipino Americans outside the initial cohort of physicians and their families, its history during the past thirty years has mainly been their history, following their careers and the growth of their children to adulthood. While CIPAS social functions have served to welcome many Filipino Americans who never took leadership roles, including such short-term residents as the fifteen "new Filipina nurses" pictured in one of its yearbooks, well into the 1990s CIPAS drew its leadership from among the physicians and their spouses. A 1995 estimate put its active membership at about 120, but membership has fallen somewhat as members of the original cohort have retired and/or moved away from central Illinois.

Two additional associations have linked "Filipino" and "physician" to define a central facet of the ethnic group's primary identity in central Illinois: the Association of Philippine Physicians in America (APPA), a national organization, and the Association of Filipino Physicians in Southern Illinois (AFPSI), founded in 1977 by Belleville's Dr. Cosme Cagas to "present a united front against discriminatory practices and unfair legislation against foreign medical graduates."[12] Both have regularly sponsored dinner dances and social events, sometimes in tandem with continuing medical education conferences. AFPSI has also enthusiastically promoted a Science Scholarship Quiz Show in which area high school students compete for cash prizes. Women of the AFPSI Auxiliary have raised money for several charitable causes in the Philippines. Not surprisingly, many of the same names rotate among the officers of each of these groups and of CIPAS.

In April 1988, with the physicians and their families long established in the Springfield area, Dr. Virgilio Pilapil launched the Filipino American Historical Society (FAHS), with twenty-two founding members, including twelve physicians. Ever since, this group has met quarterly for potlucks at members' homes, conducted programs on historical themes, and promoted its members' causes. Modeled in part after the Filipino American National Historical Society (FANHS) founded in Seattle in 1982, Springfield's FAHS continued as a separate organization even as Pilapil subsequently helped launch a Midwest chapter of FANHS and became the national FANHS president some years later.

The society's quarterly *Bulletin,* edited by Pilapil, has documented Filipino Springfield's activities, as well as those of FAHS members: the arrival and departure of the city's first Filipino Protestant pastor; the opening and closing of local Filipino American businesses; the arrival of a Filipino food market in Champaign, a ninety-mile drive from Springfield; its members' citizenship ceremonies, wedding anniversaries, and fiftieth birthday parties; their children's births and marriages; their departures from the area; and the deaths of community members and their relatives both in the United States and in the Philippines. Several brief autobiographies of members have included Lilian Torres Beams's account of her career as a nurse and community college instructor and Felicidad Hypke's memoir of her downtown café and her subsequent efforts on behalf of the Miss Teen Illinois pageant, a contest in which her daughter placed first in 1995.

From the outset, FAHS also served as a vehicle for its members' particular interests. Thus Drs. Reynaldo and Rachel Gotanco organized a monthly First Saturday rosary group that still rotates among the homes of devout Roman Catholic communicants, Filipino American and non-Filipino alike, traveling to Shelbyville, Pana, Jacksonville, Decatur, and throughout Springfield, just as do FAHS meetings. In 1992, FAHS "younger members" challenged the plaque on a Springfield Spanish American War memorial for employing the term *Philippine Insurrection* rather than *Philippine American War.* FAHS sponsored a public forum and notified the Philippine consulate in Chicago. More recently, FAHS joined the national campaign calling for legislation to increase benefits for Filipino veterans of World War II.

For more than fifteen years, FAHS has put on an annual Graduates Recognition Day program featuring a speaker, folk dancing, and sometimes a dinner dance. Many of these central Illinois Filipino American high school, college, and professional school graduates have, not surprisingly, been the children of FAHS and CIPAS members. The offspring of

the physicians' cohort have garnered many honors, often attended prestigious colleges, and frequently followed their parents into scientific and
medical fields. Springfield's second-generation Filipino Americans apparently have not experienced the downward social mobility found among
more ethnically dense immigrant communities on the West and East
Coasts.[13] Moreover, Filipino American daughters have been encouraged to
attend college away from home, despite the presence of several institutions
of higher education in Springfield. Central Illinois parents have fostered
high academic aspirations in their daughters, as well as their sons, unlike
the experiences of some of their counterparts on the West Coast.[14]

As their histories make clear, CIPAS, AFPSI, and FAHS have collectively
helped define the Filipino American ethnic community in the Land of
Lincoln. Within these organizations, Filipina women have labored alongside Filipino men to create a group identity that emphasizes sociability
and service within a family-centered framework. In the Philippines, extended family networks maintained largely by women might have provided the dominant outlet for their energies. In central Illinois, community has replaced extended family networks, yet women's importance has
not diminished.

Two women of the physicians' cohort illustrate Filipina lives in Springfield
from the 1970s onward.[15] In both cases, Philippine-educated professional
women of middle- or upper-middle-class origin settled with their husbands to the Springfield area. Both women concentrated on family, religious, and community life rather than pursue full-time careers, one of
them continuously working part time in the medical field, the other working more sporadically as a volunteer and independent travel agent. Both
have been community activists, one of them in church work as well as in
Filipino American organizations and the other in an array of social, pub-
lic-spirited, and charitable activities beyond as well as within the community. Neither woman nor her husband promoted a chain of migration among relatives from the Philippines to the United States, but both
women have befriended some of the newer female immigrants of the
1980s and 1990s.

Maria C. Lara has devoted much of her adult life to organizational activities. Born in Manila and the daughter of a lawyer, she met her physi-
cian-to-be husband, José, when she was sixteen. Married in 1959 at the age
of twenty-two after graduating in nutrition and dietetics from the Philippine Women's University, she bore two of her four children in the Phil-

ippines before José traveled to the United States on the Exchange Visitor Program in 1963. She followed a year later, and her last two children were born in Florida and Mississippi. Because the primary focus of her life has been her husband and her children, Maria has worked only intermittently as a volunteer dietician for St. John's Hospital and as an independent travel agent. More striking has been her remarkably active life in an array of organizations, by no means all Filipino American. When asked to explain her reasons for being so involved, Maria stressed the link between what she has done for her husband and children and what she has done for her community.

Seeking to balance Philippine and American patterns of child rearing, Maria and José admitted, in separate interviews, that they may have emphasized the Philippine side more in such matters as respecting elders, emphasizing education, regulating dating, and practicing Catholicism. According to José, the two aimed to instill "more Filipino conservative ways," forbidding "one-to-one" dating before age eighteen and enforcing curfews. To their children's protests, José pointed out: "Mom and I pay attention to you," implying a contrast with the less conscientious practices of American parents. Maria singled out "coming home late" as a major difference between growing up in the Philippines and in Springfield. Their youngest son, Andy, now married and working in Springfield, largely agrees. Yet despite their wish to inculcate Filipino values, Maria and José spoke English to their children, even though they have always spoken Tagalog to each other. As José put it: "We don't want them to develop an accent that would be a hindrance in [their] progress." In this, they were not atypical among Filipino Americans.[16]

Both Laras take pride in the results. Their oldest daughter trained as a nurse, married a non-Filipino physician, and produced two grandchildren, now teenagers. Their second two children, a daughter and a son, both single, took degrees in podiatry and a PhD in psychology respectively. Andy, a ceramic engineer, is married to a non-Filipina, Amy Smithson, who avidly participates in both Filipino American and nonethnic activities, many of which her mother-in-law also supports. While their oldest daughter and her family live ninety miles away in Champaign-Urbana, the other three second-generation Laras live nearby, fulfilling their parents' desire that the family "stay close together."

Like most of the Filipino migrants to the Springfield area, the Laras are practicing Catholics, and Catholicism has combined with ethnicity to structure their lives. Along with weekly attendance at mass, Maria and Jose have long participated in the First Saturday rosary group, among other religious and church-related activities. Her meticulously decorated home displays Philippine artwork and woodcarvings and expensive crystal and china—all typical of an upper-middle-class Filipino immigrant household. But in addition Maria un-self-consciously displays her religious devotion with numerous religious artifacts and statuary set prominently on an "altar" at one end of her large living room.

What is most distinctive about Maria's organizational life has been its variety. She has served as president of approximately fifteen different organizations during three decades in Springfield, many but not all of them women's groups. While being consistently active in CIPAS, FAHS, and the auxiliary of AFPSI, Maria has also served as president of the area YWCA and as an officer in the Springfield Arts Association, the Carillon Belles, the Sangamon County Historical Society, and the American Association of University Women, as well as helping lead various charitable fund-raising ventures. Asked to identify her closest friends, Maria named the Venezuelan wife of an Iranian physician, the Italian wife of an African American retired navy officer, the Sicilian widow of a Springfield businessman, and a Burmese woman.

More reserved, but articulate and friendly, Sarah Fonacier Lim is the daughter of a Cebuano elementary school teacher who raised his four daughters in Mindanao. She remembers her father's emphasis on education and his borrowing to raise tuition money. After graduating from the University of Santo Tomas Medical School in Manila in 1965, she came to the United States on the Exchange Visitor Program. While interning in New Jersey, she dated and, in 1968, married Dr. Apolinario Lim, a medical school classmate whom she had never met in the Philippines. The Lims soon joined a fellow Filipino resident of her husband's who launched a practice in anesthesiology in Springfield, and they raised four children. For a time, Sarah gave gynecological examinations at a mental hospital, but she found part-time work as a medical consultant for the Social Security disabilities program more compatible with her desire to be a full-time mother. Over the years, her household also included either her mother or mother-in-law, both of whom helped with child care but stayed in the United States only temporarily, though sometimes longer than a year. The Lim children participated in scouting, tennis, and youth baseball, activities that Sarah found overly "competitive." Firmly intending a religious upbringing for her children, Sarah is not entirely satisfied with the outcome:

"I thought erroneously that they would pick it up." In this, her experience appears to parallel that of other Filipino immigrant professionals.[17]

If not taking on their parents' religious activism, three of the four Lim children have chosen to be physicians: a psychiatrist in San Antonio, a resident anesthesiologist in Tucson, and an internist in Indianapolis. Their oldest child, a daughter, took a master's degree in comparative literature before turning to medicine and psychiatry. The only nonphysician among their children is their second child and oldest son, who took a law degree but now teaches elementary school in San Jose. He is married to a Peruvian woman and has been the only one with a significant identification with the Philippines. As an adult, this son, "the darkest" of their children in complexion, told his surprised parents that he had experienced racial discrimination in Springfield and never wanted to live in central Illinois again.

There is no doubt about the Lims' religiosity. They sent all four children to Roman Catholic schools through high school. They helped found the First Saturday rosary group. Sarah says she always felt "very welcome" in the Little Flower Parish, and her husband became a church trustee. The Lims and other Filipino Americans at Little Flower raised money for the church by selling Philippine *lumpia* (egg rolls) and other ethnic specialties, initially at the Springfield Ethnic Festival in the early 1980s, then through the FAHS group. When one FAHS member complained about the organization's support of a particular parish's fund-raising activities, Sarah "felt like it was a personal attack" and didn't want to belong to FAHS any more. Instead, Philippine food became part of a separate, successful Little Flower Heritage Days program at the Springfield Fairgrounds in the late 1980s and 1990s.

More than Maria Lara, Sarah Lim retains an active interest in the Philippines, partly for family reasons. She has sent back remittance money that helped to send her youngest sister to pharmacy school and a niece to medical school. Sarah received her green card in 1976 and became a U.S. citizen in 1981 because she was concerned about Ferdinand Marcos's martial-law rule in the Philippines. Still, she would "like to vote in Philippine elections" if given the chance. Both Sarah and Apolinario Lim lament the extent of corruption in the Philippines but have participated in and contributed to medical missions there, and Apolinario Lim speculated about "building a house" in the Philippines sometime in the future.

*

By the 1990s, the physicians of the 1970s saw their oldest children grown, their careers established, their organizations in place, and their modest numbers rarely supplemented by countrymen and women of similar ages and occupations. Their community was by no means static. Children finished school and left for other parts of the country. Some offspring married and produced grandchildren who lived both near and far. Some who reached retirement age continued in place, while others moved; not back to the Philippines permanently, but to warmer climates in the United States or to be closer to their children or other relatives. Simultaneously, during the 1990s, even as their occupational success and their social respectability confirmed their collective status as model immigrants, Filipinos in the Land of Lincoln also confronted with some trepidation the arrival of a small cohort of new immigrants from the Philippines.

In the 1990s, Springfield, Illinois, like other communities, became the home of brides who met their husbands either near American bases in the Philippines or through correspondence or later over the Internet. Calling themselves "pen pal brides" rather than the more pejorative "mail-order brides," which could connote a catalog order based on goods received for payment rendered, these women found common nationality and shared gender insufficient—*by themselves*—to bridge the gulf between older and newer immigrants.

Filipinas living in the Springfield area now differed from each other not only in time of arrival in the United States but also by age, education, command of English, and most importantly class. At the same time, even as these factors divided Filipinas in the Land of Lincoln, the distance between the two generations of women could be bridged through the shared valuing of family and religion in their lives. By acknowledging and enacting fundamental values held in common with the older women, the younger brides might win entry and welcome into the ethnic world of central Illinois Filipinos. By contrast, Filipina newcomers who lived outside these parameters came to exist only on the margins of the ethnic community. Four cases can serve to illustrate: two Filipinas incorporated, and two excluded.

Interracial marriage between a white man and a Filipina did *not* by itself arouse concern or hostility during any of the years of this study. Several of the earliest leaders of Filipino organizational life had married interracially. By contrast, class—as defined by education, occupation, and lifestyle—loomed larger in its capacity to engender division within the community. The military and pen pal brides typically married white men with less education who held nonprofessional employment and could provide considerably fewer of the trappings of material comfort than the older Filipinas in the Springfield area enjoyed. Still, as our first two examples will make clear, class differences did not prove insurmountable.[18]

Christina Parañas Cole describes the family into which she was born in 1957 in Cebu City in the Visayan Islands of the southern Philippines as "middle class," "very close knit," and "religious." Her "very strict" father, a career noncommissioned officer in the Philippine Army, and her housewife mother stressed respect for elders and also emphasized education. Despite being the oldest of eight siblings (five sons and three daughters) in a far from wealthy family, Christina graduated from college with a degree in social work in 1977. From grammar school through college, Christina attended classes conducted solely in English. In addition, through her sophomore year at the University of the Southern Philippines, she studied Tagalog, the national language, though at home her family always spoke Cebuano.

Christina's foray into the world of a distant relationship did not come early. For ten years after graduating from college, she kept the job she had while a college student rather than take the board examination in social work. Part-time work in the school supplies section of the Fairmart department store became a full-time job, and she bonded closely with three other young women there. Their locally forged network of four would ultimately cross the Pacific.

Nearing age thirty, Christina had had only one serious boyfriend, a college classmate; their relationship fractured when he "wanted more than I was willing to give." By 1987, she had spent a decade working in school supplies while continuing to live at home, her income helping rear her youngest siblings. The future promised only more of the same; a routine relieved only by an occasional movie. In the mid-1980s, one of the working-girl foursome, Linette, had peeled away by taking the radical step of marrying Jack Berry, an American postal worker from St. Paul, Minnesota, with whom she had corresponded. Lonely for her friends and yet content with the life-altering choice that she had risked, Linette, with Jack's encouragement and assistance, began advertising for correspondents for her friends. Acting as matchmakers, the Berrys assessed, screened, and forwarded only the most promising prospects to Cebu City. Eventually, all three married American men and settled down, if not "next door," at least close enough for continued contact, two in Minnesota and Christina in Springfield. After corresponding with Christina for a year and a half, David

Cole arrived in Cebu City to meet her in person. Christina recalled her fear when she told her father of David Cole, her "pen pal": "He didn't know anything about David before he arrived." Her father warned her to "be careful" but did not oppose the marriage of his thirty-two-year-old daughter and her fifty-one-year-old future husband before a justice of the peace in the Philippines in late 1989.

Several months later, in 1990, Christina Parañas Cole arrived in Springfield, where she and David, a high school graduate and divorced father of one, first lived in a trailer. Fifteen years after their marriage, Christina, David, and their eleven-year-old daughter Susan make their home in the small but spotless ranch-style home in a working-class neighborhood purchased for them by David's father. Christina has filled their living room with trendy, overstuffed furniture, a good television, and surfaces sufficient for the display of many, many family photos, including several of David's older daughter and her family who live nearby; Susan's highly polished piano bespeaks Christina's traditional goals for her adolescent daughter's accomplishments. She emphasizes strict Catholic religious beliefs and expects that her daughter, whom she closely supervises, will attend college. Although David is not Catholic, the couple married in church in 1999, ten years after their civil ceremony, and Susan is currently enrolled in a local Catholic grammar school. Every month, Christina and Susan join other Filipinos in the Springfield area to pray the rosary, and every December, the family attends the Springfield-area Filipino community's biggest bash, the annual Christmas party.

Apart from these activities, Christina is not involved in Filipino organizations. Her primary associations are with family and personal friends. Working in real estate, David has earnings sufficient to enable Christina to remain at home and focus on raising Susan and keeping their home. Christina takes pride in Susan's willingness, even at age eleven, to sacrifice some of what she might have to help her cousins in the Philippines. Christina counts herself fortunate, and she is certainly viewed as such by another Filipina wife in Springfield, Erlinda Tan Salerno, the mother of the two young sons, who juggles domestic responsibilities with full-time work as an accounting clerk in a downtown Springfield hotel.

Like Christina, Erlinda hails from the southern, Visayan-speaking Philippines, and describes her birth family as "very poor." Her father, a small farm owner, grew the corn, vegetables, and bananas that barely provided for his fourteen children. Erlinda, the tenth child among seven boys and seven girls, was born in 1960 and completed the usual six-year elementary school course in her hometown. In her early teens, Erlinda joined an older sister, who had married an American businessman, had four children, and lived near the U.S. naval base at Olongapo. Over the years, Erlinda's remittances, and those of three sisters who joined her in Olongapo City, helped support siblings still at home, and she was able to complete one year of high school. After ten years away from the southern Philippines, twenty-seven-year-old Erlinda was sent reeling by gossip forwarded by her mother. Hearing it, Erlinda "didn't want to go back home." Erlinda's long-time Filipino boyfriend, a carpenter, had gotten another girl pregnant. Shortly thereafter, her sister introduced her to a U.S. navy seaman first-class, Phillip Salerno. One year older than Erlinda, Phil Salerno had joined the navy immediately after his graduation from high school in Springfield, Illinois. The two, neither of whom had previously been wed, decided to marry a scant two weeks after they were introduced. For three years after their marriage in 1987, the couple lived in the Philippines, where their first son, Robert, was born in 1988. After eleven years in the navy, Phil moved his family back to Springfield, where the couple's second son, Daniel, was born in 1993.

With her husband holding unskilled employment, currently as an electronic gate controller at the Springfield jail, Erlinda has always earned money to supplement his earnings. After six months as a maid at the Springfield Renaissance Hotel at a starting salary of $4.25 per hour, Erlinda shifted from cleaning rooms to sewing when her supervisors discovered her skill. In 2000, thanks to an American woman with whom she frequently ate lunch, Erlinda moved from housekeeping into the hotel's business office, where her acquaintance trained her as an accounting clerk. Erlinda relishes her new job, the $10.55 per hour that it pays, and the Monday through Friday schedule that has her working from eight to five. Eager to earn more, she caters Filipino food for Filipinas with more money than time to cook. She celebrates the satisfactions that American life can bring "if you are hard working," yet she also envies Christina Cole, who can stay at home with her daughter.

With Rob and Dan Salerno enrolled at neighborhood public schools in Springfield, Erlinda maintains that she and her husband are raising their boys in ways that combine the best of American and Filipino beliefs and practices, with his Catholic and part-Italian heritage making the task easier. She singles out respect for elders, moral values, Catholic religious belief, and Sunday mass attendance and applauds the absence of gangs that might ensnare her sons in Springfield, unlike California, where they lived for the last two years of Phil's navy service. Erlinda glows as she recounts that her younger son was recently named his school's "student of the year" and firmly underscores her goal for both boys—that they "finish college."

More so than Christina Cole, Erlinda Salerno is still tied to her birth family, some in the Philippines and some now in the United States. All three of the sisters she worked with in Olongapo also married Americans and settled in the Midwest—in St. Louis, in Sycamore, Illinois, and in Ft. Wayne, Indiana. All their marriages are intact, and all have Filipino American children. Erlinda and her sisters in the United States all send money home to their parents, though she can afford only $20 per month and occasional boxes of U.S.-made items. Erlinda frequently telephones her parents in the Philippines, as well as the sister to whom she feels closest and has given charge of the money that she remits. In addition, she follows several Filipino Internet sites and watches a Filipino television program every Saturday. Visits back home have been few: a sad, fast trip in 2000 when her eldest brother, an overseas contract worker, died and a more joyful, month-long trip with Phil and her sons in 2002. Erlinda became a U.S. citizen as soon as she was legally able, as did her sisters. In consequence, her parents now hold green cards, can come and go without restriction, and have visited the United States for as long as six months.

Erlinda does not socialize with any of Springfield's Filipino professionals or participate in the monthly rosary group that Christina and her daughter attend. But she is nonetheless known and respected as a hardworking, religious woman who is devoted to the family that accompanies her each year to the annual CIPAS picnic and Christmas gala. Thus, despite her class, her lack of formal education, and her occasionally hesitant command of English, Erlinda Tan Salerno, like Christina Parañas Cole, has found a place among Filipinos in the Land of Lincoln through a gender-based devotion to family and religion.

Settling in the heartland of Illinois has been a far less positive experience for two other Filipinas whose situations and conduct have excluded them from Springfield's Filipino community. In February 1997, in Bukidnon, on Mindanao in the southern Philippines, twenty-seven-year-old Lorena Lash married an American eight years her senior. Dale W. Lash had chosen his future spouse from the photographs of eager Filipina women appearing in a mail-order bride magazine. Seven months after her marriage, in September 1997, Lorena joined Dale in Springfield, where her difficulties began almost immediately, triggered by her pregnancy and the impending birth of their child, whom Dale did not want. In July 1998,

Lash threw his pregnant wife out of their home, and that fall their son Shawn was born while Lorena was living with her brother-in-law and his family.

In July 1999, Lorena, who first worked as a housekeeper in a Springfield hotel and then at St. John's Hospital, sought an order of protection against her estranged husband and also filed for divorce. During their months together they "slept in a bed with a handgun on the headboard. When they fought, . . . he'd look at the gun or remind her that he had it."[19] Lorena said, "He doesn't want the baby because baby is not included in his plan. . . . He has made me walk miles to and from work and would be angry if I found a ride. He consistently threatens to send me back to the Philippines if I don't do as he says."[20] Although Lash had refused to pay the medical bills for the birth of his son, he later telephoned Lorena to offer a reconciliation but only on his "conditions." Dale Lash would not bedevil his Filipina wife much longer. In August 1999, he was arrested for having raped a Springfield real estate agent nine months earlier. A month later, DNA evidence connected Lash to the rape and murder of a young mother found shot in the head in a cornfield west of Springfield shortly before his arrest.[21]

Given her trauma, Lorena Lash might have expected support from her Filipino compatriots in Springfield, but her own behavior soon marginalized her in the collective view of the community. Sexually involved with the unmarried American attorney handling her divorce case, Lorena bore his child but refused his offer of marriage, citing his enormous school loans as a barrier to the sort of life she envisioned for herself. More recently, she has become the mistress of a married car dealer, himself the father of four.

In an ethnic community as small as theirs, Springfield-area Filipinos recognize Lorena Lash as a Filipina and a mother. But the sympathy and support, including a baby shower, that members extended early on to a countrywoman so abused by her husband dissipated completely as gossip about Lorena's own conduct took center stage. Despite being Filipina, Lorena is now effectively excluded. Her compatriots speak of her in hushed tones and with considerable disdain and embarrassment. Having secured their own places within the community, Christina Cole and Erlinda Salerno will not risk their reputations by open association with Lorena Lash.

Christina Cole's refusal to help another Filipina in trouble with her husband confirms the reluctance that the working-class newcomers feel to jeopardize their standing with community leaders. During an interview, Christina recounted a late-night phone call that she had received from a

Filipino physician who was trying to help a Filipina who had left her husband and had sought temporary shelter with a neighbor but could not explain her situation in English. Knowing that the woman was from the Philippines, the neighbor called a nearby hospital, whose personnel contacted the Filipino doctor, but because of the difference in their Philippine dialects, they too were unable to communicate. The physician then called Christina Cole, who was also from the southern Philippines and who agreed, with some reluctance, to telephone the neighbor and speak with the Filipina. "What is the problem?" Christina asked. Her husband was an alcoholic. "Does he beat you?" No. "Did you know that he was an alcoholic when you married him?" Yes. That was the end of their conversation. Christina said there was nothing that she could do and advised the woman to go back to her husband and try to make peace, since she had no job and nowhere to go. Christina did not volunteer her name or telephone number; she did not ask for the woman's name or telephone number; she did *not* want to be involved: "I was afraid for my family. What if I helped her and her husband came looking for me?"

From the early 1970s through the mid-1980s, Filipino immigrant families settling in the Land of Lincoln labored to create a vibrant and respected ethnic community even as they simultaneously worked to build their own families and careers and to position their lives within the broader milieu. Their incorporation within mainstream society proceeded along many lines outside their own homes—most notably on the blocks where they lived, in the places where they worked, in the churches where they worshiped, and in the schools that their children attended. By the early 1990s, these Filipino immigrants typically claimed membership in the American middle class through their professional status and their prosperity. Although racial identity and ethnic loyalty precluded seamless incorporation into white America, by emphasizing what they shared with respectable white Americans—devotion to family, hard work, and God—they established secure lives for themselves in the Land of Lincoln. Their definition of the Filipino American ethnic community in Springfield and surrounding towns continues to hold sway, even as community membership changes over time. When strengthened by shared values regarding family and religion, gender and ethnic identity among Filipinas in the Land of Lincoln have the capacity to bridge notable differences of age and class. By contrast, in the absence of these shared values, Filipinas in Springfield find little in common and scant reason to associate. Those who defy or cannot uphold the ethnic community's implicit norms are not welcome in the community's organizations and at the community's functions. Today, the inclusivity of the Filipino community in Springfield derives from shared values, as well as remembrance of the land of their birth and common identity as immigrants from the Philippines. However, these same values regarding family and religion simultaneously promote exclusivity by ostracizing Filipinas who do not share them or work to sustain them.

NOTES

1. Barbara M. Posadas, *The Filipino Americans* (Westport, CT: Greenwood Press, 1999).

2. U.S. Census Bureau, Census 2000 Redistricting Data (P.L. 94–171) Summary File, Table PL1, http://factfinder.census.gov/servlet/GCTTable.

3. Springfield's Filipino population totaled 30 in 1970, 49 in 1980, and 92 in 1990. See U.S. Bureau of the Census, *1970 Census of Population,* vol. 1, *Characteristics of Population,* pt. 15, "Illinois," Section 1, Table 23, "Race by Sex" (Washington, DC: U.S. Census Bureau, 1973), 15–104, *1980 Census of Population,* vol. 1, *Population Characteristics,* pt. 15, "Illinois," Table 15, "Persons by Race" (Washington, DC: U.S. Census Bureau, 1982), 15–76, and *1990 Census of Population,* vol. 1, *General Population Characteristics,* "Illinois," Table 6, "Race and Hispanic Origin" (Washington, DC: U.S. Census Bureau, 1992), 91.

4. U.S. Census Bureau, Census 2000, Table DP-1, Profile of General Demographic Characteristics: 2000, Geographic area: Springfield city, Carlinville city, Decatur city, Jacksonville city, Lincoln city, Pana city, Shelbyville city, Taylorville city, Illinois, www2.illinois.biz/2000census/Cities.html.

5. Posadas, *Filipino Americans,* 30, 38–40; Catherine Ceniza Choy, *Empire of Care: Nursing and Migration in Filipino American History* (Durham: Duke University Press, 2003), 41–57.

6. Ruben G. Rumbaut, "Passages to America: Perspectives on the New Immigration," in *America at Century's End,* ed. Alan Wolfe (Berkeley: University of California Press, 2001), 224.

7. Yen Le Espiritu, *Filipino American Lives* (Philadelphia: Temple University, 1995), 84–85.

8. Ann D. Bagchi, *Making Connections: A Study of Networking among Immigrant Professionals* (New York: LFB Scholarly Publishing, 2001).

9. Central Illinois Philippine American Society, *1995 CIPAS Silver Anniversary Issue* (Springfield, IL: n.p., 1996).

10. CIPAS, "Circular," July 19, 1982, copy in authors' possession.

11. In 2003, the Ethnic Festival drew participation only from Germans, Greeks,

Italians, and Spanish. Penny Zimmerman-Wills, "The Spice of Lives: Now in Its 30th Year, the Ethnic Festival Struggles in Solidarity," *Illinois Times*, August 28, 2003, www.illinoistimes.com/gbase/Gyrosite/Content?oid=oid%3A2474.

12. "Program, AFPSI, 25th Anniversary Spring Ball," May 17, 2003, 81.

13. Alejandro Portes and Ruben G. Rumbaut, *Immigrant America: A Portrait*, 2nd ed. (Berkeley: University of California Press, 1996); Nancy Foner, *From Ellis Island to JFK: New York's Two Great Waves of Immigration* (New Haven: Yale University Press, 2000).

14. Yen Le Espiritu and Diane L. Wolf, "The Paradox of Assimilation: Children of Filipino Immigrants in San Diego," in *Ethnicities: Children of Immigrants in America*, ed. Ruben G. Rumbaut and Alejandro Portes (Berkeley: University of California Press, 2001), 168. On an environment similar to that of Springfield, see Center for East Asian Studies, University of Kansas, and KTWU/Channel 11, Topeka, Kansas, *Green Pastures: Filipinos in the Heartland*, video, 1997, on Filipino immigrants and their children in the small towns of Kansas.

15. This section is based, in part, on interviews with Maria C. Lara, Springfield, IL, June 10, 2003; José Lara, Springfield, IL, June 10, 2003; Andy Lara, Springfield, IL, June 12, 2003; Amy Smithson Lara, Springfield, IL, June 12, 2003; Sarah Fonacier Lim, Springfield, IL, June 13, 2003; and Apolinario Lim, Springfield, IL, June 12, 2003. These names are pseudonyms.

16. Charles Hirschman, Philip Kasinitz, and Josh DeWind, eds., *The Handbook of International Migration: The American Experience* (New York: Russell Sage Foundation, 1999).

17. Espiritu, *Filipino American Lives*, 89, 140.

18. This section is based, in part, on interviews with Christina Parañas Cole, Springfield, IL, June 11, 2003, and Erlinda Tan Salerno, Springfield, IL, June 13, 2003.

19. "Rape Suspect Has Left Trail of Fear; Those Who Know Lash Remember Spurts of Violence," *State Journal-Register* (Springfield, IL), September 12, 1999, 1.

20. "Wife Says Lash Wanted Control; Rape Suspect Wrote Contract Forbidding Her Complaints," *State Journal-Register* (Springfield, IL), August 25, 1999, 1.

21. "Wife Says," 1; "Rape Suspect," 1.

Chapter 7

Ethnic-Language Maintenance and Social Mobility

A Historical Look at the Development of Chinese Schools in the United States

Min Zhou and Xiyuan Li

Getting resettled in a new country, immigrants are often required to learn the host language, which often differs from that of their own, and to eventually assimilate into the host society. The U.S. history of immigrant adaptation has shown a consistent trend of language shift from the ethnic to the dominant language intergenerationally. As predicted by the Fishman model, the first generation speaks the ethnic language at home, the second generation speaks the ethnic language at home but the dominant language in public, and the third generation speaks the dominant language both at home and in public.[1] In the United States, except for the somewhat more enduring pattern of Spanish-language maintenance, hardly any non-English European languages are maintained by third-generation German, Italian, French, Scandinavian, and other European Americans, and hardly any Asian languages are maintained beyond second-generation Asian Americans today.[2] In the existing literature of immigrant adaptation, intergenerational language shift to English monolingualism is often considered desirable, as it connotes assimilation and the acquisition of English the prerequisite for upward social mobility.[3]

While English proficiency is indisputably a key determinant of mobility outcomes, measured by education, occupation, naturalization, and political participation among others, the mechanisms by which ethnic languages influence these outcomes are less clear-cut and more complex. From the perspective of classical assimilation, ethnic languages are viewed as part of the ethnic enclaves from which immigrants need to detach themselves in order to move ahead in the host society. Thus maintaining ethnic languages, like participating in ethnic enclaves or institutions, constitutes a distinct liability, or a "language handicap." For example, ethnic languages are found to cause linguistic confusion and interference in the process of learning for minority children, leading to both emotional and educational maladjustment.[4] Multiculturalist scholars, on the contrary, see ethnic languages as not competing with English acquisition and as contributing to rather than inhibiting successful adaptation. From this standpoint, ethnic languages constitute assets, or advantages. Fluent bilingual children are found to score higher than English-monolingual children on a wide range of verbal and nonverbal IQ tests and to perform better on a range of educational outcomes, such as grade point average (GPA) and high school graduation rate.[5] Explanations for ethnic-language advantages are manifold, such as exposure to richer cultural repertoires, more sophisticated cognitive ability, and greater adaptability. In this chapter, we attempt to take a historical look at the development of ethnic Chinese schools in the United States, arguing that the ethnic language, as an integral component of the ethnic community, has been conducive to desirable social mobility outcomes among children of immigrants.

The Ethnic Language and the Ethnic Social Environment: A Framework for Analysis

Immigrants and their communities often consciously work to maintain their ethnic languages in the second generation as the basis for carrying on their cultural heritages.[6] In our view, what determines a child's development is not merely family socioeconomic status or other broader structure factors, such as neighborhoods and schools, but also the immediate social environment in which the child grows up. For many immigrants, this environment is ethnically specific, manifested in observable neighborhood-based ethnic institutions and interpersonal relations among those who interact in them.[7] We, thus, frame our study of Chinese-language schools in terms of how this type of ethnic institution constitutes an important part of the ethnic social environment.

Two theoretical conceptions are of vital relevance: community forces and social capital. John Ogbu conceptualizes community forces as the products of sociocultural adaptation embedded within an ethnic community, which entails specific beliefs, interpretations, and coping strategies that an ethnic group adopts in response to their societal treatment. According to Ogbu, racial minority groups may go one of two ways. Many who are looked down upon manage to turn their sense of their distinctive heritage into a kind of ethnic armor. They establish a sense of collective dignity that enables them to cope psychologically, even in the face of exclusion and discrimination, by keeping the host society at arm's length. Others, however, accept and internalize socially imposed inferiority as part of their collective self-definition, and this in turn fosters an "oppositional outlook" toward the dominant group and mainstream institutions, including education.[8] In this case, symbolic expressions of ethnicity and ethnic empowerment may hinder, rather than facilitate, social mobility. That pattern is exemplified by the forced-choice dilemma confronting black, Chicano, and Puerto Rican youth studied by Signithia Fordham, Margaret Gibson, and Philippe Bourgois, who have consistently found that black, Chicano, and Puerto Rican students who do well in school are forcefully excluded by their co-ethnic peers as "turnovers" acting "white."[9]

Community forces vary by ethnicity in affecting intergenerational mobility directly, while also intervening in the process of social capital formation to erect distinct ethnic environments. James Coleman defines social capital as consisting of closed systems of social networks inherent in the structure of relations between persons and among persons within a social group to promote cooperative behavior and to serve specific needs of its group members.[10] Despite heated debates on how social capital should be precisely defined and measured, various scholars converge on the view that social capital is lodged not in the individual, but in the structure of social organizations, patterns of social relations, or processes of interactions between individual and organizations. As Alejandro Portes suggests, "Social capital stands for the ability of actors to secure benefits by virtue of memberships in social networks or other social structures."[11] The value of social capital varies by ethnicity, however. On the one hand, community forces shape the orientation, coping strategies, and corresponding behaviors of different ethnic groups with regard to getting by or moving ahead in society. On the other hand, group-level socioeconomic characteristics influence the cultural and economic contacts and all other tangible social and material resources to which group members are exposed or have access. Both have profound implications for understanding how unique ethnic social environments facilitate, or inhibit, intergenerational mobility of individual group members.

Drawing on the concepts of community forces and social capital, we frame our descriptive analysis around three main themes: the historical conditions under which Chinese-language schools evolved and developed; the linkage between formal education and Chinese-language schools and other child/youth-centered ethnic institutions; and the social effects of Chinese-language schools and other relevant ethnic institutions on the children, the immigrant family, and the ethnic community. As we shall see in the following analysis, the emergence and development of Chinese-language schools are direct products of historical conditions, societal treatment, and constant adaptation on the part of the ethnic community.[12]

From Racial Exclusion to Social Integration: The Development of Chinese Schools

Chinese-language schools have been an integral part of the organizational structure of the Chinese diasporic community around the world. In the United States, Chinese-language schools date back to the late 1880s and served to preserve the Chinese language and cultural heritage in the second and succeeding generations, just as other ethnic-language schools have served a parallel function in the immigrant German, Scandinavian, Jewish, and Japanese communities.[13] Since World War II, however, Chinese-language schools have evolved to a much broader range of functions beyond language and culture and have joined a wide variety of children-youth-centered ethnic institutions to constitute a comprehensive system of supplementary education. Research on Chinese-language schools has been deplorably scant. Of the few studies that had been conducted, many stemmed from the assimilationist assumption that Chinese-language schools were essentially competing with the goal of public schools and found that these language schools ultimately diverted students' attention and energy from making progress in formal education.[14] With the exception of recent studies by Him Mark Lai and Joe Fong, past studies often took Chinese-language schools at their face value, placing too much emphasis on the content and curriculum of language teaching and cultural preservation and on their direct linkages to public education but overlooking their changes and indirect effects.[15]

Segregation and Early Development

As is well documented in the history of Chinese immigration to the United States, Chinese immigrants initially came to this country from the southern region of China's Guangdong Province in search of a sojourner's dream, to make money and then return home with "gold and glory," only to find themselves easy targets for discrimination and exclusion. Not only did their significant contributions to developing the American West and to building the most difficult part of the transcontinental road west of the Rockies go unrecognized, but the mere existence of Chinese immigrant labor became a nuisance when the host society experienced severe economic problems. The anti-Chinese movement, prompted by a racist ideology and the fear of unfair job competition with native white workers, led to the passage of the Chinese Exclusion Act in 1882; it lasted until 1943, forcing the Chinese into segregated enclaves and reinforcing the image of the Chinese as unassimilable aliens.[16]

Since they had no families with them, had no intention of staying for a long time, and were not allowed to participate in the host society, immigrant Chinese had no other options, but built their own Chinatowns within which they organized themselves economically and socially. Chinatowns were places of refuge that resembled the ancestral homeland, where immigrants could speak their own language, eat their own food, play their own games, exchange news from home, and share common experiences with fellow countrymen day in and day out. The level of co-ethnic interaction was high, almost entirely through working in Chinese-owned businesses and socializing in various family, clan or kinship associations, hometown (district or regional) associations, and tongs (or merchants' associations). Chinese ethnicity was heightened as an effective reaction to exclusion and, consequently, Chinatown became resistant to integration, not only because Chinese immigrants were not oriented to integrate into American society, but also because they were prohibited to do so by law.

During the exclusion era, Chinatowns across the United States were essentially bachelors' societies with few women, children, or husband-wife households. The sex ratio, which was nearly 27 males per female in 1890, dropped to 9:1 by 1910 and then gradually evened out over time. But by the 1940s, males still outnumbered females by more than 2:1. The shortage of women, combined with the "paper son" phenomenon and other illegal entry of young men, stifled the formation of "normal" families and the natural reproduction of the ethnic population. The children born in the United States prior to World War II were mostly born in the late 1920s and the 1930s and were still very young at the outbreak of the war. As of 1930, the proportion of U.S. born went up to 41 percent from under 10 percent in 1900 because of restricted immigration. Chinese children, like other racial minority children, were not permitted in public schools with white children. In the 1870s and early 1880s, Chinese children were banned from attending public school in California. A segregated elementary school for Chinese children was established by San Francisco authorities only after a successful lawsuit in 1885.[17] Few Chinese at the time were able to find jobs commensurate with their levels of education in the mainstream economy.[18]

When an ethnic group is legally excluded from participating in the mainstream host society, effective community organizing can mobilize ethnic resources to counter the negative effects of adversarial conditions. During the exclusion era, various ethnic institutions also arose to meet the sojourning needs of immigrants. It was against this historical backdrop that Chinese-language schools came into existence, first appearing in San Francisco's Chinatown in 1884, to provide a basic education for children and keep their culture, custom, heritage, and language alive in the United States in preparation for the children's eventual return to China with their families. Formal Chinese-language schools were initially established with Qing imperial government funds in Chinatowns in San Francisco, New York, and Chicago at the turn of the twentieth century. Later these ethnic schools were funded by the government of the new republic and by the Chinese Consolidated Benevolent Association (CCBA—Chinatown's quasi-government) as they spread to Chinatowns across the country.[19] During the period of exclusion, most of Chinatown's children enrolled in Chinese-language schools after their regular school days. In San Francisco's Chinatown, for example, Chinese-language schools in the late nineteenth and early twentieth centuries were mostly private, taught in Cantonese by one or two teachers in the basement of a teacher's home or in a room inside a family association building. Classes were held daily for three to four hours in the evenings and Saturday mornings, and tuition was $4 to $5 a month. Prior to World War II, there were about six Chinese schools in San Francisco's Chinatown serving more than two thousand K–12 children, four in Los Angeles's Chinatown, and a smaller number in New York's Chinatown. Wherever a sizable Chinese enclave was found, there was at least one Chinese-language school.[20]

Early Chinese-language schools were largely financed by tuition and donations from churches, temples, family associations, and Chinese businesses. Each school was governed by a board consisting of mostly elite members of ethnic organizations and businesses in Chinatown.[21] The Qing imperial government and later the new republic's government in China also supported formal Chinese education in overseas Chinese communities. The first "formal" public Chinese-language school was established at the turn of the twentieth century in San Francisco's Chinatown (the Ching School or Da Qing Shu Yuan). Sponsored by the Chinese government in China and later run by the Chinese Six Company, a quasi-governmental institution in Chinatown, this formal school, also separate from American public schools, started with two classes held daily from 3:00 p.m. to 9:00 p.m. during the week and from 9:00 a.m. to 9:00 p.m. on Saturdays, with an initial enrollment of some sixty students under the supervision of two teachers. Tuition was fifty cents a month, and the curriculum included the Four Books (*sishu*)—*The Great Learning, The Doctrine of the Mean, The Analects of Confucius,* and *Mencius*—which were Chinese classics basic for preparing students for the primary civil service exams in China.[22] Curricula in other private Chinese schools were less formal and lacked structure.

In the bachelors' society under legal and social exclusion, the immigrant Chinese community was more concerned with issues associated with labor, ethnic economy, racial discrimination, and sheer survival than with children's education. However, families with children did take their children's education, particularly Chinese education, seriously. Most children attended Chinese schools after their regular public schools. Immigrant parents believed that proficiency in the Chinese language was practical for their children, since the children's future options were limited either to returning to China or to finding jobs in Chinatowns.[23] Parents also believed that a strong Chinese identity and ethnic pride instilled in the Chinese through Chinese cultural and moral teachings were necessary to help children cope with racism and discrimination. Like other ethnic organizations in Chinatown, earlier Chinese schools had very little contact with mainstream institutions, and education in ethnic-language schools was supplementary but *not* commensurate with public schooling. Past research on early Chinese schools found no effect or some significant negative effects of Chinese schooling on academic performance and mental health well-being of immigrant Chinese children.[24] However, these studies overlooked the fact that public education and assimilation at that time were issues not immediately relevant to Chinese immigrants, who were excluded by law from participating in American society.

Integration and Post–World War II Development

The repeal of the Chinese Exclusion Act during World War II marked a new era. Despite persistent racism and institutional discrimination, Chinese were legally allowed and encouraged to participate in American society, and the immigrant Chinese community started to shift its orientation from sojourning to putting down roots. The founding of the People's Republic of China in 1949 and the subsequent political and economic sanctions of the West further reinforced the community's goal of permanent settlement and social integration. Meanwhile, the rise of a visible second generation that began in the 1930s quietly changed the demographic makeup of the bachelors' society, more and more transforming it into a family-centered community. Between 1940 and 1960, the U.S. born outnumbered the foreign born (61 percent vs. 39 percent), and the sex ratio became more balanced (133 males per 100 females). While Chinatowns concentrated the majority of the Chinese in the United States, residential out-movements of the more affluent families and of the second generation became an increasingly visible trend.

Chinese immigration since the 1960s has led to even more dramatic changes in the immigrant Chinese community. Between 1961 and 2000, more than 1.3 million immigrants have been admitted as permanent residents from China, Hong Kong, and Taiwan. Immigrant Chinese are no longer only the poor, uneducated, rural peasants from traditional sending villages in Guangdong. Instead, they have come from major cities all over China, as well as from Hong Kong, Taiwan, Southeast Asia, and other parts of the Chinese diaspora. The ethnic Chinese population increased more than tenfold, from 237,292 in 1960 to 1,645,472 in 1990 and to nearly 2.9 million in 2000. The new immigrants are socioeconomically diverse, with high numbers of college-educated professionals, skilled workers, and independent entrepreneurs. Upon arrival in the United States, many have managed to bypass Chinatowns to settle directly in more affluent outer areas or suburbs in traditional gateway cities, as well as in new multiethnic, immigrant-dominant suburban municipalities, also referred to as "ethnoburbs."[25] More than half of the ethnic Chinese population today live in suburbs, and the proportion of those living in traditional Chinatowns has shrunk significantly, even though absolute numbers have continued to grow since the 1970s. As of 2000, only 2 percent of the Chinese in Los Angeles, 8 percent of the Chinese in San Francisco, and 14 percent of the Chinese in New York live in old Chinatowns.

The openness in mainstream American society does not automatically guarantee the desirable outcomes of social integration and mobility. Decades of legal exclusion, social isolation, discrimination, and persistent racial stereotyping have left the Chinese with practically one feasible channel: public education. Whereas children's education was never an issue for survival in a society full of bachelors and sojourners, it has now become an urgent and central issue for the immigrant family and the entire ethnic group. As the ethnic community has redefined its goals from sojourning to permanent settlement, so have ethnic organizations, including Chinese-language schools. However, changes in Chinese-language schools have not been smooth, undergoing cycles of decline in the 1950s and 1960s, revival in the 1970s and 1980s, and rapid growth since the early 1990s.

Prior to World War II, Chinese-language schools existed in almost every Chinatown, and they were the only ethnic institutions serving children. Children attended Chinese-language schools in their neighborhoods after regular school as a matter of course with little questioning. Even though most children lacked enthusiasm and interest, many of them did recognize the practical value of Chinese schooling, as their future prospects were largely limited to Chinatowns or China.[26] Between World War II and the 1960s, however, Chinese-language schools experienced a period of decline due to the pressure of assimilation. The children, especially adolescents, started to question the necessity of Chinese schooling and the practical value of Chinese-language proficiency. Public schools indirectly encouraged the children to break away from the ethnic-language schools. School administrators and teachers believed that such ethnic education would place too much of a burden on the young minds of immigrant children and serve to confuse and ultimately impede their social and intellectual developments. Indeed, some prior studies, designed on the basis of this rationale, found that ethnic-language school attendees were more likely than nonattendees to show unfavorable outcomes such as sleepiness, eyestrain, a lack of outdoor and leisure activities, low academic performance on standardized tests, a lack of leadership quality, and a double identity dilemma (feeling part Chinese and part American but belonging to neither).[27] Meanwhile, demographic and structural changes in the ethnic community and the larger society, such as the aging of the teachers, who were mostly non-English speaking and slow to adjust to changes, and the rigidity of the Chinese school curricula and teaching methods, combined with greater residential dispersion and the opening of various educational and vocational opportunities outside Chinatown to contribute to the decline of Chinese-language schools. Going to Chinese school increasingly became a burden on the child and a source of parent-child conflict. Children continued to attend Chinese-language schools because their parents made them, but most dropped out by the sixth grade. Parents were ambivalent as well, especially after the war, when returning to China became impossible. While they wanted their children to learn English and excel in school, many feared that they would lose their children if their children became too Americanized.[28]

Contrary to the assimilation theories that predict a decline of ethnicity over time, however, the past thirty years have witnessed a revival and rapid growth of ethnic institutions in Chinatowns and newly developed Chinese ethnoburbs, including Chinese-language schools and a range of ethnic institutions oriented toward children's education. The National Council of Associations of Chinese Language Schools (NCACLS) was founded in 1994 by Taiwanese Chinese. In its inaugural year, it estimated that there were a total of 643 registered Chinese-language schools in the United States (189 in California) with 5,536 teachers serving 82,675 K–12 students.[29] The Chinese School Association in the United States (CSAUS), founded in 1994 by mainland Chinese, has more than three hundred member schools in forty-one states across the country, serving sixty thousand K–12 students.[30]

Traditional Chinese-language schools have been under pressure to change. For example, the New York Chinese School run by the CCBA is perhaps the largest child- and youth-oriented organization in inner-city Chinatowns. The school annually (not including summers) enrolls about four thousand children, from preschool to twelfth grade, in their 137 Chinese-language classes and over 10 specialty classes (e.g., band, choir, piano, cello, violin, t'ai chi, ikebana, dancing, and Chinese painting). The Chinese language classes run from 3:00 to 6:30 p.m. daily after regular school hours. Students usually spend one hour on regular school homework and two hours on Chinese language or other selected specialties. The school also has English classes for immigrant youths and adult immigrant workers.[31]

Since the 1970s, new Chinese-language schools have also sprung up both in and out of traditional Chinatowns and new Chinese ethnoburbs started first by educated Taiwanese immigrants and then by international students and well-educated professional immigrants from mainland China. For example, the majority of suburban Chinese schools affiliated with the Southern California United Chinese School Association were initially established by Taiwanese immigrants in the mid- or late 1970s. The Hua Xia Chinese School was established as a Saturday school in a northern New Jersey suburb in the early 1990s by immigrant Chinese from the mainland and has now expanded into fourteen branch campuses in suburbs along the northeastern seaboard from Connecticut to Pennsylvania, serving more than five thousand students and shifting its admission to "everyone, regardless of his or her gender, race, color of skin, religion, nationality and blood ties." Similarly, the Hope Chinese School started as a small weekend Saturday school in a Washington, D.C., suburb for professional Chinese immigrant families from mainland China in the early 1990s and has now grown into five campuses in suburban towns in Maryland and Virginia, enrolling more than 2,500 students.[32]

Parallel to the revival and rapid growth of Chinese-language schools is the rise of a whole range of child- and youth-oriented private institutions including after-school tutoring (also called *buxiban* in Mandarin), college preparation, arts, and sports, as well as day care and preschools. These private institutions range from transnational enterprises with headquarters or branches in Taiwan and mainland China to small-scale one-person or mom-and-pop operations. Mostly located in Chinatowns and Chinese ethnoburbs, these institutions offer various academic and cultural enrichment programs and after-school care to immigrant children.

Changing Functions of Contemporary Chinese-Language Schools

Today's Chinese-language schools, both in and out of Chinatown, differ from those prior to World War II. First, their primary goal is to assist immigrant families in their efforts to push their children to excel in American public schools, to get into prestigious colleges and universities, and to eventually attain high-paying, high-status professions that secure a decent living in the United States. This reflects, in part, the traditional pragmatism of Chinese immigrant families; only this time it is U.S. centered rather than China centered. A Chinese immigrant has said, "I hope to accomplish nothing but three things [in the United States]: to own a home, to be my own boss, and to send my children to the Ivy League." Parents are enthusiastic about sending their children to Chinese-language schools, but not because they think that Chinese is the only thing that is important. Rather, many parents are implicitly dissatisfied with American public schools and believe that Chinese-language schools and other ethnic supplementary institutions can help ensure that their children will meet parental expectations.

Second, unlike traditional Chinese-language schools, which were relatively homogeneous and rigid in institutional form and governance, today's schools have become more diverse and flexible. In general, Chinese-language schools today are formal nonprofit or for-profit organizations. Nonprofits may be church or temple sponsored, community or family association sponsored, or independent. For-profits are independent enterprises functioning in the same way as other ethnic businesses. Most schools in Chinatowns or Chinese ethnoburbs offer regular weekday (3:00–6:00 p.m. daily after school), weekend (Saturday or Sunday half-day), and summer programs (day schools or overseas camps), as well as programs during spring and Christmas breaks (day camps). Scheduling accommodates the needs of dual-worker families living in the ethnic community. Other suburban Chinese schools are mostly half-day Saturday or Sunday schools, since families tend to disperse in non-co-ethnic neighborhoods to distances as far apart as twenty to thirty miles.

Schools are mainly financed by student tuitions, but nonprofits are supported by donations and community fund-raising as well. Nonprofits are free or charge nominal fees. Tuitions in for-profits vary depending on the type of program and enrollment number, but generally range from $70 to $250 and can be as high as $400 per semester (ten to seventeen weeks) for a typical weekday after-school program or a weekend school program, with extra fees for enrollment in special programs that are offered in the schools. Private lessons range from $10 to $50 per hour. Each school has a principal, a part-time staff, and teachers. It is governed by a board consisting of parents, teachers, ethnic business owners, and community leaders. Members of the governing board also tend to be parents themselves. Nonprofits rely heavily on parents, who volunteer to act as teacher aides, chauffeurs offering pickup or dropoff services, fund-raising workers, and even janitors. Such parental volunteerism is also evident in for-profits. Many Chinese schools have Parent Volunteer Associations (PVAs) modeled after the Parent-Teacher Associations (PTAs) in public schools. Parental involvement is direct and intense in Chinese schools, but similar involvement is minimal in public schools because of language and cultural barriers.

Third, unlike traditional schools, where the teaching of Chinese language and culture was at the core of its curriculum, today's Chinese-language schools have shifted to a more comprehensive, well-rounded curriculum complementary to the requirements of public education by grade level and college admission. In fact, language teaching no longer takes priority in most of today's Chinese-language schools, and Chinese classics have been almost completely taken out of the curriculum. We have observed that teachers, staff members, and even parents habitually use a mixture of English and Chinese to communicate with the children. Instead, schools now offer a variety of academic and tutoring programs and *buxiban* in such subjects as English (including English as a Second Language), social studies, math, and sciences, as well as in college preparation such as SAT, in addition to their Chinese-language programs. They also offer extracurricular programs such as youth leadership training, public speech, modern and folk dancing, chorus, music (piano, violin, drums, and Chinese string instruments), drama, Chinese painting, calligraphy, origami, martial arts, Chinese chess and Go, and sports (tennis, ping-pong, and basketball being the most popular). Some Chinese schools do have excellent Chinese-language programs (mostly in Mandarin) that aim to assist students in gaining high school foreign-language credits from the formal education system and in excelling on the SATII Chinese Language Test.

Fourth, while Chinese-language teaching is balanced out with other academic enrichment, tutoring, and recreational programs, the focus on moral teaching and the passing of cultural heritage is more subtle in today's Chinese schools. When schools are in session, these institutions provide a cultural environment where the children are surrounded by other Chinese people and things and are thus under external pressures to feel and act Chinese. Teachers reinforce the values of filial piety, respect for authority, hard work, and discipline in classrooms. Also, during traditional Chinese holiday seasons, such as the Chinese New Year, the Dragon Festival in the spring, and the Mid-Autumn Moon Festival, Chinese schools participate in celebratory parades, evening shows, and other community events, such as sports and choral or dance festivals. Participation in these cultural activities not only exposes children to their cultural heritage, reaffirming their ethnic identity, but also provides opportunities for the children to work closely with their parents and other adults in the community on common projects.

Discussion: The Ethnic Social Environment
Conducive to Education

In essence, Chinese-language schools and the ethnic system of supplementary education are designed "by the parents, for the parents," as one school's motto says. More often than not, immigrant Chinese parents measure success not merely by their own occupational achievements, but also by their children's educational achievements. If a child goes to an Ivy League college, his or her parents feel rewarded and are admired and respected as successful parents by others around them. Otherwise, they feel as if they have lost face. In this respect, Chinese schools and the relevant ethnic institutions emerge as a direct response to parents' desires for success. On the one hand, they produce a community force driving children to attain educational success on their parents' terms. Flashy names such as "Little Harvard," "Ivy League School," "Little PhD Early Learning Center" (a preschool), "Stanford-to-Be Prep School," "IQ180," and "Hope Buxiban (Tutoring)" are illustrative. Advertisements in the Chinese-language newspapers are full of promises to "bring out the best in your child," "turn your child into a well-rounded superstar," "escort your child into *your* [emphasis added by authors] dream school," and "open the door to UC admission," all carefully crafted to attract the parents' attention. On the other hand, these ethnic institutions also provide child care and after-school care for working families, which are all too common in the immigrant community. While some of these ethnic institutions may not have many structured programs, existing just to keep children under adult supervision, most do offer a variety of programs and structured activities at flexible after-school hours along with dropoff and pickup services.

It becomes apparent that ethnic-language maintenance in light of the development of Chinese schools facilitates rather than inhibits social integration among children of immigrants. While Chinese schools offer direct after-school services supplementary to formal education, the spillover effects are significant, though less noticeable. For parents, Chinese-language schools provide an important physical site where formerly unrelated immigrants (and parents) come to socialize and rebuild social ties. As we have just mentioned, immigrant Chinese today are from diverse origins and backgrounds and are not necessarily connected to one another, even when they have the same origin. Reconnecting with co-ethnics often helps ease psychological and social isolation. The co-ethnic ties that are rebuilt may not be as strong as the ones that existed in traditional Chinatowns of the past, but they nonetheless serve as bridge ties that connect immigrants to, rather than isolate them from, the mainstream society by making their social life richer and more comfortable. In an interview, one Chinese parent likened the suburban Chinese school to a church:

> We are nonreligious and don't go to church. So coming to Chinese school weekly is like going to church for us. While our children are in class, we parents don't just go home, because we live quite far away. We hang out here and participate in a variety of things that we organize for ourselves, including dancing, fitness exercise, seminars on the stock market, family financial management, and children's college preparation. I kind of look forward to going to the Chinese school on Saturdays because that is the only time we can socialize with our own people in our native language. I know some of our older kids don't like it that much. When they complain, I simply tell them, "This is not a matter of choice, you must go."

Chinese-language schools also serve as an intermediate ground between the immigrant home and American school, helping immigrant parents, especially those who do not speak English well, learn about the American educational system and make the best of the system by serving their children without getting personally involved in formal schools and their PTAs. Through these ethnic institutions, immigrant parents are indirectly, but effectively, connected to formal schools and are well informed of the specifics crucial for their children's educational success. In this sense, social capital arising from participating in Chinese schools and other ethnic institutions is extremely valuable in serving this particular goal.

Furthermore, Chinese-language schools foster a sense of civic duty in immigrants, who are often criticized for their lack of civic participation. In ethnic institutions, many parents volunteer their time and energy in various tasks, ranging from decision making, fund-raising, and serving as teaching assistants, event organizers, chauffeurs, security guards, and janitors. Parents also take the initiative in organizing community events such as Chinese and American holiday celebrations.

The spillover effects on children are also profound. First, Chinese-language schools and other relevant ethnic institutions offer an alternative space where children can express and share their feelings of growing up in immigrant Chinese families. A Chinese school teacher said, "It is very important to allow youths to express themselves in their own terms without any parental pressure. Chinese parents usually have very high expectations of their children. When children find it difficult to meet these expectations and do not have an outlet for their frustration and anxiety, they tend to become alienated and lost on the streets. But when they are around others who have similar experiences, they are more likely to let out their feelings and come to terms with their current situation."

Moreover, these ethnic institutions provide unique opportunities for immigrant children to form a different set of peer group networks, giving them more leverage in negotiating parent-child relations at home. In immigrant Chinese families, parents are usually more comfortable and less strict with having their children hang out with Chinese friends than with having them hang out with American friends from formal schools, since they either know the parents of their children's Chinese friends or feel that they can communicate with the Chinese parents if things go wrong. So when children are doing things that would cause parents anxiety and raise their objections, they can use their Chinese friendship network as an effective bargaining chip to avoid conflict. In the case of interracial dating, for example, a Chinese girl may simply tell her mother that she is going to study with so-and-so from Chinese school (whose parents are family friends) and then run off with her non-Chinese boyfriend, thereby avoiding an intense confrontation with her mother.

Furthermore, these ethnic institutions function to nurture ethnic identity and pride that may be rejected by the children because of the pressure for assimilation. In Chinese schools, they are exposed to something quite different from what they learn in their formal schools. For example, they recite classical Chinese poems and Confucian sayings about family values, behavioral and moral guidelines, and the importance of schooling. They listen to Chinese fables and legends and learn to sing Chinese folk songs that reveal various aspects of Chinese history and culture. Such cultural exposure reinforces family values and heightens a sense of "Chineseness," helping children to relate to the Chinese "stuff" without feeling embarrassed. A Chinese school principal made it clear that "these kids are here because their parents sent them. They are usually not very motivated in learning Chinese per se, and we do not push them too hard. Language teaching is only part of our mission. An essential part of our mission is to enlighten these kids about their own cultural heritage, so that they show respect for their parents and feel proud of being Chinese." More importantly, being in this particular ethnic social environment helps alleviate bicultural conflicts that are rampant in many immigrant families. As Betty Lee Sung observed in her study of immigrant children in New York City's

Chinatown, bicultural conflicts are "moderated to a large degree because there are other Chinese children around to mitigate the dilemmas that they encounter. When they are among their own, the Chinese ways are better known and better accepted. The Chinese customs and traditions are not denigrated to the degree that they would be if the immigrant child were the only one to face the conflict on his or her own."[33]

However, there is also a downside to growing up in this unique ethnic social environment. Tremendous pressures for achievement on the children as well as on the parents can lead to intense intergenerational conflict and to children's rebellious behavior, alienation from the networks that are supposed to assist them, and even withdrawal from formal schools. Alienated children fall easy prey to street gangs. Ironically, though, pressures and conflicts in a resourceful ethnic environment can serve to fulfill parental expectations. Children are motivated to learn and do well in school because they believe that education is the only way to escape their parents' control. This motivation, while arising from parental pressure and being reinforced through their participation in the ethnic institutions, often leads to desirable outcomes. A nonprofit program organizer summed it up in these words: "Well, tremendous pressures create problems, for sure. However, you've got to realize that we are not living in an ideal environment. Without these pressures, you would probably see as much adolescent rebellion in the family, but a much *larger* [emphasis in tone] proportions of kids failing. Our goal is to get these kids out into college, and for that, we have been very successful."

Conclusion

Together with other ethnic institutions specializing in academic and extracurricular programs for children, today's Chinese-language schools have grown into an ethnic system of supplementary education that is complementary to, rather than competing with, formal education. Despite diversity in form, governance, and curriculum, today's Chinese-language schools, whether nonprofit or for-profit, have one thing in common: they are Chinese-language schools only in the name. They compete more and more intensely with one another in offering services to immigrant families that are directly relevant to children's formal public education. Our study illustrates how the value of education is supported by an ethnic community's social structures and highlights the important effect of the immediate social environment between a child's home and formal school. As a Chinese school teacher remarked, "When you think of how much time these Chinese kids put in their studies after regular school, you won't be surprised why they succeed at such a high rate." It is this ethnic environment with enormous tangible and intangible benefits to the immigrant family that helps promote and actualize the value of education.

However, it should be noted that the ethnic resources and social capital can be useful only up to a certain point: ensuring that immigrant children graduate from high school and get into college. But beyond high school, these ethnic resources may become constraining. For example, many children of Chinese immigrants tend to concentrate in science and engineering not only because their families want them to do so but also because their co-ethnic friends are doing so. After graduating from college, they often lack the type of social networks that facilitate their job placement and occupational mobility. In this respect, there is much room for improvement in the existing ethnic system of supplementary education.

Our case study of Chinese schools is ethnic specific and limited in its generalizability. But it provides evidence in support of an institutional approach to ethnicity that takes into account both structural and cultural factors in explaining interethnic differences in mobility outcomes. It begins to suggest that community forces and social capital are not intrinsic to a particular group but arise from the group's adaptation to the host society, which is largely determined by immigrant history, class backgrounds of immigrants, and societal reception. Since ethnic cultural patterns, including ethnic-language maintenance, interact with the various levels of social structures within a particular ethnic community as they do in larger society, further study is necessary to delve in greater detail into interactive effects of these two significant social contexts on social mobility of immigrants and their children.

NOTES

1. Joshua Fishman, "The Status and Prospects of Bilingualism in the United States," *Modern Language Journal* 49 (1965): 143–55.

2. David Lopez, "Language: Diversity and Assimilation," in *Ethnic Los Angeles*, ed. Roger Waldinger and Mehdi Bozorgmehr (Berkeley: University of California Press, 1996), 139–63.

3. See Richard Alba and Victor Nee, *Remaking the American Mainstream: As-*

similation and Contemporary Immigration (Cambridge, MA: Harvard University Press, 2004), for a comprehensive review of the literature.

4. Rafael M. Diaz, "Thought and Two Languages: The Impact of Bilingualism on Cognitive Development," *Review of Research on Education* 10 (1983): 23–54; Kenji Hakuta, *The Mirror of Language: The Debate on Bilingualism* (New York: Basic Books, 1986); John MacNamara, *Bilingualism and Primary Education* (Edinburgh: Edinburgh University Press, 1966).

5. Elizabeth Perl and Wallace E. Lambert, "The Relation of Bilingualism to Intelligence," *Psychological Monographs: General and Applied* 76 (1962): 1–23; Alejandro Portes and Richard Schauffler, "Language and the Second Generation: Bilingualism Yesterday and Today," *International Migration Review* 28 (1994): 640–61; Ruben G. Rumbaut and Kenji Ima, *The Adaptation of Southeastern Refugees: A Comparative Study* (Washington DC: Office of Refugee Resettlement, 1988); Min Zhou and Carl L. Bankston III, *Growing Up American: How Vietnamese Children Adapt to Life in the United States* (New York: Russell Sage Foundation, 1998).

6. Joshua Fishman, "Language Maintenance," in *Harvard Encyclopedia of American Ethnic Groups,* ed. Stephan Thernstrom (Cambridge: Harvard University Press, 1980), 629–38.

7. My conception of the ethnic environment differs from that advanced by the economist George Borjas. Borjas first introduced the concept of ethnic capital to emphasize the quality of an ethnic environment, as measured by the proportion of highly skilled professionals in a given national origin group. See George Borjas, "Ethnic Capital and Intergenerational Mobility," *Quarterly Journal of Economics* 107 (1992): 123–50.

8. John Ogbu, *The Next Generation: An Ethnography of Education in an Urban Neighborhood* (New York: Academic Press, 1974).

9. Philippe Bourgois, *In Search of Respect: Selling Crack in El Barrio* (New York: Cambridge University Press, 1995); Signithia Fordham, *Blacked Out: Dilemmas of Race, Identity, and Success at Capital High* (Chicago: University of Chicago Press, 1996); Margaret A. Gibson, *Accommodation without Assimilation: Sikh Immigrants in an American High School* (Ithaca: Cornell University Press, 1989).

10. James S. Coleman, *Foundations of Social Theory* (Cambridge, MA: Harvard University Press, 1990).

11. Alejandro Portes, "Social Capital: Its Origins and Application in Modern Sociology," *Annual Review of Sociology* 24 (1998): 4.

12. This case study is exploratory in nature. The material presented in this section draws primarily on observations that we conducted at community events, in private homes, at Chinese schools and other private educational institutions, in religious and community-based organizations, in ethnic businesses, and on main business streets in New York's Chinatown between September and October in 1994, in L.A.'s Chinatown between July 1999 and December 2001, at a suburban Chinese school in Washington, D.C., between November 2000 and May 2001, and

at L.A.'s Monterey Park between July 1999 and April 2003. Random interviews were conducted face to face on site or by phone. Both Chinese and English were used in face-to-face or telephone interviews. All quoted individuals are given pseudonyms to ensure anonymity. See Min Zhou and Xiyuan Li, "Ethnic Language Schools and the Development of Supplementary Education in the Immigrant Chinese Community in the United States," in *New Directions for Youth Development: Understanding the Social Worlds of Immigrant Youth,* ed. Carola Suarez-Orozco and Irina L. G. Todorova (San Francisco: Jossey-Bass, 2003), 57–73.

13. Walter I. Acherman, "Strangers to the Tradition: Idea and Constraint in American Jewish Education," in *Jewish Education Worldwide: Cross-Cultural Perspectives,* ed. Harold S. Himmelfarb and Sergio DellaPergola (New York: University Press of America, 1989); Barbara Beatty, *Preschool Education in America: The Culture of Young Children from the Colonial Era to the Present* (New Haven: Yale University Press, 1995); Koichi Glenn Harada, "A Survey of Japanese Language Schools in Hawaii" (MA thesis, University of Hawai'i, 1934); John N. Hawkins, "Politics, Education, and Language Policy: The Case of Japanese Language Schools in Hawaii," *Amerasia Journal* 5, no. 1 (1978): 39–56; Yukiko Kimura, "Social Significance of Japanese Language Schools Campaign in Hawaii," *Social Process in Hawaii* 20 (1956): 48; Katsumi Onishi, "A Study of the Attitudes of the Japanese in Hawaii toward Japanese Language Schools" (MA thesis, University of Hawai'i, 1948); Noriko Shimada, "Wartime Dissolution and Revival of the Japanese Language Schools in Hawaii: Persistence of Ethnic Culture," *Journal of Asian American Studies* 1, no. 2 (1998): 121–51; Marian Svensrud, "Attitudes of the Japanese toward Their Language Schools," *Sociology and Social Research* 17 (January–February 1933): 259–71.

14. A survey of prior research on Chinese-language schools in the United States shows the following: Chen Yung Fan, "The Chinese Language Schools of San Francisco in Relation to Family Integration and Cultural Identity" (PhD diss., Department of Education, Duke University, 1976); Joe Chung Fong, *Complementary Education and Culture in the Global/Local Chinese Community* (San Francisco: China Books and Periodicals, 2003); Herbert S. Foreman, "A Study of Chinese Language School" (MA thesis, San Francisco State College, 1958); Raymond K. Jung, "The Chinese Language School in the U.S.," *School and Society* 100 (Summer 1972): 309–12; Him Mark Lai, *Retention of the Chinese Heritage: Language Schools in America before World War II,* Chinese America: History and Perspectives (San Francisco: Chinese Historical Society of America, 2000) and *Retention of the Chinese Heritage: Language Schools in America, World War II to Present,* Chinese America: History and Perspectives (San Francisco: Chinese Historical Society of America, 2001); Eric Kwok-wing Leung, "A Sociological Study of the Chinese Language Schools in the San Francisco Bay Area" (PhD diss., University of Missouri-Columbia, 1975); Yi Ying Ma, "Effects of Attendance at Chinese Language Schools upon San Francisco Children" (EdD diss., University of California, 1945); Kim-

Fong Tom, "Functions of the Chinese Language Schools," *Sociology and Social Research* 25 (July–August 1941): 557–61; Xueying Wang, *A View from Within: A Case Study of Chinese Heritage Community Language Schools in the United States* (Baltimore: National Foreign Language Center, Johns Hopkins University, 1996).

15. Fong, "Complementary Education"; Lai, "Retention of the Chinese Heritage . . . before World War II," "Retention of the Chinese Heritage . . . World War II to Present," and *Becoming Chinese American: A History of Communities and Institutions* (Walnut Creek, CA: AltaMira Press, 2004).

16. Sucheng Chan, *This Bitter-Sweet Soil: The Chinese in California Agriculture, 1860–1910* (Berkeley: University of California Press, 1986).

17. Lai, *Becoming Chinese American.*

18. Gloria Heyung Chun, *Of Orphans and Warriors: Inventing Chinese American Culture and Identity* (New Brunswick: Rutgers University Press, 2001).

19. Wang, *View from Within.*

20. Fan, "Chinese Language Schools"; Foreman, "Study of Chinese Language School"; Fong, "Complementary Education"; Leung, "Sociological Study"; Tom, "Functions."

21. Fan, "Chinese Language Schools."

22. Ibid.

23. Chun, *Of Orphans and Warriors.*

24. Foreman, "Study of Chinese Language School"; Jung, "Chinese Language School"; Leung, "Sociological Study"; Ma, "Effects of Attendance"; Tom, "Functions."

25. *Ethnoburb* is a term developed by Wei Li to refer to suburban ethnic clustering of diverse groups with no single racial ethnic group dominant. L.A.'s Monterey Park is a typical ethnoburb. Wei Li, "Spatial Transformation of an Urban Ethnic Community from Chinatown to Chinese Ethnoburb in Los Angeles" (PhD diss., University of Southern California, 1997).

26. Chun, *Of Orphans and Warriors.*

27. Fan, "Chinese Language Schools"; Ma, "Effects of Attendance." But these same studies also found favorable outcomes among Chinese school attendees in terms of general health, posture, nutrition, and grade point averages.

28. Lai, *Becoming Chinese American.*

29. NCACLS was founded in 1994. See Wang, *View from Within;* also cited and tabulated by states in Fong, "Complementary Education." Also see "NCACLS Introduction," www.ncacls.org/ncacls_frm_intro.htm.

30. "Chinese School Association in the United States," www.csaus.org/about_english.asp (accessed October 12, 2005). Some of the CSAUS member schools may have dual memberships in the NCACLS.

31. Min Zhou, "Social Capital in Chinatown: The Role of Community-Based Organizations and Families in the Adaptation of the Younger Generation," in *Beyond Black and White: New Voices, New Faces in the United States Schools,* ed. Lois

Weis and Maxine S. Seller (Albany: State University of New York Press, 1997), 181–206.

32. "Hope Chinese School," www.hopechineseschool.org/ (accessed October 12, 2005).

33. Betty Lee Sung, *The Adjustment Experience of Chinese Immigrant Children in New York City* (New York: Center for Migration Studies, 1987), 126.

Chapter 8

_____

The Importance of Being Italian
Italian Americans in American Popular Culture, 1960s to 1990s

Timothy J. Meagher

As the final editing of the movie *The Godfather* wound down in the winter of 1971–72, Francis Ford Coppola, the film's young director, was nervous. He worried that he had taken an "exciting . . . novel" and "transformed it into a dark, ponderous, boring movie." Paramount Studios, which had hired Coppola, had been unsure of the movie's potential as well. Although the dark novel by Mario Puzo, the basis for the movie, had been wildly popular, some in the studio had wanted to play it safe with "a low budget production." *The Godfather* opened on March 15, 1972, in New York and soon made the unheard-of sum, for those days, of a million dollars a day. By the end of 1972 it had earned more money than any other movie in history.[1]

The *Godfather* began an extraordinary revolution in the representation of Italian Americans in American popular culture, particularly in American movies. A people who had had a marginal presence at best in American film before the 1960s suddenly became "Hollywood's favorite ethnic group" in the 1970s and would remain so through the 1990s and perhaps beyond. The explosion of images of Italian Americans in movies and television at this time is difficult to explain. First, it appeared to have no roots in the reality of Italian American life. By the 1970s and 1980s Italian Americans had long been abandoning old neighborhoods, marrying outside the group, and shedding values and customs that had once marked them as different. In short, by the time images of Italian Americans exploded across American movie screens, real Americans of Italian descent had become so incorporated into the American mainstream that they had become virtually indistinguishable from other white Americans, even white

Protestants. Second, the images of Italian Americans suddenly so popular in the films of the 1970s and 1980s actually differed little from representations of Italian Americans that had appeared in American films since the invention of movies at the turn of the twentieth century. A passionate nature, a penchant for violence, a love of family and neighborhood, and suspicion of authority had marked Italian American characters in American movies from the earliest silent films and continued to mark them in the *Godfather* era of the late twentieth century. If the screen images of Italian Americans in the 1970s and 1980s seemed much the same as before, and were even less representative of how Americans of Italian ancestry actually lived than they ever had been, why did they suddenly become so popular?

In part, stories about Italian Americans became pervasive and popular on screen after the 1960s because Italian Americans made them so. As Italian Americans became more incorporated into American life and grew more comfortable with American culture by the middle of the twentieth century, they picked up skills in acting in and in making movies and became more confident about putting their own experiences on screen. Talented Italian Americans like Robert De Niro, Al Pacino, Francis Ford Coppola, and Martin Scorsese made many of the images of Italian Americans that would appear on American movie screens from the 1970s through the 1990s.

Yet if Italian American directors and actors played a role in the revolution in Italian American representation on screen, they did not cause it. Members of any ethnic minority have only limited power over how films or other popular culture products represent them and even less to say about how popular those images might become. What made the image of Italian Americans so pervasive and popular in American movies after the 1960s was the changes in American values and desires during that tumultuous decade. Amid the turmoil of the sixties Americans of many ethnic backgrounds began to reassess their values and attitudes about sex, government, and a host of other subjects and in that reassessment began to imagine Italian Americans as embodiments of their new yearnings for personal authenticity and communal loyalty as well as rage against the state and authority. No other ethnic group, not the Irish, Jews, or the Poles, seemed to represent these fantasies as well as Italian Americans did, and thus no other ethnic image became as broadly popular and pervasive in American film.

The story of how Italian Americans became Hollywood's favorite ethnic group underlines the complexity of the processes of ethnic incorporation in America. In the 1970s and 1980s, the history of images of Italian Americans and the history of real Italian Americans followed different paths: images of Italian Americans as a distinctive, even exotic, people flourished in the movies even as Italian Americans themselves, largely indistinguishable from their fellow Americans, lived and moved among their suburban neighbors without comment. The two histories, therefore, evolved differently and for different reasons, and their curious evolution reinforces how important it is for scholars to understand ethnic incorporation as a multidimensional, contingent, and complex process.

Images of Italian Americans abounded in American movies from the 1970s through the 1990s, and box office receipts testified to their enormous popularity. Films featuring Italian Americans included *The Godfather* (1972) and its two sequels (1974 and 1990); *Rocky* (1976) and its four sequels (1979, 1982, 1985, and 1990); *Mean Streets* (1973); *Raging Bull* (1980); *Goodfellas* (1990); *Moonstruck* (1988); and *Saturday Night Fever* (1977). Four of the films, *Rocky, The Godfather, Saturday Night Fever,* and *Rocky IV,* ranked, at one time or another, among the top fifty moneymaking films of all time. In 1988, *Moonstruck* finished ninth among the top-grossing films of the year. In 1990, *The Godfather III, Rocky V,* and *Goodfellas* were among the fifty top-grossing films that year. Rentals of the *Moonstruck* video topped eighteen million in the first six months after its release in 1988, a figure that, when translated into rating points, would have made the show one of the top ten TV shows that year. Some of the profits from these movies surprised even their makers. Sylvester Stallone made *Rocky* on a shoestring for $1 million, but the film grossed over $56 million at the box office. A year later *Saturday Night Fever,* made quickly and cheaply to cash in on the disco dancing craze, earned over $70 million.[2]

Critical acclaim for films about Italian Americans in this era matched their financial success. Between 1972 and the mid-1990s, three films about Italian Americans, *The Godfather, The Godfather II,* and *Rocky,* won Academy Awards for "Best Picture." Those victories may even underestimate the critical achievements of movies about Italian Americans. *Goodfellas* did not win an Oscar in 1990, but it topped polls for the best movie of the year among critics in New York and Los Angeles. Some film critics also selected *Raging Bull,* another of Martin Scorsese's pictures that failed to cop the Academy's prize for Best Picture, as the best picture not only of its year, 1980, but of its decade.[3]

Not all movies made about Italian Americans in the 1970s, 1980s, and early 1990s earned critical or financial success. Many faded quickly into deserved obscurity, such as *Spike of Bensonhurst* (1988) and *Mr. Wonderful* (1993). Yet these films, too, testified to the pervasive popularity of Italian Americans and their image in films. So did the films that satirized that image, such as *My Cousin Vinnie* (1992), the *Freshman* (1990), and *Married to the Mob* (1988), and movies featuring African American or white Protestant heroes but including prominent Italian American characters, such as Spike Lee's *Do the Right Thing* (1988) and *Jungle Fever* (1991) and Brian De Palma's *Untouchables* (1987).[4]

Images of Italian Americans had, of course, appeared in American movies before the 1970s and 1980s, but they had never before been nearly so prominent or popular. Before the 1960s, gangster or fight films, genres that Italian Americans would later dominate, were as likely to be about Irishmen—for example, *Public Enemy* (1931) and *Angels with Dirty Faces* (1938)—or Jews or even rural white Protestants as Italian Americans. Prior to 1972 only one film focusing on Italian American life, *Marty* (1955), won an Oscar, and the few Italian American "stars" or prestigious directors rarely played in or directed movies that focused on Italian American life. Rudolph Valentino, for example, played an assortment of exotic foreign types and won his greatest fame as an Arab sheik. Similarly, Frank Capra, the most successful Italian American director before the 1970s, paid little attention to Italian Americans in his films. His work focused almost exclusively on "real Americans," rural or small-town white Protestants. Italian Americans enjoyed somewhat greater success in music. A host of Italian American "crooners," led by Frank Sinatra, became popular in the 1940s and 1950s, and many of them managed to hang on for decades after that. Sinatra also fashioned a successful movie career for himself and won an Academy Award as Best Supporting Actor for playing an Italian American character, Angelo Maggio, in *From Here to Eternity* in 1953. Yet before the 1960s, Italian American characters only rarely gained such prominence in American movies. The explosion of representations of Italian Americans into public consciousness in the 1970s and 1980s represented a truly decisive break from the past.[5]

Ironically this new prominence occurred just when sociologists began detecting a clear and rapid erosion of distinctive cultural traits and ethnic self-consciousness among Italian Americans. Richard Alba has pointed out that the cultural values and customs of third-generation Italian Americans had become virtually indistinguishable from those of white Protestants by the 1970s and 1980s. Younger Italian Americans, for example, married outside the group more often than not, cooked and ate Italian food only rarely, ignored Italian American clubs and societies, and were more liberal than most white Protestants on such family issues as premarital sex, gay rights, and abortion. Alba contended that Italian Americans had entered the "twilight" of their ethnicity. The slow demise of the Mafia in the 1970s and 1980s reflected this overall decline in Italian American ethnicity as well, as aging and weakening Italian American crime organizations succumbed to the challenges of younger and hungrier Latino, Russian, and Asian immigrants.[6]

Why, then, did images of Italian Americans become so pervasive and popular in American movies? Was it simply Italian Americans' "turn"? Was it just their time in a cycle of ethnic succession as the group's members finally acquired the skills and confidence to present their own story to all Americans?

There can be no denying the emerging abundance of talented Italian American directors, actors, and actresses in the 1960s and 1970s. They included Francis Ford Coppola, Martin Scorsese, Robert De Niro, Al Pacino, Sylvester Stallone, Marissa Tomei, John Turturro, Danny Aiello, Annabella Sciorra, Talia Shire, John Travolta, and Joe Pesci. One or another of these men or women directed or acted in movies as diverse at *The Godfather I, II,* and *III, Goodfellas, Raging Bull, My Cousin Vinnie, Do the Right Thing, Jungle Fever,* the *Rocky* films, and *Saturday Night Fever.* The Academy of Motion Picture Arts and Sciences recognized their abilities and those of other Italian Americans by nominating Americans of Italian descent thirty-one times for directing or acting Academy Awards and awarding seven to them between 1970 and 1992.[7]

The emergence of such talent was a product of Italian American upward mobility and acculturation. If those changes carried new generations of Italian Americans further and further from their immigrant roots, the same changes also made young Italian Americans more comfortable with American culture and eased their efforts to become skilled and savvy moviemakers or talented actors and actresses. Such familiarity with American life and the acquisition of those skills, in turn, made the new generation of Italian Americans more confident about putting their own or their families' experiences on screen. Even young Italian Americans like Martin Scorsese, raised in older, poorer Italian American neighborhoods, could learn how to love and make movies, while others, including Francis Ford Coppola, child of a successful classical musician, or Robert De Niro, son of aspiring artists, could naturally dream of creative careers.[8]

Yet no ethnic or racial minority, whatever its members' savvy or confidence, shapes the characteristics of its own image on its own, and group members have even less control over how popular that image will become to a broader national audience. Representations of ethnic groups do not appear and disappear or change shape in orderly, mechanical cycles of ethnic succession. If that were true, then images of Polish Americans, whose immigrant ancestors arrived in America at about the same time as Italian immigrants—in significant if smaller numbers than the Italians—at the turn of the twentieth century, would have also become more visible and prominent by the 1970s and 1980s. Yet that did not happen. Furthermore, even if a group produces hosts of talented actors and moviemakers, that hardly assures the popularity of the ethnic group's image on screen. Representations of Jews in American movies never came close to reflecting Jewish participation in the early-twentieth-century movie industry. Indeed, as the number of Jewish actors, actresses, directors, and producers rose over the first half of the twentieth century, the number of Jewish characters on screen actually fell. As Lester Friedman has pointed out, Jewish characters virtually disappeared from American movies after the 1930s. They appeared even less in the movies of the 1950s than in the films of any decade earlier in the century.[9]

No matter how talented Martin Scorsese, Francis Ford Coppola, De Niro, and a host of other Italian Americans might have been, if members of the public had not seen something they wanted in representations of Italian Americans they would not have flocked to movies featuring those images. The stunning success of movies like *Rocky* and *Saturday Night Fever* suggested the extent of the public's new hunger for stories about Italian Americans and the power of that appeal to transform relative Italian American nobodies like Sylvester Stallone and John Travolta into stars. That broad appeal not only gave Italian American directors and actors the opportunity to become successful by crafting constructions of their own people but also drew others to make or act in movies featuring Italian American characters, among them the Anglo-Canadian director Norman Jewison, the African American director Spike Lee, the Alsatian American actor Marlon Brando, and the Armenian American actress Cher. Rather than trying to explain the new, broad popularity of images of Italian American directors and actors in terms of the group's own efforts, it is more useful to analyze the images Italian American and other American moviemakers constructed of Italian Americans after the 1960s and to try to plumb why these images suddenly seemed so appealing to a broad and diverse American movie audience.

If they had been trying to depict Italian Americans as they really were in the 1970s and 1980s (or at least what they were rapidly becoming), film-makers would have made movies about men and women going to college, finding success in professions or management, settling in suburbs, and mingling easily with Americans of all nationalities. Most Italian American characters would have been modern, even sophisticated Americans at home in the world of late-twentieth-century America. Virtually no one made films about such Italian Americans.

Rather, filmmakers made movies about Italian American boxers, gangsters, and working-class urban villagers who were rarely modern and scarcely ever sophisticated. On the contrary, films about Italian Americans in the 1970s and 1980s almost invariably depicted them as what I would call white primitives: whites who were tough, passionate, and sexual but thoroughly committed to the elemental human institutions of family, community, and religion.

Makers of such films themselves often described their work in terms of the characters' primitivism. Martin Scorsese, for example, stated that his *Raging Bull* was an attempt to show "life on its most primitive level," and of his movie *Goodfellas* he stated, "I was trying to make it as practical and primitive as possible."[10]

Stanley Kaufmann, of the *New Republic,* pointed out in a review of *Goodfellas* that images of Italian Americans as primitives were common in other films as well. "Scorsese specializes in the primitive aspects of urban life, with an emphasis on the colors and conflicts of Italian Americans," Kauffman wrote, but "American films have developed a latter day line in this vein: *Rocky* both I and II, which twined movieland braids around its primitivism, and *Godfather* I and II, which aggrandized a family's bestiality into a saga." Even Kaufman's observation was too limited, however, for what he detected in *Goodfellas, Rocky,* and the *Godfather* movies characterized almost every representation of Italian Americans in movies and television after the 1960s.[11]

Yet what does it mean to claim that American movies made since the 1960s have represented Italian Americans as primitives? Two sets of characteristics, I believe, defined the Italian American white primitive in American movies from the 1970s to the 1990s. One set was relatively simple and straightforward: the Italian American white primitive in such movies operated at the most basic level of animal-like existence. He (and it was usually he) was tough, passionate, and often violent. He did not reflect or think but expressed and satisfied almost all his passions, sexual and otherwise, immediately, without regard to society and its complex restraints, particularly those imposed by the government. Reviewers of movies like *Goodfellas, Godfather, Raging Bull,* and others often used words like *bestial, savage, barbarian,* and *animal menace* to describe Italian American characters. One reviewer, for example, likened Scorsese's gangsters in *Goodfellas* to "a barrel of weasels, snarling . . . devouring each other, swimming around in a muck of their own making." Other critics labeled Sylvester Stallone's character Rocky in the movie of the same name a "rough, untutored," "uncomplicated," and "crude" if "naturally noble fellow." Stallone, who wrote the movie, delighted in the characterization and boasted of being an "intellectual caveman."[12]

The other set of characteristics defined the Italian American as the anthropological other, as the premodern member of a "primitive" but nonetheless ritualized culture. He, and in this case slightly more often she, belonged to a culture that valued elemental, "natural" institutions, such as the family and the neighborhood (substitutes for the village), or even the gang (a substitute for the tribe or clan). The Italian American white primitive also possessed a distinctive premodern language, had unique foodways, and practiced a magical religion, a primitive form of Catholicism. The *Godfather* films offered some of the best examples of this kind of Italian American primitivism. Reviewers lauded the "joyous primitivism" of the *Godfather's* "semicivilized" ritual celebrations, notably the elaborate weddings and christenings, and noted the old-fashioned formalities of address and speech the characters often used, particularly the use of the title "Godfather" itself. Several critics also commented on the prominence of food in the *Godfather* films and other gangster pictures like *Goodfellas.* One entitled her review of the latter film "Blood and Pasta." Films satirizing the image of the Italian American primitive, such as *Married to the Mob* and the *Freshman,* mocked this prominence of food and food rituals. Such movies thus underlined the importance of food to the primitive image even as they poked fun at it. In *Married to the Mob* the gangsters' favorite restaurant and the site of a mob shootout is a fast-food outlet, not an "authentic" ethnic restaurant. In the *Freshman* the plot centers on a Mafia scam to stage illegal, expensive dinners feasting on endangered animal species.[13]

The image of the Italian American primitive was not a decisively new representation of Italian Americans in American film. Representations of Italians in movies since the early twentieth century had featured many of the essential elements of the popular Italian American white primitives of the 1970s and 1980s: unfettered passion; a penchant for violence; and prominent roles as gangsters and boxers. Yet if the image had not changed much from the 1930s and 1940s to the 1970s and 1980s, America had. In the 1960s specifically, a number of changes, large and small, created the environment that helped the Italian American white primitive flourish in American popular culture.

One change came in American racial and ethnic relations. African Americans, long banished to the margins of American life, had fought their way to its center. Whites, particularly white ethnics, notably Italians or Polish Americans, who had been making progress in their efforts to integrate into mainstream American society, reacted ambivalently to the new black assertiveness. On the one hand, they resisted the claims of these new rivals to the jobs, neighborhoods, and political offices that had long been white preserves; on the other hand, black challenges to white culture inspired Polish, Italian, and other white ethnic Americans to assert their own versions of group pride.[14]

Yet the turmoil of the 1960s extended far beyond race and ethnic relations. Antiwar, countercultural, feminist, and gay rights movements also erupted in that decade. Combined with the African American crusade and white ethnic revival, as well as long-term social and economic changes, such movements not only provoked tumult but prompted a fundamental transformation of American values and attitudes. Americans, for example, became increasingly suspicious of authority and institutions. Although observers of the 1960s often identified such suspicions with the student Left, E. J. Dionne has pointed out that many working-class and other conservatives grew, if anything, even more disenchanted with the government and social and cultural elites than the more visible student protesters or counterculture hippies. Frustrated and straining against social and political authorities and their repressive rules, Americans after the 1960s became enamored of personal and communal authenticity. "Getting in touch" with one's feelings became a kind of mantra and self-expression a virtue. This concern for authenticity, like the suspicion of authority, resonated among a variety of different groups and was reflected in trends as diverse as a spreading revolution in sexual norms and behavior, the new popularity of folk music and folk culture, and the "ethnic revival"—the new pride people like Italian Americans expressed in their group's origins and culture.[15]

For many Americans the representation of Italian American white primitives came to embody powerfully the new yearnings and desires that had emerged in the wake of the 1960s' tumult. Images of Italian Americans in many movies suggested that some whites had the power to match the "natural" toughness and passion attributed to newly assertive African Americans. Italian American primitives on screen also offered a white alternative to corporate, academic, or government "moderns" who because of their emotional hollowness had become alienated from the authentic essentials of life, such as traditional gender roles, family, community, and even appreciation of food and its rituals. Italian Americans in the movies in this era knew who they were, while white "moderns" wandered in a fog of anomie. The imagined Italian American primitives had a sure sense of self, the fantasy went, because they had managed to break free of the government and other institutions that smothered and frustrated the natural desires of so many in the tangles of bureaucratic red tape and social convention. Italian American white primitives in the movies of the 1970s and 1980s treated governments, even their own government, as alien pariahs to be evaded, dismissed, or manipulated, but always suspected and despised.

Amid these broader social and cultural revolutions of the 1960s, and in part because of them, the movie industry itself also changed radically, permitting filmmakers to portray Italian Americans in all their primitive glory. During the 1960s, the Motion Picture Production Code disappeared, studios declined, and a fresh crop of directors emerged. These changes broke the shackles of official restriction and studio caution and gave moviemakers the freedom to graphically depict Italian American passion and violence and celebrate outsiders like gangsters while exposing corruption in mainstream institutions, especially the police, government, and even the church. With the demise of the old Motion Picture Production Code, moviemakers did not have to make sure the "good" guys always won and could even suggest that maybe the "good" guys—police, priests, and patriots—had not in the first place really been so "good" and the "bad" guys, gangsters, not really so "bad."[16]

Italian Americans and Race

Images of Italian Americans as white primitives drew much of their power and broad appeal from the racial tensions that rose from the 1960s through the 1980s. In 1990, trying to explore the reason for the mob movies' popularity, Richard Corliss, of *Time* magazine, argued that "directors love [the gangster movie] because it allows them to confront in code, the awful ethnic schisms of American life; Italian vs. Wasp stands in for black vs. white." Corliss suggested that Italians were depicted like imagined blacks, as white primitives or, better, "white niggers." Like blacks, Italian Americans in the movies emerged as a minority suffering from discrimination, and like imagined blacks they behaved more "naturally" than did other whites. They were passionate, sexual, tough, and violent. The perspective here suggested sympathetically that Italian Americans and blacks had much in common and that the racial boundary between them, white versus black, blurred or submerged in the opposition of both to white Protestants.[17]

The image of the Italian American white primitive, however, attracted audiences less because Italian Americans appeared as sympathetic stand-ins for blacks than because they stood as icons of white opposition or even hostility to blacks. Italian Americans proved that whites could be "natural" like blacks and, more important, that they had the toughness, willingness to use violence, and sexual prowess to meet and defeat black challenges. The Italian American, then, might have been a primitive "other," but for white audiences he also stood for "us" whites, proof of whites' potential power, proof that whites, too, in Stanley Kauffman's summation of Robert De Niro's character Jake La Motta in *Raging Bull,* could "hit and screw."

The movie *Rocky* and its many sequels most clearly illustrates the critical importance of race in defining Italian American white primitivism in the post-1960s era. Sylvester Stallone self-consciously forged his movie character Rocky Balboa as a new kind of American hero. Stallone stated shortly after the movie's opening: "People require symbols of humanity and heroism. A man who brings his family to theaters today asks, 'Is there anybody here I can identify with?' . . . He sees Rocky as a simple man, a man he can identify with . . . a man who likes America, a man who is a real man. That's what people want to see these days."[18] Stallone left unsaid that, in identifying with Rocky, such a man also identifies with a white man whose one achievement in life is fighting a black man to a standstill. As historian Daniel Leab wrote of the first movie in the series, *Rocky:* "Rocky plays on . . . old prejudices and new fears. The film's racism is not overtly stated, but if not explicit, it is still vividly (and visually) implicit." Not only is Stallone's opponent, played by Carl Weathers, a "nasty" imitation of Muhammad Ali, who made fun of American values, but, as Leab also points out, Stallone's Rocky is interviewed during the film by an "arrogantly glib," "fashionably dressed" black woman who "oozes condescension and contempt" for this Italian American working-class hero.[19]

Rocky III, the second of the sequels to Rocky, took what seemed a different tack, implying a qualified sympathy and identification between Italian and African Americans. In *Rocky III,* Apollo Creed, played again by Carl Weathers, Rocky's black opponent in the first two *Rocky* movies, becomes Stallone's trainer. He even teaches Stallone how "to fight like a black man," emphasizing quickness over toughness. But in *Rocky III,* reviewers suggested, the reconciliation between blacks and Italian Americans appeared to be a contrivance to hide the *Rocky* series' continuing play on the underlying fundamental opposition between the two groups. Stallone's *Rocky* may have had a new African American trainer, but the white champion's opponent was another black man, "Clubber Lang," played by Mr. T, a far more menacing, street-tough black (Pauline Kael described the character as a "vicious brute") than the cool, sophisticated champion Apollo Creed in the first two *Rocky* movies. Making Creed Rocky's trainer in *Rocky III* seemed to many reviewers simply part of a cynical effort to soften Stallone's possibly racist image as an icon of populist conservatives.[20]

In *Rocky IV* Rocky Balboa took time out to fight and win a battle in the Cold War over a Russian boxer, and in *Rocky V* he fought a southern white boy, his former protégé. Yet in this last Rocky film, George Washington Duke, a cartoonish black boxing promoter modeled after Don King, corrupted Rocky's young white friend Tommy "Machine" Gunn and turned Gunn against Rocky. Thus, yet again, a black man, Duke, was Rocky's real antagonist. Aside from *Rocky IV,* then, race virtually defined Stallone's wildly popular boxing hero throughout the series of films as an icon of white primitive power set against the emerging threat of African American assertion.

Italian Americans and "Moderns"

Italian Americans stood in opposition not only to blacks in movies after the 1960s, as Corliss suggested in his analysis of the popularity of gangster movies, but also to other whites. Although Corliss suggested that this contrast pitted Italian Americans against white Protestants, the opposition appeared to be less against another white ethnic group than against modern, de-ethnicized, "new class," white technocrats. The depiction of Italian American masculinity, tough, passionate, and violent, clearly marked off the Italian American white primitive from modern, liberal, excessively rational white men, so emotionally stunted by their bureaucratic jobs and emasculated by feminists that they had lost touch with their "true" natures. Italian Americans, by contrast, embodied lost roots in traditional sex roles and reaffirmed the naturalness of older values. Sasha Mitchell as the lead, Spike Fumo, in *Spike of Bensonhurst*, for example, declared emphatically: "Lesbianism is un-American, un-Catholic and un-Italian." Stallone, discussing his own role in *Rocky*, argued: "I don't think that even woman's lib wants all men to become limp wristed librarians. I don't know what is happening to men these days. . . . There don't seem to be enough real men to go around."[21]

In addition, the imagined opposition between the Italian American primitives and white moderns pitted the Italian American's primeval loyalties to family and community against the atomized individualism of the modern man or woman. In the first half of the twentieth century, this contrast in movies almost always affirmed modern individualism as opposed to Italian familism and communalism. In the 1950s, Hollywood had usually celebrated white ethnic progress out of old neighborhood ghettos to broader, less narrowly restricted lives in the mainstream of American culture. *Marty*, appearing first as a television drama in 1953 and released later as a movie in 1955, perhaps expressed that theme more poignantly than any other movie or television show of its time. In the movie, Marty, a pleasant, likable, Italian American butcher, lives a dead-end existence trapped by commitments to his family and ethnic community until he meets a non-Italian girl from outside the neighborhood. The climactic scene comes when Marty decides to break the oppressive bonds of family and ethnic village to marry his newfound love.[22]

This continued to be an important theme in Italian American movies through the 1970s. In *Rocky*, for example, Rocky's girlfriend, Adrian, played by Talia Shire, seems ensnared in family obligations until Sylvester Stallone's Rocky liberates her. Rocky's gritty neighborhood, dominated by two-bit hoodlums, hardly stands as a positive symbol of community. Spiritual despair also suffuses Martin Scorsese's Little Italy in Manhattan in his early films like *Who's That Knocking at My Door* and *Mean Streets*.[23]

The *Marty* theme emerged more fully in *Saturday Night Fever*. Here Tony Manero lives in a narrow, claustrophobic, and shallow world of oppressive family and provincial neighborhood. An authoritarian father, an Italian American culture that deadens expectations, and a rigidly oppressive Catholicism seem to strangle Tony's exuberance and talent, which finds expression only on the dance floor of the local disco club. To achieve self-fulfillment Tony has to flee, a need that is first suggested when his brother shows up after leaving the priesthood, then develops through Tony's relationship with a woman who works in Manhattan and boasts of its possibilities, and finally is confirmed in the movie's last scenes when Tony takes a train ride to Manhattan.

This theme, reminiscent of *Marty* (*Marty*'s last scene shows him getting off a bus to visit his new girlfriend), did not play as well for critics and audiences in 1977 as it had in 1955, however. *Time* magazine found the labored efforts "to get Tony out of Brooklyn" clichéd and hackneyed but raved about the primitive power of scenes showing Tony and his friends dancing at the disco. Audiences also appeared to prefer Tony in the provincial world of his Brooklyn Italian American neighborhood than in the presumably liberating stage world of Manhattan. While *Saturday Night Fever* stunned expectations and made tens of millions of dollars, the sequel *Staying Alive*, which "got Tony out of Brooklyn" and focused on his new life as a dancer in Manhattan, failed miserably at the box office and with critics.[24]

Other films about Italian Americans in the post-1960s era, movies as diverse as the fabulously successful *Godfather* series, the flop *Mr. Wonderful*, and the mob satire the *Freshman*, clearly rejected and reversed this theme of liberation through assimilation. These rejections did not just indirectly affirm the ethnic village and the family; they pointedly repudiated modern men and women and their vacuous promises of individual liberation through flight from family and community. At least in the sphere of popular media—the terms on which Italians Americans were invited into mainstream America were very much linked to their representation of traditional values of family and community.

Moonstruck made this point most clearly. The movie celebrated the ethnic village, a friendly, intimate, and even pretty neighborhood in Brooklyn. Yet the movie also specifically set the ethnic village and its values triumphantly against the values of the liberated moderns. The film made this point less through Loretta Castorini, the main character, played by Cher, than by her mother, Rose Castorini, played by Olympia Dukakis. During the movie, Rose meets Perry, a professor of communications from New York University (a perfect embodiment of the emotionally hollow modern man) played by John Mahoney. Perry has just had an embarrassing fight with his date, one of his graduate students, and one of many young women he has picked up and then abandoned in a series of shallow relationships. Perry walks Rose back to her house through her Italian neighborhood, an intimate village framed by the cold, impersonal skyscrapers of Manhattan in the distance. He asks if he can come into her house, but she replies—not with regret but with triumph—that she cannot let him do that. He is a child who treats relationships like playthings, she says, but she understands her role and her obligations. She has real roots in village and community, she implies, as she states confidently: "I know who I am." The implication, of course, is that he, Perry, the modern man, does not— possibly never can—know who he really is.[25]

An internal tension or contradiction ran through the Italian American white primitive image, which never seemed to be resolved or seemed even to need to be resolved. This contradiction set the primitive's passion, heedless of restraint, against the strict codes and rules of family, church, and neighborhood. This contradiction seemed lost or submerged in the opposition between the white primitive and the modern man and woman. White primitives could be both more natural and passionate and more committed to family, community, and neighborhood than moderns could. *Moonstruck* neatly summed up the compromise American movies made to resolve the seeming contradictions in this image. The film affirmed the passion between the two white primitives, Loretta and her lover Ronny Cammareri, played by Nicholas Cage, as natural ("Don't try to live on milk and cookies when what you want is meat!" says Ronny to Loretta, "Red meat just like me! It's wolves and nothing else! You're a wolf just like me. Come up stairs with me and get in my bed"), but it rebuked the aimless philandering of the modern Perry as self-indulgent and shallow.[26]

Italian Americans and "Society"

If Italian Americans lived in tight families and communities in the movies of the post-1960s era, they did not live in "society," to invoke the word Mario Puzo's word often used in *The Godfather*. Tight families and close knit neighborhoods functioned, in fact, as necessary private havens and strongholds in a dangerous, broader, public world, rife with government corruption and ruled by official caprice.

The depiction of government as hopelessly corrupt cropped up repeatedly in films about Italian Americans. It loomed large, for example, in the *Godfather* pictures. Don Corleone, played by Marlon Brando, wins the respect of his fellow mob chieftains because he controls a stable of officials on the take. Michael Corleone, played by Al Pacino, is initiated into the mob through the murder of a corrupt police captain. He later builds his own network of corrupt officials in Nevada, New York, and Cuba. In *Godfather III*, he tries, unsuccessfully, to prevent the corrupt Vatican bureaucracy from destroying a new pope modeled on Pope John Paul I.

Such depictions of corruption did not constitute muckraking. They did not expose official wrongdoing to encourage reform but rather affirmed the Italian American primitive suspicion that government corruption was inevitable and thus any kind of government irredeemable. Furthermore, such movies powerfully demonstrated not merely government or institutions' corruption but their deadening hand, their frustration of desires and aspirations, their deafness to the people, and their blundering ineffectiveness.

Mob movies appealed to broad audiences, at least in part, because they showed the power of the mobsters to defy government and still achieve their goals and fulfill their desires. Indeed, the gangsters' very indifference to "society's" norms made them efficient and successful. In *The Godfather*'s opening sequence, for example, an undertaker comes to the Don for retribution against the men who raped his daughter, explaining that the police can or will do nothing to help him. The Godfather can and does give him justice—ordering the beating of the two men—in a world where the law, corrupted and feeble, cannot.

More important than helping others, the Italian American primitive gangster could help himself. In an article in *American Film* in 1990, the critic Wolf Schneider said of gangsters in American movies: "Gangsters don't have to wait in line, they double park wherever they want, people buy them drinks and favors are theirs for the asking." Henry Hill, played by Ray Liotta, the lead character in *Goodfellas,* says: "If we wanted something we just took it. If anyone complained he got hit so bad he never complained again." Scorsese himself described the gangster's life more pithily: "Want. Take. Simple." Several reviewers commented on *Goodfellas'* remarkable illustration of gangster power in one scene as Hill and his wife, Karen, played by Lorraine Bracco, enter a nightclub through the kitchen, hurry into the nightclub proper, and sit "basking in privilege" at a front row table that has appeared miraculously, courtesy of the "effusively" polite headwaiter.[27]

Italian American white primitives seemed most powerful, however, when they exacted vengeance from those who showed them no respect. As Joe Pesci described his character in *Goodfellas:* "In Tommy's society if he allows people to treat him like a jerk, he loses power. He can't be taken lightly by anyone. And when he kills, he's like the doctor who performs an operation on someone whose guts are wide open—and then goes out for lunch." Robert De Niro, as Jake La Motta in *Raging Bull*, wreaks havoc on his brother, other fighters, and anyone else he suspects of even admiring his wife. Though much more calculated and carried out on a far grander scale, vengeance dominated the three *Godfather* movies as well and appeared to be a key to their popularity. The original *Godfather*, for example, builds to a climactic montage of scenes when Michael Corleone's henchmen slaughter their boss's enemies as Michael himself solemnly stands as godfather for his sister's son at the child's christening. Audiences cheered Michael's efficient vengeance, stunning the movie's director, Francis Ford Coppola, who claimed that he had never anticipated how thoroughly the public would identify with the mob boss and his bloody revenge.[28]

The opposition to government and institutions, then, did not seem necessarily revolutionary or radical or even liberal. It grew less out of the disgust over scandals like Watergate than out of the dissatisfaction with big government brewing throughout the 1970s, which finally exploded in the Reagan revolution of the early 1980s. Conservative white ethnic working- and lower-middle-class workers (the "schnooks," as Henry Hill calls them in *Goodfellas*), who felt increasingly powerless in the wake of the changes of the 1960s, found ready heroes in movie characters who defied corrupt authorities and took what they wanted with an insouciant disregard for legalities or politically correct social conventions.[29]

If the image of the white primitives seemed so powerful and appealing, perhaps necessary, in the 1970s and 1980s, why did Italian Americans in particular, and not some other group, became the white primitive icon? On a superficial level, there appear to be some real sources for the white primitive image in Italian American culture itself. Family and neighborhood ties did, in fact, loom large in the lives of Italian immigrants and their children, even if they weakened considerably in later generations. Moreover, Italian Americans such as Rocky Marciano, Rocky Graziano, and La Motta won success as boxers, and a number of Italian Americans figured prominently in the world of organized crime. In the 1960s, the Mafia received enormous attention and publicity through the congressional testimony of Joe Valachi, a self-confessed member of an organized crime gang, and this publicity, perhaps, built credibility for the later successful Mob pictures like the *Godfather* and *Goodfellas*.[30]

Yet Italian American culture, like other ethnic cultures, has always been complex, far different and richer than the cartoonish stereotypes that depicted Italian Americans as white primitives, or, for that matter, even the

202 TIMOTHY J. MEAGHER

more thoughtful, but very selective, representations of them in the best recent films. Moreover, as noted earlier, this culture had already begun to change dramatically by the time the white primitive image became broadly popular. The images in the movies of the 1970s and 1980s may have reflected some real aspects of Italian American experience in the 1920s or 1930s—if in exaggerated, caricatured form—but they hardly resembled the lives of the vast majority of Italian Americans at the time the movies appeared.

If the reality of Italian American life was, at best, a source of mixed relevance for this image, there were, as noted earlier, rich sources—though, perhaps, disassembled and still in pieces—in previous movie depictions of Italian Americans. The Italian as passionate, as prone to violence or emotional excess, and as the prisoner of family, community, or a primeval Catholicism were all standard representations of Italians in American popular culture as far back as the 1910s. Historian Carlos Cortés points to depictions of violent Italian immigrants in the 1919 film *Dangerous Hours,* for example, or depictions of "lascivious" ones in the 1924 movie *Manhandled.* Even by the 1950s, Cortés contends, American movies repeatedly hammered home that "violence—physical and verbal" was "the prime Italian American cultural characteristic."[31]

Marlon Brando, who is not of Italian ancestry but is often mistaken for an Italian American, may have also provided a key transition in the transformation of the Italian American into the white primitive. In the 1950s, Brando had perfected the image of the natural brute while playing a variety of ethnic types, such as the Irish Terry Malloy in *On the Waterfront* and the Polish Stanley Kowalski in *Streetcar Named Desire.* Indeed, the primitivism of his characters had become his hallmark: *Halliwell's Filmgoers Guide* describes him simply as an "unsmiling American leading actor whose prototype is the primitive modern male." By starring in *The Godfather,* which launched the recent explosion of "Italian Americanness" in popular culture, and then serving as a point of comparison for Robert De Niro and even Sylvester Stallone, Brando, perhaps, helped give birth to and legitimize the new, Italian American white primitive.[32]

Italian Americans also emerged as the white primitive, however, simply because no other group's image seemed to provide a better fit. Irish Americans had once provided working-class heroes. Indeed, the Irish gangster or tough guy had dominated American popular culture in the nineteenth and early twentieth centuries. Some films attempted to keep this tradition alive after the 1960s. *State of Grace* and *Miller's Crossing,* both released about the same time as *Goodfellas,* featured Irish American gangsters. Neither earned as much money or garnered the same critical acclaim; the Coen brothers' masterpiece, *Miller's Crossing,* won some plaudits, but reviewers dismissed *State of Grace* as "forgettable and graceless." One critic argued: "In *State of Grace* the Irish are Italians without style. The Irish used to be able to talk at least. But they mostly shout and mumble in this story."[33]

In part, the Irish ethnic image had become too vague or hazy to define the white primitive distinctly and believably. Most Irish immigrants had, after all, arrived in America a half-century or more before the great Italian immigration at the turn of the twentieth century and thus had moved even further down the path of social and cultural assimilation than had Italian Americans. Playwrights, vaudevillians, songwriters, and moviemakers had created distinct Irish types throughout the history of American popular culture, but images of Irish Americans in the movies had already begun to shed some of their distinctive ethnic traits by the early twentieth century. As early as the 1910s and 1920s, movies featuring Irish American characters often portrayed the Irish as a people close to the center of American culture and society, mediating between an American mainstream and other newer groups. By the 1970s and 1980s the Irishman increasingly became *the* American, the stand-in for the average American. Irish ethnicity added some color, a touch of difference that made Irish American men or women on screen more believable (Mrs. O'Brien or Mrs. McMahon selling soap rather than Mrs. Jones or Mrs. Smith), but it had no significant social or cultural meanings. In *Field of Dreams* (1990), a popular celebration of baseball as the American essence, for example, the lead character, Ray Kinsella, played by Kevin Costner, announces so matter-of-factly that most viewers might have missed it: "My father was John Kinsella. It's an Irish name."[34]

Distinct images of Irish Americans had not disappeared entirely from American popular culture by the 1970s and 1980s, however, and they sometimes still displayed some of the characteristics of the primitive. The cops in Tom Wolfe's novel *Bonfire of the Vanities,* for example, are "stone" tough, honest, loyal, and faithful to their own code (though this was hardly recognizable in the movie made from the novel in 1990). Gene Hackman in the *French Connection* (1971), Clint Eastwood in *Dirty Harry* (1971), and Sean Connery more recently in the *Untouchables* (1987) also personified tough, earthy, savvy, but basically honest Irish Americans.[35]

Yet representations of Irish Americans lacked some of the white primitive's essential characteristics. Irish Americans, for example, seemed too repressed, too incapable of indulging natural appetites for life or expressing their desires. As Hasia Diner has pointed out, they had no food of their own or even traditions celebrating eating as both the sweet satisfaction of a natural desire and a central ritual of family and community.[36] More important, perhaps, few representations of Irish Americans anywhere in twentieth-century popular culture have depicted them as passionately sexual. During the Motion Picture Production Code era this hardly counted against the Irish, since the code, backed by the power of the Irish-led Catholic Church, severely restricted display of such passion on screen. Irish American characters in the 1930s and 1940s, then, could easily model innocent, even childlike, romance or, even better, a disavowal of sex altogether for a higher cause. Such films as *Going My Way* (1944) and *The Cardinal* (1963) celebrated the heroic choices young Irish American men made for the priesthood over attractive young women.

With the demise of the code in the 1960s, however, movies could depict sexuality much more openly, and now Irish Americans seemed victims of their adherence to the tyrannical sexual discipline of Catholicism. They seemed to embody sexual prudery and repression on screen and in many films reaped the consequences in unhappiness or tragedy. The best-known film representation of tragic Irish American sexuality in the post-1960s era was *Looking for Mr. Goodbar*, made in 1977 by director Richard Brooks and based on a novel by Judith Rossner. In that movie an Irish American girl, Theresa Dunn, played by Diane Keaton, escapes her oppressive Catholic family, only to find abuse and death in the seamy pickup bars of New York. Even films made by Irish Americans and sympathetic to them, like the *Brothers McMullen* (1995), portrayed Irish Americans as, at best, romantically dysfunctional.

Irish Americans in popular culture and real life also seemed too tightly connected to authority to serve as primitive rebels. Most of the tough Irishmen, for example, have been cops, who, though celebrated by Wolfe and some others for their ability to operate outside the system, were nonetheless the enforcers of civilization's rules and thus became implicated in government corruption and inefficiency. *True Confessions* (1981), a film portraying Irish American malfeasance at the highest levels of government and the Catholic Church, notably summed up this corruption of the Irish by power, but many other movies made since the 1960s—such as *Serpico* (1973), *Q & A* (1990), and *LA Confidential* (1997)—made the same point.

In short, then, the Irish could not typify the white primitive because they did not "screw" and because, when they "hit," they often fought on behalf of civilization and corrupt government. They defended the white Protestant elite as its accomplices; they did not attack it as its opponents. Indeed, in one of the first and most vivid films to focus on white ethnic workers' reactions to the cultural and political tumult of the 1960s, *Joe* (1970), Peter Boyle played a crazed right-wing Irish American, "hard hat," blue-collar worker, Joe Curran, who helped a rich white Protestant, Bill Compton, played by Dennis Patrick, take revenge on the counterculture that Patrick believed had destroyed his daughter.[37]

Few other white ethnics might have served as symbols of the white primitive. Jews scarcely fit the criteria. If anything, they suffered from being overcivilized, as Woody Allen's many movies make clear. German ethnicity had so faded by the 1970s that it would scarcely be recognizable. Poles, Ukrainians, and other Slavic groups offered better possibilities. In fact, Michael Cimino, an Italian American director, made Slavs, not Italians, the central characters in some of his important movies: Ukrainian Americans from Pennsylvania in the Academy Award–winning *Deer Hunter* (1978) and a Pole from the outer boroughs of New York City in the *Year of the Dragon* (1985). Yet, like the Irish, the Slavic image lacked the elements necessary for the white primitive of the 1970s and 1980s. Images of Slavic Americans suggested stolid, hardworking, guileless peasants transformed into American coal miners and industrial workers. Such images lacked the passion of the Italians for either sex or violence. Slavs might make sympathetic victims. They would not make icons of primitive power.

In the two decades following the cultural upheavals of the 1960s, images of Italian Americans exploded across American movie screens. Some of the makers of these movies were Italian American, but many were not. All, Italian Americans and others, were responding to the revolutions in American life that had erupted in the 1960s, transforming conceptions of race and perceptions of authority and institutions and introducing new standards of sexual practice as well as notions of emotional and personal authenticity. Italian Americans—once demeaned in stereotypes for their overripe sexuality, emotional excess, penchant for violence, and unquestioning family loyalty—now embodied like no other group the easy sexuality, passion, toughness, and familism that Americans came to crave after the 1960s revolutions. Hence they emerged as Hollywood's favorite ethnic group and a vital part of a new American discourse or symbolic system.

Yet real Italian Americans did not embody such characteristics, certainly not in the late twentieth century, if they ever had. Real Italian Americans had entered the "twilight" of their history as a distinct ethnic people and thus a final phase in their incorporation into American society by the 1970s and 1980s, even as American movies began to celebrate the group's differences as never before.

Did this sudden explosion of images of their people in American film slow or roll back that process of incorporation? Spokesmen for Italian Americans clearly thought so, complaining loudly and virulently about movies' depictions of their people as gangsters and criminals. Suspicions that Italian Americans had a natural penchant for underworld vice did seem to create, or at least exacerbate, the problems that some Italian American politicians confronted in attempting to break into the highest circles of American politics. This was clearly true for Geraldine Ferraro, candidate for vice president in 1984 and later for senator from New York. Reporters constantly questioned her and her husband's associations with shady crime figures.[38] The charge of Mafia ties, though never made as explicitly against him as against Ferraro, seemed to haunt Mario Cuomo, longtime governor of New York. Cuomo clearly worried about how his Italian American heritage could hurt his image. There were many reasons why Cuomo ultimately decided to forego a run for the presidency, but many observers believed that his fear that the public would naturally suspect him as an Italian American of having gangster links was one of them.[39]

On the other hand, American movies after the 1960s, though often depicting Italian Americans as gangsters or crude boxers, also made them attractive as natural and familial, tough and "cool." They were so attractive that, as Mary Waters found in her studies of ethnic identification in the 1990s, Americans of mixed ancestry with some Italian blood were far more likely to identify with their Italian heritage in census surveys than with their other ancestries. Waters noted with some surprise: "Italian is a good ancestry to have, people told me, because they have good food and warm family life. This change in the social meaning of being Italian is quite dramatic, given that Italians were subject to discrimination, exclusion and extreme negative stereotyping in the early part of the twentieth century."[40] Even Cuomo seemed to benefit in many ways from the new popularity of Italian Americans in popular culture. Political observers, for example, seemed to find many of the same virtues in him that moviemakers had created in their films' Italian American characters. Reporters and pundits lauded his toughness, his passion, and his commitment to family, for example, and Cuomo himself frequently played on his Italian American heritage. Cuomo's "Italian Americanness" thus may have helped inoculate him from the derisive criticisms hurled at most Democratic liberal leaders of his era as passionless "stiffs," aloof elitists, or soft weaklings.[41] Even though he may have declined to run for president partly because of it, then, the new image of Italian Americans may have enhanced his political popularity and his political stature—in short, aided his political incorporation. And Cuomo was not the only person who seemed to take a new delight in his Italian American identity.[42]

Donald Tricario found that after movies like *Saturday Night Fever* young Italian Americans in New York's outer borough neighborhoods eagerly embraced in "Guido" images they saw on screen and began to imitate them. As part of a broad cultural and social change in the 1960s that helped undermine an old WASP ideal and celebrate white ethnic origins —the triumph, as Matthew Jacobson would say, of "Ellis Island whiteness" over "Plymouth Rock whiteness"—the celebration of Italian Americans on screen seemed to help many Italian Americans further integrate into American life without denying their cultural heritage or pride in their lineage.[43]

Whatever its effect on the social mobility, acculturation, or growing political power of real Italian Americans, the post-1960s revolution in the representation of Italian Americans on American movie screens raises some more fundamental and puzzling questions about processes of ethnic incorporation generally. Most importantly, for example, it suggests that the evolution of group images is not directly and inevitably tied to the history of the group itself. Representation of Italian Americans in the 1970s and 1980s, as noted, had little or no relation to how real Italian Americans lived in those decades. Indeed, at that point the history of images of Italian Americans and Italian American cultural and social life seemed to be moving in opposite directions: in the one, an explosion of images of distinctiveness; in the other, real social and cultural distinctiveness rapidly melting away. Though some Italian Americans thought otherwise, the explosion of Italian American images in the 1970s and 1980s was also not a deliberate effort aimed at defining their people as a threat by demeaning them and mobilizing their opponents, as the stereotyping of Italian Americans in the early decades of the twentieth century or longtime racist imaginings of African Americans or Jews had been.

Though many people made movies about Italian Americans in the post-1960s era, Italian American writers, directors, and actors themselves

—people like Francis Ford Coppola, Martin Scorsese, and Robert De Niro —played vital roles in creating some of the most important such films, and these and other films seemed to make Italian Americans more attractive to a broad American public, not less so. Indeed, it appears that the image of Italian Americans had almost become detached from the people themselves and proceeded on its own path of incorporation to its own end, becoming part of an American popular culture vocabulary of imagery that movie makers and other cultural producers could readily deploy to talk about important trends and issues in their society. Thus, after the dramatic cultural changes of the 1960s disrupted old definitions of race, sexuality, family, and gender roles, images of Italian Americans became a vital part of a national conversation about the changes that had altered American culture and society.

What the experience of Italian Americans might suggest for the future of more recent immigrants, is, of course, hard to discern. It is possible, that, as with the Italian Americans, images of new groups may persist even after real group members fully incorporate into American society and that those images may become important elements in the language Americans use to talk about critical trends and issues in their society. Asian Americans, for example, have been constructed as a model minority since the 1960s, paradoxically highlighting their very success at incorporation as ethnically distinctive. That image first emerged during the midst of African American civil rights struggle, when, Robert Lee has argued, white conservatives held up Asian Americans as models of self-reliance and achievement to counter black claims for government help in achieving equality. More recently, movies like *Harold and Kumar Go to White Castle* (2004) and *National Lampoon's Van Wilder: The Rise of Taj* (2006) seem to have adapted the Asian American model minority image to new uses, such as playing on age-old theme of adolescent rebellion against parental authority.[44]

Critical differences between the new immigrants' situation and that of Italian Americans, however, make it difficult to foresee the future of new immigrant images or how they would affect the incorporation of real Latinos or Asians into American life. First, Latinos and Asians continue to come into the country and will continue to do so for the foreseeable future, but the explosion of Italian American representation came almost half a century after Italian immigration had substantially ended. Since immigration is likely to be a contested issue for a long time and Latinos and Asians will be at the center of it, debates over immigration policy are likely to have a significant impact on the image construction of these newcomers in ways that they never did for Italian Americans in the 1970s and 1980s. What also complicates the usefulness of the Italian American experience as an analogue for new immigrants is the impossibility of foreseeing major shifts in American cultural values and attitudes. What made images of Italian American popular in the 1970s and 1980s was the cultural revolution of the previous decade, and it is hard to predict when conditions like those that rocked the nation in the 1960s might occur again and how they might reshape American attitudes and values, or what ethnic images might be deployed in new discourses prompted by such changes.

In the end, perhaps the very inability to mechanically predict such changes serves a useful purpose by reminding us that processes of incorporation are specific to each group, contingent on historical events and circumstances, always subject to change, and above all multidimensional, simultaneously occurring on several fronts—symbolic, political, and social. In other words, they are historical processes and should be understood as such.

NOTES

1. Peter Courie, *Coppola: A Biography* (New York: Da Capo Press, 1994), 79.

2. *World Almanac and Book of Facts, 1990* (New York: World Almanac, 1990), 361; *World Almanac and Book of Facts, 1994* (New York: World Almanac, 1994), 297; *World Almanac and Book of Facts, 1992* (New York: World Almanac, 1992), 308: David Ansen, "A Macho for All Seasons," *Newsweek,* May 30, 1988, 44; Wayne Walley, "Moonstruck Video Tracked," *Advertising Age,* October 17, 1988, 59.

3. Patrick McGilligan and Mark Rowland, "Can Eighty Critics Be Wrong?" *American Film* 16 (April 1991): 28–33; *World Almanac, 1994,* 357; Lawrence Cohn, "National Critics Group Favors Goodfellas," *Variety,* January 14, 1991, 14; "N.Y., L.A. Critics Go for Goodfellas," *Variety,* December 24, 1990, 3.

4. *My Cousin Vinny* placed a respectable twenty-eighth among money makers in 1992; *World Almanac, 1994,* 297.

5. *World Almanac, 1994,* 357; Richard Alba, *Italian Americans: Into the Twilight of Ethnicity* (Englewood Cliffs, NJ: Prentice Hall, 1985), 84–86, 99–101; Humbert Nelli, *From Immigrants to Ethnics: The Italian Americans* (New York: Oxford University Press, 1983), 162–66, 186–88; Lee Lourdeaux, *Italian and Irish Filmmakers in America: Ford, Capra, Coppola and Scorsese* (Philadelphia: Temple University Press, 1990), 65–86; Daniel Sembroff Golden, "The Fate of La Famiglia: Italian Images in American Film," in *The Kaleidoscopic Lens: How Hollywood Views Ethnic Groups,* ed. Randall Miller (Englewood Cliffs, NJ: Jerome Ozer, 1980), 72–97; Ian

C. Jarvie, "Stars and Ethnicity: Hollywood and the United States, 1932–1951," in *Unspeakable Images: Ethnicity and the American Cinema,* ed. Lester Friedman (Urbana: University of Illinois Press, 1991), 82–111; Stuart Kaminsky, *American Film Genres* (Chicago: Nelson Hall, 1985), 32.

6. Alba, *Italian Americans,* 132–58, 146. On the slow decline of the Mafia, see Peter Reuter, "The Decline of the American Mafia," *Public Interest,* no. 120 (Summer 1995), 89–100; Mark Bernstein, "Lamefellas," *New Republic,* August 4, 1997, 9–10.

7. Based on last names and biographical information and drawn from the Web site of the Academy of Motion Picture Arts and Sciences: www.oscars.org/.

8. Courie, *Coppola,* 15–24; Andy Dougan, *Untouchable: A Biography of Robert De Niro* (New York: Thundermouth Press, 1996), 13–19; Mary Katherine Connelly, *Martin Scorsese: An Analysis of His Films with a Filmography of His Entire Directorial Career* (North Carolina: McFarland Press, 1998), ix–x; Peter Brindle, ed., *Martin Scorsese: Interviews* (Jackson: University of Mississippi Press, 1998), 37–51.

9. In 2000, the U.S. Census counted 8,977,444 people claiming Polish ancestry and 15,723,555 claiming Italian ancestry. U.S. Census Bureau, "American Factfinder: 2000 US Census: QT-P13 Ancestry: 2000.," http://factfinder.census.gov/servlet/QT-Table?_bm=y&-geo_id=01000US&-qr_name=DEC_2000_SF3_U_QTP13&-ds_name=DEC_2000_SF3_U&-_lang=en&-_sse=on. It is difficult to estimate Polish immigration, since Poland was divided among Russia, Germany, and Austria Hungary through the First World War. Roger Daniels estimates that about 45 percent of Polish immigrants came from Russia, 35 percent from Austria Hungary, and 20 percent from Germany. There is also the difficulty of distinguishing Polish Jews and Polish Catholics. Nonetheless, Victor Greene estimates that about 2.5 million Poles emigrated to America between 1850 and 1918, compared to the approximately 4.2 million Italians who came to America between 1850 and 1920. Victor Greene, "Poles," and Humberto Nelli, "Italians," both in *Harvard Encyclopedia of American Ethnic Groups,* ed. Stephan Thernstrom (Cambridge, MA: Harvard University Press, 1980), 792 and 547 respectively; Roger Daniels, *Coming to America: A History of Immigration and Ethnicity in American Life* (New York: HarperPerennial, 1991), 215; Patricia Erens, *The Jews in American Cinema* (Bloomington: Indiana University Press, 1984), 256; Lester Friedman, *Hollywood's Image of the Jew* (New York: Frederick Ungar, 1982), 61–64; Robert Sklar, *Movie Made America: A Cultural History of American Movies* (New York: Random House, 1994), 161–246; Gary Gerstle, *American Crucible: Race and Nation in the Twentieth Century* (Princeton: Princeton University Press, 2001), 165–77; Neal Gabler, *An Empire of Their Own: How the Jews Invented Hollywood* (New York: Doubleday, 1988), 79–150.

10. Anthony De Curtis, "The Rolling Stone Interview: Martin Scorsese," *Rolling Stone,* November 1990, 59; Gavin Smith, "Martin Scorsese," *Film Comment* 26 (September 1990): 27–30.

11. Stanley Kauffmann, "Stanley Kauffmann on Films: Look Back in Anger," *New Republic,* December 6, 1980, 26; Richard Schickel, "Contender," *Time,* November 15, 1976, 99; "Italian Stallion," *Time,* October 17, 1976, 101; "The Godfather: Triumph for Brando," *Newsweek,* March 13, 1972, 56; "The Godsons," *Time,* April 3, 1972, 70; Some qualifications may be useful at the outset. First, and hopefully obviously, there is no suggestion here that Italian Americans really are white primitives —merely that they are represented as such in American popular culture. The representation of Italian Americans as white primitives in movies or other forms of popular culture is not the essential or only meaning of those films. They can and do have many meanings. The argument here is simply that some elements of Italian American white primitivism figure in their public representation and have something to do with their popularity.

12. Richard Corliss, "Animal House," *Time* November 24, 1980, 100; Robert Hatch, "Films," *Nation,* December 13, 1980, 652; Ralph Novak, "Picks and Pans: Screen," *People Weekly,* October 1, 1990, 15; Richard Corliss, "Married to the Mob," *Time,* September 24, 1990, 84.

13. "The Godfather Triumph for Brando"; "The Making of the Godfather," *Time,* March 13, 1972, 61; Amy Taubin, "Blood and Pasta," *New Statesman and Society,* November 9, 1990, 12; Kauffman, "Blood Money," *New Republic,* 28; Jay Cocks, "What Is the Godfather Saying?" *Time,* March 13, 1972, 58.

14. Timothy J. Meagher, "Racial and Ethnic Relations in America, 1965–2000," in *Race and Ethnicity in America: A Concise History,* ed. Ronald Bayor (New York: Columbia University Press, 2003); Manning Marable, *Race, Reform and Rebellion: The Second Reconstruction in Black America, 1945–1982* (Jackson; University of Mississippi Press, 1984); Tamar Jacoby, *Someone Else's House: America's Unfinished Struggle for Integration* (New York: Basic Books, 1998); Joshua Fishman et al., *The Rise and Fall of the Ethnic Revival: Perspectives on Language and Ethnicity* (New York: Mouton, 1985).

15. Morris Dickstein, *Gates of Eden: American Culture in the Sixties* (Cambridge, MA: Harvard University Press, 1997), 51–88; Maurice Isserman and Michael Kazin, *America Divided: The Civil War of the 1960s* (New York: Oxford University Press, 2000), 95–97, 147–86, 205–20; William O'Neill, *Coming Apart: An Informal History of America in the 1960s* (Chicago: Quadrangle Books, 1980), 200–227, 360–95; E. J. Dionne, *Why Americans Hate Politics* (New York: Touchstone, 1991), 214–24, 89–94.

16. Peter Biskind, *Easy Riders, Raging Bulls: How the Sex, Drugs and Rock and Roll Generation Saved Hollywood* (New York: Touchstone, 1998), 13–80.

17. Corliss, "Married to the Mob," 83; Carrie Fisher, "True Confessions: The *Rolling Stone* Interview with Madonna," *Rolling Stone,* June 3, 1991, 46. Questions of Italian "whiteness" or "nonwhiteness" have recently aroused substantial scholarly interest. See Jennifer Guglielmo and Salvatore Salerno, *Are Italians White?*

How Race Is Made in America (New York: Routledge, 2003); James R. Barrett and David Roediger, "Inbetween Peoples: Race, Nationality and the 'New Immigrant' Working Class," *Journal of American Ethnic History* 16, no. 3 (1997): 3–44.

18. Judy Klemesrud, " 'Rocky Isn't Based on Me,' Says Stallone, 'But We Both Went the Distance,' " *New York Times,* November 28, 1976, 111.

19. Daniel Leab, "The Blue Collar Ethnic in Bicentennial America: Rocky," in *American History/American Film: Interpreting the Hollywood Image,* ed. John O'Connor and Martin Jackson (New York: Frederick Ungar, 1970), 267.

20. Pauline Kael, "The Current Cinema," *New Yorker,* May 31, 1982, 84, 85.

21. Gregory Waller, "Rambo: Getting It Right This Time," in *From Hanoi to Hollywood: The Vietnam War in American Film,* ed. Linda Ditmar and Gene Michaud (New Brunswick: Rutgers University Press, 1990), 119; *City Paper,* November 18, 1988; Klemesrud, "Rocky."

22. George Lipsitz, *Time Passages: Collective Memory and American Popular Culture* (Minneapolis: University of Minnesota Press, 1990), 40; Judith Smith, *Visions of Beloved: Family Stories and Postwar Democracy, 1940–1960* (New York: Columbia University Press, 2004), 278–79.

23. Janet Maslin, "Knockout," *New York Times,* November 28, 1976.

24. Janet Maslin, "Screen: The Prince of Bay Ridge," *New York Times,* December 16, 1977, 82; Frank Rich, "Discomania," *Time,* December 19, 1977, 69.

25. This scene was cited by many critics as the most important scene in the movie and is credited by some with winning Dukakis her Oscar. See, for example, John Simon, "Long Faces," *National Review,* March 4, 1988, 54; Peter Travers, "Picks and Pans: Screen," *People Weekly,* January 18, 1988, 8.

26. "Dialogue on Film; John Patrick Shanley," *American Film* 14 (September 1989): 22.

27. Wolf Schneider, "Blood Ties; Blood Shed," *American Film* 15 (December 1990): 4; Simon, "Mob and the Family," 64; Gavin Smith, "Martin Scorsese," *Film Comment* 26 (September 1990), 27; David Denby, "Meaner Streets," *New York,* January 24, 1990, 78; Kathleen Murphy, "Made Men," *Film Comment* 26 (September 1990): 25.

28. Lourdeaux, *Italian and Irish Filmmakers,* 186; Gene Philips and Rodney Hall, eds., *Francis Ford Coppola: Interviews* (Jackson: University of Mississippi Press, 2004), 27; Chris Messenger, *The Godfather: How the Corleones Became Our Gang* (Albany: SUNY Press, 2002), 202.

29. Denby, "Meaner Streets," 78.

30. Peter Maas, *The Valachi Papers* (New York: Bantam Books, 1969), "Mafia: The Inside Story," *Saturday Evening Post,* August 10, 1963, 19–25, and "The Killer Who Told on the Mob," *Saturday Evening Post,* November 23, 1963, 21–23.

31. Carlos Cortés, "Italian Americans in Film: From Immigrants to Icons," *Melus* 14 (Fall–Winter 1987): 92. Italian emotionalism and violence, of course, were even more evident in such films as *Little Caesar* (1930) and *Scarface* (1932),

but passion was also a hallmark of Italian Americans in such films as *They Knew What They Wanted* (1940), about a grape grower.

32. Leslie Halliwell, *Halliwell's Filmgoers Guide* (New York: Hill and Wang, 1977), 97. In Charles Van Doren, ed., *Webster's American Biographies* (Springfield, MA: G. C. Merriam, 1974), 131, Brando is described as an actor who "received widespread popular and critical acclaim for his powerful portrayal of the primitive, brutal but, nonetheless vulnerably human."

33. Brian D. Johnson, "Reign of Terror: Gangster Movies Battle It Out at the Cinema," *McLeans,* October 1, 1990, 55; Corliss, "Married to the Mob," 83.

34. Lourdeaux, *Italian and Irish Filmmakers,* 55, 64; Joseph Curran, *Hibernian Green and the Silver Screen: The Irish and American Movies* (Westport, CT: Greenwood Press, 1989), 106–8, 121.

35. Tom Wolfe, *Bonfire of the Vanities* (New York: Farrar, Straus and Giroux, 1987).

36. Hasia Diner, *Hungering for America: Italian, Irish, and Jewish Foodways in the Age of Migration* (Cambridge, MA: Harvard University Press, 2001).

37. Curran, *Hibernian Green,* 121.

38. Wayne Barrett, "Ethics and Ethnics," *Village Voice,* September 8, 1992, 11; Wayne Barrett and William Bastone, "Gerry and the Mob," *Village Voice,* August 25, 1992, 11; Denise Kelp, "A 'Bold Stroke': Ferraro as VP Pick," *Off Our Backs,* September 30, 1984, 7.

39. "In 1985 he blurted out angrily to a startled group of reporters: 'You're telling me that the Mafia is an organization and I'm telling you that's a lot of baloney.'" Sidney Blumenthal, "The Coward," *New Republic,* March 16, 1992, 12, and "Cuomo Vadis," *New Republic,* May 6, 1991, 23.

40. Mary Waters, "Optional Ethnicities: For Whites Only?" in *Origins and Destinies: Immigration, Race, and Ethnicity in America,* ed. Silvia Pedraza and Ruben G. Rumbaut (Belmont, CA: Wadsworth, 1996), 449.

41. Blumenthal, "Cuomo Vadis," 24; "Unsupermario," *New Republic,* January 20, 1992, 7; Calvin Trillin, "After Seeing Mario Cuomo Interviewed on Television," *Nation,* December 23, 1991, 13; John Leo, "Mario's Passionate Monologue," *U.S. News and World Report,* November 25, 1991, 19.

42. Blumenthal, "Cuomo Vadis," 24; Donald Baer, "The Urban Log Cabin Legend," *U.S. News and World Report,* November 12, 1990, 41.

43. Matthew Frye Jacobson, *Roots Too: White Ethnic Revival in a Post–Civil Rights America* (Cambridge, MA: Harvard University Press, 2006), 59–70.

44. Robert G. Lee, *Orientals: Asian Americans in Popular Culture* (Philadelphia: Temple University Press, 1999), 145–46.

Part III

Contemporary Immigration and Incorporation

Chapter 9

The Immigrant as Threat to American Security

A Historical Perspective

Gary Gerstle

For most of its history, America has been remarkably open to immigrants from most parts of the world. So many have come—more than fifty million in the last 120 years alone—that the very history of America is incomprehensible apart from a consideration of who these immigrants were and what manner of life they made in their new home. Oscar Handlin, a pioneer in the field of immigration history, captured this truth in his Pulitzer Prize–winning book, *The Uprooted: The Epic Story of the Great Migrations That Made the American People.* "Once I thought to write a history of the immigrants in America," he wrote in 1951. "Then I discovered that the immigrants were American history."[1] From the seventeenth-century Pilgrims to the nineteenth-century Germans to the late-twentieth-century Cubans, immigrants and their children have left their mark on virtually every period and aspect of American history: as workers and revolutionaries, entrepreneurs and inventors, scholars and artists, entertainers and politicians, journalists and reformers. Americans have lavished praise on many individual immigrants and their offspring, including the Puritan John Winthrop, the farmer Hector St. John Crèvecoeur, the industrialist Andrew Carnegie, the reformer Lillian Wald, the filmmaker Frank Capra, the labor leaders Walther Reuther and Cesar Chavez, and Chief of Staff and Secretary of State Colin Powell.[2]

But Americans, at a variety of moments, have also feared immigrants and lashed out at specific groups of newcomers who were thought to imperil the nation's present or future. Those singled out for attack have included the Irish and Chinese in the nineteenth century, Germans in World

War I, foreign-born radicals and the groups allegedly nourishing them (Jews and Italians) in the 1920s, Mexicans in the 1930s, and Japanese in World War II. Extensive literatures exist on each of these episodes of anti-immigrant agitation, but few attempts have been made, especially in the last twenty years, to compare these episodes with each other and to understand their similarities and differences.[3] Little effort has been made as well to explain how, when, and why mild or inchoate anti-immigrant sentiments, which are almost always present, metamorphose into coherent and powerful crusades that seek to deprive immigrants of their civil liberties, personal safety, and sometimes even the right to live in America.[4] Undertaking this kind of inquiry seems especially important in light of September 11, 2001, and the ongoing fear that current immigrant populations are harboring or supporting terrorists intent on striking against the American people, their leaders, and their institutions. What can history tell us about how Americans of past generations identified subversiveness among immigrants, the legitimacy of such accusations, and the consequences of policies adopted to counter the threats that immigrants were thought to pose? Can previous responses to fears of immigrant subversion illuminate how we will, or should, respond today? This essay will attempt to answer these and related questions.

The essay has three parts. The first attempts to group into four general categories immigrant behaviors and identities that historically Americans have labeled subversive. The second examines several situations in which Americans became obsessed with particular groups of immigrants and took action. And the third attempts to situate the current fear about the threat that immigrants pose into the previously developed historical context.

Threats of Immigrant Subversion: A Typology

While a cumulative list of the specific ways in which immigrants "threatened" America in the past would occupy many pages, it is possible to identify in only a few pages four generic kinds of "subversive" behavior and identities that immigrants were commonly accused of embodying: religious, political, economic, and racial. This typological exercise requires us first to understand not what kind of threat immigrants really posed but how the "protectors" of America constructed that threat in their own minds. It requires us, in other words, to see the immigrants as those whom

historians have labeled "nativists" saw them. Nativists are those who believe that America belongs to its native population (usually meaning its
white, native population) and that the country's welfare is threatened by
the presence, beliefs, and actions of the foreign born. In some cases, it will
be obvious that what past generations of nativists considered threatening
and subversive was nothing of the sort; in other cases, we will have to un-
dertake careful analysis to disentangle the real from the perceived threat.

Fear of Religious Subversion

At its origins, and for much of its history, the United States wanted
to be a Protestant country. That did not mean only that Protestants of all
varieties would be able to worship free of interference from the state (or
some state-endorsed religious establishment). It meant as well that the
country should do everything in its power to create a society in which Catholicism, and more specifically, papal influence, would have no purchase.
This fear of Rome is difficult for twenty-first-century Americans to understand because it is no longer a motive force in our politics or immigration
policy. But for most of our history the Catholic Church's theology, liturgy,
and rituals, its life-and-death struggle with European Protestants, its sheer
international size and power, and the control that it was thought to exercise over rank-and-file Catholics alarmed American Protestants. Catholicism was depicted not only as the enemy of God but as the enemy of republicanism. To Protestant Americans, the church stood for monarchy,
aristocracy, and other reactionary forces from which America was seeking to escape. Where the pope "ruled," Protestants charged, "the people"
most certainly did not. Thus Catholic influence had to be resisted, even
eradicated.[5]

The Catholic group in America that bore the brunt of American Protestant fury were the Irish, who, when they arrived in the 1830s and 1840s,
constituted the first mass immigration of Catholics to America. Fleeing
an Ireland devastated by colonial rule and famine, these Irish immigrants
were largely destitute; they had few skills, little access to good jobs, and not
much familiarity with urban living. Many native Protestants viewed them
as an urban underclass, cut off from "American" values and traditions,
their assimilation to their new land blocked by what these Protestants
took to be a fanatical and unholy devotion to the Catholic Church. America's first mass nativist movement, the Know-Nothings, arose in the 1840s
and 1850s in reaction to the "Irish peril." The Know-Nothings stirred up

anti-Irish sentiment and sparked vigilante attacks by Protestant gangs on Irish neighborhoods, Catholic schools, and even, in some cases, Catholic churches themselves. In their more "respectable" moments, the Know-Nothings organized politically to end Irish immigration, to remove the children of Irish Catholic immigrants from parochial schools so that they could be educated in a proper Protestant environment, and to bar immigrants from holding public office and, in some cases, from voting.[6]

The politics of sectionalism and the impending Civil War sent the Know-Nothings into eclipse and also provided opportunities for Irish immigrants to demonstrate their loyalty to the Union, to rise in the social order, and to gain more respectability for their Catholic ways. But even so, the religiously motivated discrimination that Irish Catholics had experienced in the antebellum era persisted for another hundred years. As late as 1928, the Republicans defeated the Democratic, Irish Catholic nominee for president, Al Smith, by arousing anxiety about the threat that a Catholic president would pose to the United States. And even in 1960, another Democratic hopeful and Irish Catholic, John F. Kennedy, had to appear before a group of Protestant ministers in Houston to prove to their satisfaction that his election would not make the Vatican the ruler of Washington.[7]

It is easy for us to critique our forebears for their small-minded and intolerant hostility to Catholicism. But before we congratulate ourselves on our current broad-mindedness, we should note that we are once again living in an intensely religious age more akin to the nineteenth century than to the twentieth and that, in this current age, many Americans are once again talking about the threat that a "foreign" religion, in this case Islam, poses to American values, traditions, and security. Thus the early history of Irish Catholics in America may have more relevance than we might at first have imagined to current problems, particularly in terms of how American society as a whole is reacting and will react to the presence of eight million Muslims in its midst.

Fear of Political Subversion

The second kind of threat that immigrants were thought to pose was political. If America wanted to be a Protestant country, it also wanted to be a republic, one in which the people ruled. A republic had to guarantee not only popular sovereignty but also political and economic liberty for its citizens. In the late eighteenth and early nineteenth centuries, America was virtually unique among the nations of the world in its republicanism, and its creators feared that this system of politics would not last long, giving way to monarchy, aristocracy, or democracy, then pejoratively equated with mob rule. Republicanism, it was believed, depended on citizens who were fierce in defense of their independence and liberty and abundantly endowed with virtue. Citizens had to resist the temptations of excessive wealth and power. Those Americans who saw themselves as the guardians of their country's republican inheritance kept a close eye on immigrants who, especially in the nineteenth century, might not comprehend republicanism's value or fragility. In this respect, the antebellum fear of Irish Catholics was not just religiously grounded but politically grounded as well: Could these immigrants, who owed so deep an allegiance to Rome, be counted on to embrace and defend American republican and libertarian principles? Would not their subservience to the monarchical pope incline them to favor authoritarian forms of secular rule in America?[8]

By the late nineteenth and early twentieth centuries, the threat to American republicanism was thought to emanate as much from the revolutionary Left, comprising the followers of Marx, Proudhon, Bakunin, and Lenin, as from the Catholic Right. Significant numbers of these leftists had come to the United States as immigrants: from France, Germany, Finland, Russia, the Balkans, Italy, Mexico, Cuba, and elsewhere. Many participated in continent-spanning international networks; some, such as those of the anarchists, were similar to Al-Qaeda in their decentralized character and in their refusal to put allegiance to any nation ahead of their loyalty to their revolutionary cause. Many also were contemptuous of American political principles and the state that embodied them. A few were saboteurs and terrorists. They contributed to the roiling class conflicts of the industrial era and aroused fears that America, as a result of their agency, would soon be gripped by proletarian revolution. To many Americans, such a revolution incarnated the threat that republicans had discerned in democracy in the eighteenth century—mob rule, violence, contempt for individual liberties and private property. Should it occur in the United States, American republicanism would be subverted in the most profound sense, a denouement that helps to explain both the extraordinary hostility of so many Americans to anarchism, socialism, and communism and the large-scale violations of civil liberties that would be justified on the grounds of the need to eliminate those revolutionary movements from American soil.[9]

Sometimes the charge that immigrants posed a political threat was leveled at entire populations of immigrants and not just at the comparatively small groups of agitators who resided within them. This happened in the

1920s, when many native-born Americans argued that Jewish and Italian immigration to America had to be stopped altogether because the communities they formed here bred Bolsheviks and anarchists. It also happened in World War I and World War II, when all immigrants who had come from an enemy's land—Germany in the first instance, Japan in the second—were tarred with the charge of disloyalty. An immigrant group would not always be stigmatized in this way—it happened to Germans in World War I but not in World War II—making it necessary for us to explain the circumstances in which this kind of charge took hold (a topic that will be taken up in a subsequent section of this essay).

Fear of Economic Subversion

The third kind of threat that immigrants were thought to pose was economic. Most immigrants came to America to work. The heaviest immigrations occurred during economic upturns, when labor demands were acute. But immigrant flows could never be perfectly synchronized with the business cycle. It took time for news of economic downturns to reach foreign shores. And even those immigrants who came during boom years might experience a depression a year or two after they arrived, their presence then swelling a labor surplus and no longer filling a labor need. The scarcity of jobs during downturns meant rising unemployment, falling wages, and the inability of wage earners to support their families. It is hardly surprising that, in such circumstances, native-born Americans often accused immigrants of causing unemployment and depressing wages and called on their labor leaders and political representatives to curtail further immigration. Virtually every immigrant group that has come to America has been, at one time or another, the target of these accusations and demands: the Irish in the 1840s and 1850s, the Chinese in the 1870s and 1880s, the "New Immigrants" from eastern and southern Europe in the early decades of the twentieth century, and the Mexicans in the 1930s and 1990s and 2000s.[10]

Fear of Racial Subversion

The fourth kind of threat that immigrants were thought to pose was racial: the belief that some immigrants belonged to racially inferior groups unsuitable for American life. Racism, of course, was a defining feature of the American republic from the moment of its creation and remained so for 150 years. Though the Constitution outlawed slavery in 1865, its Supreme Court interpreters failed to put it squarely on the side of racial equality until the 1950s and 1960s. In 1790, the first Congress passed a law stipulating that to be eligible for naturalization an immigrant had to be both free and white. In 1870, Congress amended this law to permit the naturalization of black immigrants, but the law continued to bar the naturalization of East and South Asian immigrants until it was progressively repealed between 1943 and 1952. From the earliest days of the Republic, many Americans justified their hostility toward immigrants by arguing that certain groups simply did not—and would never—possess the intelligence, character, independence, and regard for republicanism that the country demanded of its citizens. By the 1840s and 1850s groups such as the Irish and the Mexicans (whom the United States was fighting in Texas) were being compared unfavorably to the racially superior "Anglo-Saxons," who had allegedly first brought liberty to England in the Middle Ages and then brought even greater liberty to America in the seventeenth and eighteenth centuries.[11]

Nineteenth-century romantic nationalists in England and America invented these Anglo-Saxons as part of their effort to locate the greatness of their nations in the special genius of a people who were thought to form both nations' core. These early romantic nationalists had not yet fully developed the racial implications of their Anglo-Saxonism; that task would be left to their Social Darwinist successors of the late nineteenth century. By that time, the shapers of both educated and popular opinion were attempting to measure the "racial character" of each of the world's peoples and to arrange these peoples in a hierarchy of racial aptitude. Intelligence, honor, virtue, sobriety, and capacity for self-government became traits that were thought to inhere in some groups more than others. Those groups that possessed these traits in abundance—invariably western and northern Europeans who were labeled Anglo-Saxon, Nordic, or Caucasian —ended up on top of racial hierarchies, and those groups thought to lack them—principally blacks, "Orientals," and "brown" peoples such as Indians and Mexicans—ended up on bottom. Diverse groups emanating from eastern and southern Europe—Italians, Poles, Jews, Greeks, and so on— were precariously poised on the middle rungs of these hierarchies, higher than blacks, Asians, and Indians but lower than the Anglo Saxons, whose status, more often than not, was judged to be out of reach. Even the Irish came in for some racial drubbing, especially in popular cartoons that depicted the Irish as gorillas or as black.[12]

In this climate, immigration restrictionists and eugenicists began arguing that it was the obligation of the United States to maximize the number
of racially superior immigrants and to minimize the number of racially
inferior ones. Without that kind of policy, America as a land of liberty,
popular sovereignty, and economic strength would cease to exist. This racially motivated restriction campaign emerged in the 1880s when Congress
passed the Chinese Exclusion Act, the first of a series of laws that barred
most Chinese from immigrating to the United States for a period of sixty
years. It continued in 1907–8 with the Gentlemen's Agreement with Japan,
which ended mass Japanese immigration to the United States, and it cli-
maxed in 1924 when, in addition to all East and South Asians, most people
from eastern and southern Europe, the Near East, and Africa were barred
from entering America. Racism defined American immigration policy, a
phenomenon that would not end until the 1960s.

Threats of Immigrant Subversion: Cases

Occasionally, any one of the four kinds of subversive behavior that immigrants were accused of embodying—religious, political, economic, and
racial—could generate an anti-immigrant crusade on its own. But more
commonly the greatest obsessions with the threats posed by immigrants
and the most sustained movements against them occurred in instances
where two or more kinds of subversive behavior were believed to be reinforcing each other. Thus the Know-Nothings, who conducted the most determined campaign against the Irish, charged these immigrants with religious *and* political subversion. The campaign against Chinese immigrants
arose in the West not just because Chinese workers were thought to be
competing with American workers but also because the Chinese were alleged to be racially incapable of striving for decent standards of work and
pay.[13] The indiscriminate attacks on German Americans in World War I
for their alleged political subversiveness depended on the transformation
of the once-honored German immigrant into the racially feared "Hun."
And the draconian campaigns against eastern and southern Europeans after World War I and against Japanese immigrants and their offspring in
World War II rested on the charge that their disloyalty was grounded in a
racial character that chronically predisposed these groups to subversion.
The greatest civil libertarian peril we face today, in handling the terrorist
threat, is probably a similar kind of merger of different kinds of subversive

charges in which the protectors of America construe the threat as residing not simply in terrorist bands that want to destroy America but in Arab or Muslim peoples whose racial or religious character is thought to be antithetical to American cultural values and political principles.

To illuminate these points further, I will discuss three different cases of alleged immigrant subversion and responses to them: the Germans in World War I; eastern and southern Europeans during the Red Scare after World War I; and the Japanese in World War II. Each of these cases of alleged subversion occurred in war or near-war situations; considered together, they offer the best historical framework within which to understand the current "War on Terror."

Germans in World War I

The Germans form one of the most interesting historical cases of immigrants charged with subversion because of their high status prior to the First World War. In the late nineteenth and early twentieth centuries, they ranked among the most economically successful of immigrants. They developed a reputation for cultural accomplishment, founding centers for learning and the arts in their communities. Their ethnic communities also drew praise for the family-oriented and wholesome character of their popular culture. German immigrants did not, of course, escape all suspicion. A substantial minority were Catholics, who experienced the general anti-Catholic prejudices of the time. A significant number were socialists who, for a time, dominated radical political organization in the United States. Germans also tended to be avowedly pluralist in their cultural politics, proclaiming that they would cultivate their German language and traditions, newspapers and schools, in the United States. This proud and public display of Germanness generated an undercurrent of anxiety among many native-born Americans who expected all immigrants not to hold themselves apart but to shed their "Old World" habits and to embrace American culture completely.[14]

To mobilize a fractious American population for war in 1916 and 1917, Woodrow Wilson's administration first exhorted Americans to rally around the country's ideals of freedom, democracy, and self-determination and to view the war as a crusade to bring these beliefs to the peoples of Europe. But when that effort failed to produce the requisite social harmony and war enthusiasm, the government's campaign for unity turned harsh, now intent on punishing those who were slow to demonstrate their allegiance and loyalty. In the most far-reaching federal restriction on free speech enacted since 1798, Congress passed the Espionage and Sedition Acts in 1917 and 1918, empowering the government to prosecute aliens and citizens for writing or uttering any statement that could be construed by government attorneys as profaning the flag, the Constitution, or the military.[15]

The Germans were especially vulnerable to this government loyalty campaign. On the eve of war, they still constituted the largest immigrant group in America—four million strong. If one were to add to that total the number of immigrants who had come from some part of the Austro-Hungarian Empire—Germany's ally—that figure doubled to eight million. Any government would have been worried about those numbers; even if the number of loyalists to the Kaiser or the Austrian emperor among those eight millions was infinitesimally small, they could still have formed a subversive force large enough to harm American security.[16] The government might have made every effort to limit its security campaign to those Germans who could be identified as truly subversive. That would have meant exposing and arresting actual agents of the German government and putting under careful surveillance those who were outspoken in their support of German war aims and the Kaiser. It would have meant, additionally, resisting the temptation to arrest or punish those German immigrants who were simply fond of their Old World culture or who opposed America's entry into war because they believed that a victory by either side would bring no benefit to the working man or woman. And it would have meant refusing to ostracize individuals whose only subversive act was the possession of German ancestry.

Instead of making such distinctions, the government began to regard (and racialize) all Germans as "Huns." This epithet tied modern-day Germans to the barbaric tribes who had emerged from Europe's forests a millennium and a half earlier to devastate European civilization and plunge the continent into the Dark Ages. The latter-day Huns, like their forebears, were depicted as brutish and apelike men who did not understand the meaning of compassion, mercy, restraint, or democracy. The Committee on Public Information, the American government agency charged with arousing popular support for the war, spread images of the "German as beast" in posters it plastered everywhere. It tied the German army's atrocities against the Belgian people to the subhuman character of the German people. It encouraged the public to see anti-German movies, such as *The Prussian Cur* and *The Beast of Berlin*.[17]

Unleashing an anti-German hysteria justified the government's campaign to arrest thousands of German and Austrian immigrants whom it suspected of subversion. Congress, meanwhile, passed the Trading with the Enemy Act, which required German-language publications (as well as other foreign-language publications) to submit all war-related stories to post office censors for approval. It also passed the Volstead Act, prohibiting the manufacture and distribution of alcohol, at least in part because of the belief that the German American brewers who controlled substantial sectors of the beer industry would ply loyal Americans with alcohol and thus weaken their will to fight.

At the popular level, and at the level of state and local governments, German Americans became the objects of popular hatred. Boston's city government banned performances of Beethoven's symphonies, and the German-born conductor of the Boston Symphony Orchestra was forced to resign. Although Americans would not give up the German foods they had grown to love, they would no longer call them by their German names. Sauerkraut was rechristened "liberty cabbage," hamburgers became "liberty sandwiches." Libraries removed works of German literature from their shelves, and politicians urged school districts to prohibit the teaching of the German language. Patriotic school boards in Lima, Ohio, and elsewhere actually burned German-language books in their districts.

German Americans risked being fired from work, losing their businesses, and being assaulted on the street. Even before Prohibition went into effect, German American brewers found it difficult to sell their beer and thus to keep their enterprises afloat. A St. Louis mob lynched an innocent German immigrant whom they suspected of subversion. After only twenty-five minutes of deliberation, a St. Louis jury acquitted the mob leaders, who had brazenly defended their crime as an act of patriotism.

These sorts of experiences devastated the once-proud German American community. Its members began hiding their ethnic identity, changing their names, speaking German only in the privacy of their own homes, and celebrating their holidays out of the public view. While the physical assaults on individual Germans, the violation of their civil liberties, and the racialization of Germans as Huns stopped soon after the Armistice was signed in November 1918, many German Americans would take far longer to recover from the shame and vulnerability they had experienced in 1917 and 1918. Many would never again celebrate their Germanness in public; quite a few abandoned their heritage entirely, choosing to assimilate into a white Protestant culture or, if they were Catholic, into an Irish American culture. It can be argued that this assimilatory process would have happened anyway, as second- and third-generation German Americans succeeded the immigrants in their communities and saw less reason to maintain Old World language and culture. But had not the war intervened, this process would have unfolded more slowly and unevenly than it did.[18] So thoroughly did Germans assimilate that twenty-five years after World War I ended, important Americans, such as Dwight D. Eisenhower and Walter Reuther, would not be known or thought about as German Americans. They were simply, and 100 percent, American.

It is a measure of the assimilative capacities of American society that members of a group who had been so despised in the 1910s could reach the highest levels of government and labor movement power only a generation later. The fear of Germans subsided so completely that already by 1924, when the United States was putting its immigration restriction system into place, the government gave Germany one of its largest and most coveted quotas. The quickness of this about-face only served to underscore how bizarre and shameful the indiscriminate assaults on the German American population in World War I had been.

The Red Scare and Immigration Restriction, 1919–24

The patriotic emotions whipped up by the government and private patriotic groups during World War I carried over into the postwar period, now focusing primarily on political radicals as the chief threat to American security. Suspicion of political radicals had emerged during the war itself, especially once the principal radical organizations, the Socialist Party and the Industrial Workers of the World, declared themselves to be opponents of the war. This suspicion grew when the Bolsheviks took power in St. Petersburg in November 1917, withdrew Russia from the war, and called on workers everywhere, including those in the United States, to fight capitalist power rather than the armies of the Triple Alliance. The Bolshevik Revolution stirred considerable interest in the United States, not only among radicals, about two-thirds of whom would soon leave the Socialist Party to form two Communist parties, but also among hundreds of thousands of American workers, many of whom had immigrated from Russia or countries proximate to Russia in eastern Europe. Most of these immigrants never became socialists or communists, but they were stirred by the dream, embodied by the Bolshevik Revolution, that workers could successfully revolt against their capitalist masters and thus transform the conditions of their labor.

Labor militancy among American workers had risen during the war itself and intensified once the war ended. In January 1919 a general strike paralyzed the city of Seattle when 60,000 workers walked off their jobs. By August, walkouts had been staged by 400,000 coal miners, 120,000 textile workers, 50,000 garment workers, and 300,000 steel workers. Altogether, four million workers—one-fifth of the nation's manufacturing workforce —went on strike in 1919. This reality of massive labor unrest, combined with the fear that this unrest would enable Bolshevik sympathizers to stage a revolution in the United States, forms the essential background to the Red Scare of 1919.[19]

The trigger for the Red Scare occurred on April 28 and 29, 1919, when mail bombs arrived at the office of Mayor Ole Hanson in Seattle and the home of former U.S. Senator Thomas W. Hardwick in Atlanta. The bomb meant for Hanson did not explode, but the one for Hardwick did, blowing off the hands of the maid who opened the bomb package and seriously burning Hardwick's wife. On April 30, a clerk in the New York City Parcel Post Division discovered sixteen more bombs that had been set aside in his office because they contained insufficient postage. Another eighteen bombs already traveling through the mail were then intercepted before they could reach their recipients. Altogether thirty-six mail bombs were identified, targeted either at capitalists, such as John D. Rockefeller and J. P. Morgan, or at government officials who had been deemed "class enemies." Nor was this episode the last to involve explosives: on June 2, 1919, bombs exploded within the same hour at the homes of manufacturers and government officials in eight different cities on the East Coast.

One of these June 2 bombs was meant to destroy Attorney General A. Mitchell Palmer's home in Washington, D.C., but the device exploded prematurely, blowing up the bomb thrower on the steps leading up to Palmer's abode. Enough of the man's body was recovered to identify him as an Italian immigrant from Philadelphia. That he was an anarchist seemed confirmed by an anarchist pamphlet found near the door to Palmer's house. It contained these words: "There will have to be bloodshed; we will not dodge; there will have to be murder; we will kill . . . there will have to be destruction; we will destroy. . . . We are ready to do anything and everything to suppress the capitalist class. . . . The ANARCHIST FIGHTERS."[20]

Radicals charged that the June 2 bombings had been executed and the pamphlet planted by those who wanted to discredit the Left and whip the American people into an anti-radical frenzy. To support their case, they pointed to the fact that the government, despite massive manhunts, failed to arrest or to bring to trial a single person accused of making or planting these bombs. More likely, however, these bombs were the work of anarchists, some of whom espoused violence as the only way to upend capitalist power. The terrorist streak in anarchism had first surfaced in the United States in the late nineteenth century, causing injury and death to Americans—to workers and police involved in the Haymarket protest of 1886; to Henry Clay Frick, Andrew Carnegie's right-hand man, wounded by the anarchist Alexander Berkman in 1892; and to President William McKinley, assassinated by anarchist Leon Czolgosz in 1901. But while many anarchists defended the use of violence as a matter of principle, very few of them engaged in it themselves. The bombings of 1919 were probably the work of a small, clandestine group of anarchist terrorists. Not only were the prominent anarchists of the period, such as Emma Goldman, uninvolved in these acts, but they also probably did not know the identity of the perpetrators. Anarchism was a decentralized movement, its adherents organized into many different cells and groups, often acting independently of each other. Adding further to the complexity of the situation, the two larger and more influential wings of radicalism in 1919, the socialists and the communists, had repudiated assassinations as legitimate techniques of class struggle.[21]

These different attitudes toward violence among the various radical groups and within the anarchist movement itself, however, made little impression on either government authorities or the public at large. The bombings of the spring of 1919, combined with the year's labor unrest, convinced most Americans that a Bolshevik-style revolution was unfolding in the United States and that every measure had to be taken to stop it. Suspicion fell most heavily on communities of immigrants, especially those who had originated in eastern and southern Europe and who were thought to be vulnerable to Bolshevik propaganda. These immigrants, predominately Catholic, Christian Orthodox, and Jewish, had never possessed the social prestige enjoyed by the Germans prior to World War I. In the language of the time, they were "new immigrants," a pejorative shorthand for those newcomers whose religion, politics, customs, personal hygiene, racial fitness, and capacity for self-government did not match the standard expected of American citizens or set by such "old immigrant" groups as the Germans and the Swedes. These new immigrants were easy targets for charges of subversion and treachery.[22]

Attorney General Palmer and state law enforcement authorities struck against the new immigrant Reds in November 1919, arresting 750 aliens in

New York and deporting 249 of them a month later. Most of these aliens were immigrants from Russia or other countries in eastern Europe. On January 2, 1920, the authorities struck again, arresting more than four thousand suspected radicals in thirty-three cities spread across twenty-three states. Meant to expose the extent of revolutionary activity, these massive raids netted exactly three pistols, no rifles, no explosives, and no plans for insurrection. Nevertheless, those arrested were jailed for weeks and, in some cases, months without being charged with a crime and often under harsh conditions. Of these, 591 would be deported by the spring of 1920 and the rest would be released.[23]

In some respects, the Red Scare of 1919–20 ebbed rather quickly. The cases of those aliens arrested during the scare were largely resolved within six months. Congress refused to give Palmer and his energetic young assistant, J. Edgar Hoover, the peacetime sedition law they needed in order to prosecute native-born radicals.[24] Moreover, significant opposition to Attorney General Palmer's methods had already surfaced among federal judges, who began ruling, as early as January 1920, that evidence gathered in illegal seizures of papers could not be used in criminal proceedings. By April, Assistant Secretary of Labor Louis Post, in charge of immigration control, had thrown out hundreds of warrants issued by Palmer and released almost half of those arrested on January 2. Threatened with impeachment by Congress for his "leniency," Post demanded and received a congressional hearing, during which he convinced his accusers that the Attorney General's Office had violated the civil liberties of hundreds of innocent individuals. These hearings diminished Attorney General Palmer's prestige. Palmer then discredited himself altogether when the radical violence he had predicted for May 1, 1920, failed to materialize. By the summer of 1920, the Red Scare had largely subsided.[25]

The effects of the Red Scare lingered in two ways, however. First, the raids and arrests had decimated the communist Left, reducing its membership from seventy thousand to sixteen thousand in 1920 alone. By 1927, that number stood at eight thousand.[26] Reliable figures on anarchist membership do not exist, but there can be little doubt that the arrests and deportations of 1919–20, combined with the seven-year ordeal of Nicola Sacco and Bartolomeo Vanzetti, Italian anarchists convicted of murdering a Brockton, Massachusetts, paymaster in 1920 and executed in 1927, damaged the anarchist movement.[27] Other radical movements, including the Socialist Party and the Industrial Workers of the World, also would suffer from the calumny that the Red Scare had heaped on all "Red" ideologies.

Second, the Red Scare lingered in the attempt by federal authorities to target entire groups of "new immigrants" for their alleged role in nurturing radicals. Bolshevik sympathy probably was stronger among Jewish immigrants, most of whom had fled the tyranny of czarist Russia and celebrated the czar's fall, than among any other single immigrant group; anarchism drew a disproportionate number of its immigrant supporters from Italians. In both cases, the numbers of Bolsheviks and anarchists constituted only a small percentage of the total immigrant Jewish and Italian populations living in the United States. Most government authorities, however, refused to make this distinction. Increasingly, they treated Italians as constitutionally hot-tempered and prone to criminality and violence, and Jews as parasitic, immoral, yet clever—precisely the qualities that had allegedly allowed a small "Judeo-Bolshevik" clique in Russia to seize power and embark on a program of world revolution. Because these qualities were thought to be inborn, no amount of exposure to the ennobling American environment would erode them. The political subversion of Jews and Italians was now thought to rest on these two groups' racial character.[28]

Once the problem was defined in this way, the only solution was to bar such groups from coming to the United States, which Congress did, first in emergency legislation in 1921 and then as a permanent measure in 1924. The 1924 legislation established an immigration quota for each of the world's nations pegged at 2 percent of that nation's population present in the United States in 1890. At that date, very few Jewish, Italian, or other "new immigrants" resided in the United States, guaranteeing that those groups' post-1924 quotas would be small. Indeed, those quotas reduced immigration from eastern and southern Europe to a trickle, from a prewar annual average of 738,000 to only 18,439, a 97 percent decrease.[29]

Racialist language permeated discussions of the 1924 immigration restriction legislation when it was being discussed on the House and Senate floor. For example, Congressman Fred S. Purnell of Indiana (Republican) declared: "There is little or no similarity between the clear-thinking, self-governing stocks that sired the American people and this stream of irresponsible and broken wreckage that is pouring into the lifeblood of America the social and political diseases of the Old World." Ira G. Hershey of Maine (Republican) alleged that all eastern and southern European revolutionaries—"soviets and the socialists and the bolshevists, the radicals and anarchists"—were "mixed bloods" who would mongrelize America, sapping it of its morality and good sense. America's salvation from the

Bolsheviks, degeneracy, and other evils, declared Congressman R. E. L. Allen of West Virginia (Democrat), lay in "purifying and keeping pure the blood of America."[30] The legislation favored by these racial purists passed both houses of Congress by overwhelming margins and kept most eastern and southern European immigrants out of the United States for the next forty years. Among other things, it made the admission of eastern European Jews fleeing the Holocaust virtually impossible. In such ways did the effects of the Red Scare endure.

Japanese in World War II

No group that had voluntarily immigrated to the United States suffered what 120,000 West Coast Japanese Americans experienced for almost three years in the 1940s: incarceration by the government in ten "relocation centers" in California, Arizona, Utah, Wyoming, Colorado, and Arkansas. Next to the slavery and the confinement of Native American populations on reservations, this policy arguably constituted the worst violation of civil liberties in American history. On February 19, 1942, President Roosevelt signed Executive Order 9066, authorizing the removal of people deemed dangerous from "military areas." Though Japanese Americans were not actually named in this order, they were its targets. The general roundup began in March 1942. The government made no distinction between those Japanese Americans who were likely to be subversives and those who were not, or even between those who were immigrant aliens and those who were native-born citizens. Many were advised to sell their homes, businesses, and the possessions that they could not personally carry with them. They were then transported by the U.S. Army to sixteen assembly centers. Across a five-month period, from June through October 1942, they were distributed to the ten camps. These camps were, in fact, federal prisons. Barbed wire surrounded them and armed guards patrolled their perimeter. No one was permitted to leave or enter without permission. Some Japanese Americans who signed loyalty oaths would be allowed to leave camps to work in cities or agricultural regions of the Midwest or to serve in the U.S. military. By early 1945, those who had passed loyalty tests were permitted to return to the West Coast, and many did. But eighteen thousand who failed them were held until 1946. And many others were afraid to leave the camps.[31]

It is not surprising, of course, that Americans feared the Japanese in the aftermath of Pearl Harbor. The December 7, 1941, attack was the most devastating assault by a foreign power on American territory since the War of 1812. Incredulity and fear only mounted in the months after December 7, especially as the Japanese military, sweeping through the Southeast Asian colonies of Great Britain, the Netherlands, France, and the United States, demonstrated that the ease of its victory at Pearl Harbor had been no fluke. Americans began to wonder whether Japanese nationals and their descendants living in Hawaii—158,000 strong—had assisted the Japanese military in its surprise attack. But such concerns did not necessarily lead to the conclusion that all Japanese Americans in Hawaii or on the mainland had to be rounded up. Indeed, no government agency would ever attempt to round up the entire Japanese population in Hawaii; and initially the federal government did not even attempt such a roundup on the mainland. Rather, in the days following Pearl Harbor, the Department of Justice and the Federal Bureau of Investigation deployed the techniques they had developed to deal with the Germans in World War I and the anarchists and communists in 1919: they arrested twelve thousand immigrants from Japan, Germany, and Italy whom they suspected of political subversion. Only two thousand of those arrested were Japanese Americans, signaling that U.S. governmental institutions had not yet singled out the Japanese.[32]

By the standards of World War I and the Red Scare (and of the Radical Islamicist Scare of 2001), the arrest of 7,500 to 9,500 people was itself staggering. The FBI, under the command of J. Edgar Hoover, believed that this extensive dragnet had snared most pro-Axis political subversives and thus ensured the internal security of the United States. Continued surveillance netted another 5,500 to 7,500 suspects by October 1943. Of the cumulative 13,000 to 15,000 detained in this way, about 6,000 were interned in U.S. Immigration and Naturalization Service (INS) camps administered by June 1944, and the rest were released.[33] A roundup of alleged political subversives of this magnitude had never occurred in America before, and the laws and techniques used to accomplish it established precedents for future programs of surveillance and arrest, including the anticommunist campaign of the late 1940s and early 1950s. Only in comparison to the mass evacuation and incarceration of 120,000 West Coast Japanese Americans does the scope and intensity of this roundup of political subversives begin to seem tame.

The program of Japanese incarceration resulted from pressure that politically powerful groups of white Americans in the western states and military authorities stationed there were able to exert on the federal government. Declaring that the sabotage of key military installations and perhaps even a Japanese military invasion on the West Coast were imminent, these groups demanded the immediate and mass evacuation of the area's Japanese American population. For a few weeks, Attorney General Francis Biddle resisted these demands. But by February the evacuation arguments had carried the day, and FDR signed Executive Order 9066 after barely a moment of reflection.

The allegations made by white westerners and the Western Defense Command were grounded not in reality but in fifty years of racist stereotypes about the Japanese. These stereotypes ascribed a variety of negative and threatening qualities to the Japanese race: its members were too clannish to assimilate to American life; they possessed the mentality of a herd, readily submitting to emperors and strongmen and unable either to cultivate their own individualism or to appreciate the importance of self-government; they labored like beasts of burden, working themselves, their wives, and their children to the bone. Not only did such habits of work undermine Japanese family life, but they also subverted the wages, hours, and working conditions that "American" workingmen had fought so hard to attain. Finally, the Japanese were accused of being inscrutable and unknowable, possessing an "Oriental-like" habit of stealth and subversion. The combination of their stealth and hard work, white Americans feared, endowed these people with superhuman qualities that might enable them to conquer the white race militarily and economically. Because these qualities were thought to be racial in origin, they could never be shed. The Japanese could never become true Americans.[34]

White Americans had expressed their hostility to the Japanese as early as 1905. Their protests soon compelled President Theodore Roosevelt to persuade the Japanese government to halt further emigration of Japanese laborers to the United States. In 1913, California passed an Alien Land Law, prohibiting Japanese and other Asian aliens from owning property in the state. In 1924, the Immigration Act barred almost all Japanese immigrants from coming to the United States.[35] The treatment of Japanese Americans after Pearl Harbor drew directly on this history of racial stereotyping and exclusion. General John L. DeWitt, the head of the Western Defense Command in 1942, was simply repeating an off-repeated slur of the era when he declared, "A Jap's a Jap." In his report urging internment, DeWitt argued that "the Japanese race is an enemy race and while many second- and third-generation Japanese born on United States soil, possessed of United States citizenship, have become 'Americanized,' the racial strains are undiluted."[36] Fears of racial subversion had joined fears of political subversion, with profound consequences both for Japanese Americans and America itself.

Significantly, the government in World War II ordered no mass evacuation or incarceration of the German American or Italian American populations. Of course, it would have been much harder to execute such a policy given that those groups numbered in the millions, not the hundreds of thousands. The Japanese Americans in Hawaii themselves escaped mass incarceration because, at 35 percent of the Hawaiian population, they were simply too vital to the local economy to be locked away in prisons. But the arguments about expediency can only be carried so far. Had the Germans and the Italians numbered in the hundreds of thousands, it is still unlikely that they would have been rounded up en masse.[37]

This is true even though a good case could have been made, in the 1940s, that Germans posed a greater internal security risk than did the Japanese. Not only was the German American Bund a dangerous pro-Nazi organization that, in size and influence, had no pro-emperor counterpart in the Japanese American population, but the German military possessed an ability to strike the mainland United States that the Japanese military lacked. German submarines regularly prowled the Atlantic coastline of the United States in ways that Japanese subs did not do in the Pacific. The German military actually executed on Long Island what American alarmists on the West Coast falsely charged the Japanese military with planning to do in California: they landed saboteurs to blow up key American army, munitions, and communications facilities.[38] Yet despite the evidence pointing to the greater danger to the East Coast posed by the Germans, fears of subversion and sabotage focused almost entirely on the Japanese on the West Coast.

Those fears might have subsided sooner had critical government intelligence been allowed to surface and influence the deliberations of the Supreme Court when it began considering the constitutionality of internment in 1943. The U.S. Solicitor General's Office had in its possession at that time a detailed report assembled by the Office of Naval Intelligence arguing that the Japanese population on the West Coast posed no loyalty threat to the United States and that its incarceration was therefore not a military necessity. But the solicitor general suppressed the report, making it impossible for any of the Supreme Court justices to view it. We cannot know how that report might have affected the internal deliberations of the Court, but it would have made it possible for those justices, such as Frank

Murphy, who were disturbed by the policy of internment to challenge the stigmatization of the Japanese as an "enemy race" capable of extraordinary treachery.[39]

The Germans and Italians escaped the worst effects of the government's antisubversion campaign because they were no longer racially suspect. In their case, fear of political subversion was not compounded by the fear of racial subversion. That U.S. authorities and public opinion no longer construed the German and Italian populations as racially threatening can be interpreted as evidence that egalitarian sentiments had made progress against racist ones since the 1910s and 1920s. Yet the treatment of Japanese Americans reveals how far the United States still had to go in ridding itself of its racist habits.[40]

Using the Past to Illuminate the Present

The historical record instructs us that war or near-war situations often put immigrants at risk, especially if those immigrants have come from a part of the world or belong to a race or religion perceived to be the enemy of the United States. Fears of internal subversion during wartime are probably inevitable. Governments are charged with protecting the nation they represent and the people who comprise it. In wartime, governments will usually demand and receive an authority to pursue subversives that, in republican or democratic polities, they would not be given in peacetime. In most wartime situations, governments will have to discharge their responsibilities to provide security while possessing imperfect information about the sources and likelihood of subversive acts. The lack of adequate information usually leads, not to caution, but to overreaching in the form of indiscriminate violations of civil liberties that would not be tolerated during peacetime. Immigrant groups associated through nationality, race, or religion with America's enemy have been especially vulnerable to government overreach. Marked as different, they are easily construed as dangerous.

Such groups are commonly accused of wanting to aid our enemies and thus to subvert the political integrity of the United States. But in the first half of the twentieth century, the groups that suffered the most—the Germans in World War I, the southern and eastern Europeans during the Red Scare, and the Japanese in World War II—were those whose political subversion was thought to be grounded in another kind of subversion, most commonly that of race. Leveling the charge of racial subversion imperiled an entire group, for the tendency to political subversion could now be construed as inhering in any individual born into that group. This joining of political subversion to racial subversion suited the needs of Americans trying to arouse hysteria as well as those of government officials who could now relieve themselves of the difficult task of distinguishing between actual subversives and those who were innocent.

An evaluation of government efforts across the last five years to provide security to America in the ongoing "War on Terror" allows us to say that, in some respects, we have learned from past experiences. While Arabs and/ or Muslim terrorists are considered to be the chief threat to American security, no attempt is being made to eradicate from American society all aspects of Islamic or Arab culture, a policy that governments and private citizens pursued against German culture in World War I. To the contrary, public and private organizations have understood the urgency of learning more about Arab and Muslim civilizations, past and present, and have undertaken projects in schools, universities, and interfaith assemblies to do just that. Nor is any attempt being made to round up all Arab or Muslim Americans, as was carried out against the Japanese in World War II. While some Americans have verbally abused or physically attacked individual Arabs and Muslims since September 2001, the highest public authorities have refused to condone such popular prejudice and vigilantism. President George Bush has made it clear in ways that Woodrow Wilson and Franklin Roosevelt never did that it is simply not acceptable to stigmatize an entire racial or religious group because of the small number of terrorists and enemies who reside in its ranks.

In other respects, however, we may not yet have learned the lessons of the past well enough. The anti-Red campaign of 1919–20 is the episode in American history that most closely resembles the current War on Islamic Terror, and paying close attention to the similarities will reveal the danger America runs of repeating past mistakes. Both campaigns crystallized around terrorist acts—mail bombs sent to the homes of "class enemies" in the first case, airplanes turned into bombs and directed toward buildings (and their inhabitants) that symbolized American power in the second. Both acts were the work of revolutionists who were willing to sacrifice anything, including their lives, to achieve their aims (though the revolutionists of 1919 did not celebrate the killing of innocent civilians in the way that the revolutionists of 2001 did). The terrorists in both instances belonged to small cells that were virtually impossible for outsiders to penetrate but that drew on global networks of supporters. Both acts of terrorism occasioned frenzied roundups by U.S. government authorities of thousands of immigrant suspects who were held for a long time, often without access to bail, attorneys, or decent conditions. Both of these roundups yielded remarkably little information about those who had been involved in terrorist acts while spreading fear in America at large about those populations of immigrants with whom the terrorists shared a nationality or religion. In the 1920s, as we have seen, this fear led to the racialized stigmatization of entire groups of immigrants and the decision to bar them from the United States.

This has begun to happen in regard to Arab or Muslim immigrants, not through a blanket immigration restriction act of the sort passed by Congress in the 1920s, but by a series of administrative measures taken by federal authorities. Several months after September 11, 2001, the government asked five thousand men from Middle Eastern and Muslim countries to "volunteer" for interviews with immigration officials; some of these interviews have triggered deportations. About the same time, the INS ordered public and private universities to provide it with information about their Middle Eastern and Muslim students. Hundreds, perhaps thousands, of university students from Middle Eastern countries have already dropped out of school and gone home, and applications from prospective new students have plummeted. In February 2003, the INS began registering and fingerprinting forty-four thousand immigrants from specified Arab and Islamic countries. A federal noose has tightened around Muslim and Arab immigration, giving the government the ability to choke it.

Whether the United States cuts off this immigrant stream may well depend on whether the charge of political subversion leveled at Muslim terrorists becomes compounded by the charge of racial or religious subversion. The charge of racial subversion would be leveled at Arabs, who would be depicted as harboring a racial affinity for terror. The charge of religious subversion would be leveled at Muslims, who would be accused of adhering to a faith fundamentally hostile to the political ideals that Americans hold most dear and exercising a grip among its adherents so strong that no one who is exposed to it can escape it. The precedent for religious subversion accusations lies in the charges made against Catholicism in the nineteenth century. Those who charged Catholicism with putting America in mortal danger stressed, as critics of Islam do today, its incompatibility with democracy and its lack of regard for individual rights and liberties. No Muslim figure parallels that of the pope, since Islam is a decentralized religion and is split between Sunni and Shiites, but the charge that Muslims prefer to live in theocracies, autocratic polities controlled by clerics, is similar to the allegation that American Protestants made against Catholics 150 years ago.

The defense against stigmatizing entire groups as threats to America lies in the willingness of Americans to insist that charges of political subversion be separated from those of racial or religious subversion and that the arrest, prosecution, and deportation of individuals be limited to those whose actions, separated from a consideration of race and religion, can be shown to be subversive. Attorney General Palmer was partially stymied in his anti-Red campaign because judges and government officials had the courage to take a stand against his methods. The postwar Red Scare also brought into being the American Civil Liberties Union, an organization committed to fighting illegal campaigns to strip individual Americans and aliens of their rights. The ACLU still exists and has mounted vigorous protests since 2001 against the indiscriminate surveillance and prosecution of Arab and Muslim populations. Its work draws support from a large number of other groups, ranging from the U.S. Civil Rights Commission to an array of ethnic and racial antidiscrimination organizations larger and more influential than what existed in 1920. But the counterparts of the judges and government officials who, in 1920, did so much to thwart Attorney General Palmer, have take much longer to surface in post-2001 America than they did after the Red Scare of 1919.[41] And even that robust anti-Palmer opposition, it must be said, did little to stop the campaign for racialized immigration restriction that came on the Red Scare's heels.

In times of war or near-war, it is not easy to resist demands for unity, conformity, and homogeneity. Yet the record of the twentieth century reminds us how important it is for private citizens and public officials to be vigilant in defense of constitutional rights and to resist the temptation to stigmatize entire immigrant groups as threats to the American republic.

NOTES

This essay is a revised and updated version of the article of the same title that appeared in *The Maze of Fear: Security and Migration after 9/11*, ed. John Tirman (New York: New Press, 2004).

1. Oscar Handlin, *The Uprooted: The Epic Story of the Great Migrations That Made the American People* (New York: Grosset and Dunlap, 1951), 3.

2. Lazarus, Powell, and Reuther were the children of immigrants, not immigrants themselves.

3. On the Irish, see Oscar Handlin, *Boston's Immigrants, 1790–1865: A Study in Acculturation* (Cambridge, MA: Harvard University Press, 1941); on the Chinese, see Andrew Gyory, *Closing the Gate: Race, Politics, and the Chinese Exclusion Act* (Chapel Hill: University of North Carolina Press, 1998), and Erika Lee, *At America's Gates: Chinese Immigration during the Exclusion Era, 1882–1943* (Chapel Hill: University of North Carolina Press, 2003); on the Germans during World War I, see Frederick C. Luebke, *Bonds of Loyalty: German-Americans and World War I* (De Kalb: Northern Illinois University Press, 1974); on eastern and southern Europeans in the 1920s, see John Higham, *Strangers in the Land: Patterns of American Nativism, 1860–1925* (1955; reprint, New Brunswick: Rutgers University Press, 1992), and Gary Gerstle, *American Crucible: Race and Nation in the Twentieth Century* (Princeton: Princeton University Press, 2001); on Mexicans in the 1930s, see Abraham Hoffman, *Unwanted Mexican Americans in the Great Depression: Repatriation Pressures, 1929–1939* (Tucson: University of Arizona Press, 1974), and Mae Ngai, *Impossible Subjects: Illegal Aliens and the Making of Modern America* (Princeton: Princeton University Press, 2004); on Japanese internment, see Roger Daniels, *Concentration Camps USA: Japanese Americans and World War II* (New York: Holt, Rinehart, and Winston, 1971).

4. One of the oldest and still one of the best efforts of this sort is Higham, *Strangers in the Land*; for a more recent effort, see David H. Bennett, *The Party of Fear: From Nativist Movements to the New Right in American History* (Chapel Hill: University of North Carolina Press, 1988).

5. For a history of this country's anti-Catholic origins, see Higham, *Strangers in the Land*, 4–7, and Bennett, *Party of Fear*, Part I, passim.

6. Handlin, *Boston's Immigrants*; Bennett; *Party of Fear*; Tyler G. Anbinder, *Nativism and Slavery: The Northern Know Nothings and the Politics of the 1850s* (New York: Oxford University Press, 1992); David R. Roediger, *The Wages of Whiteness: Race and the Making of the American Working Class* (London: Verso, 1999).

7. Bennett, *Party of Fear*, 233–37, 319–21.

8. On the importance and meaning of republicanism to American political culture in the nineteenth century, see Sean Wilentz, *Chants Democratic: New York City and the Rise of an American Working Class* (New York: Oxford University Press, 1984). On its troubling implications for immigrants and others thought to lack the necessary political independence and virtue, see Gary Gerstle, "Ideas of the American Labor Movement," in *Ideas, Ideologies, and Social Movements: The U.S. Experience since 1800*, ed. Stuart Burchey and Peter Coclanis (Charleston: University of South Carolina Press, 1999), 72–89; Matthew Frye Jacobson, *Whiteness of a Different Color: European Immigrants and the Alchemy of Race* (Cambridge, MA: Harvard University Press, 1998).

9. Higham, *Strangers in the Land*, 54–58. This fear of what radicalism and rev-

olution would do to the American republic can best be grasped by reading what politicians such as Theodore Roosevelt wrote and said in reaction to Haymarket, the strikes of the 1890s, and the assassination of William McKinley. See, for example, Theodore Roosevelt, "American Ideals," in *The Works of Theodore Roosevelt, National Edition*, ed. Hermann Hagaedorn (New York, 1926), 13:7; Howard Lawrence Hurwitz, *Theodore Roosevelt and Labor in New York, 1880–1900* (New York: Columbia University Press, 1943), 11, 181, 283.

10. Gary Gerstle, "Immigration and Ethnicity in the American Century," in *Perspectives on Modern America: Making Sense of the Twentieth Century*, ed. Harvard Sitkoff (New York: Oxford University Press, 2000), 275–95.

11. Gerstle, *American Crucible*, 4–5; Jacobson, *Whiteness of a Different Color*; Reginald Horsman, *Race and Manifest Destiny: The Origins of American Racial Anglo-Saxonism* (Cambridge, MA: Harvard University Press, 1981).

12. Richard Hofstadter, *Social Darwinism in American Thought* (Boston: Beacon Press, 1955); Jacobson, *Whiteness of a Different Color*; Roediger, *Wages of Whiteness*; James R. Barrett and David Roediger, "Inbetween Peoples: Race, Nationality, and the 'New Immigrant' Working Class," *Journal of American Ethnic History* 16 (Spring 1997): 3–44.

13. Gyory, *Closing the Gate*; Lee, *At America's Gates*; Alexander Saxton, *The Rise and Fall of the White Republic: Class Politics and Mass Culture in Nineteenth-Century America* (London: Verso, 1990).

14. Would the preservation of German traditions include an admiration for the German Kaiser and thus constitute a threat to republicanism? Most German immigrants addressed this problem by insisting that their cultural affection for Germany entailed no political loyalty. To the contrary, they insisted, Germans were committed to American political traditions. They were German only in culture, not in politics. And most Americans believed them—until World War I. Luebke, *Bonds of Loyalty*; Russell A. Kazal, "Becoming 'Old Stock': The Waning of German-American Identity in Philadelphia, 1900–1930" (PhD diss., University of Pennsylvania, 1998). In the space of three years, 1916–18, Germans went from being one of America's most celebrated and public ethnic groups to one of its most feared and private ones. As the American government prepared itself to fight in 1916, it worried that the American people would not support America's entry into war. A large and diverse antiwar movement had cohered, drawing on large number of progressives, women's peace party activists, Protestant ministers, socialists, and Irish and German immigrants. Moreover, America in the 1910s was a society deeply divided between workers and bosses, immigrants and the native born, city dwellers and farmers. It would not have been easy for any government, no matter how enlightened or skillful, to overcome those divisions and to secure everyone's support for a hard, difficult fight, especially a government that was as small as the American one and so inadequately endowed with administrative capacity.

15. David Kennedy, *Over Here! The First World War and American Society* (New

York: Oxford University Press, 1982); Gerstle, *American Crucible*, ch. 3; Higham, *Strangers in the Land*, 194–263.

16. The situation of the Germans was made more precarious by the long period of official neutrality—two and a half years (August 1914–April 1917) that preceded America's entry into war. For most of that time, the American government insisted that it would not take sides in the conflict and that it would continue to maintain trade and other kinds of relations with both the Entente and Central Powers. German Americans interpreted this neutrality to be genuine, meaning that they were free to express their neutrality, their belief (if they were socialists) that the working people had nothing to gain from this war, their continued love of German culture, their suspicions of England, and, in some cases, their sympathies with Germany's war aims. But America's neutrality was never as evenhanded as the Germans immigrants interpreted it to be. Owing to a large volume of trade between the United States and England and a common cultural and political inheritance, a majority of Americans felt closer to England than to Germany. In 1915 and 1916, public and official opinion in America moved steadily in the direction of England and the Triple Entente and against Germany and the Central Powers. Luebke, *Bonds of Loyalty*.

17. This paragraph and the ones on the German American experience that follow are largely based on the following sources: ibid.; H. C. Peterson, *Propaganda for War: The War against American Neutrality* (Norman: University of Oklahoma Press, 1939); George Sylvester Viereck, *Spreading Germs of Hate* (New York: H. Liveright, 1930); Christopher Gildemeister, "*My Four Years in Germany:* Progressivism, Propaganda and American Film in World War I," unpublished seminar paper, Catholic University of America, 1994; Kennedy, *Over Here!*; Ronald Schaeffer, *America in the Great War: The Rise of the War Welfare State* (New York: Oxford University Press, 1991); Higham, *Strangers in the Land*; Kazal, "Becoming 'Old Stock.'"

18. Kazal, "Becoming 'Old Stock.'"

19. Robert K. Murray, *Red Scare: A Study in National Hysteria, 1919–1920* (Minneapolis: University of Minnesota Press, 1955); William Preston Jr., *Aliens and Dissenters: Federal Suppression of Radicals, 1903–1933* (Cambridge, MA: Harvard University Press, 1963); Higham, *Strangers in the Land*, 194–263; Gerstle, *American Crucible*, 81–127; David Montgomery, *The Fall of the House of Labor: The Workplace, the State, and American Labor Activism, 1865–1925* (New York: Cambridge University Press, 1987); Joseph A. McCartin, *Labor's Great War: The Struggle for Industrial Democracy and the Origins of Modern American Labor Relations, 1912–1921* (Chapel Hill: University of North Carolina Press, 1997); Nell Irvin Painter, *Standing at Armageddon: The United States, 1877–1919* (New York: W. W. Norton, 1987); Steve Fraser, *Labor Will Rule: Sidney Hillman and the Rise of American Labor* (New York: Free Press, 1991); H. C. Peterson and Gilbert C. Fite, *Opponents of War, 1917–1918* (Madison: University of Wisconsin Press, 1957).

20. R. Murray, *Red Scare*, 79.

21. The best work on the history of anarchism in the United States has been done by Paul Avrich. See, in particular, *The Haymarket Tragedy* (Princeton: Princeton University of Press, 1984), and *Sacco and Vanzetti: The Anarchist Background* (Princeton: Princeton University Press, 1991).

22. Higham, *Strangers in the Land*; Gerstle, *American Crucible.*

23. R. Murray, *Red Scare.*

24. This refusal made it impossible for federal law enforcement agencies to target citizens and explains why most of those arrested and virtually all of those deported were immigrants, who were vulnerable to the antisedition provisions of the Alien Act of 1918.

25. R. Murray, *Red Scare,* 239–62; Stanley Coben, *A. Mitchell Palmer: Politician* (New York: Columbia University Press, 1963).

26. R. Murray, *Red Scare,* 276.

27. Avrich, *Sacco and Vanzetti.*

28. Gerstle, *American Crucible,* 95–104.

29. Ibid., 95–109.

30. *Congressional Record,* March 17, 1924, 4389; April 8, 1924, 5868–69; April 5, 1924, 5693.

31. This account of Japanese internment is based on the following: Daniels, *Concentration Camps, USA*; Roger Daniels, *Prisoners without Trial: Japanese Americans in World War II* (New York: Hill and Wang, 1993); Peter Irons, ed., *Justice Delayed: The Record of the Japanese Internment Cases* (Middletown: Wesleyan University Press, 1989); Jacobus tenBroek, Edward N. Barnhart, and Floyd W. Matson, *Prejudice, War and the Constitution: Japanese American Evacuation and Resettlement* (Berkeley: University of California Press, 1958); Dillon S. Myer, *Uprooted Americans: The Japanese Americans and the War Relocation Authority during World War II* (Tuscon: University of Arizona Press, 1971); Gary Y. Okihiro and Joan Myers, *Whispered Silences: Japanese Americans and World War II* (Seattle: University of Washington Press, 1996); Alice Yang Murray, ed., *What Did the Internment of Japanese Americans Mean?* (Boston: Bedford, 2000); Greg Robinson, *By Order of the President: FDR and the Internment of Japanese Americans* (Cambridge, MA: Harvard University Press, 2001).

32. Alice Yang Murray, "The Internment of Japanese Americans," in A. Murray, *What Did the Internment of Japanese Americans Mean?* 3.

33. Stephen Fox, *The Unknown Internment: An Oral History of Italian Americans during World War II* (Boston: Twayne, 1990), 151, 163–64.

34. In addition to the sources listed above, see John Dower, *War without Mercy: Race and Power in the Pacific War* (New York: Pantheon, 1986).

35. Yuji Ichioka, *The Issei: The World of First Generation Japanese Immigrants, 1880–1924* (New York: Free Press, 1988); Gerstle, *American Crucible,* 60–62, 109–13.

36. U.S. Commission on Wartime Relocation and Internment of Civilians, *Personal Justice Denied: The Report of the Commission on Wartime Relocation and In-*

ternment of Civilians (Washington, DC: Civil Liberties Public Education Fund, 1997), 66; Lt. Gen. J. L. DeWitt, U.S. Army, *Final Report: Japanese Evacuation from the West Coast, 1942* (Washington, DC: Government Printing Office, 1943), 97.

37. Western Command, under General DeWitt's command, did draw up plans for mass expulsion and internment of West Coast Italians and Germans, but these proposals never attracted the kind of support from Western politicians, Western public opinion, or Washington bureaucrats that Japanese internment did.

38. In 1942, the Germans landed eight soldiers disguised as American civilians on Long Island with instructions to blow up key U.S. military installations. They were captured before they could do any harm and were tried and executed under military law. Louis Fisher, *Nazi Saboteurs on Trial: A Military Tribunal and American Law* (Lawrence: University Press of Kansas, 2003).

39. Peter Irons, "Gordon Hirabayashi v. United States: 'A Jap's a Jap,'" in *The Courage of their Convictions,* ed. Peter Irons (New York: Free Press, 1988), 37–62.

40. Though the effects of internment on the Japanese American population are beyond the purview of this essay, it should be said those effects, in terms of loss of wealth, status, freedom, family integrity, and culture, were extreme and would not be overcome for two generations. The disgraceful episode would finally elicit from the U.S. government a formal apology in 1990.

41. It should be said that an additional reason why the Red Scare of 1919–20 declined more quickly than the Radical Islamicist Scare of today lies in the changing foreign policy of the Soviet Union in the early 1920s. It stopped making international revolution its chief priority, choosing instead to consolidate its power within the confines of the nation and empire it had wrested from the czars. This change made other countries fear the Soviet Union and communism less than they had and diminished what these other countries had construed as a campaign of international terror. The Soviet Union had become more of a conventional nation-state and easier to deal with through traditional diplomatic channels. This has not happened, of course, with Al Qaeda.

Chapter 10

Post-9/11 Government Initiatives in Comparative and Historical Perspectives

Mehdi Bozorgmehr and Anny Bakalian

On several occasions, the U.S. government has targeted immigrant and ethnic groups (e.g., German Americans during World War I and Japanese Americans during World War II) when their country of origin has waged war on America. During the Palmer Raids and the Red Scare against the Bolshevik threat between 1919 and 1920, the communists were targeted by the government. Furthermore, Iranian students were subjected to deportation if found out of legal status during the "Iran Hostage Crisis" in 1979–81. President Bush declared the "Attacks on America" as an act of war against the United States, and his administration launched the "War on Terror" internationally and domestically. This chapter analyzes the post-9/11 government initiatives against Middle Eastern and Muslim Americans from a historical perspective, examining the similarities and differences between this case and its precedents in the twentieth century.

Historians have produced a wealth of information on the mistreatment of German Americans and Japanese Americans,[1] but little attempt has been made to draw comparisons among these watershed cases and post-September 11 backlash. Two notable exceptions are a book chapter by Gary Gerstle and a short essay by Roger Daniels in the *Chronicle of Higher Education.*[2] This may be due to historians' disciplinary constraints. As Daniels himself has noted, "Historical analogies are always tricky, particularly when one of the things being compared is a current event. Contemporary history is, after all, a contradiction in terms. Nevertheless, the ways in which our memory of what was done to Japanese Americans has evolved over six decades can shed some light on our contemporary situation."[3]

Rarely is nativist and patriotic backlash to a major national crisis studied when unfolding. Given the political climate of the early to mid-twentieth century, it was not prudent to carry out such research, which ran the risk of being labeled unpatriotic. Historians usually analyze such conflicts at a later date when sources become available, and no doubt the domestic backlash from the "Attacks on America" will be examined in due course. Sociologists, however, can make a contribution by examining a crisis as it unfolds, especially if it involves fieldwork, a common research tool. We have been engaged in research on this topic from the outset, following the impact of the backlash on Middle Eastern and South Asian Americans. As sociologists, we are also interested in going beyond descriptions of what happened. Our goal here is to compare and contrast the consequences of government targeting on specific immigrant/ethnic groups during times of national crisis, that is, war or threat of war. To that end, we review cases of minority mistreatment in U.S. history in the last century. We conclude by assessing the cumulative effects of the post-9/11 backlash in a comparative and historical context, looking for similarities and differences between this case and its precedents.

Historical Precedents

Fear of "enemy aliens" and sweeping, often unwarranted, government programs of investigation, incarceration, and deportation have been recurrent in U.S. history during times of war or confrontation with a foreign enemy. Federal and state administrations have in the past targeted national origin groups during times of crisis as scapegoats.

German Americans during World War I

Soon after its entrance into World War I in 1917, the U.S. government implemented the Alien Enemies Act of 1798 as a justification to arrest 6,300 German Americans. This act authorized the U.S. president to imprison or deport aliens associated with any nation that the United States had declared a war against. As aptly put by David Reimers, "It seemed as if the war against Germany in Europe had degenerated into a 'War against German America.'"[4] German men over the age of fourteen were not allowed to own guns, radios, or explosives and were not allowed to live near munitions factories or military areas. Over 250,000 German immigrants, so-called "enemy aliens," were required to register at their local post office and carry their card at all times. Fifteen states passed laws making English the official language. These and other measures encouraged some zealous groups to spy on and harass German Americans. Altogether, during the Great War, over six thousand Germans were arrested and over two thousand Germans were interned.

As soon as the United States entered the war, a new ideological movement euphemistically called "100 Percent Americanism" targeted German Americans. "Unhyphenated Americanism" became the new popular expression. German immigrants—perceived until then as industrious, thrifty, and honest—suddenly faced severe hostility. German ethnic organizations were attacked, and there were serious efforts to eliminate German language and culture in German American institutions and organizations. Many Lutheran churches switched to English, and many German Americans anglicized their names and publicly denounced Germany.[5] Conformity to the demands of superpatriots was almost universal. Only left-wing radicals denounced these repressive policies.[6]

The Palmer Raids

As World War I came to a close, Americans' new fear became Bolshevism, leading to the "Red Scare," shorthand for communism. Unrest at home, including women's fight for suffrage, the temperance movement's advocacy of prohibition, racial riots, inflation, and economic recession, stirred fear of encroaching "Bolshevik menace." Topping that, on June 2, 1919, bombs exploded in eight cities, including one in Washington, D.C., that partially destroyed the house of A. Mitchell Palmer, the attorney general in Woodrow Wilson's administration. Palmer had harbored strong antipathy to communism, claiming that it was "eating its way into the homes of the American workman," and had attributed the country's problems to socialists. It is important to note that anticommunism had developed in the last quarter of the nineteenth century as a reaction to labor unrest. "Red-baiting offered anti-union employers a way to legitimize opposition to organized labor without having to refer to economic issues."[7]

Under the Espionage Act of 1917 and the Sedition Act of 1918, Palmer and his young assistant J. Edgar Hoover amassed a list of supposedly subversive elements and then proceeded to raid a large number of labor union offices and headquarters of communist clubs and organizations without search warrants. In December 1919, a total of 249 individuals were arrested and deported to the Soviet Union, including prominent radicals such as Emma Goldman and Alexander Berkman, and on January 1920, over six thousand communist aliens were arrested in cities across the nation.[8] Unmistakably, Palmer manipulated public hysteria to go after revolutionaries and anarchists whom he deemed enemies of the United States.

The Japanese Internment

Some historians believe that the mistreatment of Germans during World War I provided the blueprint for the evacuation of Japanese Americans and their internment in World War II. Immediately after the bombing of Pearl Harbor in 1941, President Roosevelt directed government agencies to arrest all Japanese aliens. They were forced to liquidate their property and were transported in large numbers to remote locations in detention camps. By 1942, about 120,000 West Coast Japanese were behind barbed wire. Of these, about two-thirds were American born. Later in the war, even when American-born men of Japanese ancestry joined the armed forces and proved their valor and loyalty to their country, the government was slow in freeing them.

Ironically, the vast majority of the second-generation Japanese (Nisei) were oriented toward the United States. The Nisei participated in American-style organizations, and the majority of the Nisei organizations had a mainstream American content. The Japanese American Citizens League (JACL), the most prominent national Nisei organization, was established in 1930, growing out of several local and regional organizations.[9] As a citizens' league, the JACL barred the immigrant first generation (Issei) from joining. According to Daniels, immediately after Pearl Harbor the JACL wired President Franklin Roosevelt, pledging their loyalty.[10] But regardless of their superpatriotism, the Nisei were identified as the enemy when war came. The internment not only destroyed the Japanese American community but imprisoned the Nisei for four years. It also altered their lives, so much that afterwards they divided their lives into two distinct periods, "before the war" and "after the war."

A Japanese American leader wrote to the American Civil Liberties Union (ACLU), wondering about the constitutionality of drafting interned citizens who were behind barbed wire. However, the ACLU director disassociated his organization from the Japanese in a letter that was made public. The ACLU supported the JACL's decision of submission to government orders. Since the war, the major political activities of the JACL have been directed at eradicating anti-Japanese discrimination. It remembers the war years on its Web site as follows: "The organization argued for and won the right of Japanese Americans to serve in the U.S. military, resulting in the creation of a segregated unit, the famous 442nd Regimental Combat Team, which joined with the 100th Battalion from Hawaii and became the most highly decorated unit in U.S. military history despite having only served in combat for a little over a year in the European theater of the war."[11]

Some historians argue that the major cause of evacuation was the pressure exerted by special interest groups in California and on the Pacific coast generally. However, the Japanese were unpopular in the entire nation. If the Japanese were a threat to security in California, where they constituted less than 2 percent of the population, then why were they left alone in Hawaii, where they constituted almost one-third of the population? Although Hawaii was at the center of the war, fewer than 2,000 of the 150,000 Japanese were rounded up. There is also little support for the argument that military necessity required the evacuation and internment.

Iran Hostage Crisis

The Iran hostage crisis began on November 4, 1979, when a group of Iranian students seized the U.S. embassy in Tehran, taking the American employees hostage. Relations between the United States and Iran had been strained since the Iranian Revolution of 1978–79, when Iran's new revolutionary leaders denounced the United States for its longtime support of Mohammad Reza Shah Pahlavi. When the exiled shah entered the United States in October for medical care, Iranian revolutionaries feared a repetition of the CIA-assisted coup that had put him back on the throne in 1953. In retaliation, a crowd of about five hundred militants stormed the U.S. embassy in Tehran and captured the American personnel inside. The ordeal of the fifty-two American hostages lasted 444 days. During the "Iran Hostage Crisis," both the federal government and several states enacted measures that specifically targeted Iranian students in the United States. In November 1979, the attorney general, at the direction of President Carter, required all foreign Iranian college students to report to the U.S. Immigration and Naturalization Service (INS) for registration by mid-December. Each nonimmigrant alien was required to provide proof of residence and full-time school enrollment and a passport with a valid visa. The regulation claimed that failure to comply would be considered a violation of the conditions of the alien's stay in the United States and would be grounds for deportation under the Immigration and Nationality Act.

The hostage crisis prompted a presidential order referred to as the Iranian Control Program. The program screened, on a case-by-case basis, almost fifty-seven thousand Iranian students, the single largest group of foreign students at the time, to make sure that they were legally in status. The program was not aimed at students only. In the INS's own words, the new policy "effectively prohibited the entry of most Iranians into this country."[12] In light of the permanent closure of the American embassy in Iran, even over a quarter of a century later, Iranians must still first travel to another country to obtain a U.S. visa.

In response to President Carter's decree, several Iranian students sued the government to challenge the order. The plaintiffs used the protection of personal rights under the Fifth Amendment to argue that the U.S. government had unfairly singled out Iranians. In its defense, the government argued that the regulation served "overriding national interests." The district court dismissed this claim, finding that there was a dubious connection between protecting the lives of American hostages in Iran and singling out Iranians for registration with the INS. Rather, it argued that the regulation seemed to serve a psychological purpose only, namely appeasing the American public's demand that the United States take some action in response to the hostage crisis. When the government appealed, the U.S. Court of Appeals for the D.C. Circuit reversed the lower court's order, noting that the Immigration and Nationality Act had given the attorney general sufficiently broad authority to screen aliens of certain nationalities.[13] It should also be pointed out that the hostage crisis occurred right after the revolution in Iran, which had led to a massive influx of Iranian exiles into the United States. Ironically, these exiles faced targeting and scapegoating despite their opposition to the Iranian regime that had instigated the hostage crisis.

Post-9/11 Government Initiatives against Middle Eastern and Muslim Immigrants

Within a few weeks of 9/11, the Bush administration set in motion a series of initiatives and policies that targeted Middle Eastern and Asian communities and in particular profiled Arab and Muslim immigrant men. Even though these directives were part of the new policies of the Bush administration in fighting terrorism, they sent the reverse message. From the perspective of the affected communities, there was little difference in the outcome between the hate crimes and bias incidents perpetrated by ordinary Americans and the government's reaction. In fact, the government's dragnet was more pervasive and dangerous. As a background, it is important to note that men and women of Middle Eastern ancestry had long been subjects of stereotyping and discrimination in U.S. history. Ever since the 1967 Arab-Israeli war, the political events in the Middle East have reverberated in acts of bias and discrimination against people of Middle Eastern descent in the United States.[14] The list is long but includes the 1973 Arab oil embargo, the Iran Hostage Crisis, the 1983 suicide bombing of the U.S. Marine barracks in Beirut, the 1985 hijacking of TWA fight 847 to Beirut, the 1990–91 Gulf War, and the 1993 bombing of the World Trade Center in New York.[15] Knee-jerk reactions to Middle Eastern crises had become so pervasive that the 1995 bombing in Oklahoma City was initially attributed to Middle Eastern terrorists, but it turned out to be of the home-grown variety. A *Newsweek* headline read, "Jumping to Conclusions—Many in the press and public were quick to assume the crime had Mideast origins. But 'John Doe' is one of us."[16] What is different about the events of September 11, 2001, is that it brought the Middle Eastern conflict to American soil. No longer were terrorist events a foreign policy issue; they allegedly made Arab and Muslim Americans a threat to national security.

The popular media—Hollywood movies, inflammatory news shows, infomercials, the tabloid press—have been especially liable in perpetuating stereotypes of Middle Easterners historically as savages, womanizers, deceitful persons, and more recently as terrorists.[17] Anti–Middle Eastern racism is pervasive in the United States, condoned and manipulated by the government and politicians in support of U.S. policy in the Middle East.[18] Not surprisingly, hijackings, suicide bombings, hostage taking, and other such events in the Middle East often result in prejudicial, even discriminatory reactions against people of Middle Eastern descent in the United States because of the way the administration and the press plays up these incidents.

The USA Patriot Act, an acronym for Uniting and Strengthening America by Providing Appropriate Tools Required to Intercept and Obstruct Terrorism, is perhaps the most monumental piece of legislation to date that aims to ensure the security of the land and its citizens. It was passed by Congress with little debate or opposition on October 25, 2001, and was signed into law the next day by President Bush. The PATRIOT Act intro-

duced sweeping changes in domestic law and intelligence agencies overseas, giving unprecedented powers to the government with little oversight
from the courts. Due process provisions, protections against unreasonable
searches and seizures, detentions without hearings or probable cause, and
denial of bail if not a flight risk are some of the issues that have concerned
constitutional scholars about this act.[19]

Detentions and Deportations

Detentions and deportations were the first of a series of initiatives issued by the U.S. Attorney General's Office in its effort to catch terrorists.
Starting on September 17, 2001, immigrants became subject to detention.
If suspected of terrorism, detainees could be kept without charge for an
extended period of time, hearings could be "secure," that is closed to the
public, bond could be denied, and attorney-client communications privilege could be disregarded. According to the report entitled *The September
11 Detainees,* issued by the inspector general of the U.S. Department of Justice, 762 illegal immigrant men from Arab and/or Muslim countries were
detained, some for weeks and months, but none were charged with terrorism. Secrecy shrouded the entire process. Estimates on the number of detainees vary from 500 to over 1,200.[20] Even Congress did not receive an answer when it questioned the Department of Justice about the detainees.
The inspector general was critical of the treatment of the detainees; in
many cases their civil liberties were abused.[21] Most were housed in the
Metropolitan Detention Center in Brooklyn, New York, and the Passaic
County Jail, in Paterson, New Jersey. Pakistanis were the largest proportion
of the detainees, followed by Egyptians, Turks, and Yemenis,[22] suggesting
that both Arabs and other Muslims were targeted.

Voluntary Interviews and Absconder Initiative

Profiling men from Arab and/or Muslim countries has been a persistent problem in the government initiatives after September 11. The initiative known as "voluntary interviews" enabled the attorney general to order
the FBI to interview some 5,000 men, ages eighteen to thirty-three, who
had entered the United States between January 2000 and November 2001
from countries suspected of Al Qaeda presence or activity. On February
26, 2002, the *Final Report on Interview Project* was released, revealing that
out of the 5,000 Arab and/or Muslim men on the list, 2,261 had been

interviewed, and fewer than 20 had been taken into custody, three on criminal violations and the rest for immigration charges.[23] In spite of the ineffectiveness of this policy to find terrorists, on March 19, 2002, the Department of Justice declared that it would conduct an additional 3,000 interviews. Then in November 2002, the Department of Justice sought more than 10,000 individuals born in Iraq for questioning, many of whom were naturalized U.S. citizens.

The "absconder initiative" was named for the announcement made by the INS commissioner James Ziglar on December 6, 2001, to make public the names of over three hundred thousand immigrants who were still in the United States in spite of deportation orders. This was followed on January 8, 2002, by an announcement by the Department of Justice to enter into the FBI database the names of about six thousand male absconders, Arab and/or Muslim nationals from predominantly Muslim countries, believed to be Al Qaeda–harboring countries. These men were to be identified and removed. The measure singled out Middle Easterners, even though the vast majority of absconders are Latino.

SEVIS and NSEERS

Securing the nation's frontiers is an important strategy in tracking terrorists. The administration set in motion several measures to regulate the traffic of people, goods, and money across borders. The Student and Exchange Visitor System (SEVIS) is one example. It is a computer system that tracks foreign student enrollment. SEVIS was implemented across the board for all foreign students and not only for students from predominantly Muslim countries. Officials at institutions of higher education, and U.S. embassies, enter data on details such as start date of each semester, failure to enroll, dropping below nine credits per term, disciplinary action by the institution, and early graduation. SEVIS became law on January 30, 2003, though there were many glitches in the system that continued to create backlogs even a year afterwards. Critics argue that these problems have contributed to the decrease in foreign students in U.S. colleges and universities, reversing a trend that had showed a steady growth between 1948 and 2001.[24]

Another initiative in regulating borders was the National Security Entry-Exit Registration System (NSEERS) which required immigrants from twenty-six countries (Afghanistan, Algeria, Bahrain, Djibouti, Egypt, Eritrea, Indonesia, Iran, Iraq, Jordan, Kuwait, Lebanon, Libya, Malaysia, Morocco, Oman, Pakistan, Qatar, Saudi Arabia, Somalia, Sudan, Syria, Tunisia, United Arab Emirates, and Yemen) to be registered, fingerprinted, and photographed upon their arrival and periodically afterwards. This initiative named only immigrants from predominantly Arab and Muslim nations. NSEERS has been criticized for ethnic profiling, a violation of the equal-protection principle in U.S. law.[25] On December 2, 2003, the Department of Homeland Security suspended the NSEERS program.

Though careful inspections of all passengers are a legitimate procedure at airports and on airlines, singling out individuals with Arab/Muslim looks or names is discriminatory and illegal. It has been a particularly hurtful policy for members of the Sikh community. Their characteristic turban and unshorn hair have singled them out as "the other." Even though Sikhs are neither Arab nor Muslim, their looks have been mistakenly associated with Osama bin Laden and his followers. They were also the target of misdirected hostility when the turbaned Ayatollah Khomeini urged Iranian students to take the employees of the American embassy in Tehran hostage. Even a year after 9/11, a flight attendant on Delta Airlines informed a Sikh software consultant who was traveling from Newark, New Jersey, to Dayton, Ohio, that he and his fellow Middle Easterners should keep a low profile. When he tried to explain who he was, he was told to "shut up" and "stay seated" and "not to cause any problems." Sikh Mediawatch and Resource Task Force (SMART) and their counterparts in the Arab and Muslim American communities have been helping victims of racial profiling take their case to court. More importantly, these communities have been actively educating the general public about who they are and what they believe in.

Special Registration

Another legally problematic initiative was the "special registration" that required men older than sixteen who were citizens of Iran, Iraq, Libya, Sudan, and Syria, who had entered the United States before September 10, 2002, and who planned to remain at least until December 16, 2002, to register with the INS before December 16, 2002. Other countries were later added to the list. Failure to report to the INS was cause for deportation. Ironically, more than thirteen thousand individuals who obeyed the order risked deportation.[26] Special registration increased the workload of an already strained INS staff. These men complained of harsh treatment by staff and long waits without access to food or water.[27] But more seriously, the lives of many families were disrupted as husbands were detained and deported, leaving wives and American-born children without any means of support and no opportunity to rejoin the men unless they returned to his country of origin. By early May 2003, over eighty thousand Arab men had registered. Special registration resulted in the arrest of several hundred Iranians who were deemed in violation of their visas. In Los Angeles, these orders created unprecedented demonstrations and protests from the Iranian American population, the largest such concentration in the United States. Up until NSEERS and the special registration, Iranians had avoided being caught in the governmental dragnet, but these initiatives suggested that all immigrants from predominantly Muslim countries would be subject to government scrutiny and control sooner or later.

Closure of Charitable Organizations

In December 2001, the U.S. government froze the assets of three large Muslim charities in an effort to crack down on laundering of money to terrorist organizations in the Muslim world. The Holy Land Foundation for Relief and Development, established in 1989 and based in Texas, was the first casualty. The humanitarian and disaster relief organization had its assets and accounts frozen because of allegations that it provided financial support to Hamas, which has assumed responsibility for many terrorist attacks against civilians in Israel. The problem is that Hamas is also a social support organization and it is hard to separate these dual, often contradictory objectives. The Holy Land Foundation is the largest Muslim charity in the United States. The charity collected over $13 million from American Muslims in 2000. The Holy Land Foundation released a statement denying the allegations made against it, saying it does not support terrorists groups or individuals. However, the Holy Land Foundation was not the only one targeted.

The assets of the Illinois-based Global Relief Foundation as well as the Benevolence International Foundation (BLF) were also frozen, both under investigation for alleged connections to terrorism. Reporting $3.6 million in contributions for 2001, the BLF is also one of the largest Muslim charities in the United States. From the point of view of Muslims, the problem with the closure of Muslim charities is that it curtails the ability of Muslim Americans to fulfill their *zakat* (almsgiving) duties. Giving alms is one of the five pillars or tenets of Islam and is a religious duty of all Muslims.

Muslims are required to give charitable donations annually, consisting of 2.5 percent of their entire wealth, not just income.

Arab and/or Muslim immigrant men suffered the most from these policies, and their ethnic/religious communities were left feeling extremely vulnerable. As men from traditional societies are often the household breadwinners and have extended families, their wives, children, and other family members were drawn into the dragnet unwittingly. Elsewhere, we assess the repercussions on the Arab and/or Muslim immigrant communities.[28] The Pakistani immigrant community in Coney Island, New York, for example, has experienced the closure of many businesses.[29] Even some supporters of the government are concerned about the permanent consequences of the sweeping changes that are executed with little time for debate and reflection, such as the requirement that public libraries inform the government of their patrons' reading habits.

Moreover, the government's appropriation of unprecedented powers to catch terrorists within its borders has not been successful. Perhaps the closest the FBI came to arresting anyone remotely related to Al Qaeda was the capture on September 14, 2002, of six U.S. citizens of Yemeni descent in Lackawanna, New York. This is not to say, however, that some of the government initiatives in the aftermath of 9/11 were not necessary. Indeed, many immigration procedures were lax and flawed, and stricter border controls are a basic requirement in this age of globalization and terrorism. However, the targeting and profiling of a specific population is widely considered abusive. Moreover, searching for leads to terrorist cells requires the trust and collaboration of the very ethnic communities that were angered and alienated by the government's presumption of guilt by association. Instead of winning the hearts and minds of Middle Eastern and Muslim Americans, the government's policies of singling out their co-ethnics and co-religionists had the opposite effect. Furthermore, the government initiatives enflamed the suspicions and stereotypes of the general public and heightened the climate of fear and insecurity.

Similarities and Differences in Treatment of Ethnic Groups in Times of Crisis

There are some basic similarities and differences among the five historical examples explored in this chapter—the Germans in World War I, the Red

Scare between 1919 and 1921, the Japanese internment during World War II, the Iran hostage crisis in 1979–81, and the backlash against Arab and Muslim immigrants after September 11, 2001. As Gerstle has argued, "The anti-Red campaign of 1919–1920 is the episode in American history that most closely resembles the current war on (Islamic) Terror, and paying close attention to the similarities will reveal the danger America runs of repeating past mistakes. Both campaigns crystallized around terrorist acts —mail bombs sent to the homes of 'class enemies' in the first case, airplanes turned into bombs and directed toward buildings (and their inhabitants) that symbolized American power in the second."[30] Gerstle also points out that both cases involved revolutionaries belonging to small cells who were willing to sacrifice their lives to achieve their goals. Both resulted in extended roundups of thousands of immigrants, ironically yielding little intelligence to locate the perpetrators of terrorist acts.[31]

Our goal is to analyze these cases using a variety of criteria. These include the historical event itself; its scope; the characteristics and citizenship status of the targeted group(s); the government's reaction and the measures taken; and yield or outcome. The first four cases of the twentieth century were initiated by nation-states, whereas a terrorist organization network, extending beyond national boundaries, masterminded the 9/11 attacks. On the issue of scope, the United States entered the war in 1917 against Germany in Europe; the Japanese attack on Pearl Harbor was launched on the island of Hawaii, minimally involving the majority of the mainland population. The Iran hostage crisis, which occurred in Tehran, involved fifty-two U.S. government employees. As for the Red Scare, it was the Bolshevik menace that was deemed threatening to the United States. In stark contrast, the 9/11 terrorist attack took 3,021 innocent lives on American soil.

In retribution, the U.S. government targeted persons of German, Japanese, and Iranian origin, as well as communists. Bin Laden, on the other hand, the assumed architect of 9/11, was born in Yemen, became a national of the Kingdom of Saudi Arabia, and operated Al Qaeda out of Afghanistan. Because the nineteen terrorists who hijacked the airplanes that crashed into the World Trade Center, the Pentagon, and in Pennsylvania held a variety of passports, including Egyptian, Saudi, and Lebanese, the administration went after immigrants from a wide range of Arab and Muslim countries. Another dimension must be considered, that is, population size. The estimates of the Arab population in the United States range from 1.2 million, according to the 2000 U.S. Census, to 3 million, according to the Arab American Institute. The census does not collect data on religion, and as a result the estimates in the number of Muslims are even wider, ranging from 2 million to 6 or 7 million. Even when African Americans are excluded from these calculations (estimated at one-third of all Muslims in the United States), the figure is still substantial. Clearly, even the low estimates are more significant than the numbers of Japanese and Iranians during their periods of crises. Population size, however, does not explain the governmental response to 9/11. After all, there were at least 2 million Germans in the United States in 1917.[32]

Perhaps the most outstanding difference among these five cases is that the German and the Japanese victims were both *citizens* and *noncitizens*. The Red Scare targeted mostly aliens, while Iranians who were subject to deportation were exclusively nonimmigrants (aliens). The Bush administration may invoke the Iran Hostage Crisis case in support of the post-9/11 law enforcement measures being implemented against Middle Eastern and South Asian immigrants. However, the challenged regulation that required Iranian students to register with the INS had a narrower focus than the post-9/11 initiatives and was based on national origin, not ethnicity or religion.[33] This also perhaps accounts for why the civil rights community did not step in to help Iranians, especially as there was no organized challenge from the Iranian community itself. At that time there was no Iranian immigrant advocacy group, since most Iranians were either vulnerable foreign students or newly arrived exiles. Since the 2001 hijackers had come to the United States to carry out their goal, the government initiatives sought out those who resembled their characteristics, including their ethnic and religious identity. Yet Aristide Zolberg correctly reminds us that these hijackers could not be regarded as immigrants in the traditional sense of the term. Their immigration status was much more akin to visitors.[34]

The fact that the government initiatives after 9/11 have by and large targeted *noncitizens* is very significant. Unlike the many immigrants who were detained, deported, and subjected to a number of procedures, the cases of U.S. citizens Jose Padilla and Zacarias Moussaoui indicate that they were charged on specific violations. Similarly, as the case of Lackawanna Six, which involved U.S.-born Yemenis, shows, the FBI refrained from arresting them until a witness was able to testify that they had attended Al Qaeda training camp in Afghanistan.[35] It is clear that government initiatives have not targeted American citizens in the September 11 case. This cannot be attributed to the nature of the threat. If anything, terrorism on American soil can just as easily be carried out by citizens (e.g., the Oklahoma bombing).

Constitutional scholars have addressed the citizen versus noncitizen issue, though with different interpretations. To their book *Terrorism and the Constitution,* Cole and Dempsey have aptly given the subtitle *Sacrificing Civil Liberties in the Name of National Security.*[36] Devoting a chapter to fighting the war against terrorism, they argue that in delicately balancing the two, the United States should not trample on the rights of vulnerable immigrants. They state that "while the post–September 11 response does not yet match these historical overreactions, it nonetheless features some of the same mistakes of principle."[37] Elsewhere, Cole argues that "while there has been much talk about the need to sacrifice liberty for a greater sense of security, in practice we have selectively sacrificed *noncitizens'* civil liberties while retaining basic protections for citizens. It is often said that civil liberties are the first casualty of war. It will be more accurate to say that noncitizens' liberties are the first to go."[38] Cole challenges the justification of this "double standard" to ensure citizens' security normatively and constitutionally. He argues that "contrary to widely held assumptions, the Constitution extends fundamental protections of due process, political freedoms, and equal protection to all persons subject to our laws, without regard to citizenship."[39]

David Cole further elaborates these arguments in his book *Enemy Aliens.*[40] From his perspective as a constitutional legal expert, the line between citizen and noncitizen can easily be crossed. He illustrates this by using several historical examples. The Sedition Act of 1918, which was used during the Palmer Raids, brought charges against all forms of disrespect to the government of the United States. The raids punished political dissidents—noncitizens and citizens alike. In the case of the Japanese during World War II, the U.S. government interned aliens and citizens together as likely to engage in subversive action. This can be interpreted as an antecedent of today's risk of "sleeper cells." In reality, however, it was racism that blurred the boundary between Japanese citizens and noncitizens. The repressive measures of the Bush administration are not limited to noncitizens, Cole argues; they may still be used on American citizens, U.S. born and naturalized, as they were during the "Red Scare."

Susan Akram and Maritza Karmely challenge the widely held assumption that discriminatory treatment of Arab and Muslim noncitizens is permissible because of the constitutional exceptionalism of treatment of immigrants.[41] They take issue with David Cole's earlier distinction between citizens and noncitizens and critique governmental overreaction in time of historical crisis. They argue that the mistreatment of Arabs and Muslims predates 9/11. Elsewhere, Akram and Kevin Johnson have argued that U.S. laws and policies have targeted Arab and Muslim noncitizens at least since the 1970s.[42] Others, such as Leti Volpp, have extended the definition of citizenship to include identity. Because of the legitimacy of racial profiling, and the redeployment of Orientalism as a stereotypical ideology, she argues that those who appear as Middle Eastern, Arab, or Muslim, regardless of their formal rights, are excluded from being American.[43] Nonetheless, this argument goes too far in stripping citizenship from its legal meaning and the rights bestowed on citizens. Despite these divergent interpretations and even extrapolations, it is patently clear that citizen versus noncitizen issue distinguishes the post-9/11 case from its historical precedents.

Conclusion

Governmental reaction to wartime threats has taken different forms in various historical periods, depending not only on the nature and scale of the crisis but also on the political and legal atmosphere in the country. If one measures the numbers of persons directly affected by the government initiatives, then the most extreme case is that of the Japanese during World War II because over 120,000 Japanese were interned in "relocation centers." The next most extreme case is the arrest of over 6,000 and the internment of 2,000 German Americans, as well as the registration of over 250,000 German aliens during World War I. During the Red Scare, at least 4,000 aliens were arrested, one-quarter of whom were deported and the rest of whom later released.[44]

The reaction to the hostage crisis was manifested in terms of a deportation threat of over 50,000 Iranian foreign students in the United States. According to the INS, after holding a total of 7,177 deportation hearings, 3,088 students were ordered to leave the United States, and the departure of 445 was verified. Even though the cases of the treatment of the Germans and the Japanese are probably the most similar to the post-9/11 situation, the case of Iranian students is the closest analogy, since it involves Middle Easterners.

It is not yet known how many of the Arab and/or Muslim immigrant men who were detained, interviewed, and registered have been deported because the government has not published these statistics. It will probably be never known how many decided to leave the country voluntarily. It is also difficult to quantify the suffering of the Middle Eastern and Muslim American communities, which were left feeling extremely vulnerable in the aftermath of all the initiatives. However, the available evidence suggests that about 6,000 Arab/Muslim absconders were sought; 42 percent of them were invited for "voluntary interviews" and were questioned; about 20 were arrested on immigration and criminal charges; at least 231 individuals were deported, more than half of them Pakistanis; and fewer than 1 percent of the 5,000 Iraqis were detained after interviewing. Estimates of the detainees vary between the inspector general's quote of 762 illegal immigrants from the Middle East or South Asia and over 1,200 from other sources. Almost 1,200 were detained as a result of NSEERS and special registration.

Clearly, numbers alone cannot be used to categorize the pain and suffering of different groups. Nonetheless, it appears that the tangible government reactions to 9/11, at least so far, have been more limited than in the past, given that the terrorist attacks were the most abhorrent acts perpetrated against the United States on domestic soil. While at first glance the post-9/11 governmental initiatives seem reminiscent of the abuses of the Japanese internment during World War II, Daniels argues otherwise. He writes, "Many commentators have compared the two cases—some seeing a disturbingly similar pattern in the reaction against a feared nonwhite population, others praising what they see as the relative moderation of today's government. . . . But when compared with what was done to Japanese Americans during World War II, government actions before and after September 11 do not seem to amount to very much. Indeed, many media commentators have objected that even to mention them in connection with the massive violations of civil liberties by the Roosevelt administration is inappropriate."[45] Zolberg concurs with Daniels's analysis:

> In contrast with previous surges of securitarian nationalism provoked by international conflicts, most notoriously in the wake of Pearl Harbor when the U.S. government treated all ethnic Japanese as suspects, including American citizens, governmental responses were restrained. Not only were there no wholesale denunciations of particular groups, but instead, the President pointedly visited a mosque and the mayor of New York explicitly admonished the city's residents not to seek revenge on Arabs or Muslims. Again in contrast with the past, while the events stimulated considerable talk of the need to modify American immigration policy, in practice the

proposed changes were almost entirely circumscribed to matters of "border control," and there were no widespread calls to reduce immigration.[46]

We draw two conclusions from this analysis: first, the Bush administration spared citizens after September 11 but mistreated immigrants; and second, qualitatively and quantitatively the government's actions were comparatively restrained. Therefore the question is: What accounts for this change?

The most plausible explanation for not targeting U.S. citizens is that the civil rights movement of the 1960s improved the civil liberties of all minorities in American society, even Middle Easterners, who are not legally considered a minority group. As Richard Alba and Victor Nee remind us, "*In the post-civil rights era, the institutional mechanisms for monitoring and enforcing federal rules have increased the cost of discrimination in non-trivial ways.*"[47] Even the government is not spared from abiding by federal rules. Moreover, the Japanese redress movement, which resulted in the passage of the Civil Liberties Act of 1988, cost the U.S. government $1.6 billion. More importantly, it appears that a new consensus has emerged at the highest levels of government not to repeat "our worst wartime mistake," that is, the internment of the Japanese.

We suggest that the answer to our question is the passage of civil rights bills and the growth of the civil rights community since the 1960s. The networks of civil rights and civil liberties organizations at the national level, and the growth of the grassroots advocacy groups, have become effective watchdogs for the nation's Constitution and legal framework. The activists are able to mobilize their constituencies and challenge whenever they see threats. A clear example of the effectiveness of these groups is what happened to the Justice Department's Terrorism Information and Prevention System (TIPS) program. On November 25, 2002, President Bush signed TIPS, which proposed to enlist thousands of truck drivers, mail carriers, and bus drivers as "citizen observers." TIPS was never implemented when extensive media exposure resulted in outrage among the American public. The ACLU took credit for orchestrating the media blitz and the subsequent repeal.

There are, of course, other plausible explanations. The role of the media in exposing some of the government civil rights abuses is another factor. As global communications have made news dissemination instantaneous, the Arab/Muslim world—including communities in the diaspora

—watches U.S. actions closely. When the U.S. government profiles American Muslims and violates their human rights, its proposals to improve human rights in the Middle East appear hypocritical. This ferments anti-American sentiments and potentially leads to more terrorist acts against the United States, the very root of the problem that the government is trying to eradicate. The multicultural nature of American society today, as opposed to the dominant assimilationist ideology before World War II, is another important consideration. Indeed, one of the few silver linings of the post-9/11 backlash is the greater awareness and understanding of Islam and the Middle East among the American public.

NOTES

This chapter is based on research supported by a grant from the National Science Foundation (SGER 014027). The arguments are our own and do not reflect the views of the National Science Foundation. We acknowledge the editorial assistance of Danielle Zack-Kalbacher.

1. Frederick Luebke, *Bonds of Loyalty: German Americans and World War I* (De Kalb: University of Northern Illinois Press, 1974); Roger Daniels, *Prisoners without Trial* (New York: Hill and Wang, 1992), and *Concentration Camps USA: Japanese Americans and World War II* (New York: Holt, Rinehart and Winston, 1972).

2. Gary Gerstle, "The Immigrant as Threat to American Security: A Historical Perspective," *The Maze of Fear: Security and Migration after 9/11,* ed. John Tirman (New York: New Press, 2004); see also the preceding essay in this collection. Roger Daniels, "Detaining Minority Citizens, Then and Now," *Chronicle of Higher Education,* February 15, 2002.

3. Ibid., B10.

4. David Reimers, *Unwelcome Strangers: American Identity and the Turn against Immigration* (New York: Columbia University Press, 1998), 19.

5. Ibid.; Luebke, *Bonds of Loyalty.*

6. John Higham, *Strangers in the Land,* 2nd ed. (New Brunswick: Rutgers University Press, 1988).

7. Ellen Schrecker, *Many Are the Crimes: McCarthyism in America* (Princeton: Princeton University Press, 1988), 49.

8. Ibid., 59.

9. David O'Brien and Stephen Fugita, *The Japanese American Experience* (Bloomington: Indiana University Press, 1991).

10. Daniels, *Concentration Camps USA.*

11. See Japanese American Citizens League, "About Us" (under "History"), 2007, www.jacl.org/about_history.php (accessed March 26, 2007).

12. Mehdi Bozorgmehr, "Does Host Hostility Create Ethnic Solidarity? The Experience of Iranians in the United States," *Bulletin of the Royal Institute for Inter-Faith Studies (BRIEFS)* 2 (Spring 2000): 159–78.

13. Muzaffar A. Chishti et al., *America's Challenge: Domestic Security, Civil Liberties, and National Unity after September 11* (Washington, DC: Migration Policy Institute, 2003).

14. Nabeel Abraham, "Anti-Arab Racism and Violence in the United States," Ronald Stockton, "Ethnic Archetypes and the Arab Image," and Michael W. Suleiman, "Arab-Americans and the Political Process," all in *The Development of Arab-American Identity,* ed. Ernest McCarus (Ann Arbor: University of Michigan Press, 1994).

15. Mehdi Bozorgmehr and Anny Bakalian, "Discriminatory Reactions to September 11, 2001 Terrorism," in *Encyclopedia of Racism in the United States,* ed. Pyong Gap Min (Westport CT: Greenwood Press, 2005).

16. Jonathan Alter, "Jumping to Conclusions," *Newsweek,* May 1, 1955, 55.

17. Jack G. Shaheen, *The TV Arab* (Bowling Green: Bowling Green State University Popular Press, 1984), and *Reel Bad Arabs: How Hollywood Vilifies a People* (New York: Olive Branch Press, 2001).

18. Shaheen, *TV Arab* and *Reel Bad Arabs*; Abraham, "Anti-Arab Racism."

19. David Cole, *Enemy Aliens* (New York: New Press, 2003); David Cole and James Dempsey, *Terrorism and the Constitution* (New York: New Press, 2002).

20. U.S. Department of Justice, *The September 11 Detainees: A Review of the Treatment of Aliens Held on Immigration Charges in Connection with the Investigations of the September 11 Attacks* (Washington, DC: U.S. Department of Justice, 2003); Chishti et al., *America's Challenge*; American-Arab Anti-Discrimination Committee (ADC), *Report on Hate Crimes and Discrimination against Arab Americans: The Post–September 11 Backlash. September 11, 2001–October 11, 2002* (Washington, DC: ADC, 2003).

21. ADC, *Report on Hate Crimes.*

22. Ibid.

23. Kenneth L. Wainstein, Director, Executive Office for U.S. Attorneys, U.S. Department of Justice for the Attorney General, *Final Report on Interview Project,* February 26, 2002. A later version is the General Accounting Office's Report to Congressional Committees, *Homeland Security, Justice Department's Project to Interview Aliens after September 11, 2001,* GAO-03-459 (Washington, DC: U.S. Department of Justice, 2003).

24. Jennifer Jacobson, "In Visa Limbo: American Colleges Report a Decline in Foreign-Student Enrollment as Tighter Consular Regulations Make Scholars Wait or Look Elsewhere," *Chronicle of Higher Education,* September 19, 2003, A37–38, and "U.S. Foreign Enrollments Stagnate: New Security Measures Keep Out Students from Muslim Countries," *Chronicle of Higher Education,* November 7, 2003, A1, 44–47.

25. Jacobson, "U.S. Foreign Enrollment," 44–47; Chishti et al., *America's Challenge.*

26. See "U.S. Threatens Mass Expulsions," BBC News, June 10, 2003, http://news.bbc.co.uk/1/hi/world/americas/2974882.stm (accessed March 26, 2007).

27. Arab American Family Support Center, Brooklyn, press conference, June 12, 2003.

28. Mehdi Bozorhmehr and Anny Bakalian, "Discriminatory Reactions to September 11, 2001 Terrorism," in Min, *Encyclopedia of Racism.*

29. American Civil Liberties Union, *Worlds Apart: How Deporting Immigrants after 9/11 Tore Families Apart and Shattered Communities,* (New York: ACLU, 2004), 10–11.

30. Gerstle, "Immigrant as Threat," 106.

31. Ibid., 107.

32. Higham, *Strangers in the Land.*

33. Chishti et al., *America's Challenge.*

34. Aristide Zolberg, "Guarding the Gates," in *Understanding September 11,* ed. Craig J. Calhoun, Paul Price, and Ashley Timmer (New York: Social Science Research Council, 2002).

35. Mathew Purdy and Lowell Bergman, "Unclear Danger: Inside the Lackawanna Terror Case," *New York Times,* October 12, 2003, A1, A35–37.

36. Cole and Dempsey, *Terrorism and the Constitution,* ch. 11.

37. Ibid., 151.

38. David Cole, "Enemy Aliens," *Stanford Law Review* 54 (2002): 955.

39. Ibid., 221.

40. Cole, *Enemy Aliens.*

41. Susan Akram and Maritza Karmely, "Immigration and Constitutional Consequences of Post-9/11 Policies Involving Arabs and Muslims in the United States: Is Alienage a Distinction without a Difference?" *University of California Davis Law Review* 38, no. 3 (2005): 609–99.

42. Susan Akram and Kevin Johnson, "Race and Civil Rights Pre-September 11, 2001: The Targeting of Arabs and Muslims," in *Civil Rights in Peril: The Targeting of Arabs and Muslims,* ed. Elaine Hagopian (London: Pluto Press, 2004).

43. Leti Volpp, "The Citizen and the Terrorist," *UCLA Law Review* 49 (2002): 1575–1600.

44. Gerstle, "Immigrant as Threat."

45. Daniels, "Detaining Minority Citizens," B10.

46. Zolberg, "Guarding the Gates," 287–88.

47. Richard Alba and Victor Nee, *Remaking the American Mainstream* (Cambridge, MA: Harvard University Press, 2003), 54, emphasis in the original.

Chapter 11

Immigrant "Transnationalism" and the Presence of the Past

Roger Waldinger

At the turn of the twenty-first century, the view that nation-state and so-ciety normally converge has waned. Instead, "globalization" is the order of the day, with international migration bringing the alien "other" from Third World to First, and worldwide trade and communications amplify-ing and accelerating the feedbacks traveling in the opposite direction. Consequently, social scientists are looking for new ways to think about the connections between "here" and "there," as evidenced by the interest in the many things called "transnational." The excitement is particularly great among those studying international migration: observing that migration produces a plethora of connections spanning "home" and "host" societies, scholars detect the emergence of "transnational communities," from which they conclude that the era of nation-state societies successfully keeping themselves distinct has now been eclipsed.

But does transnationalism—as idea or reality—represent anything new? For contributors to the foundational document—the proceedings of a 1990 New York Academy of Science meeting organized by the anthropol-ogists Nina Glick Schiller, Linda Basch, and Christina Blanc-Szanton—the answer was a resounding yes.[1] The development of social fields linking *par-ticular* sending and destination countries, they argued, represented a deci-sive break with the past. Contrary to historical patterns and received social science notions, neither settlement nor the severing of ties to a home coun-try was inevitable. In the contemporary age of migration, rather, "trans-migrants . . . maintain, build, and reinforce multiple linkages with their countries of origins."[2] In so doing, the long-distance movers of the con-temporary age expanded the range of "home" to encompass both "here" and "there," a change so fundamental that entirely new conceptualizations were required. *Transnationalism* became the label used for identifying the social connections between receiving and sending countries, and *trans-migrants* denoted the people who forged those ties and kept them alive.

Even at the very moment of this debut, however, the historians were there to say that nothing, or at least, not much, was new under the sun. While the social scientists were simply accepting the dictionary's definition of *immigration* as movement for the purposes of settlement, the historians knew better, reminding their colleagues that the last era of mass migration was characterized by a continuous ebb and flow across and indeed around the trans-Atlantic. Nor was an immigrant or ethnic preoccupation with homeland politics anything new; *au contraire*, the literature told us, nothing was as American as agitating in favor of the homeland earlier abandoned.

Roughly fifteen years after debate began, we now all know better. Concerns generated by research on the international migrations of the contemporary era directed historians to patterns of which they had been aware but perhaps not fully attentive. The social scientists have agreed that connections between here and there were indeed seen before—though most still insist that there is something distinctive about the host-home linkages of today. More importantly, there is a steady stream of publications seeking to make systematic past-present comparisons—as opposed to the original practice of just pushing the issue off the table.

But from my vantage point, the record of the past decade and a half provides scant ground for satisfaction. On the one hand, the phenomenon that immigration scholars call transnationalism is fundamentally mislabeled and misunderstood. After all, connectivity between source and destination points is an inherent aspect of the migration phenomenon—no surprise, given the social networks that channel the process. However, those networks generate, not one, but a multiplicity of "imagined communities," organized along different, often conflicting principles, whether related to the scale of aggregation (local vs. national) or opposing visions of the "community" in question. Before the demise of the late, lamented workers' movements of the late nineteenth to mid-twentieth centuries, those "imagined communities" often conformed to the root meaning of *trans*national—extending *beyond* loyalties that connected to any specific place of origin or ethnic or national "group." But that was then, this is now: what contemporary immigration scholars describe as "transnationalism" is just long-distance particularism—a form of social action antithetical to transnationalism in any meaningful sense.[3]

Nor do the scholars of transnationalism do better when thinking about the possible relationships between present and past. To begin with, they dehistoricize the present, forgetting that it is but a moment in the flow of history, and therefore tomorrow's past. Likewise, they take temporal boundaries for granted, assuming, rather than explaining, just when and why the "past" stopped and the "present" began.

As to the existing debate, it has barely begun, having highlighted just one form of past-present connection—namely recurrence, by which I refer to the continued reappearance of trans-state immigrant and ethnic ties linking "here" and "there." The finding is surely important—but it simply reminds us that networks of goods, information, and people repeatedly and regularly extend beyond the limits of state institutions. To a large extent, long-distance migrant networks operate in much the same way whether extending within or across state boundaries—which is why much of the transnational literature concerns bilocal connections bearing no inherent relationship to international migration whatsoever.

However, the relationship between past and present takes more than one form, extending beyond recurrence to include secular change and contingency. Secular change entails direction, not just cyclicality. In this case, movement involves a historical shift toward a world increasingly divided by states, seeking to control movement across territorial boundaries, regulating the internal boundaries of membership, and nationalizing their peoples. Consequently, while social networks do connect nation-state societies—allowing *some* migrants to live both here and there—they don't always penetrate state boundaries.

If possessing direction, history is nonetheless indeterminate, reason for contingency to matter. Because international migration entails movement between states, it is a phenomenon of an inherently political sort. Therefore, the political uncertainties inherent in the relationships among states impinge on the ability of immigrants and their descendants to engage in activities that link "here" and "there." In particular, the security/solidarity nexus waxes and wanes with the degree of interstate tension, with the "dual loyalty" issue becoming particularly intense when belligerency develops between host and sending countries. While the shadow of war repeatedly falls over the trans-state social ties of immigrants and their descendants, it does so unpredictably—and thus contrasts with the regular, recurrent activation of migrant networks.

Having outlined these four different modalities by which past and present relate, I will now elaborate on each one.

Dehistoricization

Right from the start, historians scoffed at the notion that migratory experiences organized by both "here" and "there" represented something not seen before. Indeed, attention to the persistence and significance of migrants' trans-state ties had long been on the historians' agenda. As noted by the manifesto of modern immigration historiography—Frank Thistlethwaite's celebrated 1960 address—the migrations of the turn of the *last* century entailed trans-oceanic, back-and-forth traffic of such amplitude that only some portion of the phenomenon fell into the standard categories of settlement and acculturation.[4] Thus, by the time that sociologists and anthropologists "discovered" transnationalism, the historians were documenting—in copious detail—that all was *not* new under the sun. A trio of books, published in the early 1990s by Dino Cinel, Bruno Ramirez, and Mark Wyman, and focusing on return migration, long-distance nationalism, and immigrant associational life at the turn of the twentieth century, underlined the many commonalities between "now" and "then."[5]

That point has now been so frequently made that it has actually been heard. Even so, the argument for discontinuity has proven remarkably hard to abandon. As case in point, consider the writings of Alejandro Portes, our foremost sociologist of immigration. Portes and his associates first argued that the case for studying transnationalism rested on the very novelty of the phenomenon itself.[6] Shortly, thereafter, these same authors made due note of the historical precedents but sought to rescue the concept by invoking the "fallacy of adumbration." Conceding that the phenomenon was not new, the authors found that transnationalism illuminated previously unnoticed parallels linking "contemporary events with similar ones in the past" and therefore concluded that the concept yielded significant added value.[7]

Today, the scholars of immigrant transnationalism repeat this very mantra, telling us that the transnational phenomenon may be old hat, but little matter, as the transnational concept does "new analytical work," to quote Robert Smith.[8] Yet a close look at the writings of such diverse authors as Robert Smith, Luis Guarnizo, Peggy Levitt, and Nina Glick Schiller shows that the emphasis on past-present divergence remains in place.[9] According to these authors, a complex of factors makes "now" fundamentally different from "then":

- The effects of technological change—reducing the costs and time entailed in communication and travel
- The shift from the melting pot to multiculturalism—legitimating the expression of and organization around home-country loyalties
- The nationalization of home-country societies—increasing the salience of the national identities with which immigrants arrived
- The advent of a new international human rights regime (labeled *postnationalism*)—diminishing the difference between "nationals" and "foreigners" by circumscribing the power of receiving states

But whether the concept or the phenomenon is thought to be new, the same basic problems remain. In claiming discontinuity, the scholars of immigrant transnationalism have fallen victim to the presentism characteristic of their disciplines and times. After all, the distinction they draw between today's world of migrant connectivity and yesterday's world of migrant uprooting simply reproduces the familiar antinomies of social science, most notably that of a "closed" past and an "open" present.[10] As with the study of globalization or transnational relations, the original framing of the question has therefore produced exactly the same so-called discovery—that the phenomenon happened before and in surprisingly similar ways.[11] On the other hand, if one hadn't started with these particular blinders, one might have asked more productive questions.

Moreover, the second line-defense, emphasizing the novelty of the transnational concept and the new illumination it sheds, convinces only if the concept correctly specifies the salient aspect of the situation at either point in time. But that is precisely what contemporary scholarship fails to do, emphasizing parallels while obscuring the fundamental contrast: that contemporary migrations, because they occur in a world carved up by nation-states, are both international and political in ways that were simply not true before. No doubt, parallels exist between now and then; for that reason, one has to note that they probably also extend to the factors that brought the earlier era to an end. While scholarship is right to emphasize the recurrence of migration, a point to which I will return to in a moment, one need be attentive to other, less predictable events that can work in the opposite direction. And so, if we take past-present parallels seriously, we need to concede that the current state of affairs is not inevitable but rather a contingent outcome, subject to unpredictable pressures that could burst today's era of global interconnection asunder, as occurred in the past.

To begin with, the technological determinism asserted by the proponents of immigrant "transnationalism" surely deserves second thought: after all, the simple letter did a remarkably effective job of knitting together transoceanic migration networks, as the reader of *The Polish Peasant* will surely recall.[12] As the historians of globalization point out, moreover, the impact of the telegram was almost as fundamental as that of the Internet; yet neither the telegram nor any other, contemporaneous advances in communications and transportation technology prevented the slide into autarchy experienced for much of the twentieth century.[13] On the other hand, a political environment supportive of immigrant and ethnic long-distance nationalism should hardly be taken for granted. The evidence for the influence of international norms, or of an international human rights regime, is far from compelling.[14] If, instead, domestic political actors have been responsible for relaxing the distinction between nationals and foreigners, movement in the other direction is no less possible. Likewise, the greater legitimacy accorded expression of homeland loyalties is better understood as a product of the moment, not a permanent feature of advanced democracies. The liberal universalism of those social and political groups supportive of immigrant rights does not naturally converge with the highly particularistic attachments of immigrant long-distance nationalists, especially if the latter create new fissures among groups that first encounter one another in the American context, as for example, when African Americans and Cubans clashed over the visit of Nelson Mandela to Miami.[15] The key point is that immigrants' ability to act here in pursuit of objectives located there is chronically a subject of contestation, which is why what the scholars call transnationalism the public labels "dual loyalty." Regardless of what scholars think of such views, they matter and are ignored at our own peril.

Recurrence

Conventional social science views overlap with folk understandings: both assume that nation-states normally contain societies (as implied by the concept of "American society"), which is why the appearance of foreigners and their foreign attachments are viewed as anomalies expected to disappear.

The scholarship on migration tells us exactly the opposite: the advent of international migration is the *normal,* recurrent social outcome: networks of information, goods, and services *regularly* extend beyond the economy, which is why outsiders keep on showing up. In part, it is simply a story of capitalist economies relentlessly expanding beyond the ambit of any national society, even as they generate positions into which a newly activated labor force can move. In part, it is a story of the problem-solving strategies of the migrants, who use their most important resource—namely, each other—to consolidate networks linking "here" and "there" and in turn making it easier for the poor to try to exploit the rich for purposes of their own. Whatever its causes, international migration is a native, *not* alien phenomenon—even though nation-state societies would like to pretend otherwise.

Consequently, the proliferation of ties extending beyond the territory that states seek to enclose reappears in virtually every migrant context—whether "now" or "then," whether in the United States or in any of the world's other major receiving nations. Moreover, population flows across borders leave large numbers of persons moving back and forth in a state of transition, not yet certain where to settle, let alone how much importance to place on the connections "here" as opposed to "there." Over the long term, the networks that breach the nation-state society also pull the migrants away from home environments and encourage settlement. The short- to medium-term horizons, however, may look quite different. As long as migration increases, so too does the density of persons for whom home is not "here," a factor affecting the predispositions of veteran migrants as well as the opportunities they confront. More migration tends to cause more cross-border ties.

But if connections linking here and there are a recurrent feature of the migratory phenomenon, they are not a feature distinguishing international from other forms of population movement. Social networks lubricate long-distance migrations of all types, whether extending across borders or linking country and city within the same state. In some respects, long-distance migrants are all one of a kind: as Michael Piore argued years ago, what matters is not the color of the identity card or passport but rather that migrants are social outsiders, evaluating conditions here in light of the standards there.[16] Using a different terminology, the economic historians have confirmed this point of view: after the 1920s, when international migration was cut off, displaced rural Americans provided most, if not all, of the substitutes that employers needed.[17] And for further evidence, one can reference New York's own history of ethnic succession, where one group of migrant laborers has been more or less interchangeable with any other, regardless of whether their origins were to be found within the United States or beyond its borders.[18]

Consequently, long-distance migrants, whether international or internal, undergo a similar experience: displaced from familiar ground, they get treated as strangers, which is why they suddenly discover a commonality in people originating from the same place. Whether we call them *landsmann* or *paisano*, immigrant hometowners and their organizations are at once ubiquitous but also *fundamentally bilocal*—that is to say, oriented toward attachments and activities linking *particular* places here and there. While these bilocal ties define the principal subject matter of the literature on immigrant transnationalism, the phenomenon bears no intrinsic relationship to international migration as such.[19]

Moreover, even migrations internal to modern, nation-state societies can be sufficiently displacing as to generate new connections around the place left behind. As an uprooted New Yorker, I both know whereof I speak and connect with a long-standing tradition of strangers trying to adapt to the strange land called California. In the 1920s, for example, midwestern migrants to Los Angeles created state-based associations that picnicked, through the 1960s, in the very same L.A. public parks where Salvadoran and Guatemalan associations now gather.[20] Indeed, the Iowa association of Long Beach survives to this very today. In the 1930s, the displaced southwestern farmers made into "Okies" and "Arkies" by fearful Californians not only held on to their local attachments but kept shuttling back and forth between the golden state and their old homes, in a fashion quite similar to that of the Mexican field hands who replaced them when times improved.[21] In the 1950s, as Deborah Dash Moore has told us, second-generation Jewish migrants to Los Angeles thought it necessary to form *landsmannschaften* to bring together, not ex-Bialystokers or ex-Pinskers, but rather the displaced New Yorkers from various parts of the Bronx or Brooklyn.[22]

Of course, we do need to take the international dimension of migration seriously: transborder bilocalism differs from intrastate bilocalism and more so now, when regional differences within the United States have declined, than before. But the key point, to invoke the stilted language of social science, is that discovering connections between "villages" or "communities" here and there simply confirms the null hypothesis: social networks both lubricate long-distance migrations *and* provide the basis around which new forms of community are constructed after the move has taken place. However, these relationships also arise in almost any migratory context, whether within or across state boundaries. Therefore, they do not identify the distinctive traits of international migration, regardless of whether our focus falls on the world of "now" or that of "then."

Secular Change

The "concept of transnationalism," contend Alejandro Portes and his associates in their widely cited and hailed reformulation, should be delimited "to occupations and activities that require regular and sustained social contact over time across national borders for their implementation."[23] It is not for me to contest the claim. But I can note that this reformulation makes freedom of movement the point of departure, as if this were not a world divided by states, many of them expelling their undesirable residents, whose humanity proves insufficient reason for the so-called liberal democracies to open their doors. In this respect, the proponents of transnationalism turn out to share the same biases as the advocates of assimilation, who tell us that "assimilation" is the decline of an ethnic difference,[24] without noting that it is also the *making* of difference between national "peoples." As the sociology of assimilation obscures the coercion involved in excluding outsiders—via control of external borders—and in distinguishing between members and unacceptable residents of the territory—through regulation of the internal boundaries leading to citizenship and legal residence—it also reveals itself to be ideology of the nation-state society.[25] Consequently, the usual distinctions between assimilation and transnationalism mislead.

Neither transnationalism nor assimilation grapples with the inherently political nature of the phenomenon in question; for these reasons, the literature has yet to confront the alternative hypothesis, regarding past-present contrasts, advanced by Hannah Arendt more than a half century ago. Because of the global spread of the state system and the nation-state society, argued Arendt, the condition of having *no* home—*not two homes*—is what distinguishes "now" from "then."[26]

For Arendt, the old order exploded with World War I, though she conceded that the episodes of persecution and forced migration that followed the Great War represented nothing new. "In the long memory of history," as she wrote, developments of this sort "were everyday occurrences." What had changed, rather, was the emergence of a world completely organized into nation-states, conceived of and understood in familistic and communitarian terms. Entire classes of peoples found themselves expelled, "not because of what they had done or thought, but because of what they unchangeably were." And those deprived of a state found "themselves thrown out of the family of nations altogether," as "the loss of home and political status became identical with the expulsion from humanity altogether."[27]

While the Arendtian world and the world at the turn of the twenty-first century may not be fully identical, she fully captured the underlying trend. In the long run, the rise of massive state apparatuses *controlling* population movements between states, and rationalizing distinctions between foreigners and citizens, represents the most striking development. Unlike the situation at the turn of the century, persons migrating across international boundaries are not simply assessing the right mix of costs and benefits, as the economists insist. Today, they must also confront "a problem of political organization," just as underscored by Arendt.

To begin with, international migration is a pervasive, yet quantitatively minor exception to the system by which states bound mutually exclusive populations: after all, only 2.5 percent of the world's population is currently living in a state different from the country of birth. What the liberal democracies dignify by the name of immigration policy is utterly mislabeled: rather, it is an exclusion policy, designed and maintained with the intent to keep out. Looking at the numbers of aliens who have entered the territory of this particular state, some large portion of whom have also been accepted into its nation, one might say that exclusion is pursued without effect. But if we consider the potential pool of migrants, not to speak of the lines patiently waiting for visas—whether permanent or temporary—in U.S. consulates and embassies all over the world, then the success of the fundamental policy is beyond doubt.

Moreover, the state-building efforts entailed in immigration restriction and the state-spanning processes that occur when migration networks extend beyond the state container inevitably collide, yielding a set of cross-pressures that have increased, not diminished, the political impediments to international migration. Thus the United States earlier had a border but scant territoriality, which is why immigrants could come and go as they pleased. As the historical studies have shown us, restriction did not so much choke off movement as alter its pattern. Bottling up established ports of entry simply pushed new flows toward less regulated areas, in turn eliciting yet a further exercise of state power to gain control over space.[28] Though the process has been exceedingly protracted, the once near-open, informally regulated border, long managed in response to regional or local preferences, has now been completely politicized and formalized, with control extending to the entire perimeter of the United States. Of course, the border is leaky—which border isn't? But notice the intensity of the effort to keep people out, as evidenced by the steady militarization of the U.S.-Mexico border and the extension of checkpoints to a zone well north of the border itself.[29] Note also the rising toll of mortality among unauthorized border crossers—an outcome produced only when one prefers to extinguish rather than recognize the humanity of people not like oneself, just as Arendt would have predicted.[30] And though unsuccessful in deterring movement to *el norte,* and therefore derided as "smoke and mirrors" by the leading sociological authorities, current border policies have significantly discouraged unauthorized Mexican migrants from returning home—thus highlighting the newly created political obstacles to the sort of "regular and sustained social contact" across borders that supposedly distinguishes the immigrant transnationalism of today.[31]

Of course, the students of immigrant transnationalism will insist that the political trends work the other way: today's world is increasingly governed by a trans- or postnational human rights regime, which is why immigrants can pursue their various forms of long-distance particularism with a freedom unknown before. But in making this argument, they get the time order all wrong, as one can see by focusing on the refugee regime, an example of transnationalism in the very truest sense of the world. As implicitly argued by Arendt, and later reformulated with precision by Aristide Zolberg, the refugee is a product of the modern world.[32] The migrants of the turn of the twentieth century certainly included people fleeing political hostility but few, if any, for whom a failure to find safe haven would have meant death. Nor was that search for safe haven a desperate venture, as the immigration countries of the times exercised so little border control that they greeted revolutionaries and peasants with the same welcome. What case better exemplifies this unhappily long-lost world than that of Leon Trotsky, in February 1917 a Bronx man, in October 1917 a leader of the Russian Revolution?[33]

It was the subsequent actions of states—expelling their undesirables, while closing themselves off to the unwanted—that impelled the creation of the interwar refugee regime. And the career of our same revolutionary highlights the limits of this interwar transnationalism: once unarmed and outcast, the prophet Trotsky discovered that virtually no place on earth would harbor the likes of him.[34]

Like its interwar predecessor, the contemporary transnational refugee regime is not just a creation of and adaptation to the actions of states; it remains the weaker party, giving way when it clashes with claims to state sovereignty, as illustrated most notably by the experience of the United States. The United States never acceded to the 1951 UN Refugee Convention, even though the convention largely applied to refugees from the Soviet bloc, precisely the outcome desired by the United States. In 1967, the United States finally agreed to observe most of convention's obligations but retained its own narrow view of how refugees were to be defined, which in practice made refugee policy a matter not of humanitarianism but of U.S. foreign policy. While things changed significantly with the passage of the 1980 Refugee Act, the executive branch lost little of the latitude it had long possessed. Politics, not humanitarian considerations, determined where external boundaries would be enforced and with what degree of vigilance, as evidenced by the very different treatment accorded persons fleeing to the United States by boat from Haiti, as opposed to those coming from Cuba. Although land borders have been more difficult to enforce, the insistence on sovereign control of internal boundaries is clear. Asylum remains granted for those coming to the United States for reasons approved by the executive branch, as Salvadoran and Guatemalan refugees have learned to their distress. These unhappy experiences notwithstanding, the relatively liberal asylum regime introduced by the 1980 Refugee Act is already a thing of the past, with the advent of expedited removal reducing rights of review and increasing the state's power to deport.[35]

Of course, none of this precludes international migrants from seeing "themselves as transnational, as persons with two homelands," to quote Glick Schiller and Georges Fouron.[36] Likewise, they can imagine themselves as "transnationals" and construct individual and social identities in transnational form, as Levitt and Mary Waters have recently suggested.[37] Those views, however, are hardly binding on anyone else. Not only do states not only exercise control over who enters the territory and enjoys rights of membership once there, but their capacity to do so has increased significantly between the last age of mass migration and today's.

Contingency

Whatever can be said for sociologists or anthropologists, the historians always knew that homeland attachments loomed large in the lives and communities of immigrants—with some significant degree of retention extended to second and third generations. But in those bad old days, before the correct terminology had been learned, scholars conceived of homeland attachments in terms of "dual loyalty"—as can be seen by opening the canonical 1980 *Harvard Encyclopedia of American Ethnic Groups,* where an essay on just that topic is to be found.[38]

Chronological time does not measure the distance between 1980 and 1989, when the short twentieth century, as Hobsbawm called it, seemingly came to a close.[39] With the Berlin Wall dismantled and the Cold War concluded, the onset of a more pacific era appeared to signal the end of the mutually exclusive national loyalties that had earlier prevailed. In this more relaxed context, states no longer had the same reason to greedily control the allegiance of members and residents. This was all the more so for the world's hegemon, whose newcomers mainly came from poor, weak, and often small states—not of the sort to present a threat to anyone.

How quickly things change! While hindsight is always 20/20, the possibility that tolerance of dual loyalties would respond to the ebb and flow of international tensions should be no surprise. After all, national identity is relational: we define ourselves in contrast to alien peoples and external states. From this perspective, international migrants are the internal aliens, whose links to foreign people and places, so emphasized by the students of immigrant transnationalism, are precisely what renders them suspect.

It is the relationships among states that determine whether persons with foreign attachments are viewed benignly, as adding to the spice of social life, or malignly, as Trojan horses. In general, a peaceful world encourages states to relax the security/solidarity nexus; by contrast, international tension, let alone belligerence, provides the motivation to tighten up on those whose loyalties extend abroad.[40] Of course, predicting just when such tensions will rise or fall seems to exceed the capacity of social science: no one forecast the sudden demise of the Soviet Union, let alone the bombing of the Twin Towers. On the other hand, history does seem to teach us that the pendulum inevitably shifts, which means that international phenomena can be expected to intrude on the political bona fides of persons whose social identities are largely framed by their connections to two very distinct, sometimes opposing states.

War provides the supreme challenge. One can *try,* when war breaks out, to profess allegiance to two mutually belligerent states, but that often proves a difficult effort to pursue. No one is more threatening than the detested and feared Other who happens to be located within the boundaries of one's own state. Moreover, the popular nature of modern wars threatens to transform immigrants from enemy countries into potential enemies, as happened in all the liberal democracies during each of the world wars.[41]

Hopefully, we won't face this test again, at least not in our lifetimes. Even so, the relative international tranquillity of the 1990s should not have blinded analysts to the threats on the horizon. Well before 9/11 one could have seen that immigrants originating from countries with unfriendly or tense relationships with the United States ran the risk of falling into the "enemy alien" trap. As shown by the Wen Ho Lee case, one only had to question a single person's loyalty for America's political rivalry with China to suddenly cast a shadow over the political legitimacy of an entire group. Though the shadow of suspicion receded after the case against Lee collapsed, the latent threat posed by potential conflict between an ever-more-powerful China and a United States prone to saber-rattling never fully disappeared. Before the Trade Tower bombings one could have also noted that long-distance nationalism in all its forms (including that of the time-honored ethnic lobby) did not come so easily to Arab Americans, reason to conclude that the exception proves the rule: when loyalty is in question, long-distance nationalism is a hazardous game.

Just how the sudden inflection of international tension in the early twenty-first century will affect the pursuit of immigrant and ethnic homeland loyalties is anyone's guess. But the lessons of history do indicate that the perception of external threat builds support for a more restrictive view of the national community. Past experience also shows that the American state has the *capacity* to monitor, control, and restrict the trans-state social action of international migrants and their descendants; whether and to what extent that capacity will be activated is a matter to which scholars of immigrant "transnationalism" will now surely want to attend.[42]

Conclusion

The "transnationalism" field emerged with the conviction that the case of contemporary migrants living "here" and "there" represented something new. Understandably, critics responded by saying, *Plus ça change, plus c'est la même chose.* Alas, this sort of discussion is nothing but a trap. History involves change, which is why any particular historical constellation is distinct from other like developments encountered before. But no phenome-

non lies beyond history or exists in and of itself. Consequently, historical knowledge develops through comparison: the task involves specifying
both the similarities and the differences that distinguish one historical
period from another. As I have argued in these pages, the periodization
of the contemporary era needs to be taken seriously; but in the end, we
do want to know how and why "now"—whenever that may be—differs
from "then."

If the historical project is to progress, we cannot proceed by making
ourselves prisoners of our age. One understands that self-congratulation is
no more alien to social scientists than to the man or the woman in the
street, which is why we continue to construct oppositions between a supposedly open present and closed past. But the reality is quite different.
While long-distance, trans-state migration has been seen many times before, the efforts of nation-states to keep themselves apart from the world
represents something relatively new. Therefore, our question is how the
recurrent, state-spanning processes of migration collide with the reactive,
often illiberal, often coercive, efforts to enclose nation-state societies and
bound a national community. As I have contended in this essay, the advent
of that collision is a historical event, entailing an ongoing process encom-
passing us all. While contemporary immigrants living "here" certainly act
in ways that yield leverage "there," they do so in ways that reflect the continuing presence of the past. It is possible that the foreign attachments of
America's immigrants will continue to experience the acceptance enjoyed
in recent years. But the storm clouds stirred up since September 2001
should leave us all wondering whether the present may not also yield place
to the past.

NOTES

1. Nina Glick Schiller, Linda Basch, and Cristina Blanc-Szanton, *Towards a
Transnational Perspective on Migration: Race, Class, Ethnicity, and Nationalism Reconsidered* (New York: New York Academy of Sciences, 1992).

2. Nina Glick Schiller, Linda Basch, and Cristina Blanc-Szanton, "From Immigrant to Transmigrant: Theorizing Transnational Migration," *Anthropological
Quarterly* 68, no. 1 (1995): 52.

3. For further discussion of the scholarship on immigrant "transnationalism,"
as well as the distinction between "long-distance particularism" and a transnationalism consistent with the word's meaning, see Roger Waldinger and David
Fitzgerald, "Transnationalism in Question," *American Journal of Sociology* 109, no.
5 (2004): 1177–95.

4. Frank Thistlethwaite, "Migration from Europe Overseas during the Nineteenth and Twentieth Centuries," in *Population Movements in Modern European History,* ed. Herbert Moller (New York: Macmillan, 1964), 73–92.

5. Mark Wyman, *Round-Trip to America* (Ithaca: Cornell University Press, 1992); Bruno Ramirez, *On the Move: French Canadian and Italian Migrants in the North Atlantic Economy, 1860–1914* (Toronto: McClellan and Stewart, 1991); Dino Cinel, *The National Integration of Italian Return Migration, 1870–1929* (New York: Cambridge University Press, 1991).

6. Alejandro Portes, Luis E. Guarnizo, and Patricia Landolt, "The Study of Transnationalism: Pitfalls and Promise of an Emergent Research Field," *Ethnic and Racial Studies* 22, no. 2 (1999): 217–37.

7. Alejandro Portes, William J. Haller, and Luis Eduardo Guarnizo, "Transnational Entrepreneurs: An Alternative Form of Immigrant Economic Adaptation," *American Sociological Review* 67, no. 2 (2002): 184.

8. Robert C. Smith, "Diasporic Memberships in Historical Perspective: Comparative Insights from the Mexican, Italian, and Polish Cases," *International Migration Review* 37, no. 3 (2003): 725.

9. Nina Glick Schiller, "Transmigrants and Nation-States: Something Old and Something New in the U.S. Immigrant Experience," in *The Handbook of International Migration: The American Experience,* ed. Charles Hirschman, Philip Kasinitz, and Josh DeWind (New York: Russell Sage Foundation, 1999), 94–119; Luis E. Guarnizo, "On the Political Participation of Transnational Migrants: Old Practices and New Trends," in *E Pluribus Unum? Contemporary and Historical Perspectives on Immigrant Political Incorporation,* ed. Gary Gerstle and John H. Mollenkopf (New York: Russell Sage Foundation, 2001), 213–63; Peggy Levitt, *The Transnational Villagers* (Berkeley: University of California Press, 2001); Robert C. Smith, "Comparing Local-Level Swedish and Mexican Transnational Life: an Essay in Historical Retrieval," in *New Transnational Social Spaces,* ed. Ludger Pries (New York: Routledge, 2001).

10. Jean-Loup Amselle, "Globalization and the Future of Anthropology," *African Affairs* 101 (2002): 213–29.

11. Harold James, *The End of Globalization: Lessons from the Great Depression* (Cambridge, MA: Harvard University Press, 2001); Audie Klotz, "Transnational Activism and Global Transformations: The Anti-apartheid and Abolitionist Experiences," *European Journal of International Relations* 8, no. 1 (2002): 49–76.

12. William I. Thomas and Florian Znaniecki, *The Polish Peasant in Europe and America* (1927; repr., New York: Octagon Books, 1974).

13. On the ways in which earlier transformations affected both sending and receiving societies, see Jose C. Moya, *Cousins and Strangers: Spanish Immigrants in Buenos Aires, 1850–1930* (Berkeley: University of California Press, 1998).

14. As argued by, among others, Christian Joppke, *Immigration and the Nation-State: The United States, Germany, and Great Britain* (Oxford: Oxford Univer-

sity Press. 1998), and Virginie Guiraudon, "Citizenship Rights for Non-citizens: France, Germany and the Netherlands," in *Challenge to the Nation-State: Immigration in Western Europe and the United States,* ed. Christian Joppke (Oxford: Oxford University Press, 1998).

15. For background on the conflicts produced by divergent long-distance loyalties among ethnic Miamians, see the account in Alejandro Portes and Alex Stepick, *City on the Edge: The Transformation of Miami* (Berkeley: University of California Press, 1993). Of course, events in contemporary Miami are neither new nor particular to that place. As the historical record shows, disputes based on home-country polarities yield internecine conflicts that belie claims of a transnational "community"—as in "the war of the little Italies" earlier in the century (John P. Diggins, *Mussolini and Fascism: The View from America* [Princeton: Princeton University Press, 1972]) or clashes between nationalists and communists in contemporary U.S. Chinatowns (Zai Liang, "Rules of the Game and Game of the Rules: The Politics of Recent Chinese Immigration to New York City," *Migration, Transnationalization, and Race in a Changing New York,* ed. Hector Cordero-Guzman et al. [Philadelphia: Temple University Press, 2001]). Alternatively, opposing home-country loyalties can create adoptive-country cleavages, as illustrated by contemporary disputes among Arab Americans and Jewish Americans (Yossi Shain, *Marketing the American Creed Abroad: Diasporas in the U.S. and Their Homelands* [New York: Cambridge University Press, 1999]) and the earlier frictions between African Americans and Italian Americans spurred by Italy's invasion of Ethiopia during the 1930s, or the discord between Japanese Americans and Chinese Americans provoked by Japan's invasion of China (John F. Stack Jr., *Ethnic Conflict in an International City* [Westport, CT: Greenwood Press, 1979]).

16. Michael Piore, *Birds of Passage* (Cambridge: Cambridge University Press, 1979).

17. Henry Gemery, "Immigrants and Emigrants: International Migration and the U.S. Labor Market in the Great Depression," in *Migration and the International Labor Market, 1850–1939,* ed. Timothy J. Hatton and Jeffrey G. Williamson (New York: Routledge, 1994), 175–203.

18. As I argued in Roger Waldinger, *Still the Promised City? African-Americans and New Immigrants in Postindustrial New York* (Cambridge, MA: Harvard University Press, 1996).

19. For further evidence, see David Fitzgerald, "A Nation of Emigrants? Statecraft, Church-Building, and Nationalism in Mexican Migrant Source Communities" (PhD diss., University of California, Los Angeles, 2005).

20. Joseph Boskin, "Societies and Picnics as Stabilizing Forces in Southern California," *California Historical Quarterly* 44, no. 2 (1965): 17–26.

21. James N. Gregory, *American Exodus: The Dust Bowl Migration and Okie Culture in California* (New York: Oxford University Press, 1989).

22. Deborah Dash Moore, *To the Golden Cities: Pursuing the American Jewish Dream in Miami and L.A.* (New York: Macmillan, 1994).

23. Portes, Guarnizo, and Landolt, "Study of Transnationalism," 219.

24. Richard Alba and Victor Nee, *Remaking the American Mainstream: Assimilation and Contemporary Immigration* (Cambridge, MA: Harvard University Press, 2003).

25. For a fuller development of this argument, see Roger Waldinger, "Foreigners Transformed: International Migration and the Making of a Divided People," *Diaspora* 12, no. 2 (2003): 247–72.

26. Hannah Arendt, *The Age of Totalitarianism* (1951; reprint, New York: Harcourt, 1996).

27. Ibid., 294 and passim.

28. On the extension of border controls following passage of the 1924 Immigration Act, see Ramirez, *On the Move,* and Mae M. Ngai, *Impossible Subjects: Illegal Aliens and the Making of Modern America* (Princeton: Princeton University Press, 2004).

29. Timothy J. Dunn, *The Militarization of the U.S.-Mexico Border, 1978–1992: Low-Intensity Conflict Doctrine Comes Home* (Austin, TX: CMAS Press, 1996).

30. Wayne Cornelius, "Death at the Border: Efficacy and Unintended Consequences of US Immigration Control Policy," *Population and Development Review* 27, no. 4 (2001): 661–85.

31. Douglas Massey, Jorge Durand, and Dumas Malone, *Beyond Smoke and Mirrors: Mexican Immigration in an Era of Economic Integration* (New York: Russell Sage Foundation, 2002).

32. Aristide Zolberg, "Matters of State: Theorizing Immigration Policy," in Hirschman, Kasinitz, and DeWind, *Handbook of International Migration.*

33. Isaac Deutscher, *The Prophet Armed* (New York: Vintage Books, 1965).

34. Isaac Deutscher, *The Prophet Outcast* (New York: Oxford University Press, 1963).

35. Gil Loescher and John Scanlon, *Calculated Kindness: Refugees and America's Half-Open Door, 1945 to the Present* (New York: Free Press, 1986).

36. Nina Glick Schiller and Georges Fouron, "Everywhere We Go, We Are in Danger: Ti Manno and the Emergence of a Haitian Transnational Identity," *American Ethnologist* 17, no. 2 (1990): 341.

37. Peggy Levitt and Mary Waters, eds., *The Changing Face of Home: The Transnational Lives of the Second Generation* (New York: Russell Sage Foundation, 2002).

38. Mona Harrington, "Loyalties: Dual and Divided," in *Harvard Encyclopedia of American Ethnic Groups,* ed. Stephan Thernstrom (Cambridge, MA: Harvard University Press, 1980), 676–86.

39. Eric J. Hobsbawm, *The Age of Extremes: A History of the World, 1914–1991* (New York: Pantheon, 1994).

40. John A. Armstrong, "Proletarian and Mobilized Diasporas," *American Political Science Review* 70, no. 2 (1976): 393–408.

41. As I argued in Waldinger and Fitzgerald, "Transnationalism in Question."

42. See David Cole, *Enemy Aliens: Double Standards and Constitutional Freedoms in the War on Terrorism* (New York: New Press, 2003); Gary Gerstle, "The Immigrant as a Threat to American Security," in *The Maze of Fear: Security and Migration after 9/11,* ed. John Tirman (New York: New Press, 2004), 87–108.

About the Contributors

Anny Bakalian is Associate Director of the Middle East and Middle Eastern American Center (MEMEAC) at the Graduate School and University Center of the City University of New York (CUNY). The leading authority on Armenian Americans, she is the author of *Armenian Americans: From Being to Feeling Armenian* (1993).

Elliott R. Barkan has been a Professor of History and Ethnic Studies at California State University, San Bernardino, since 1968 and became an Emeritus Professor in 2003. He is the author of editor of numerous books, including *And Still They Come* (1996), *A Nation of Peoples* (1999), *Making It in America: A Sourcebook on Eminent Ethnic Americans* (2001), and *From All Points: America's Immigrant West, 1870s–1952* (2007).

Mehdi Bozorgmehr is Associate Professor of Sociology at City College and Graduate Center, City University of New York (CUNY), and the founding Co-Director of the Middle East and Middle Eastern American Center (MEMEAC) at the Graduate Center, CUNY. He is coeditor of the award-winning book *Ethnic Los Angeles*.

Caroline B. Brettell is Dedman Family Distinguished Professor in the Department of Anthropology at Southern Methodist University and Chair of the department since 1994. She is the author of, among many works, *We Have Already Cried Many Tears: The Stories of Three Portuguese Migrant Women* (1982, 1995), and *Anthropology and Migration: Essays on Transnationalism, Ethnicity and Identity* (2003), and she is coeditor of *Gender in Cross-Cultural Perspective* (1993, 1997, 2001, 2005), and *Migration Theory: Talking across Disciplines* (2000).

Barry R. Chiswick is Distinguished Professor and Chair, Department of Economics, University of Illinois at Chicago, and Program Director, Migration Studies, IZA—Institute for the Study of Labor (Bonn). He is also President of the European Society for Population Economics.

Hasia Diner is the Paul and Sylvia Steinberg Professor of American Jewish History at New York University (Departments of History and Hebrew and Judaic Studies) and Director of the Goldstein Goren Center for American Jewish History. A specialist in immigration and ethnic history, American Jewish history, and the history of American women, she has authored numerous books, including *In the Almost Promised Land: American Jews and Blacks, 1915–1935* (1977, 1995), *A Time for Gathering: The Second Migration, 1820–1880* (1992), and *Hungering for America: Italian, Irish, and Jewish Foodways in the Age of Migration* (2001), and has coauthored a history of American Jewish women, *Her Works Praise Her* (2002), as well as *The Jews of the United States* (2004).

Gary Gerstle is Professor of History at Vanderbilt University. Among his works are *American Crucible: Race and Nation in the Twentieth Century* (2001, winner of the Saloutos Prize), *Working-Class Americanism: The Politics of Labor in a Textile City, 1914–1960* (1989), and the coedited *E Pluribus Unum: Contemporary and Historical Perspectives on Immigrant Political Incorporation* (2001).

Roland L. Guyotte is Professor of History at the University of Minnesota, Morris. He has published widely in U.S. history, including works on the history of U.S. higher education and the history of immigration. His article "Aspiration and Reality: Occupational and Educational Choices among Filipino Migrants to Chicago, 1900–1935," coauthored with Barbara M. Posadas, received the Harry Pratt Memorial Award of the Illinois State Historical Society.

David W. Haines is currently an Associate Professor of Anthropology at George Mason University but was formerly a policy analyst for the U.S. refugee program in the early 1980s. Among other works, he edited (most recently) *Refugees in America in the 1990s* (1996), coedited *Illegal Immigration in America* (1999) and *Manifest Destinies* (2001), and authored *The Limits of Kinship: South Vietnamese Households* (2006).

Alan M. Kraut is Professor of History at American University in Washington, D.C. He has authored or edited seven books, including the award-winning *Goldberger's War: The Life and Work of a Public Health Crusader* (2003) and *Silent Travelers: Germs, Genes and the "Immigrant Menace"* (1994). Other books include *The Huddled Masses: The Immigrant in American Society, 1880–1921* (1982, 2001), *American Refugee Policy and*

European Jewry, 1933–1945 (1987, coauthored), and *American Immigration and Ethnicity: A Reader* (2005, coedited). His most recent book, coauthored with Deborah Kraut, is *Covenant of Care: Newark Beth Israel and the Jewish Hospital in America* (2007).

Xiyuan Li, PhD, is an Associate Professor at the Center for Research on Hong Kong, Macau, and the Pearl Delta River Region at Zhongshan University, China.

Timothy J. Meagher is Associate Professor of History and Curator of American Catholic History Collections at Catholic University. He has written *Inventing Irish America: Generation, Class and Ethnic Identity in a New England City, 1880 to 1928* (2001) and the *Columbia Guide to Irish American History* (2005) and has edited two collections of essays, including *The New York Irish* (1996).

Paul W. Miller currently holds an Australian Professorial Fellowship in the Business School at the University of Western Australia, Perth. He has over one hundred publications in refereed journals on labor market issues.

Barbara M. Posadas is Professor of History at Northern Illinois University. She is the author of *The Filipino Americans* (1999) and numerous articles on Filipino American history, particularly in the Midwest.

Paul Spickard is Professor of History, Asian American Studies, and Religious Studies at the University of California, Santa Barbara. He is the author or editor of a dozen books, including *Revealing the Sacred in Asian and Pacific America* (2003), *Racial Thinking in the United States* (2005), *Race and Nation: Ethnic Systems in the Modern World* (2005), and *Is Lighter Better? Skin-Tone Discrimination among Asian Americans* (2007) and *Almost All Aliens: Immigration, Race, and Colonialism in American History and Identity* (2007).

Roger Waldinger is a Professor in the Department of Sociology at the University of California, Los Angeles. He is the author of numerous books, including *How The Other Half Works: Immigration and the Social Organization of Labor* (coauthored, 2003), *Strangers at the Gates: New Immigrants in Urban America* (2001), *Still the Promised City? New Immigrants and African-Americans in Post-Industrial New York* (1996), and *Ethnic Los Angeles* (coedited with Mehdi Bozorgmehr, 1996).

Karen A. Woodrow-Lafield has focused on U.S. immigration, especially legal and undocumented immigration. She was Director of Border and Inter-American Affairs (2002–4) in the Institute for Latino Studies at the University of Notre Dame, an Associate Professor of Sociology at Mississippi State University (1996–2002), and Statistician and Demographer on the Population Analysis Staff at the U.S. Census Bureau (1984–92). From 1995 to 1997, she collaborated on the *Report of the Binational Study of Migration between Mexico and the United States.* She has authored essays in, among others, the *International Migration Review, Population Research and Policy Review,* and *Demography,* as well as chapters in *Illegal Immigration in America: A Reference Handbook* (1999) and *Undocumented Migration to the United States: IRCA and the Experience of the 1980s* (1990).

Min Zhou, PhD, is a Professor of Sociology and the Inaugural Chair of the Department of Asian American Studies at the University of California, Los Angeles. She is the author of *Chinatown: The Socioeconomic Potential of an Urban Enclave* (1992), coauthor of *Growing Up American: How Vietnamese Children Adapt to Life in the United States* (1998), and coeditor of *Contemporary Asian America* (2000) and *Asian American Youth* (2004).

Index

100th Battalion, 250
442nd Regimental Combat Team, 250

1840–1860, 2–3
1880–1920s, 3, 138
1910–1930, 60
1920s, 9, 17, 18
1930s, 9, 17, 60
1940s, 60
1950s, 60
1960s, 60
1965 on, 17–18
1970, 76
1970s, 76
1970s on, 5–7
1978–1991, 70
1980, 76
1980s, 76
1990, 76
1990s, 76
mid-1990s, 74–75
2000, 76
2005, 20

absconder initiative, 253–254, 262
Academy of Motion Picture Arts and Sciences, 189
acculturation: acceptance of, 10–11; *versus* assimilation, 15; Italian Americans, 189
ACLU (American Civil Liberties Union), 240, 249, 263
Adams, Herbert Baxter, 5
adaptation: *versus* assimilation, 15; English-language proficiency, 48; integration, 15; refugees, 48; Spanish language, 57n16
Addams, Jane, 3, 11–12
"affinity group goods." *See* "ethnic goods"
Afghan immigrants, 48, 254–255

AFPSI. *See* Association of Filipino Physicians in Southern Illinois
African Americans: assertiveness, 193, 194; assimilation, 99; civil rights movement, 208; films featuring, 188; Herberg and, 99; Muslims and, 259; opposition to white Protestants, 195; race, 100; racist imaginings of, 207; *Rocky* films, 195–196; West Indian immigrants and, 15
African immigrants: 1965 on, 17; 1970s on, 6; assimilation model of migrant experience, 96; ethnicities of, 97; Immigration Act (1965, the Hart-Cellar Act), 18; naturalization levels, 70, 76; North Africans, 97; race, 94, 95; refugees, 45, 50, 53, 55n9; religion, 94
Afroyim v. Rusk (1967), 14, 19
Aiello, Danny, 189
Akram, Susan, 260–261
Al Qaeda: absconder initiative, 254; Afghanistan, 258; countries harboring, 253; Lackawanna Six, 257, 259; non-state status, 245n41
Alba, Richard: concerning assimilation, 21; cost of discrimination, 263; ethnic community, definition of, 129; race, 27–28, 99, 100; third-generation Italian Americans, 188–189
Algerian immigrants, 254–255
Ali, Muhammad, 195
Alien Act (1918), 244n24
Alien Enemies Act (1798), 247
Alien Land Law (California, 1913), 235
Allen, R. E. L., 233
Allen, Woody, 205
Amerasians, 47
American Anthropological Association, 4–5
American Anthropological Society, 4
American Civil Liberties Union (ACLU), 240, 249, 263
American Film (magazine), 200

assimilation: acculturation, as part of, 15; adaptation, as part of, 15; African Americans, 99; Chinese immigrants, 167; decline of ethnic difference, 275; definition, 15, 19; ethnic exclusivity, 15; ethnic traditions, 15; in films about Italian Americans, 198–199; German Americans, 227–228; globalization, 16; identificational assimilation, 60; Irish Americans, 203–205; Latinos, 99; length of the process, 16; making of differences between national "peoples," 275; marital assimilation, 60; melting pot, 271; Mexican immigrants, 99; Native Americans, 99; race, 4, 21, 27–28, 96; religion, 27; segmented assimilation, 15; structural assimilation, 60; transnationalism, 14, 16, 275; as two-way street, 84

assimilation model of migrant experience, 96–97

Association of Filipino Physicians in Southern Illinois (AFPSI): Filipina women, 150; founding and events, 148; Lara (Maria) and, 152; Science Scholarship Quiz Show, 148; Springfield, Illinois, 146

Association of Philippine Physicians in America (APPA), 148

asylees, 47, 61

At Heaven's Door (Borjas), 74

Atlanta, 124, 137–138

Australia, 52

Austrian immigrants, 227

Bagchi, Ann, 146

Bahrainian immigrants, 254–255

Bakalian, Anny, 32–33

Bakunin, Mikhail Aleksandrovich, 221

Balkans, immigrants from, 6, 221

Bancroft, George, 3

Barkan, Elliott, 15

Basch, Linda, 267

Beam, Lilian Torres, 149

Beast of Berlin (film), 226

Beethoven, Ludwig van, 227

Belgium: bilingualism, 89; German atrocities against, 226; post–World War II refugees, 52, 55n10

Bend It Like Beckham (film), 135

Benedict, Ruth, 4

Benevolence International Foundation (BLF), 256

Berkman, Alexander, 230, 249

Berry, Jack, 155

Berry, Linette, 155

Biddle, Francis, 235

"Big 6" immigrant-receiving states, 80

bilocalism, 269, 274–275

bin Laden, Osama, 255, 258

Blanc-Szanton, Christina, 267

Blumenthal, Sidney, 213n39

Boas, Franz: *Mind of Primitive Man*, 4

Bodkin, Karen, 9

Bodnar, John, 10

Bolshevik Revolution, 33

Bolsheviks: fear of, 248; Jewish immigrants, 232; "new immigrants," 230; Red Scare, 228–229

Bon Odori festival (Seattle), 101

Bonacich, Edna, 121

Bonfire of the Vanities (Wolfe), 203

border policies, 277

Borjas, George, 74, 181n7

Bosnian immigrants, 48

Boston Symphony Orchestra, 227

Bourgeois, Philippe, 165

Boyle, Peter, 205

Bozorgmehr, Mehdi, 32–33

Bracco, Lorraine, 200

bracero program, 61

Brando, Marlon: ethnicity, 190; in *Godfather I*, 199; portrayals of natural brutes, 202, 213n32; as white primitive, 202

Brazil, 66

Brettell, Caroline, 24–25

Brimelow, Peter, 12–13

Brooks, Richard, 204

Brothers McMullen (film), 204

Buddhism: Asian Americans, 108; *butsudans*, 106; Hawaii, 103; Japanese Americans, 103–105, 106, 107; White Buddhists, 108

Bulletin (Filipino American National Historical Society), 149

Burns, Bethany, 46

Bush, George W.: Muslim immigrants, 20, 238; nativism, 20; USA PATRIOT Act (2001), 252; "War on Terror," 246

Bush administration (George W.): post-9/11 initiatives, 251–252; post-9/11 law enforcement measures, 259; treatment of immigrants, 263

Busto, Rudy, 104

butsudans, 28

Caballero-Dauz, Virginia B., 146, 147

race (*continued*)
  immigrants, 94, 95; assimilation, 4, 21, 27–28, 96; assimilation model of migrant experience, 96; Chinese immigrants, 95, 169; citizenship, 18; Ellis Island, 95–96; European immigrants, 95; fears of subversion, 237–238; immigration history, 94, 99–100; immigration law, 18; incorporation, 96; Italian Americans as imagined blacks ("white niggers"), 195; Japanese Americans, 107, 235–236; Japanese immigrants, 95; Latinos, 100; Native Americans, 100; naturalization, 223; "race relations cycle," 99; racial formation model of migrant experience, 96, 97; racial hierarchy, 223; racial inferiority/superiority, 3–5; racial/religious profiling, 105, 255; racial subversion, 222–224, 237–238, 239; racial tensions (1960s–1980s), 194–195; racialization, 107–108; religion, 28, 99–100, 107
Radical Islamicist Scare/"War on Terror," 238–240, 245n41
Raging Bull (film): Italian Americans as primitives, 191, 192; Jake La Motta (character), 195, 201; Scorsese on, 191
Rahman, A. R., 132
rakhi, 133, 141n18
Ramirez, Bruno, 270
Reagan administration, 51
recurrence of ties, transnationalism and, 269, 272–275
Red Scare (1919–1920): American Civil Liberties Union, 240; anarchism, 231; Bolshevik Revolution, 33; Bolsheviks, 228–229; communist Left, 231; East European immigrants, 237–238; ending of, 240, 245n41; immigrant restriction, 228–233; mail bombings, 229–230, 238; Palmer Raids, 33, 248, 260; southern European immigrants, 237–238; targets, 259; treatment of immigrants during times of crisis, 257–258; "War on Terror"/Radical Islamicist Scare, 238–240, 245n41
Refugee Act (1980): asylees, 61; employment of refugees, 51, 57n21; geographical origins of refugees, 55n9; humanitarianism, 278; persecution, fear of, 45–46; provisions, 61
refugee policies, post–World War II, 22–23, 52
refugees, 41–59; 1939–2005, 41–42, 53; post-9/11, 53; adaptation, 48; admissions, 41–42, 44–49; adults, 48; Africans, 45, 50, 53, 55n9; Amerasians, 47; anti-communism, 44; anti-Semi-

tism, 42–43; Asians, 44, 50; assistance to, 41–42; asylees, 47; boat people, 54n2, 278; Cambodians, 44; Central Americans, 47; children, 48; circumstances of, 43; Cubans, 44, 45, 46–47, 48, 50–51; deportations, 53; displaced persons (*see* displaced persons); diversity of, 48–49, 52; eastern European Jews, 233; eastern Europeans, 44; employment, 49–52, 57n21; *fair share,* 45; foreign policy, 278; foreign relations with refugees' homeland, 43; fraud/persecution of other refugees, 42; gender, 48; geographical origins, 55n9; German Jews, 42–43, 46; Guatemalans, 278; Haitians, 47, 278; humanitarianism, 278; Hungarians, 44; "incountry processing," 55n7; interdictions at sea, 53; Lao, 44; media attention, 41; moral commitments to, 42–46, 53–54; Orderly Departure Program (ODP), 47, 55n7; persecution, fear of, 45–46; "pipeline" to U.S., 47; policy changes, 41, 52; as product of modern world, 277–278; Reagan administration, 51; refugee processing centers (RPCs), 47; refugees worldwide, 45; rejection (repatriation) of, 42–43, 95, 109n3; resettlement, 46–50; restitution for American inaction, 45; Roosevelt, Eleanor, and, 46; Roosevelt, Franklin, and, 46; Salvadorans, 278; self-sufficiency, achieving, 51–52, 57n21, 58n23; social transformation of, 47–48, 50–51; Southeast Asian boat people, 54n2; Southeast Asians, 44–45, 45, 47; Soviets, 44; *S.S. St. Louis,* 22, 42, 54n2; summary deportations, 53; transnational refugees, 277–278; U.S. links to refugees' homelands, 43; U.S. State Department, 41, 47; Vietnamese, 44–45, 48, 49, 50–51, 54n2, 55n7; Wagner-Rogers bill (1939), 42, 54n2
Reimers, David, 247
religion: African immigrants, 94; Asian American panethnicity, 102; Asian American studies, 98; Asian immigrants, 94; assimilation, 27; Chinese immigrants, 101–102, 108; ethnic identity, 25; ethnic studies, 98; ethnicity, 102; immigration history, 94, 97–100; incorporation, 28; Indian immigrants, 128; Japanese Americans, 100–105; Latin American immigrants, 94; lived religion, 105–107; race, 28, 99–100, 107; religious institutions, 101–102; religious leaders, 102–105, 107; religious subversion, 219–220, 239; social scientists, 98; South Asian immigrants, 102